Heidegger and the Human

SUNY series in Contemporary Continental Philosophy
Dennis J. Schmidt, editor

Heidegger and the Human

Edited by

Ingo Farin *and* Jeff Malpas

Cover art based on Ilona Schneider, *Warehouse Living* (© Ilona Schneider)

Published by State University of New York Press, Albany

© 2022 State University of New York

All rights reserved

Printed in the United States of America

No part of this book may be used or reproduced in any manner whatsoever without written permission. No part of this book may be stored in a retrieval system or transmitted in any form or by any means including electronic, electrostatic, magnetic tape, mechanical, photocopying, recording, or otherwise without the prior permission in writing of the publisher.

For information, contact State University of New York Press, Albany, NY
www.sunypress.edu

Library of Congress Cataloging-in-Publication Data

Names: Farin, Ingo, editor. | Malpas, Jeff, editor.
Title: Heidegger and the human / [edited by] Ingo Farin, Jeff Malpas.
Description: Albany : State University of New York Press, [2022] | Series: SUNY series in contemporary continental philosophy | Includes bibliographical references and index.
Identifiers: LCCN 2022005499 | ISBN 9781438490496 (hardcover : alk. paper) | ISBN 9781438490502 (ebook) | ISBN 9781438490489 (pbk. : alk. paper)
Subjects: LCSH: Heidegger, Martin, 1889–1976. | Human beings. | Humanism. | Philosophical anthropology. | Continental philosophy. | Philosophy, German—20th century.
Classification: LCC B3279.H49 H342225 2022 | DDC 193—dc23/eng/20220711
LC record available at https://lccn.loc.gov/2022005499

10 9 8 7 6 5 4 3 2 1

Contents

Acknowledgments — ix

Introduction — 1
Ingo Farin and Jeff Malpas

Part I.
Anthropology and Philosophy

Chapter One
Heidegger's Engagement with and Critique of Philosophical Anthropology — 7
Ingo Farin

Chapter Two
From Heidegger's *Da-Sein* to the "Prince of the World" — 47
Babette Babich

Chapter Three
The Unfought Battle: Heidegger and Plessner — 83
Thomas Schwarz Wentzer

Chapter Four
On the Twofoldness of Human Beings: Husserl's "Reply" to Heidegger's Critical Remarks — 111
Sara Heinämaa

Part II.
Human Being, Otherness, and World

Chapter Five
Returning to Place: Retrieving the Human from "Humanism" 137
Jeff Malpas

Chapter Six
Being Human and Being Open: Heidegger's Radicalization of the Transcendental after Husserl 155
Niall Keane

Chapter Seven
Play, World, and the Human 185
Bruce Janz

Chapter Eight
Bio-logies of Being: On Human and Animal Life in Heidegger and Beyond 205
Hans Ruin

Chapter Nine
Heidegger's Race 227
Laurence Paul Hemming

Part III.
Life, Identity, and Finitude

Chapter Ten
Dasein and Intersectional Identity 261
Tina Fernandes Botts

Chapter Eleven
Natality vs. Mortality: Turning Heidegger Inside Out 281
Anne Granberg

Chapter Twelve
Having Some Regard for Human Frailty: On Finitude and Humanity 307
Katherine Withy

Chapter Thirteen
Dwelling after 1945: Heidegger among the Architects 325
   Tobias Keiling

List of Contributors 353

Index 355

Acknowledgments

As editors, we would like to express our thanks to all of the contributors for their participation in this volume as well as to Michael Rinella and Dennis Schmidt at SUNY Press for supporting the project through to publication, to the anonymous reviewers of the original proposal and manuscript, and to Diane Ganeles at SUNY Press for her great work in guiding the volume through the production process. We would also like to acknowledge Joanna Hodge, Thomas Sheehan, Thomas Nenon, and Steven Crowell, who were involved in earlier stages of the project. Finally, thanks are also due to Randall Lindstrom for assisting with editing and final manuscript preparation.

An earlier version of chapter 5 appeared as "Die Wende zum Ort und die Wiedergewinnung des Menschen: Heideggers Kritik des 'Humanismus,'" in *Heideggers Weg in die Moderne: Eine Verortung der "Schwarzen Hefte,"* ed. Hans-Helmuth Gander and Magnus Streit (Frankfurt: Klostermann, 2016), 115–34. We are grateful to be able to include a reworking of the essay, in its original English, in this volume.

Special acknowledgment is also due to Ilona Schneider for kindly allowing the use of her image *Warehouse Living*.

Introduction

INGO FARIN AND JEFF MALPAS

"No time has known so much and such a variety about the human being as is the case today. No time has been able to present its knowledge of mankind so urgently and in so captivating a manner as is the case today. No time has previously been able to offer this knowledge as quickly and easily as today. But also, no time has known less about what the human being is than today. In no other time has the human being become as questionable as in ours."[1] Heidegger wrote these lines in *Kant and the Problem of Metaphysics*, published in 1929. World War I was still a fresh memory; World War II was not even a remote possibility. The relatively "stable" phase of the Weimar Republic (from 1925 onwards) was just coming to an end with the rise of the National Socialists and the Great Crash in the autumn of 1929. Seen in a somewhat broader historical context, Heidegger's note about the unsolved enigma of the human has even more salience, for it was written before Auschwitz; Hiroshima and Nagasaki; before the wars in Vietnam and the Middle East; before the digital revolution, artificial intelligence, and the emergence of the internet; before the Human Genome Project; before the threat of global climate change and the declaration of our geological epoch as the Anthropocene(a declaration that is not without problems of its own). In the last decades, we have also seen the entrenchment of excessively bureaucratic and technocratic forms of governance in many parts of the world, and, more recently, a reemergence, around the world, of populist authoritarianism. After the global financial crisis in 2008, we have witnessed staggering disparities in wealth and income in the world. At no point in human history were there more people fleeing their home countries because of war and violence. The global pandemic that began in 2019 has ushered in a new period of crisis—not merely a crisis of public health, but also of the balance of private rights and public good, of state control and personal autonomy. The war in the Ukraine with its unspeakable horrors casts a dark shadow on the future of Europe, indeed the future of the world at large.

All of this shows that Heidegger's lines, as quoted above, are as relevant today as they were almost a century ago. While scientific knowledge is growing at ever faster speed, we know less and less about the human being qua *human* being. Our current perplexity is quite real. Human ingenuity in controlling and mastering nature through science and technology has somehow failed to produce a more just society, lasting peace, and the enjoyment of life. The twenty-first century begins with a return to the struggle for bare life. However, we no longer live under the dictates of nature. Our world is shaped by human design, human intervention, and human responses. We find ourselves in a thoroughly "humanized" world and are still haunted by our real ignorance about the human being qua *human* being. Are we really just machines to propagate our genes? Are we just raw material of life, carefully protected and ordered around by an opaque state-bureaucracy? Are we merely passive consumers with an illusionary choice, pried upon and manipulated by an invasive and manipulative surveillance capitalism? We do protest any such notion or tendency. But on what basis? Do we know?

When Heidegger writes that "no time has known less about what the human being is than today," we can easily note the Socratic inflection and the philosophical determination to fend off ready-made or dogmatic answers.[2] For Heidegger, it is a question that stares each one of us in the face: What am I as a human being? In fact, Heidegger argues that the real conundrum is not so much that we do not know the answer to this question as it is that "we do not even know *how* to pose the question concerning the human being."[3] Thus, Heidegger aims to keep the question *open*, and he invites us to experience the truly unsettling nature of it. As Heidegger presents matters, we first must submit to the space of thinking and engage the question concerning the human from a proper philosophical perspective, without any recourse to unexamined concepts. For this reason, he does not mouth pious assurances that philosophy is committed to "humanism," as if to seek public approbation for philosophy. For Heidegger, every humanism is metaphysical, and every metaphysics implies humanism.[4] Moreover, since he rejects metaphysics, he also rejects metaphysical humanism. However, Heidegger warns against the fallacy in concluding that the philosophical critique of metaphysical humanism equals the advocacy of barbarism and the inhuman. As Heidegger puts it, he "opposes humanism because it does not set the *humanitas* of the human high enough."[5] The proper essence of the human, on Heidegger's account, resides in the capacity to respond to what there is, *being*. Thus, Heidegger asserts that "the human occurs essentially in such a way that he is the 'there' [das Da], that is the clearing of Being."[6] As such, the human is never an objectively present entity, and least of all is the human thought when defined in abstraction from the essential relation to being and the world in which the human lives.

How Heidegger's thought on the human can be brought to bear on our own situation is the main theme addressed in the chapters that make up this volume. In the spirit of Heidegger, none of the essays sets out from a dogmatic position, Heideggerian or otherwise. Many of Heidegger's key-terms are rethought, expanded upon, and also critiqued, as well as defended against popular misunderstandings. In this way, this volume aims to contribute to a renewed debate about the human in these very unsettling times, as well as to a renewed understanding of the way in which the human arises as a question for Heidegger—and the way in which he responds to that question. The latter question is perhaps more pressing now than it has been previously. Since the publication of Heidegger's *Black Notebooks* from the 1930s onwards, and in the light of the anti-Semitic comments they contain, as well as Heidegger's seeming willingness, at certain key moments, to prioritize a certain notion of the "philosophical" over and above the human,[7] the question of the place of the human in Heidegger's thought appears more difficult and more urgent.[8] Surprisingly, there have been few previous works that have directly thematized the topic of the human in Heidegger's philosophy, and so one aim of the volume is to stimulate a wider and more sustained engagement with the topic. Although there are a very small number of chapters that focus solely on Heidegger, the majority of the contributions adopt a comparative approach, exploring issues of the human in ways that bring Heidegger's thinking on this matter into conjunction with a wide range of other thinkers from Immanuel Kant to René Char. To some extent this reflects the way in which the questions that concern the human have frequently been at the center of critical engagement with Heidegger's work. But the volume is not only focused on such comparisons—also important are engagements with a broad sweep of topics from architecture and animality to identity, race, and genocide.

The volume is divided into three parts. Part 1 explores a set of questions around the idea of philosophical anthropology in Heidegger's work as it relates to a range of thinkers from Kant onwards. Part 2 explores a set of issues concerning the place of the human in the world, including the relation of the human to forms of otherness, whether the otherness at issue within the idea of the human itself or with respect to that which is beyond the human, as well as ideas of place, play, and openness. Part 3 explores a set of issues that are more directly related to human identity, self, and finitude. There is much that the volume does not address, but that is inevitable given the nature of the topic. The aim is indeed to open up the issues rather than provide a definitive or comprehensive survey.

Notes

1. Martin Heidegger, *Kant und das Problem der Metaphysik*, vol. 3 of *Gesamtausgabe*, ed. Friedrich-Wilhelm von Herrmann (Frankfurt: Klostermann, 1991), 209. Heidegger himself refers to Scheler's similar statement in his *Die Stellung des Menschen im Kosmos*, first published in 1928.

2. Hegel writes: "*Dogmatism* as a way of thinking, whether in ordinary knowing or in the study of philosophy, is nothing else but the opinion that the True consists in a proposition which is a fixed result, or which is immediately known." See Georg Wilhelm Friedrich Hegel, *Phänomenologie des Geistes* (Hamburg: Felix Meiner, 1952), 34.

3. Martin Heidegger, *Der deutsche Idealismus (Fichte, Schelling, Hegel) und die philosophische Problemlage der Gegenwart*, vol. 28 of *Gesamtausgabe*, ed. Claudius Strube (Frankfurt: Klostermann, 1997), 17.

4. See Martin Heidegger, "Brief über den 'Humanismus,'" in *Wegmarken*, vol. 9 of *Gesamtausgabe*, ed. Friedrich-Wilhelm von Herrmann (Frankfurt: Klostermann, 2004), 321.

5. Heidegger, "Brief über den 'Humanismus,'" 330.

6. Heidegger, "Brief über den 'Humanismus,'" 325.

7. See Ingo Farin and Jeff Malpas, "On Overestimating Philosophy: Lessons from Heidegger's *Black Notebooks*," *Journal of Aesthetics and Phenomenology* 4, no. 2 (2017): 183–95.

8. The *Black Notebooks* are a stimulus to the questions at issue here but are nevertheless not themselves a focus of this volume. They are dealt with in considerable detail, however, in Ingo Farin and Jeff Malpas, eds., *Reading Heidegger's "Black Notebooks 1931–1941"* (Cambridge, MA: MIT Press, 2016).

Part I

Anthropology and Philosophy

Chapter One

Heidegger's Engagement with and Critique of Philosophical Anthropology

Ingo Farin

Every philosophical question inquires into the whole.
—Martin Heidegger, *Vom Wesen der menschlichen Freiheit: Einleitung in die Philosophie*

Introduction

Without a doubt Heidegger's path of thinking passes through the field of philosophical anthropology, and he inscribes his own lines of thought in it. However, by 1928 Heidegger turns away from any constructive engagement with philosophical anthropology, providing, instead, an ever more radical critique of it, which he upholds to the very end of his life. Any assessment of Heidegger's view on philosophical anthropology must reckon with this evolution in Heidegger's thinking. It is as easy to overestimate Heidegger's early engagement with anthropological thought as it is to underestimate his continued emphasis on the human and the essence of the human when he breaks with anthropologism. Simple slogans about Heidegger's "anthropological machine" or his supposed "anti-humanism" do not do justice to his very complex and changing thought on the matter. A further complication arises out of the curious fact that, although Heidegger and Husserl are both opposed to "anthropologism"—for which opposition they actually provide structurally similar arguments—they nevertheless end up charging each other with just that: anthropologism. Adepts of Heidegger or Husserl are quick to recycle these criticisms, according to which Heidegger is falling back into historicism, psychologism, anthropologism, and so on, whereas Husserl is supposedly succumbing to the ills of subjectivism, which is just another form of anthropologism. If anything, my paper wants to challenge these simplistic views.

After delineating the relative ease with which Heidegger appropriates the anthropological theme in his early lecture courses up to 1926, I turn to Heidegger's position in *Being and Time* that is characterized by a certain containment strategy, that is, Heidegger's attempt to keep open the possibility of a philosophical anthropology within the confines of a philosophy of Being and Dasein. Next, I turn to Heidegger's philosophical arguments against any philosophical anthropology in 1928, before addressing Husserl's charge of Heidegger's supposed anthropologism. Following that, I review Heidegger's interpretative shift toward an onto-historical account of the prevalence of (philosophical) anthropology in modernity. This shift occurs already in 1929 and Heidegger continues this line of thought until the end of his career. Lastly, I return to Husserl and Heidegger's embroilment over the issue of each other's supposed anthropologism and offer concluding remarks about Heidegger's relation to the anthropological theme, and the role of the human being and Dasein in his philosophy.

Factical Life and Hints of a Hermeneutical Anthropology

If Heidegger's lecture courses from the early 1920s show anything, it is that he is not preoccupied with the question of Being, nor does he adopt Husserl's philosophy of consciousness or the phenomenological reduction (although he is committed to phenomenological and hermeneutical descriptions of phenomena). The watchword of early Heidegger is life, factical life, and the interpretation of factical life, or the "hermeneutics of facticity."[1] For Heidegger, life, life experiences, and the interpretation of life constitute ground zero for philosophy. Philosophy starts from the "primacy of factical life."[2] He provides the following formal indication of factical life: "Factical life in its facticity, its richness of relations, is closest to us: we are it."[3] Put differently, we as human beings live factical lives, and, therefore, what is at issue in Heidegger's philosophy of factical life is nothing other than *der*

Mensch, "the human being."⁴ Thus, Heidegger explicitly declares that "the subject matter of philosophical research is human existence [*das menschliche Dasein*]."⁵ Heidegger wants to describe or interpret this factical life that each one of us lives: "Life—my life, your life, your lives, our lives—we want to comprehend in its most general typical features."⁶ More specifically, the focus is on the ontological structure of the life of the human being in conjunction with its embeddedness within the world. Heidegger calls this the "world-character of life," for, so he argues, without a world in which factical life finds itself and without relations to other livers, no human being can live or exist.⁷

In short, early Heidegger aims at an account of what it means to live a life, a *human* life, and he does that in clear opposition to the standard academic conception of philosophy, according to which philosophy revolves around supposedly fixed epistemological or ontological "problems." Set against the complacent continuation of hoary themes in the philosophical tradition, the turn to human life has its own urgency, for it addresses nothing less than the meaning of human life. Heidegger begins his 1926 lectures on Dilthey with the following ironic and, yet, serious statement: "The theme of these lectures will appear somewhat remote and unfamiliar perhaps, but it involves a fundamental problem pervading the whole of Western philosophy: the problem of the meaning of life. What kind of reality is life?"⁸ Heidegger underscores that, in asking this question, the questioner is immediately implicated, because he or she lives a factical life.

Thus, Heidegger undertakes to explicate what he calls the "categories of life,"⁹ categories in which life understands itself. Many of these categories, for instance, care, distantiality, anxiety, and so on, reappear in the form of *existentialia* in *Being and Time*, but, and this is the important point, in Heidegger's early lecture courses they stand alone, as it were; they are not part of an overarching architectonic, because early Heidegger did not have a "system," and certainly not a grand philosophy of Being.

Now, if we take philosophical anthropology to mean the study of man, Heidegger's philosophy of factical life—that is, the study of the factical life of human beings—qualifies as anthropology in that sense. Heidegger's anthropological life philosophy is decidedly anti-academic, emancipatory, pragmatic, and historical, and to that extent, consciously or not, reviving the anthropological turn in German popular philosophy during the early Enlightenment, which was also favored by the early Kant and the young Herder.¹⁰ In fact, Heidegger's philosophy of factical human life brings philosophy down to earth in a manner that is also reminiscent of Feuerbach's attempt to put philosophy on a thoroughly anthropological footing, even though Heidegger would not subscribe to Feuerbach's naturalism and sensualism.[11] But Heidegger would certainly agree to Feuerbach's principle that philosophy has to start in the here and now, or what Feuerbach calls "Dasein."[12]

To continue with Heidegger, his life philosophy is primarily geared toward self-clarification and self-emancipation with the obvious intent to enable a better self-understanding of the human being qua human being. Thus Heidegger writes that the aim of the hermeneutics of factual life is to prepare a proper understanding of oneself in order to address and thus potentially overcome the "self-alienation" (*Selbstentfremdung*) with which each factical life is "smitten."[13] Since Heidegger is interested primarily in individual life, rather than the species being of man (as Feuerbach and Marx are), it is not surprising that he happily fuses his life philosophy with "the great truth," discovered in ancient Greece, that philosophy is the search for self-knowledge. Glossing the *gnothi seauton* as "know yourself, that is, know what you are and be as what you know yourself," Heidegger adds the following comment: "This self-knowledge [*Selbsterkenntnis*] of humankind [*Menschheit*] in the human [*im Menschen*], i.e., the essence of the human, is philosophy, and as far as possible removed from any psychology or morality."[14] That is to say, Heidegger combines the phenomenological and hermeneutical investigation of factical life—What are the ontological structures of factical life as such?—with the self-reflective quest for self-clarification and self-emancipation of the concrete individual human being—What or who am I as this particular human being? For Heidegger, giving an account of oneself, to take over one's life and own it, to live it in "self-responsibility" (*Selbstverantwortung*), is the indispensable motivational ground of philosophizing about factical life.[15] This is hardly the stuff of academic university philosophy with its neatly developed "problems" in carefully managed special "disciplines" like epistemology, metaphysics, and logic.

Heidegger holds that the philosophy of factical life is the very cornerstone or foundation of philosophy as such; it is not a mere regional ontology or a branch of philosophy. According to Heidegger, the factical life that we as human beings live is the primary, unsurpassable, real, and concrete ground for understanding everything we encounter in the world, and in which all theory, including all philosophy, is rooted, knowingly or not. This is the real import of Heidegger's "primacy of life."[16] It directly challenges the traditional assumption of the primacy of consciousness, the cogito (the "subject"), or the "primacy of theory" (as upheld by the neo-Kantians, as well as Husserl). With the "primacy of life," which is the primacy of human life, Heidegger also throws down the gauntlet to the friends of apriorism and eternal truths, and all those who appeal to a life-transcendent or absolute ground, over and above the life-relations within *this* world, *here and now*.

This last point can be elucidated by bringing in another crucial feature of Heidegger's concept of factical life: its historicity or *Geschichtlichkeit*. For Heidegger, factical life is "historical," because it is "stretched out" from birth to death; it projects itself into the future, recollects the past and attends to the present. In this sense, each human being or Dasein is itself "time" or "history."[17] Essentially embedded in the world and history, no human being can ever speculate him or herself out of this historical world. Moreover, since "philosophy springs from factical life experience,"[18] it follows that all philosophy is itself historical, or "historical cognition,"[19] which means that it is not cognition from "a priori principles." Philosophy is inextricably involved in a historical-hermeneutical horizon; it is influenced by past concepts and motivations, which, when taken up and projected into the future, generate new insights, which recoil onto the understanding of the past. In other words, there is no over-historical standpoint, according to Heidegger. Therefore, Heidegger asserts that "the dream" of "absolute knowledge" must be given up, because philosophy is ineluctably "historical knowledge."[20] In almost Feuerbachian terms, Heidegger calls "the idea of absolute truth" a mere "opiate," and he severely rebukes academic philosophers who still bandy it about at universities.[21] It is entirely in line with this that Heidegger also rejects all "religious ideology and delusion" and categorically declares that philosophy "is in principle a-theistic."[22] Just as Feuerbach proclaims that "the human [*das Menschliche*] alone is the real and the true," such that "man [*der Mensch*] is the measure of reason,"[23] so Heidegger makes historical, factical life the unsurpassable reality.

Given that factical life is inescapably historical, it follows that it is always embedded in a particular historical situation, or the "intellectual situation" (*geistige Situation*) of the time.[24] However, the historical situation is the opening in which the past is reviewed and reinterpreted in light of future possibilities. Consequently, Heidegger argues that one cannot blithely philosophize about man's historicity as such and then pass over in silence the actual intellectual historical situation in which one happens to philosophize. In other words, philosophy as historical cognition is "critique of the present time" (*Kritik der Gegenwart*).[25] Moreover, since the "intellectual situation" is also very much articulated in and through the sediments of "historical consciousness," Heidegger also advocates a "critique of history," insisting again, against all antiquarian tendencies, that "the critique of history is always only the critique of the present."[26]

A prime target of Heidegger's critique is the barren academic philosophy of the early twentieth century, which, far removed from the vicissitudes of human affairs, constructs a make-believe world, "an objective refuge" that comes with "the prospect of tranquilizing certainty and security."[27] It is in opposition to this soporific philosophizing of school philosophy that Heidegger presents his historical life philosophy. In turning to the structures of factical life and paying close attention to the way humans live, Heidegger at the same time forges the tools for a critical engagement with the contemporary situation. In other words, Heidegger's conception of "critical philosophy" breaks with the objective assurances of complacent school philosophy.

The idea to make philosophy relevant to life, to employ it for the elucidation of one's own historical situation and one's own role in it, is certainly reminiscent of early German Enlightenment philosophy and its preference for a distinctive historical mode of philosophizing and its turn toward the human being. As John Zammito has shown, the very creation of philosophical anthropology is a direct result of Enlightenment impulses.[28] In its impetus and orientation, Heidegger's early life philosophy is very close to this. While it is true that Heidegger does not refer to this chapter in German philosophy or employ the term "anthropology" in a positive sense in his early lecture courses,[29] he certainly must have been aware of the emergence of anthropological philosophy in the eighteenth century, especially that of Kant and Herder, but also Feuerbach. Be that as it may, to the extent that Heidegger's life philosophy is about human life as the central fulcrum around which everything revolves, it is a philosophical anthropology of its own kind. Had Heidegger never undertaken to write *Being and Time* or any of his later works, he would be remembered today as a philosopher working on an unfinished phenomenological and hermeneutical anthropology. The main systematic reason for this is that early Heidegger carefully sidesteps any commitment to a transcendental move.

Philosophical Anthropology within the Bounds of *Being and Time*

At first blush, *Being and Time* constitutes a break with Heidegger's earlier lecture courses, because here the question of Being takes center stage, and not the hermeneutics of factical life. And yet, the anthropological theme is not forgotten at all, for Heidegger not only explicitly affirms the significance of "philosophical anthropology," albeit only as a branch of philosophy, but he also casts the essential ground or base of the human being, that is, Dasein, as *the* pivot for the question of Being as such. Put differently, in *Being and Time* Heidegger reconceptualizes the essence of the human being as Dasein and reinserts it at the very center not only of philosophy, but reality at large.

While the primacy of Dasein in *Being and Time* can hardly be missed, it is worthwhile recalling Heidegger's argument for what he calls "the ontic-ontological priority of Dasein."[30] He argues that the question of Being can be advanced only by first determining who could even *ask* that question. This must be a kind of entity that in its being can pose questions, seek clarifications about its own being, inquire into the structure of other beings, and, generally, must have an "understanding of Being" (*Seinsverständnis*).[31] Heidegger designates this entity as "Dasein," adding that "each one of us" is such Dasein.[32] Dasein signifies nothing other than the site (the *Da*) where the understanding and the putting into question of Being (*Sein*) occurs. Hence, Dasein is the ontological/transcendental principle or necessary condition not only of all ontology, all science or *Wissenschaft*, including philosophical anthropology, but also of the very *concept* of the human itself. Neither ontology or science, nor the concept of the human is possible without a basic understanding of what it means for something to be, and the understanding of being is what distinguishes Dasein from all other entities. In *Being and Time*, Dasein is the ontological and transcendental sine qua non. Dasein is "the ontic-ontological condition for the possibility of all ontologies,"[33] all science, and also all conceptualization and self-understanding of the human being as well.

One can argue that just as "the human standpoint" reigns supreme in Kant's *Critique of Pure Reason*, so too Dasein designates the ultimate ground from which the sciences and the question of Being can be accessed in Heidegger's *Being and Time*. According to Heidegger, the primacy of Dasein requires that it must be investigated before the question of Being can be tackled. With an obvious nod to Kant, Heidegger calls this investigation "the analytic of Dasein." This is "fundamental ontology," because Dasein is the foundation, the original site or ground, for all scientific and ontological investigations whatsoever.[34]

However, since Dasein is also the basic and essential ontological ground for any conception of the human, for Dasein is nothing other than the "understanding" of beings and Being as such, Heidegger holds that the analytic of Dasein "also makes headway with a task *which is hardly less pressing than that of the question of Being itself* [my emphasis]—the task of laying bare the *a priori* basis which must be visible before the question of 'what man is' can be discussed philosophically."[35] This is certainly proof that in *Being and Time* Heidegger has not dropped the question "What is man?" Rather, Heidegger argues that Dasein, that is, the ability to relate to one's own being and the being of others in the midst of Being at large, in short, the understanding of Being, is a necessary condition for the human being to come to an understanding of itself *as* a human *being*—in contrast to other beings and Being as such.

In a lecture course from 1930, Heidegger writes: "If man did not possess an understanding of Being, he could not comport to himself as a being: he could not say 'I' and 'you,' he could not be 'he' himself, he could not be a person. *Man would be impossible in his essence. Accordingly, the understanding of being is the ground for the possibility of the essence of man.*"[36] Without Dasein, no concept of man, no recognition of human beings as such, would be possible. Dasein is thus the ground for the possibility of the human.

Dasein is certainly not to be confused with a Cartesian cogito, for it is thrown into the world not of its own making, and it is exposed to other beings and Being at large, always within the horizon of its own finite time. All of this bespeaks the finitude of Dasein. Nonetheless, and in keeping with his earlier mentioned rejection of a postulated absolute, Heidegger insists that truth is relative to Dasein.[37] Ultimately, it also underwrites his further claim that "Being (not entities) is something which 'there is' only in so far as and as long as Dasein is."[38] It is highly significant that Heidegger joins truth and the human in Dasein, as if to recall Plato's insight that "the soul which has never seen the truth can never pass into human form."[39]

Since "Dasein" designates, as already mentioned, the entity "which each of us is," there can be little doubt that in *Being and Time* Heidegger's term "Dasein" refers to individual human beings,[40] insofar as "each one of us" has an understanding of Being, has the capacity to inquire and ask questions concerning our very own being vis-à-vis other beings and Being at large. This alone circumscribes the connotation of Dasein. It is the essential, ontological ground in each human being. Thus "Dasein" is what one may call an "open" or "indicating" concept, which points to Dasein in each one of us, without delimiting any supposed unchanging or substantive nature.

Historicity is built into Dasein; it is not a static or material essence. Hence, Dasein must not be associated with traditional meanings of the human (rational animal, ego cogito, *ens creatum*, will to power, and so on[41]), all of which define the human as if it was a given object in the world, which runs counter to the hermeneutic-transcendental capacity of Dasein, that is, its understanding of Being.

Heidegger clearly indicates that *Being and Time* is not intended as "a comprehensive ontology of Dasein"[42] nor, more broadly, as an ontology of the human, because (1) Dasein designates the ontological ground of the human, not Dasein's or the human's reality in its epic fullness and concreteness, and (2) the analytic of Dasein is geared toward explicating the meaning of Being at large, and not the human condition as such. Nevertheless, Heidegger insists that the analytic of Dasein provides, as he puts it, "no inessential pieces" for such a complete ontology, which in turn would yield the necessary basis for the attempt to build a " 'philosophical' anthropology" worth its name.[43] That is to say, the analytic of Dasein serves also, and not just incidentally, the ends of a philosophical anthropology aiming at addressing the question "What is man?"[44] In line with this, Heidegger also supports empirical anthropological research and the discovery of new ontic facts about the human being.

Quite reasonably, Heidegger holds that, as a positive science, empirical anthropology can hardly "wait" for the philosophical clarification of the ontological basis of the human in its essential ground in Dasein. Therefore, Heidegger suggests that philosophy would have to limit itself to "revisiting" whatever ontic results empirical anthropology would unearth, providing merely the critical and ontological clarification of such research on the basis of the ontology of Dasein.[45] This is in sync with Heidegger's general idea that ontological research may be able to "correct" assumptions and theoretical positions in the positive sciences if they conflict with it, but philosophy cannot delineate or direct the research projects of positive sciences as such.[46] This is a remarkably flexible conception, for it keeps open the communication between the empirical and positive sciences and philosophy.

Overall, we can see that Heidegger separates three levels of ontological research: (1) the analytic of Dasein, and, based on it, (2) the comprehensive ontology of Dasein, and, again based on it, (3) a complete philosophical anthropology.[47] Independently of these philosophical research themes, there is room for an empirical anthropology, supplying ontic research results to philosophy, which, theoretically at least, could be "revised" by the "corrections"

16 | Ingo Farin

from the side of philosophy. Not surprisingly, Heidegger explicitly, and without reservations, welcomes Cassirer's work on myth, which is much indebted to empirical anthropological findings.[48] Schematically, this can be depicted as in figure 1.1.

In conclusion we can say that, in *Being and Time*, Heidegger does not lose sight of the anthropological theme. Rather, he transforms and sublates the issue by focusing on the ontological ground of the human being in Dasein. Inscribed within a philosophy of Being and Dasein, the question of the human being is still very much present, but no longer reducible to traditional anthropology or psychology. It is for this reason that Heidegger insists on the demarcation (*Abgrenzung*) of the analytic of Dasein from anthropology,[49] especially if such anthropology starts out from an already assumed concept of the human that is no longer open to philosophical questioning.

Heidegger's Break with Philosophical Anthropology

After *Being and Time*, Heidegger severs his philosophy from any anthropological thematic, marking a fundamental shift in his thinking. Moreover, Heidegger moves to a more pronounced Dasein-centric view and makes freedom the basis of Dasein.[50] To begin with the first point, in his *Kant and*

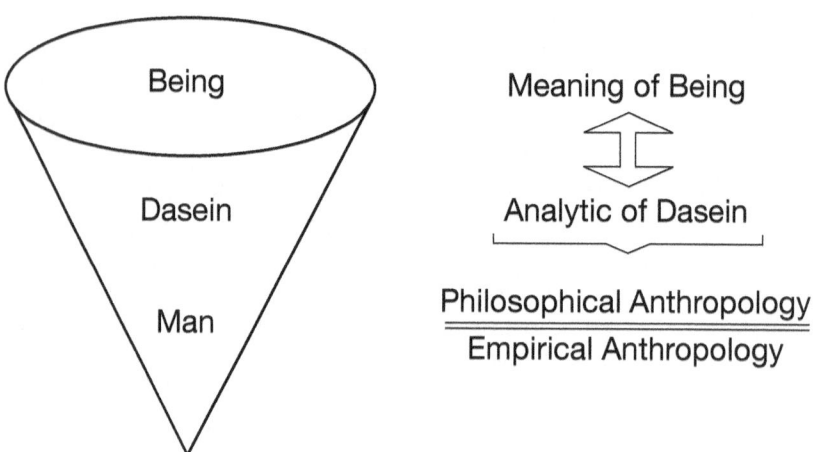

Figure 1.1.

the Problem of Metaphysics,[51] and his lecture on "Philosophical Anthropology and the Metaphysics of Dasein,"[52] both from the year 1929, Heidegger subjects the "anthropological tendencies" of his time to a decisive and devastating critique,[53] signaling the end of any toleration or accommodation of philosophical anthropology in his philosophy. That is to say, from 1929 Heidegger situates his philosophy at the opposite pole to the anthropological tendencies of his time.

Heidegger's critique of (mostly contemporary) anthropological thought aims at what he considers the broad anthropological current or tendency in society and philosophy at large, rather than a particular doctrine or position. First, referring to the plethora of (unnamed) anthropological works, essays, and treatises, mostly of an empirical character, Heidegger notes that it is very easy to relate everything under the sun to the human being by means of so many different rubrics, for instance, its somatic or psychological structure, or its biological, linguistic, or cultural capacities, its historical malleability, its propensity for various worldviews, and so on. However, the very concept of the human that is posited in such investigations remains woefully inadequate, indeterminate, and without the prospect of an emerging inner unity.[54] The charge here is that the constant, widespread, and very extensive use of anthropological investigations comes at the cost of the resultant indeterminacy and emptiness of the very concept of the human to which these studies refer.

Leaving these empirical studies of the human being to one side, Heidegger then turns to anthropological thought with a decidedly philosophical angle. Here, he differentiates between an anthropology pursued in a "philosophical manner" (*in philosophischer Weise*) and an anthropology undertaken with an explicit "philosophical intent" (*philosophischer Absicht*).[55] The former aims at a philosophical account of the human, distinguishing it from other entities, such as plants, animals, God, and so on. This kind of philosophical anthropology aims at a "regional ontology of man." Here, Heidegger's criticism is that this approach fails to explain why it is essential for the concept of philosophy to thematize man, or why the human is more essential to philosophy than any other regional ontology.[56] In other words, this approach does not explain why the study of the human is intrinsically related to the concept of philosophy, or why the concept of philosophy requires a clarification of the ontology of the human.

By contrast, an anthropology undertaken with an explicit "philosophical intent" holds that the "the question concerning the human being has an especially relevant function for philosophy itself and its realization."[57] Here, man is not just a being among other entities, whose ontological features can be studied next to the ontology of plants and animals, and so on; rather, man is singled out and accorded a special significance for the very task of carrying out philosophy. Unsurprisingly, such philosophical anthropology aims at an "ethics" or a "worldview" as the ultimate goal of philosophy, or, alternatively, attempts to secure a foundation for philosophy in man's presumed special position, as in, for instance, Descartes's cogito.[58] Often the two motifs blend together, giving rise to the view that in some general fashion "man becomes the origin and end of all philosophizing."[59] Heidegger's main objection here is that in this kind of philosophical anthropology the very concept of the human remains undertheorized, for it is either taken over from the tradition without further scrutiny or quickly established on the spot by way of ad hoc definitions. Hence Heidegger argues that this idea of a philosophical anthropology is too indeterminate and fluctuating to serve as the intended "master discipline of philosophy."[60]

According to Heidegger, this indeterminacy is also at play in the indecisive debates between advocates and critics of philosophical anthropology. When the critics denounce "anthropologism," mostly on the grounds of its supposed "empiricism," "subjectivism," and "scepticism,"[61] they usually propose some other, more or less arbitrarily selected entity as central for philosophy, without being able to provide a much more compelling argument for this choice than the friends of philosophical anthropology can muster for their choice of the special position of man.[62] According to Heidegger, the interminable debate between proponents and critics of philosophical anthropology points to the absence of any compelling argument that could either validate or invalidate the purported singular significance of the human for the task of philosophy. In short, Heidegger holds that the friends and foes of philosophical anthropology are united in wanting a proper philosophical base. They fail to demonstrate, philosophically, why man is necessarily the central thematic in philosophy, or why not.

To expand on Heidegger's point here, it may be helpful to note that it will not do to argue that, because humans create philosophy, they must be the decisive theme in philosophy too. After all, painting, music, and writing are human endeavors, and, as far as we know, human endeavors only, but it does not follow that, therefore, the human being is of central significance, let alone of exclusive thematic import within these fields, as if painting humans, or singing or writing about humans would be a defining feature of these respective activities. Hence, although philosophy is certainly dependent on human beings, it does not follow that the human being has to be the central theme in philosophy, which, however, is the underlying supposition in anthropology with a philosophical intent.

In laying bare the fundamental weakness in philosophical anthropology, Heidegger is certainly also engaged in an implicit self-correction of his earlier anthropological leanings, which we have discussed above.[63] Therefore, it is not surprising that Heidegger's aim is not only destructive. Indeed, he aims at a "radical" transformation of the entire debate about philosophical anthropology by supplying what is missing in it, that is, the proper philosophical account that determines the human significance in relation to philosophy. But to accomplish this, one must draw on a determinate idea of philosophy itself.[64] This alone can overcome the stalemate between the proponents and critics of "anthropologism."

Heidegger begins his argument by claiming that the very idea of philosophy or metaphysics (he does not differentiate between the two) is distinct from the positive sciences in that philosophy does not thematize this or that particular region of entities, but rather problematizes beings at large, the totality of all beings, and thus Being as such.[65] However, for Heidegger "the question concerning Being as such [*Sein als solchem*]" is inseparable from "the possibility of the understanding of Being."[66] Without an understanding of Being, there is no foothold for asking the explicit question about Being in order to explicate it. Using terminology that is familiar from *Being and Time*, Heidegger holds that this understanding of Being is present in the entity that "each one of us" is, an entity we commonly "designate" as "the human being."[67] Next, Heidegger claims that the understanding of Being is not merely a characteristic that we empirically find in humans and that we could delineate by investigating the nature of the human being. Rather, the understanding of Being first of all opens up the space, or rather the world, where entities appear, in the midst of which we also find ourselves as human beings, distinct from other entities but always involved, in one way or another, with the things that "are," as present at hand, or ready to hand, and so on.

Heidegger's point is that we understand ourselves as human *beings* only on the basis of an understanding of other beings and Being. But we cannot deduce the understanding of Being from the (theoretically or scientifically determined) nature of human beings, for the concept of the latter is derivative of the former; the human being as an existing entity is grasped as such only by way of the prior understanding of Being. Heidegger designates this original understanding of Being "Dasein";[68] it is the "there" for all beings in the midst of which there is the human being too. It is for this reason that Heidegger holds that Dasein, or the understanding of Being, is the ground or origin of the human. In other words, the human being is "founded" upon Dasein.[69] Dasein is the essence that defines the human. The human does not define Dasein.[70] Heidegger once even suggests that in virtue of its Dasein (its being "there" in the world) the human being (or Dasein) is "more than a human being,"[71] by which he means more than an empirically present at hand entity.

Thus, Dasein takes center stage and the human being is philosophically significant only to the extent that it appropriates its ground in Dasein. Moreover, since Dasein is characterized by an understanding of Being, each Dasein, in its own way, practices ontology or philosophy, however preconceptual that may be. Kant's claim that metaphysics is a "natural disposition" of the human being is here vindicated with regard to Dasein.[72]

For Heidegger, Dasein and philosophy are interdependent, hermeneutically entailing each other. There is no (explicit or implicit) philosophy unless there is Dasein, and there is no Dasein unless there is philosophy (at least in its inchoate form as a preontological understanding of Being). Since Dasein's prephilosophical understanding of Being is the only foothold for the question of Being, the very clarification of Dasein (of its understanding of Being) intrinsically belongs to philosophy, if and when philosophy addresses the question of Being. Put differently, Dasein cannot "be" or "own" itself as an existing being without a comprehensive grasp of Being, even if it is not fully articulated and/or systematically laid down. In other words, Dasein is dependent on a philosophy that investigates the question of Being.

Heidegger now calls the clarification of Dasein "the metaphysics of Dasein," which replaces the earlier terminology of the "analytics of Dasein."[73] Compared to *Being and Time*, this indicates a much stronger Dasein-centric orientation. Partly using Kantian language, Heidegger writes that "the laying of the ground of metaphysics is grounded in a metaphysics of Dasein."[74] This certainly underscores the importance of this "metaphysics of Dasein" as the essential and unavoidable entry into metaphysics or philosophy. Following Heidegger's own clue, it also shows a certain affinity to Kant's "metaphysics of a metaphysics," that is, the critical preparation for an undogmatic system of metaphysics.[75] Thus, Heidegger insists that the clarification of the idea of Being must revert to Dasein and advance Dasein's self-clarification, insofar as it is a being and ontological in itself.

To illustrate that Dasein not only calls forth philosophy, but is also called into question by philosophy, it is instructive to recall, for example, that, according to Heidegger, the very question of Being is to be laid out in terms of time. This entails an investigation into that entity where time shows itself, that is, Dasein or Dasein in the human being.[76] In other words, "the basic question concerning Being and time forces us into the question concerning the human being."[77] More specifically, the philosophical thematic of time cannot be dealt with as the time of the other or the time of history, but only as one's *own* time. Hence, philosophy does not only abstractly refer to Dasein as the home of time; it also throws the philosophizing Dasein back onto itself as time. Each Dasein "has" its own time; its time runs out, and Dasein therefore stands in question as this individual, finite temporal Dasein.

To summarize, Dasein and philosophy are intrinsically related, indeed mutually implicated in each other. Hence, they are not merely contingently or externally juxtaposed, as is the case when philosophical anthropology merely stipulates the centrality of the human being for philosophy.

In making the "metaphysics of Dasein" the lynch pin of philosophy, Heidegger decisively bids farewell to philosophical anthropology,[78] for it is not the human being as such, but rather Dasein that is the beginning and end of philosophy. Dasein is not reducible to the empirically existing individual, or any supposedly prominent characteristic of the human.[79] Dasein is the understanding of Being without which we as humans could not even conceive of ourselves as human *beings*. Moreover, Dasein is not something we possess or discard at our discretion. Thus, Heidegger writes that we as humans "are thrown into the original happening of Dasein's understanding of being,"[80] which means that we cannot claim control and mastery over Dasein, or Being for that matter.[81]

However, this does not mean submission to an unalterable objective Dasein or anonymous happening in humans. Rather, Dasein is free to relate to and involve itself with the beings that are disclosed to be there. It is often ignored, sometimes for ulterior motives, that Heidegger thinks freedom an essential attribute of Dasein: "Liberation of the freedom of Dasein is a basic act of the understanding of Dasein."[82] In being there, Dasein is the very openness to relate itself to itself (what Heidegger calls existence) as well as other beings. There is no "fixed" nature in Dasein that materially circumscribes its possibilities, if, as Heidegger always insists, possibility "stands" higher than actuality."[83] Precisely this intrinsic openness also undergirds Heidegger's thesis of the "neutrality" of Dasein,[84] which, as such, is incompatible with any deterministic or static conceptions of human nature in philosophical anthropology.[85]

Here, we have reached the crucial point of Heidegger's principled rejection of philosophical anthropology, apart from his charge of its lack of philosophical rigor and the indeterminacy and arbitrariness of the presupposed concept of man. If it is true, as Odo Marquard has persuasively argued, that philosophical anthropology as such tends to be antithetical to a historical conception of the human and vice versa,[86] then it is clear that Heidegger's explicitly temporal and historical conception of Dasein and its freedom stands in principled opposition to philosophical anthropology.

However, to preempt misunderstanding, one must hasten to add that Dasein's freedom must be seen in its proper ontological dimension. Freedom is neither determined by reason, nor embedded in a law or some transcendent order. Rather, Dasein's freedom is its freedom to determine itself in its response to what it encounters in the world. In fact, it is the ontological condition for the relation to beings: "Freedom is the condition of the possibility of the disclosedness of the Being of entities, of the understanding of Being."[87] It is impossible to overestimate the radical nature of this thought. In effect, freedom here is not only the basic foundation of Dasein, or, as Heidegger puts it, "the ground of the possibility of Dasein" itself,[88] but also the free response to Being, and is, as such, inscribed in Being itself. That is, freedom is "not some particular thing" within the whole of beings, but "primary" and "permeating precisely the whole in its entirety" (*durchherrschend gerade das Ganze im Ganzen*).[89] Dasein's freedom is more original than the human being. Freedom possesses man; man is not the possessor of freedom. At best, he is the "functionary of freedom."[90] As Heidegger puts it, this freedom of the human is quite "uncanny" and "strange"—stranger even "than any God could be," precisely because of the absence of any determinate nature to which Dasein would be beholden.[91]

Although one may grant that Heidegger's Dasein-centric view of philosophy nominally breaks with standard conceptions of philosophical anthropology, there is the lingering doubt that, under the new guise of a metaphysics of Dasein, Heidegger ends up introducing something that is quite analogous to the anthropocentrism that he officially decries. However, the decisive point here is that Dasein is not identical with the human being, for Dasein is the free and open onto-hermeneutical ground of the human, that is, the unfettered understanding of entities and Being as such, in light of which alone the human can be conceived as a human being in the midst of other entities and the world at large. To this extent, the human being (especially in isolation from other beings) is in no way the decisive reference point for Heidegger's philosophy, and the charge of anthropologism leveled against Heidegger's metaphysics of Dasein is untenable.

Of course, Dasein's understanding is only actually manifest in factically existing Dasein, that is, the individual human being. Thus, Heidegger concedes that, while one could say that "the human being" stands at the center of philosophy, one would have to add, the human "not *as human being*," "but as Dasein."[92] Moreover, Dasein is not a *fundamentum inconcussum*, a self-same essence or nature; it is not a return to the notion of a subject. In fact, Dasein itself is temporal and finite, as we have seen, thrown into the world, and as such bound up with the changing world itself. What is important for Heidegger is that as human beings we owe it to ourselves to leap into the "the primordial happening of being-there" (*Urgeschehen des Daseins*),[93] instead of simply resting content with whatever supposed nature we ascribe to the human being. There is freedom in the original disclosure of Being, not a chartered way to a determinate, ultimate goal. Schematically, this can be depicted as in figure 1.2.

Still, Dasein is not unconnected to the human being, for it is the very ground of the human. Thus, it is important to emphasize that, as much as Heidegger wants to avoid anthropocentrism, he is not falling for its opposite, anti-anthropocentrism. The emphasis on the freedom and openness of Dasein indicates that, to the extent that the human being appropriates Dasein, or leaps into it, there is no merging with a given objectivity. In this sense, then, Heidegger keeps his conception of philosophy equally distant from

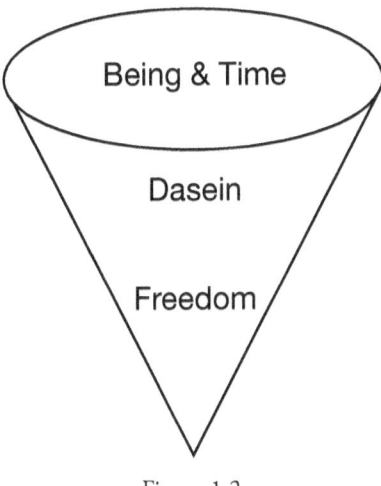

Figure 1.2.

anthropocentrism and its opposite, without losing sight of the human being as such, for Dasein exists factically only in the concrete human being.[94]

Husserl contra Heidegger

Just two and a half years after Heidegger had given his presentation on "Philosophische Anthropologie und Metaphysik" at the Kant Society in Frankfurt, Husserl gave his lecture on "Phänomenologie und Anthropologie"[95] at the same place, on June 1, 1931, with Paul Tillich chairing the meeting.[96] Husserl repeated this lecture in Berlin and Halle in the next two weeks. The lecture in Berlin, also organized by the Kant Society, took place in the auditorium maximum, with 1,600 people attending the meeting, and 136 people joining the post-lecture informal get-together.[97] We can assume that one reason why Husserl's lecture attracted so much attention was that everyone assumed that in this lecture Husserl would finally and publicly break with Heidegger and Scheler, on the grounds that their supposed leanings toward anthropology was incompatible with transcendental phenomenology, as represented by Husserl. Heidegger, for one, did interpret Husserl's lecture in this sense as "a settling of accounts" with him in public, effectively excommunicating him from the guild of right-thinking phenomenologists.[98]

However that may be, the important point here is that Husserl, without ever naming Heidegger in person, charges Heidegger's philosophical project with anthropologism, apparently unaware or unwilling to take note of the fact that Heidegger had officially broken with philosophical anthropology in his *Kant and the Problem of Metaphysics* and his lecture "Philosophical Anthropology and the Metaphysics of Dasein."[99] So, in some fundamental sense, Husserl's criticism does not address the actual position Heidegger held in 1931. Since Husserl gave his talk at the very same Kant Society in Frankfurt where Heidegger had given his rebuttal of philosophical anthropology, one may think that at least some people would have noticed the double irony that Husserl not only charged Heidegger with anthropologism, which Heidegger had already dismissed and critiqued, but that both philosophers also defended the high office of philosophy in fairly similar terms, using arguments and motifs against anthropologism in an almost interchangeable manner. Thus, Husserl's public break with Heidegger was an event that concealed far more than it revealed.

In his lecture Husserl is content with a fairly generic description of what he considers the newly emerging anthropological leanings within "the phenomenological movement." He notes that, according to "these new tendencies," "the true foundation of philosophy" is to be sought "in man alone, and, more specifically, in the essence of his concrete-worldly existence [Dasein]."[100] With even clearer reference to Heidegger, Husserl argues that the anthropological trend in phenomenology aims to put phenomenology on a firmly anthropological footing according to which "phenomenological philosophy is to be newly reconstructed from the basis in human existence [*menschliche Dasein*]."[101] However, as we have seen, Heidegger is not proposing to make "man," let alone "man alone" or the empirical human being, the foundation of philosophy, but rather the metaphysics of Dasein, that is, the understanding of beings and Being in the midst of which alone the human appears. As a criticism of Heidegger, Husserl's charge goes astray from the very start.[102] The reason is that Husserl, contra Heidegger's clear and unambiguous clarifications, first anthropologizes Dasein in order to then turn around and accuse Heidegger of anthropologism.

Still, what are the details of Husserl's argument? First of all, Husserl takes issue with the unexamined nature of the concept of man in philosophical anthropology, because "every doctrine of man, be it empirical or a priori, presupposes an actual or possible world" and this necessary background, without which we would not have the concept of man, is naively taken over without any examination, precisely because man is the designated sole subject matter.[103] In other words, philosophical anthropology draws on "the sense of being" (*Seinssinn*) of the world as well as the "validity of the world" (*Weltgeltung*) (into which man supposedly seamlessly fits), but, in failing to thematize this, necessarily remains caught in a naivete from which it cannot extricate itself on its own accord.[104] This argument is structurally and, even in terms of its material content, strikingly similar to Heidegger's charge that in positing man as something that *is*, philosophical anthropology already moves within an understanding of beings and Being at large, without, however, being able to adequately problematize it. In this sense, philosophical anthropology remains within the domain of "positive" knowledge, and thus outside genuine philosophical questioning concerning the undergirding sense of Being.[105] This convergence in Husserl and Heidegger is predicated on their shared view that any special domain of beings, including that of the human being, is made transparent if and only if it is elucidated within the whole of beings, that is, "all beings in their entirety" (*das Seiende im Ganzen*) (Heidegger),[106] or all "beings in their totality," or "the universe of beings as such" (Husserl).[107] Moreover, this elucidation must take into account the sense of Being or the validity of Being as such that permeates the totality of entities, for otherwise it would be a mere aggregate of positivities. It follows that philosophical anthropology fails to meet this standard, because it operates with a more or less arbitrary concept of man, which it first plucks from some particular and limited positive object sphere (psychology, biology, theology, sociology, economics, history, etc.) and then passes this off, without much ado, as *the* basic concept in philosophy.

But the similarities do not stop here. For just as Heidegger claims that Dasein is the ultimate sphere that opens up the field of beings and Being, so Husserl claims that the *epoché* opens up the very field of transcendental consciousness in which experiences of the world, including the experience of other human beings, and even one's very own being as an empirical person, is grounded. Since Husserl and Heidegger share the idea that the empirical concept of man, as all other empirical concepts, is derivative, and therefore not a "principle" that could yield the "basic" ground for philosophy, they also share the idea of the extraordinary diremption at the heart of the factical human being, where Dasein or the transcendental ego is the prior ground or condition for the very possibility of understanding or experiencing the mundane or factical human, *including its very own being*. For Husserl, the transcendental *epoché* is "a happening in me, albeit concealed from reflection, in which world and human personality are constituted for me," such that even my "existence as man" is constituted in this way as well.[108] In a similar way, Heidegger holds that "more primary than the being of the human being is this basic happening [*Urgeschehen*] of the understanding of Being in Dasein, into which the human being as factically existing is thrown."[109] For every human being, and certainly the philosophically inclined one, the task is to execute the transcendental *epoché* (Husserl) or the leap into Dasein (Heidegger), in order to understand oneself from out of the origin of what there *is*, instead of just swimming along with the maelstrom of mere opinions, scientific or otherwise.

Having laid out that in their rejection of philosophical anthropology, Husserl and Heidegger are much closer to each other than they would ever admit themselves, I should hasten to add that it is not my intention to assimilate one to the other. Fundamental differences remain. Most importantly, for Husserl the ascent to the transcendental ego always comes with the rather philosophical relativization of all worldly affairs, as if the transcendental ego was somehow immune to the hustle and bustle of merely human affairs. For instance, Husserl writes that "as transcendental ego I am thus the absolutely responsible subject of whatever has existential validity for me," which means that "thanks to the transcendental reduction I stand now above all worldly existence, above my own human life and existence as man."[110] Husserl quite rightly adds that this position is that of "the philosopher." There is no such serenity or detachment in Heidegger. Rather, the "leap of the philosophical man into Dasein"[111] looks more like a leap into the ground of the world, as if factical Dasein could roll up its sleeves and get to work in the boiler room of the world and influence the happenings from there.

There are other differences as well. Husserl attempts to establish essential or invariant structures as such, whereas Heidegger emphasizes the finitude of factical Dasein, its dependence on what is "given" to it, and the need to make decisions in a world into which it is thrown, without any recourse to some extraworldly or suprahistorical plane. Of course, the greatest difference is that Husserl's departure point is transcendental consciousness, whereas Heidegger's is Dasein. As we shall see, just as Husserl charges that Heidegger's Dasein veers toward anthropologism, so does Heidegger insinuate that Husserl's subjectivism borders on anthropologism. But, before we can deal with this, we need to return to Heidegger's development after 1929.

Heidegger against the Hegemony of Anthropological Discourse

In his 1929 lecture course on German idealism (Fichte, Schelling, Hegel),[112] Heidegger recapitulates many of his criticisms of philosophical anthropology as laid out in his Kant book and his 1929 talk on "Philosophical Anthropology and Metaphysics of Dasein." But in addition to the largely immanent and systematic critique of the shortcomings of philosophical anthropology, Heidegger now also notes something new. This is the sheer ubiquity of the anthropological thematic, the prevalence of the anthropological angle in philosophy and society at large: "Anything whatsoever that occurs cannot any longer be seen for its own sake and on its own terms, but rather whatever comes to pass is already enveloped by the invisible tentacles of the anthropological interpretation."[113] The hegemony of the anthropological discourse itself becomes the phenomenon to be investigated. While the early Heidegger argues against the primacy of the theoretical and, in *Being and Time*, inveighs against the dominant interpretation of "existence" in terms of what is present-at-hand, Heidegger now addresses the threat of the ascendancy of the anthropological paradigm in theory and everyday conversation.

The threat is that unless a theme or topic is secured by way of "this kind of anthropological cognition"[114] it simply does not count, is not recognized as real or true, for everything is seen through this anthropological prism.

For Heidegger, the predominance of the anthropological discourse is "uncanny" (*unheimlich*) not only because it takes from things their independence, but also because "no one can extricate" him- or herself from this dominant intellectual current.[115] Although Heidegger insists that acknowledging this state of affairs does not imply "surrendering to it," he also cautions that "some scholarly program" alone will not suffice to overcome it.[116] The peculiar "uncanniness" (*Unheimlichkeit*) of the hegemony of the anthropological discourse is this: at the very moment when everything is related to the human being, the very essence of the human is "hollowed out," precisely because the very dependence of the human being on Dasein, the understanding of Being, is increasingly ignored.[117] In other words, Heidegger now interprets the anthropological tendency as a widespread but misguided subjectivism, which is oblivious to the very opening of Dasein or the understanding of Being, on the basis of which alone the human being can form a (philosophical) concept of him- or herself and *exist* as a human being.

After 1929, Heidegger engages philosophical anthropology only *en passant* and only within the context of his broader philosophical critique of modernity, representationalism, and subjectivity, developing and deepening the motif that first emerges in his 1929 lecture course on German idealism, as we have seen above. In short, after 1929, Heidegger eschews any detailed, immanent criticism of philosophical anthropology; instead, he rests content with a transcendent assessment from within his own philosophical framework of a philosophy of Dasein and Being, and, increasingly, the forgetfulness of Being.[118]

Heidegger's point in this regard is quite straightforward. He holds that Descartes is the original philosopher who put metaphysics on a thoroughly subjectivist footing, the cogito, thereby making everything that there is a mere representation or *cogitatum* of the cogito only. For Heidegger, the shift toward the subject in Descartes marks the anthropological moment as such, the first beginning of philosophical anthropology, way before there is any particular philosophical anthropology to speak of. Heidegger writes: "With the interpretation of man as *subiectum*, Descartes created the metaphysical precondition for future anthropology of every kind and tendency. In the rise of anthropologies, he celebrates his greatest triumph."[119] This is so because already in Descartes man becomes the absolute reference point for everything that is, and, with that, the new modern world is born, with man at the center of all things.

For Heidegger, this is a kind of free human self-assertion: "But when man becomes the primary and genuine *subiectum*, this means that he becomes the being upon which every being, in its way of being and its truth, is founded. Man becomes the referential center of beings as such."[120] This revolutionizes the former embeddedness of man in the world: "Beings in their entirety are now taken in such a way that a being is first and only in being insofar as it is set in place by man, representing and producing it."[121] This seals man's assumed superiority, for man is now the sole "representor" and "representative" (*Repräsentant*) of beings, which are just "objects" vis-à-vis the subject, or man.[122]

Heidegger goes out of his way to emphasize that the subjectivity of man can be shaped in many different ways: "Man as the rational being of the Enlightenment is no less subject than man who grasps himself as nation, wills himself as people, breeds himself as race, and, finally, empowers himself as lord of the world."[123] According to Heidegger, the more entrenched the principle of subjectivity becomes, the more central becomes the human being as such; thus, anthropology reigns supreme in modernity. The anthropological stance is a fitting outward expression of the victorious principle of subjectivity that permeates all aspects of life: "The more completely and comprehensively the world, as conquered, stands at man's disposal, and the more objectively the objects appear, all the more subjectively, that is peremptorily, does the *subiectum* rise up, and all the more inexorably, too, do observations and teachings about the world transform themselves into an anthropology."[124] For Heidegger, even humanism is a kind of "moral-aesthetic anthropology."[125]

No wonder, then, that Heidegger thinks that philosophy, too, has surrendered to the anthropological turn in modernity, that is, the ultimate reduction of all reality to man's representation and production thereof, thanks to the unchallenged primacy of scientific thought and technology, which themselves are but consequences of the modern principle of subjectivity.[126] Indeed, Heidegger holds that philosophy has come to an end in the contemporary scientific-technological age. Referring to the enormous weight put on communication theory, cybernetics, and so forth, all of which make sense only if man takes center stage in reality and its theoretical reflection, Heidegger writes that "philosophy turns into empirical science of man, of all that can become for man the experiential object of his technology, the technology by which he establishes himself in the world by working on it in the manifold modes of making and shaping."[127] The very anthropological turn ushered in by philosophy (thanks to Descartes's cogito) finally catches up with it and turns philosophy into just an arm of anthropological knowledge. Thus, Heidegger writes: "Philosophy is ending in the present age. It has found its place in the scientific attitude of socially active humanity."[128]

Heidegger's point has hardly been proven wrong in the fifty years since he wrote these lines. Quite to the contrary. However, it is important to note that his critique of the underlying subjectivism in anthropological thought is entirely consistent with a continuation of his earlier, more immanent criticisms of the theoretical deficiencies of anthropologism.

Heidegger contra Husserl

In the course of his onto-historical interpretation of anthropological thought as a culmination of Cartesian subjectivism, Heidegger also insinuates, although without ever directly saying so, that Husserl's philosophy is part and parcel of the anthropological turn in modernity. For instance, Heidegger argues that Husserl's "principle of all principles" presupposes "absolute subjectivity" and would legitimize "the primacy of method."[129] However, *pace* Heidegger, in prioritizing untutored intuition, Husserl shows that consciousness is dependent on what it cannot produce, that is, the given or the things themselves. Husserl's principle of principles does not postulate the supremacy of consciousness nor does it bespeak the primacy of method, for in attending to the things themselves Husserl opens up the very space for things to show themselves as they are, without any imposition of a preconceived program, plan, or method. Moreover, Heidegger's charge that Husserl's philosophy imprisons the object in "the immanence of consciousness"[130] is likewise ill-founded, for Husserl's concept of intentionality means that consciousness is defined by its relation to what it is not, that is, the objects it intends. For Husserl, consciousness without intentionality is no consciousness at all. Consciousness cannot exist all by itself, but only in relation to what it opens up by means of intentionality, or what is given to it.[131] It is difficult to grasp what it could mean to say that what consciousness intends is nonetheless "immanent" to it, for in that case consciousness would not intend objects at all, but only itself. But such auto-affection of consciousness is not Husserl's idea of intentionality. Arguably, Heidegger's very own notion of being-in-the-world is a deformalization and concretization of Husserl's concept of intentionality.[132]

Moreover, Heidegger argues that the "primacy of consciousness" in Descartes and the philosophers working in his footsteps comes with the thesis of "the primacy of the human being" (*Vorrang des Menschen*),[133] effectively shoehorning the entire "subjectivist" tradition from Descartes to Kant and up to Husserl into the anthropological tendency.[134] But whatever we may think of the alleged "primacy of consciousness" in Husserl's phenomenology, it is patently clear that Husserl is not bound to the "primacy of the human," for transcendental consciousness is at a crucial philosophical distance from "the human," just as Dasein is. In other words, it is Heidegger who, almost mirroring Husserl's ill-founded attempt to implicate Heidegger's philosophy in anthropology, first anthropologizes Husserl's concept of "consciousness," in order then to attribute this anthropologized concept to Descartes, Kant, and even Husserl. But neither Descartes, nor Kant, let alone Husserl would entertain the notion that the pure or transcendental ego is identical to the empirical human being, least of all as it is thematized in (empirical or philosophical) anthropology.

Heidegger's attempt to implicate Husserl in anthropologism is certainly Heidegger's reprisal for Husserl's earlier charge about Heidegger's supposed anthropologism. It is as unfounded as Husserl's attack on Heidegger. More significantly, it also hides the fundamental convergence in Husserl and Heidegger, at least between 1927 and 1931, for both argue against anthropologism from a decidedly philosophical and, in particular, transcendental or transcendental-hermeneutical position. In a letter from 1927, Heidegger agrees with Husserl that what makes up "transcendental constitution" cannot be "an entity at all" and certainly not an empirically present at hand object.[135] However, Heidegger continues that Dasein is precisely "a mode of being" that is "totally different from all other entities," and that, as such, it has "within itself the possibility of transcendental constitution."[136] For Heidegger, Dasein is transcendental, just as Husserl's consciousness is.[137] Dasein is the transcendental ground, the opening or clearing that permits the very encounter of entities, things, and people within the world. Dasein is not an occurrent thing, but that does not mean that it is decoupled from the world.[138] Rather, Dasein is the ground or essence of the factical self, without which a self could not even "be." Therefore, Dasein or transcendental constitution "is a central possibility of the eksistence [*Eksistenz*] of the factical self."[139]

Both Heidegger and Husserl assume a philosophical standpoint that is decidedly not human-centric or anthropological. Thought occurs at a critical distance from the human being as an object. Husserl emphasizes that qua transcendental ego "I am not a human ego,"[140] while Heidegger argues that qua Dasein the human being is "already *more* than human."[141]

Nonetheless, Heidegger also insists that transcendental consciousness or Dasein is "a possibility of the human being."[142] In reality, Husserl is committed to this too, for the transcendental reduction is a possibility of the human being as it exists in the natural attitude, and the entire content of the natural attitude is preserved in transcendental consciousness.[143] Moreover, Husserl explicitly acknowledges that the transcendental I is not only "a conscious subject *for* the world," but it also always exists as a subject "*in* the world."[144]

In fact, what unites Husserl and Heidegger, this side of their carefully cultivated mutual "misunderstanding," is the idea that the human being exists at a distance from itself. World-disclosing thought, be it Dasein or transcendental consciousness, separates the human being from itself, ruling out any fixed "nature" as its essence, any identity with which it could coalesce, and that would make it a determinate and fixed object, let alone the unquestioned base for philosophy. Starting from the primacy of thinking, both Heidegger and Husserl reject the alleged primacy of man, and, a fortiori, anthropologism. What the human being is can be determined only in and through that tension with what is "more" than human; that is, Dasein or transcendental consciousness. Put differently, both agree that by clinging to the surface phenomenon of man, the very depth-dimension from which alone the meaning of man can be made transparent is occluded. Consequently, the Husserl/Heidegger feud over anthropology rests on a mistake, for both philosophers willfully misunderstand each other. This is but a special case of the mutual misreading of Husserl and Heidegger that Steven Crowell has systematically delineated.[145]

It bears emphasizing that in critiquing anthropologism Husserl and Heidegger are in no way assuming an anti-humanist stance. Quite to the contrary, they aim at establishing the right measure of the human, and that measure cannot be the human itself, but must be sought in a region that opens up the human *as* a human being in the world. Unlike philosophical anthropology, Husserl and Heidegger do not start from the human as the terminus a quo; rather, the human is the terminus ad quem. It is through Dasein or transcendental consciousness that one can lay bare the structures of the human within the world.

The Human This Side of Anthropologism

In order to assess Heidegger's thought on philosophical anthropology, we must take into account its complex development over many decades, as I have tried to do in the foregoing sections of this essay. While there are certainly changes in Heidegger's thought, they do not amount to dramatic reversals, sudden new departures, and so on. Instead, Heidegger refines, expands, and deepens the anthropological theme, both in terms of what he critically rejects and what he transforms and sublates into his own philosophy. Throughout, there is a commitment to thinking the human reality, without surrendering to a naturalistic or spiritualistic conception of the human, or dogmatically stipulating the ontological primacy of the human.

As we have seen, the early Heidegger puts factical life and the human being at the center of his thought. Yet he has no conception of Being as such to accompany it. Thus, the impression might be given that early Heidegger is embracing an anthropological philosophy, especially because Heidegger does not clarify the transcendental dimension in factical life. On the other hand, the pronounced hermeneutical cast of his early lectures rules out a naturalistic or empirical conception of the human being. Therefore, there is no real basis for the claim that the early Heidegger is advocating anthropologism, least of all the anthropologism that he himself criticizes from the late 1920s onward.

From around the period of *Being and Time*, Heidegger makes the essential correlation, or "correspondence," between Dasein and Being the major theme of his philosophy, never to lose sight of it again, even in his later work.[146] Differentiating between the ground of the human being—that is, Dasein—and the human being as an existing entity, Heidegger leaves behind the apparent human-centric language of his earlier philosophizing. Still, the possibility of a philosophical anthropology, subordinate to and under the auspices of a philosophy of Being, is kept open in *Being and Time*. Moreover, *Being and Time* does not abandon the human but rather turns toward the very essence of the human, that is, Dasein, which undercuts all hasty identification of the human with a set of (empirically or a priori) given properties. Arguably, Heidegger "sublates" anthropological thought by returning it to what he considers its proper philosophical depth-dimension in Dasein's being-in-the-world.

Subsequently, Heidegger develops a critical rebuttal of all philosophical anthropology, based on his argument that, for all its seeming emphasis on and concern for the human, philosophical anthropology misses the very dimension of the essence of the human being in Dasein and Dasein's free response to Being. Consequently, Heidegger is no longer open to any philosophical anthropology, which he did countenance in *Being and Time*, provided it would be aligned with and subordinated to the philosophy of Being. In retrospect, Heidegger strongly contests the view that *Being and*

Time fell back into anthropologism, although he also self-critically concedes that "some formulations" could indeed give rise to this misconception.[147] However, as Heidegger makes clear, any such anthropological "misreading" of *Being and Time* is based on equating Dasein with the human being, which implies the complete loss of the philosophical or ontological import Dasein has in *Being and Time*.

However, neither Heidegger's repudiation of anthropologism nor his shift toward the idea of *Ereignis* and the relative greater weight he attaches to Being comes at the price of abandoning human existence as such. Rather, it enables Heidegger to provide the proper philosophical perspective on the human being, without absolutizing or, more importantly, humanizing Being, nor falling for an arbitrary fixation of the human. In a conversation with Medard Boss in 1963, Heidegger summarizes it as follows: "Until now, psychology, anthropology, and psychopathology have considered the human being as an object in a broad sense, as something present-at-hand, as a domain of beings, and as the sum total of what can be stated about human beings experientially."[148] Heidegger then points out what is missing in this approach: "The question concerning what the human being is and how the human being exists as a human being has been omitted entirely; namely, that in accordance with its unfolding essence, it basically comports itself to other beings and to itself and that this is only possible on its part because of its understanding of Being."[149] In other words, Dasein, and the understanding of Being are still essential for late Heidegger.

To be sure, later Heidegger would sometimes accentuate much more Dasein's topological character or embeddedness in the world.[150] This goes together with a stronger foregrounding of the idea of Being.[151] As Capobianco notes, the later Heidegger claims that "the truth of Being does not exhaust itself in Dasein."[152] Nonetheless, Heidegger continues to take Dasein as "the place," or "the locality," or the very "region," of the truth of Being.[153] That is to say, while there is a stronger accentuation of (the history of) Being in his later works, Heidegger never renounces the idea of Dasein and, indeed, the freedom that pervades Dasein. Since it is through Dasein that we can determine the human, it follows that Heidegger's later philosophy is not downplaying the human at all.[154] Quite to the contrary. As Heidegger puts it in the *Zollikoner Seminare*: "All presencing is dependent on the human being, but this dependence on the human being consists precisely in the fact that the human being as Dasein and being-in-the-world is able to allow beings to come to presence [. . .]."[155] For the sake of this openness to what there is, Heidegger puts Dasein at the midpoint of his philosophy, equally apart from subjectivism and objectivism, that is, anthropologism and naturalism.

In his "Introduction to 'What Is Metaphysics?,'" Heidegger reminds his readers that in *Being and Time*, Dasein is defined by its "existence" (*Eksistenz*), and that existence is the way of being attributable to the human being alone.[156] Therefore, to the extent that Heidegger investigates the relation between Dasein and Being, the human being is always in question too. The human being is never absorbed by some anonymous happening of Being. Thus, Heidegger says that "for me everything depends on this, that the human being be a *human* being,"[157] separate from, but intrinsically related to the world or Being in which it finds itself.

Notes

1. Martin Heidegger, *Ontologie: Hermeneutik der Faktizität*, vol. 63 of *Gesamtausgabe*, ed. Käte Bröcker-Oltmanns (Frankfurt: Klostermann, 1995).

2. Martin Heidegger, *Grundprobleme der Phänomenologie*, vol. 58 of *Gesamtausgabe*, ed. Hans-Helmuth Gander (Frankfurt: Klostermann, 1992), 173.

3. Heidegger, *Grundprobleme der Phänomenologie*, 173.

4. Martin Heidegger, *Phänomenologische Interpretationen zu Aristoteles: Einführung in die phänomenologische Forschung*, vol. 61 of *Gesamtausgabe*, ed. Walter Bröcker and Käte Bröcker-Oltmanns, 2nd ed. (Frankfurt: Klostermann, 1994), 167.

5. Martin Heidegger, "Phänomenologische Interpretationen zu Aristoteles," in *Phänomenologische Interpretationen ausgewählter Abhandlungen des Aristotles zur Ontologie und Logik*, vol. 62 of *Gesamtausgabe*, ed. Günther Neumann (Frankfurt: Klostermann, 2005), 348.

6. Heidegger, *Grundprobleme der Phänomenologie*, 30.

7. Heidegger, *Grundprobleme der Phänomenologie*, 33.

8. Martin Heidegger, "Wilhelm Diltheys Forschungsarbeit," in *Vorträge* (part 1), vol. 80.1 of *Gesamtausgabe*, ed. Günther Neumann (Frankfurt: Klostermann, 2016), 110.

9. Heidegger, *Phänomenologische Interpretationen zu Aristoteles*, 84–155.

10. On the Enlightenment and Kant and Herder's role in the formation of philosophical anthropology, see John H. Zammito, *Kant Herder and the Birth of Anthropology* (Chicago: University of Chicago Press, 2002).

11. See, for instance, Ludwig Feuerbach, "Grundsätze der Philosophie der Zukunft," in *Sämtliche Werke*, vol. 2, ed. Wilhelm Bolin and Friedrich Jodl (Stuttgart-Bad Cannstatt: F. Fromann Verlag, 1959), 317, where he writes (my translation):

"The new philosophy makes *man* [. . .] the *exclusive, universal, and highest* object of philosophy; [. . .] it makes *anthropology* [. . .] the universal science."

12. "To-be-there [Dasein] is the primary being, the primary determination. Here *I* am—that is the first sign of a *real and living* being. The index finger shows the way from nothingness to being. Saying *here* is the first boundary, the first demarcation. I am here, you are there; in between there is a distance separating us; this is what makes it possible for both of us to exist without jeopardising each other; there is enough room." Feuerbach, "Grundsätze der Philosophie der Zukunft," § 44, 306–7.

13. Heidegger, *Ontologie: Hermeneutik der Faktizität*, 15.

14. Martin Heidegger, *Einleitung in die Philosophie*, vol. 27 of *Gesamtausgabe*, ed. Otto Saame and Ina Saame-Speidel (Frankfurt: Klostermann, 2001), 11–12.

15. Martin Heidegger, *Der Begriff der Zeit*, vol. 64 of *Gesamtausgabe*, ed. Friedrich-Wilhelm von Herrmann (Frankfurt: Klostermann, 2004), 54 and also 56.

16. Heidegger, *Grundprobleme der Phänomenologie*, 173.

17. Heidegger, *Der Begriff der Zeit*, 57, 86.

18. Martin Heidegger, *Phänomenologie des religiösen Lebens*, vol. 60 of *Gesamtausgabe*, ed. Matthias Jung and Thomas Regehly (Frankfurt: Klostermann, 1995), 8.

19. Heidegger, *Phänomenologische Interpretationen zu Aristoteles*, 163.

20. Heidegger, *Phänomenologische Interpretationen zu Aristoteles*, 61, 163.

21. Heidegger, *Phänomenologische Interpretationen zu Aristoteles*, 164.

22. Heidegger, *Phänomenologische Interpretationen zu Aristoteles*, 197.

23. Feuerbach, "Grundsätze der Philosophie der Zukunft," 313.

24. Heidegger, *Phänomenologische Interpretationen zu Aristoteles*, 168. See also, Heidegger, *Phänomenologische Interpretationen ausgewählter Abhandlungen des Aristoteles*, 347.

25. Heidegger, *Der Begriff der Zeit*, 94 and also 103.

26. Heidegger, *Phänomenologische Interpretationen ausgewählter Abhandlungen des Aristoteles*, 350.

27. Heidegger, *Ontologie: Hermeneutik der Faktizität*, 64.

28. See note 11, above.

29. However, Heidegger once writes, contra Husserl and the neo-Kantians, that "with the attack [*Bekämpfung*] on anthropological thought existential problems [*Existenzprobleme*] have been once more suppressed in philosophy, although they are something essentially different." See Martin Heidegger, *Phänomenologie der Anschauung und des Ausdrucks: Theorie der philosophischen Begriffsbildung*, vol. 59 of *Gesamtausgabe*, ed. Claudius Strube (Frankfurt: Klostermann, 2007), 63. At another passage, Heidegger notes that "the attack [*Bekämpfung*] on 'psychologism' has gone too far." See Heidegger, *Grundprobleme der Phänomenologie*, 214.

30. Martin Heidegger, *Sein und Zeit*, vol. 2 of *Gesamtausgabe*, ed. Friedrich-Wilhelm von Herrmann (Frankfurt: Klostermann, 1977), 18.

31. Heidegger, *Sein und Zeit*, 16.

32. Heidegger, *Sein und Zeit*, 10. At first sight, this is a strange formulation; it is meant to capture the idea that Dasein is something in which each and every one is implicated—each one of us is Dasein.
33. Heidegger, *Sein und Zeit*, 18.
34. Heidegger, *Sein und Zeit*, 18.
35. Heidegger, *Sein und Zeit*, 60.
36. Heidegger, *Vom Wesen der menschlichen Freiheit*, 125.
37. "'There is' truth only in so far as Dasein is and so long as Dasein is." See Heidegger, *Sein und Zeit*, 299.
38. Heidegger, *Sein und Zeit*, 304.
39. Plato, *Phaedrus* 249b6–7.
40. That "Dasein" refers to individual human beings must be qualified in one important way. Strictly speaking, Dasein is the "base" or "ground" for the human being, not the human being as such. Put differently, the human being can understand itself as a human being only on the base of its being a case of Dasein, the site of inquiry where entities show up for it within the context of the world that matters to it. Heidegger designates human beings as Dasein because he wants to prevent that traditional Greek or Christian definitions adulterate the concept of man. For an excellent discussion of this issue, see Taylor Carman, *Heidegger's Analytic* (Cambridge: Cambridge University Press, 2003), 35–43, esp. 35; Frederick A. Olafson, "The Unity of Heidegger's Thought," in *The Cambridge Companion to Heidegger*, ed. Charles B. Guignon (Cambridge: Cambridge University Press, 1993), 97–121, esp. 100; Frederick A. Olafson, *What Is a Human Being?* (Cambridge: Cambridge University Press, 1995), esp. 227–55; Wayne Martin, "The Semantics of 'Dasein' and the Modality of *Being and Time*," in *Heidegger's Being and Time*, ed. Mark A. Wrathall (Cambridge: Cambridge University Press, 2013), 100–128. For the view that Dasein cannot be restricted to human beings, or rather, the essence of human beings, see John Haugeland, "Heidegger on Being a Person," in *Dasein Disclosed: John Haugeland's Heidegger*, ed. Joseph Rouse (Cambridge: Cambridge University Press, 2013), 3–16.
41. Heidegger, *Sein und Zeit*, 66.
42. Heidegger, *Sein und Zeit*, 23.
43. Heidegger, *Sein und Zeit*, 23.
44. Heidegger, *Sein und Zeit*, 60.
45. Heidegger, *Sein und Zeit*, 69.
46. Martin Heidegger, "Phänomenologie und Theologie," in *Wegmarken*, vol. 9 of *Gesamtausgabe*, ed. Friedrich-Wilhelm von Herrmann, 3rd ed. (Frankfurt: Klostermann, 2004), 65. For Heidegger's distinction between ontological and positive sciences, see his 1926 talk "Begriff und Entwicklung der phänomenologischen Forschung," in *Vorträge*, vol. 80.1 of *Gesamtausgabe*, 159–78.
47. While Heidegger has never put forward a complete philosophical anthropology, not least because of his increasingly critical view on the limitations of such a

project after *Being and Time* (see part 3, below), Eugen Fink's study—*Grundphänomene des menschlichen Daseins* (Freiburg: Karl Alber Verlag, 1979)—is a remarkable philosophical anthropology that is in close proximity to Heidegger's thought.

48. Heidegger, *Sein und Zeit*, 69n. See also, Heidegger's review essay, "Ernst Cassirer: Philosophie der Symbolischen Formen. 2. Teil: Das mytische Denken. Berlin 1925," in *Kant und das Problem der Metaphysik*, vol. 3 of *Gesamtausgabe*, ed. Friedrich-Wilhelm von Herrmann (Frankfurt: Klostermann, 1991), 255–70.

49. Heidegger, *Sein und Zeit*, §10, 61–67.

50. In his notes on his own publications, *Zu eigenen Veröffentlichungen*, Heidegger skips over this direction taken in the years between 1928 and 1930. He makes it appear as if after *Being and Time*, he more or less directly worked on the ideas that issued into his *Beiträge*. One of the reasons for this omission is that he started to write down notes on his own publications only from 1936 onwards. Martin Heidegger, *Zu eigenen Veröffentlichungen*, vol. 82 of *Gesamtausgabe*, ed. Friedrich-Wilhelm von Herrmann (Frankfurt: Klostermann, 2018).

51. Heidegger, *Kant und das Problem der Metaphysik*.

52. Martin Heidegger, "Philosophische Anthropologie und Metaphysik des Daseins," in *Vorträge*, vol. 80.1 of *Gesamtausgabe*, 213–51.

53. See §37 of Martin Heidegger, "The Idea of a Philosophical Anthropology," in *Kant und das Problem der Metaphysik*, vol. 3 of *Gesamtausgabe*, 208–14.

54. "Insofar as all of these things, and ultimately the totality of beings in general, in some way can always be referred to humans and, accordingly, can be reckoned as belonging to anthropology, it [anthropology] becomes so encompassing that the idea of it becomes mired in complete indeterminacy." See Heidegger, *Kant und das Problem der Metaphysik*, 209.

55. Heidegger, "Philosophische Anthropologie und Metaphysik des Daseins," 223.

56. Heidegger, "Philosophische Anthropologie und Metaphysik des Daseins," 224.

57. Heidegger, "Philosophische Anthropologie und Metaphysik des Daseins," 224.

58. Heidegger, "Philosophische Anthropologie und Metaphysik des Daseins," 224.

59. Heidegger, "Philosophische Anthropologie und Metaphysik des Daseins," 224.

60. Heidegger, "Philosophische Anthropologie und Metaphysik des Daseins," 225.

61. Heidegger, "Philosophische Anthropologie und Metaphysik des Daseins," 226.

62. Heidegger, "Philosophische Anthropologie und Metaphysik des Daseins," 228.

63. For instance, when in his earlier lecture courses Heidegger argues for the primacy of factical life for philosophy and remarks that "philosophy springs from factical life experience" and that "factical life experiences are the beginning and end of philosophy," he comes close to short-circuiting the human and philosophy in a way that he criticizes here. See Heidegger, *Phänomenologie des religiösen Lebens*, 8, 15.

64. Heidegger, "Philosophische Anthropologie und Metaphysik des Daseins," 227.

65. Heidegger, "Philosophische Anthropologie und Metaphysik des Daseins," 232.

66. Heidegger, "Philosophische Anthropologie und Metaphysik des Daseins," 233.

67. Heidegger, "Philosophische Anthropologie und Metaphysik des Daseins," 235.

68. Heidegger, "Philosophische Anthropologie und Metaphysik des Daseins," 236–37.

69. Heidegger, "Philosophische Anthropologie und Metaphysik des Daseins," 236–37.

70. "The Dasein in man determines him as that being which, being in the midst of beings, comports itself to them as such. Further, as this comporting to beings, man is determined in his own being as essentially other than all remaining beings which are manifest in Dasein." See Heidegger, *Kant und das Problem der Metaphysik*, 234.

71. Heidegger, "Philosophische Anthropologie und Metaphysik des Daseins," 237.

72. Immanuel Kant, *Kritik der reinen Vernunft*, B21.

73. For Heidegger's concept of the "metaphysics of Dasein," see Steven Crowell, "The Middle Heidegger's Phenomenological Metaphysics," in *The Oxford Handbook of the History of Phenomenology*, ed. Dan Zahavi (Oxford: Oxford University Press, 2018), 229–50.

74. Heidegger, *Kant und das Problem der Metaphysik*, 230. See also Heidegger, "Philosophische Anthropologie und Metaphysik des Daseins," 238–41.

75. Heidegger, *Kant und das Problem der Metaphysik*, 230. See also, Martin Heidegger, *Metaphysische Anfangsgründe der Logik*, vol. 26 of *Gesamtausgabe*, ed. Klaus Held (Frankfurt: Klostermann, 2007), 171–202.

76. "Time is not to be found somewhere or other like a thing among things, but in ourselves." See Heidegger, *Vom Wesen der menschlichen Freiheit*, 120.

77. Heidegger, *Vom Wesen der menschlichen Freiheit*, 121.

78. "If man is only man on the grounds of the Dasein in him, then in principle the question as to what is more original than man cannot be anthropological. All anthropology, even philosophical anthropology, has already posited man as man." See Heidegger, *Kant und das Problem der Metaphysik*, 229–30.

79. Thus, Heidegger explicitly holds that Dasein is "not the egocentric individual, the ontic isolated individual." See Heidegger, *Metaphysische Anfangsgründe der Logik*, 172.

80. Heidegger, "Philosophische Anthropologie und Metaphysik des Daseins," 237.

81. Thus, Heidegger writes that what is opened up in man's understanding of Being is a world of entities that bear him along and on which he depends, such that "for all his culture and technology" he "can never become master" of these. See Heidegger, *Kant und das Problem der Metaphysik*, 228.

82. Heidegger, "Philosophische Anthropologie und Metaphysik des Daseins," 239.

83. Heidegger, *Sein und Zeit*, 51–52.

84. Heidegger, *Metaphysische Anfangsgründe der Logik*, 171.

85. Heidegger does not claim that Dasein does not have a body and a nature in that sense. In fact, he explicitly states that Dasein, as factically existing, is "dispersed" in a body, inhabiting a lived and sexed body. See Heidegger, *Metaphysische Anfangsgründe der Logik*, 173. But Heidegger insists that this does not determine Dasein, precisely because Dasein is defined by freedom and openness, not some static and unchanging nature.

86. Odo Marquard, "Zur Geschichte des philosophischen Begriffs 'Anthropologie' seit dem Ende des achtzehnten Jahrhunderts," in *Schwierigkeiten mit der Geschichtsphilosophie* (Frankfurt: Suhrkamp, 1973), 128.

87. Heidegger, *Vom Wesen der menschlichen Freiheit*, 303.

88. Heidegger, *Vom Wesen der menschlichen Freiheit*, 134.

89. Heidegger, *Vom Wesen der menschlichen Freiheit*, 134.

90. Heidegger, *Vom Wesen der menschlichen Freiheit*, 134.

91. Heidegger, *Vom Wesen der menschlichen Freiheit*, 135.

92. Heidegger, "Philosophische Anthropologie und Metaphysik des Daseins," 240–41.

93. Heidegger, "Philosophische Anthropologie und Metaphysik des Daseins," 240.

94. See Heidegger, *Metaphysische Anfangsgründe der Logik*, 172.

95. Edmund Husserl, "Phänomenologie und Anthropologie," in *Aufsätze und Vorträge (1922–1937)*, ed. Thomas Nenon and Hans Rainer Sepp (London: Kluwer Academic, 1989), 164–81.

96. Karl Schuhmann, *Husserl-Chronik: Denk- und Lebensweg Edmund Husserls* (The Hague: Martinus Nijhoff, 1977), 381.

97. Schuhmann, *Husserl-Chronik*, 381. According to Hans Blumenberg, one newspaper reported the event under the headline "2500 Philosophers at the University," while another newspaper first noted that "droves of people" had to be turned away because of the overflowing auditorium, then adding the ill-fated speculation that with Husserl "one could fill the Sportpalast in Berlin." See Hans Blumenberg,

Beschreibung des Menschen (Frankfurt: Suhrkamp, 2006), 17–18. Apparently, this line gave rise to the persistent but entirely *false* rumor that Husserl had actually given a speech at the Sportpalast (which, it should be mentioned, could seat 14,000 people, and is, of course, today primarily associated with the Nazi propaganda shows there in the 1930s and 1940s). In fact, just as it is *untrue* that Husserl ever gave a speech at the Sportpalast, so it is *true* that Heidegger repeated this rumor in writing. In the printed version of the *Der Spiegel* interview, Heidegger does say that "Husserl spoke in the Berlin Sports Palace before the student body. Erich Mühsam reported it in one of the large Berlin newspapers." See Martin Heidegger, "Nur noch ein Gott kann uns retten," interview by Rudolf Augstein and Georg Wolff, *Der Spiegel*, no. 23 (May 30, 1976): 199. In the published version of the *Der Spiegel* interview, in the *Gesamtausgabe*, Hermann Heidegger changed this incriminating sentence by removing Heidegger's incorrect reference to the Sportpalast and correcting the reference to the journalist Heinrich Müsam. See Martin Heidegger, *Reden und andere Zeugnisse eines Lebensweges*, vol. 16 of *Gesamtausgabe*, ed. Hermann Heidegger (Frankfurt: Klostermann, 2000), 660, 817.

98. Heidegger, *Reden und andere Zeugnisse*, 660. See also Heidegger's long entry, from around 1948, in *Anmerkungen I–V (Schwarze Hefte 1942–1948)*, vol. 97 of *Gesamtausgabe*, ed. Peter Trawny (Frankfurt: Klostermann, 2015), 462–63.

99. We know that Husserl had read *Being and Time* as well as *Kant and the Problem of Metaphysics* in 1929. See Schuhmann, *Husserl-Chronik*, 349. See also, Edmund Husserl, *Psychological and Transcendental Phenomenology and the Confrontation with Heidegger (1927–1931)*, trans. and ed. Thomas Sheehan and Richard Palmer (Dordrecht: Kluwer, 1997), xiii–xiv. (This volume also has Husserl's marginal notes to *Being and Time* and *Kant and the Problem of Metaphysics*.)

100. Husserl, "Phänomenologie und Anthropologie," 164.

101. Husserl, "Phänomenologie und Anthropologie," 164.

102. Arguably, Husserl's critique is more apt when directed at Scheler.

103. Husserl, "Phänomenologie und Anthropologie," 179.

104. Husserl, "Phänomenologie und Anthropologie," 173, 179.

105. Heidegger, "Philosophische Anthropologie und Metaphysik des Daseins," 230–231.

106. Heidegger, "Philosophische Anthropologie und Metaphysik des Daseins," 232.

107. Husserl, "Phänomenologie und Anthropologie," 166, 167.

108. Husserl, "Phänomenologie und Anthropologie," 174; see also 171.

109. Heidegger, "Philosophische Anthropologie und Metaphysik des Daseins," 237.

110. Husserl, "Phänomenologie und Anthropologie," 174.

111. Heidegger, "Philosophische Anthropologie und Metaphysik des Daseins," 240.

112. Martin Heidegger, *Der Deutsche Idealismus (Fichte, Schelling, Hegel) und Die Philosophische Problemlage Der Gegenwart*, vol. 28 of *Gesamtausgabe*, ed. Claudius Strube (Frankfurt: Klostermann, 1997).

113. Heidegger, *Der Deutsche Idealismus*, 15.

114. Heidegger, *Der Deutsche Idealismus*, 15.

115. Heidegger, *Der Deutsche Idealismus*, 16.

116. Heidegger, *Der Deutsche Idealismus*, 16.

117. Heidegger, *Der Deutsche Idealismus*, 18, 17.

118. Even in his 1929–30 lecture course on the "Basic Concepts of Metaphysics: World, Finitude, Solitude," which arguably touches on many themes that traditionally would fall under philosophical anthropology (the difference of man and animal, the role of the environment, etc.), Heidegger roundly declares that knowledge about the human being is "most definitely" not to be had in "anthropology, psychology, and characterology," and, unsurprisingly, insists that "the question of what the human being is," can only be approached from Dasein and its understanding of Being. See Martin Heidegger, *Die Grundbegriffe der Metaphysik: Welt, Endlichkeit, Einsamkeit*, vol. 29/30 of *Gesamtausgabe*, ed. Friedrich-Wilhelm von Herrmann (Frankfurt: Klostermann, 1983), 407–8.

119. Martin Heidegger, "Die Zeit des Weltbildes," in *Holzwege*, vol. 5 of *Gesamtausgabe*, ed. Friedrich-Wilhelm von Herrmann (Frankfurt: Klostermann, 2003), 99.

120. Heidegger, "Die Zeit des Weltbildes," 88.

121. Heidegger, "Die Zeit des Weltbildes," 89.

122. Heidegger, "Die Zeit des Weltbildes," 91.

123. Heidegger, "Die Zeit des Weltbildes," 111. Heidegger clearly believes that the trajectory of this subjectivism finds its ultimate conclusion in planetary imperialism: "In the planetary imperialism of technically organized man the subjectivism of man reaches its highest point from which it will descend into the flatness of organized uniformity and there establish itself. This uniformity becomes the surest instrument of the total, i.e., technological, domination over the earth." See Heidegger, "Die Zeit des Weltbildes," 111.

124. Heidegger, "Die Zeit des Weltbildes," 93.

125. Heidegger, "Die Zeit des Weltbildes," 93. The context makes it clear that Heidegger thinks here of what is known as the German neo-humanism of the nineteenth century. A much more fine-grained analysis would be needed to support this broad argument. In any case, it is clear that Heidegger's implication of humanism in modern anthropology cannot apply to Renaissance humanism, which predates the Cartesian turn to the subject.

126. "In the meantime, philosophy has become anthropology and in this way prey to the derivatives of metaphysics, that is, of physics in the broadest sense, which includes the physics of life and man, biology and psychology. Having become anthropology, philosophy itself perishes of metaphysics." See Martin Heidegger,

"Überwindung der Metaphysik," in *Vorträge und Aufsätze*, vol. 7 of *Gesamtausgabe*, ed. Friedrich-Wilhelm von Herrmann (Frankfurt: Klostermann, 2000), 85.

127. Martin Heidegger, "Das Ende der Philosophie und die Aufgabe des Denkens," in *Zur Sache des Denkens*, vol. 14 of *Gesamtausgabe*, ed. Friedrich-Wilhelm von Herrmann (Frankfurt: Klostermann, 2007), 71–72.

128. Heidegger, "Das Ende der Philosophie und die Aufgabe des Denkens," 72.

129. Heidegger, "Das Ende der Philosophie und die Aufgabe des Denkens," 78.

130. Martin Heidegger, *Seminare*, vol. 15 of *Gesamtausgabe*, ed. Curd Ochwadt (Frankfurt: Klostermann, 2003), 382.

131. Transcendence is built into consciousness itself. That consciousness would only deal with itself (immanent content) in opposition to what is transcendent, and "outside" consciousness is as nonsensical as the idea that everything is swallowed up by consciousness, leaving nothing outside it. Husserl writes: "Just as the reduced Ego is not a piece of the world, so, conversely, neither the world nor any worldly Object is a piece of my Ego, to be found in my conscious life as a really inherent part of it, as a complex of data of sensation or a complex of acts. This 'transcendence' is part of the intrinsic sense of anything worldly [. . .]." Edmund Husserl, *Cartesian Meditations: An Introduction to Phenomenology*, trans. Dorion Cairns (Dordrecht: Kluwer Academic, 1999), 26.

132. In fact, Heidegger expressly acknowledges the positive impact that Husserl's concept of intentionality had on him. See Heidegger, *Seminare*, 384. See also Niall Keane's reconstruction of Heidegger's critique and transformation of Husserl's concept of intentionality in this volume.

133. Heidegger, *Seminare*, 387.

134. In fact, in a more nuanced analysis, also during the seminar in Zähringen, Heidegger himself acknowledges that the very changeover to an anthropological paradigm occurred when Feuerbach stood Hegel on his feet and made "man"—and "not the absolute"—the chief matter of philosophical thought. Heidegger also points out that Marx followed Feuerbach in this regard, and he even quotes Marx's famous statement that "the critique of religion ends with the doctrine that for man the supreme being is man" (Heidegger, *Seminare*, 393). But surely Feuerbach and Marx are not starting from any "primacy of consciousness," since they define their anthropological shift in stark opposition to it. In other words, historically, the turn toward anthropology is actually predicated on turning away from the philosophy of consciousness, not adopting it! See Heidegger, *Seminare*, 393.

135. Edmund Husserl, "Heidegger's Letter," in *Psychological and Transcendental Phenomenology and the Confrontation with Heidegger*, 138.

136. Husserl, "Heidegger's Letter," 138.

137. For the transcendental dimension in Heidegger, see Steven Crowell, *Husserl, Heidegger, and the Space of Meaning: Paths Toward Transcendental Phenomenology* (Evanston, IL: Northwestern University Press, 2001).

138. For this, see also Sara Heinämaa's and Niall Keane's illuminating essays in this volume.

139. Husserl, "Heidegger's Letter," 138.

140. Husserl, *Psychological and Transcendental Phenomenology and the Confrontation with Heidegger*, 130.

141. Heidegger, "Philosophische Anthropologie und Metaphysik des Daseins," 237.

142. Husserl, *Psychological and Transcendental Phenomenology and the Confrontation with Heidegger*, 130.

143. For the Husserlian understanding of the human being as having a transcendental function while also being immersed in the world, see Sara Heinämaa's essay "On the Twofoldness of Human Beings" in this volume.

144. Edmund Husserl, *The Crisis of European Sciences and Transcendental Phenomenology*, trans. David Carr (Evanston, IL: Northwestern University Press, 1970), 181.

145. Steven Galt Crowell, "Does the Husserl/Heidegger Feud Rest on a Mistake? An Essay on Psychological and Transcendental Phenomenology," in *Husserl Studies* 18 (2002): 123–40. The most relevant point for our discussion of anthropology is Crowell's thesis number 5 (123): "Heidegger's 'being-in-the-world' is not in the world in Husserl's sense; Husserl's 'transcendental subject' is not a subject in Heidegger's sense. Many misunderstandings between the two philosophers flow from failure to recognize these points."

146. For a good statement of this, see Thomas Sheehan, *Making Sense of Heidegger: A Paradigm Shift* (London: Rowman and Littlefield, 2015).

147. Heidegger, *Zu eigenen Veröffentlichungen*, 31; see also 121, 150, 158, 197, 231, 278, 330–38, 344–50.

148. Martin Heidegger, *Zollikoner Seminare*, vol. 89 of *Gesamtausgabe*, ed. Peter Trawny (Frankfurt: Klostermann, 2018), 637.

149. Heidegger, *Zollikoner Seminare*, 637.

150. See Jeff Malpas, *Place and Experience: A Philosophical Topography*, 2nd ed. (London: Routledge, 2018).

151. See Richard Capobianco, *Heidegger's Way of Being* (Toronto: University of Toronto Press, 2014).

152. Martin Heidegger, "Einleitung zu 'Was ist Metaphysik?,'" in *Wegmarken*, vol. 9 of *Gesamtausgabe*, 373–74; Capobianco, *Heidegger's Way of Being*, 63.

153. Heidegger, "Einleitung zu 'Was ist Metaphysik?,'" 373.

154. Capobianco concedes this point quite clearly, even though he overinterprets Heidegger's shift toward Being. Thus, he writes: "The core matter for Heidegger—and those inclined to his thinking—is that *physis* is the measure, not Dasein. Nevertheless, this by no means diminishes the human being, not at all. It is simply to recognize the *limit* of our marvellous *logos*, our comprehensibility

(*Verstehbarkeit*), our taking-as, our meaning-making." See Capobianco, *Heidegger's Way of Being*, 63.

155. Heidegger, *Zollikoner Seminare*, 664.

156. Heidegger, "Einleitung zu 'Was ist Metaphysik?,' " 373, 375. See also *Zu eigenen Veröffentlichungen*, 282–93.

157. Heidegger, *Zollikoner Seminare*, 663.

Chapter Two

From Heidegger's Da-Sein to the "Prince of the World"

Babette Babich

In Memoriam: Tracy Burr Strong, 1943–2022

Beyond Heidegger's "Authenticity"

This essay thematizes the posthuman along with the transhuman on the way to revisiting Heidegger's thinking on Da-sein,[1] authenticity, and the "human condition" (as Hannah Arendt speaks of this) along with Augustine's "becoming" a question to oneself. With respect to the human "situation," as Günther [Stern] Anders speaks of this, Heidegger's "pseudo-concreteness"[2] can be criticized. Anders's denunciation is multilayered, but it is also indebted to Heidegger not only because it uses Heidegger's language of concretion but because it draws from Heidegger's specifically Augustinian conception of Da-sein: "*Das 'Wesen' dieses Seienden liegt in seinem Zu-sein*" (the "essence" of this entity [that is, this Da-sein] lies in its to-be), which essence, always distinctive, resides in its overt mineness: *je meines*, specifically "*meines wiederum je in dieser oder jener Weise zu sein*" (mine to be in one way or another).[3]

Post transhuman, we find ourselves otherwise than *who* and *what* and *where* we formerly were, quite as Giorgio Agamben recalls this question for us today—*Where Are We Now?*[4]—in the midst of a protracted "pandemic" but also via genetically modified foodstuffs unmarked and everywhere around us, amidst similarly genetically modified/modifying vaccines, but also digitally: as 'cyborgs' connected via social media, variously attached to this here and that now, our new screen-being/old screen-being (reading Anders and Adorno and Baudrillard on media, along with Heidegger), nowhere and everywhere. Following Heidegger's critique of technology, Anders argued our sense of Promethean inadequacy, our *conviction* that the human needs correction, improvement, "updating," whether by way of culture, that would be education, or else via programming using social media (the Frankfurt School), or given the recent acceleration of invasive "testing protocols," today's pharmaceutical body hacks: via swabbing onto/into nasal epithelial layers, inhaled, ingested, injected, or otherwise "patched" into the organism.[5] Thus, in *The Antiquatedness of Humanity*,[6] Anders argued that the human being regarded him- or herself as an animal to be "overcome." The defining terminology Anders lifted from Friedrich Nietzsche, who used the same language to argue that the human being *ought/should* go to ground. A number of enthusiastic advocates for transhumanism read Nietzsche on this question, perhaps wrongheadedly, taking him (or his Zarathustra) as their prophet.[7]

With his definition of the human being as indeterminate, "as *the not yet finished animal*" (*das noch nicht festgestellte Thier*),[8] Nietzsche would appear to make the case for a negative Heideggerian *authenticity*, reminding us of the deficient condition as the rule: among "human beings as among every other species there is a surplus of failures, of the sick, the degenerate, the fragile, of those who are bound to suffer."[9] By contrast, the "successful cases among human beings" always remain "the exception . . . the rare exception."[10]

With respect to the human, Anders follows Heidegger just where Heidegger (quite in accord with the cybernetic transforms of his day)[11] notes the untenability of "merely instrumental, merely anthropological definitions of technology"[12] such that the human is caught up in the technical constellation or *Ge-stell*—"the man at the switchboard, the engineer in the drafting room"[13]—"set up" thereby as "standing reserve." To this extent, Heidegger's example of "human resources," as we speak today, given our increasingly medicalized global polity, references "the supply of patients for a clinic."[14]

Longstanding in the Western tradition, triumphalist humanism sets the human as deiform—*imago dei*. In consequence, the human can be perfected to the limit of a god, as the human imagines deity. Thus Descartes can argue that had he, Descartes, been the maker (deity), he, Descartes, would have done a better job (he would have created a being without defect).[15]

Reference to religion persists in what Heidegger names "Nietzsche's word" on the death of God, a theological claim Nietzsche proposes in *The*

Gay Science, beginning with the death of Buddha (and his shadow) and continuing with the madman in the marketplace,[16] complete with a reference to Hegel and Christological traditions. From this perspective, as Anders writes, echoing Heidegger, the human is mere "raw material," as Paul Virilio also writes, citing the human in his *Art and Fear* as "bioresource": "standing reserve" on the level of tissues and cell lines since Auschwitz-Birkenau.[17]

In a 1979 annotation included in the 1980, second volume of *The Antiquatedness of the Human*, Anders reflected on the utilization or exploitation of body parts parallel to the case of concentration camp victims,[18] as an age of "cannibalism," likewise beginning in Auschwitz and including the extraction, as he explicates: of "gold teeth and hair." Here Anders gives his account of the "American soldiers [who] returned home from the Pacific with Japanese gold teeth," emphasizing the horror of witnessing with his "own eyes," GIs who proudly displayed "bags full of gold teeth."[19] The body and its hair, the metal of extracted, enemy teeth is so much "raw material."[20] Both Virilio and Anders remind us of details we prefer to forget as Virilio writes of human tissue extracted from the fetuses that were already an object of research in Auschwitz, "material" remains that continue to be deployed in many ways, via cell lines and fetal serum extracts, today's vaccines including (but not limited to) today's efforts against the current "medical" crisis.[21] To this extent, Anders underlined that this very industrial production corresponds to the "manufacture," in Heidegger's infamous words, "of corpses."[22] Above I noted that Anders uses the language Nietzsche uses with reference to Empedocles (and this ancient Greek's horror of eating flesh): "dining on oneself" (*sich-selbst-verspeisen*). To this extent, what Anders names "cannibalism" is more "concrete" and given the anthropic temerity of our modern technological age, a sheerly logical extension, we are "eaters" as Anders speaks of us, who regard the world as "raw material" whether we meant to use it heedlessly or to conserve it in some green new deal. Both consumer visions set the human at the center:

> This terrible general-license, which renders nothing taboo apart from the human and which assumes that everything has been created for the human, that is, that everything is at his disposal, has never existed apart from the monotheistic domain of the Judeo-Christian tradition (Genesis 1, 26–28): neither in the systems of the magi nor in the multifarious systems of polytheism. . . . Only in the framework of the anthropocentric tradition in which the world was regarded as "subordinated" to the human being, as servant, object, and means of survival; and in which the human, although still *creatura*, was not regarded as part of nature but as unlimited

lord of all creation; solely within this frame could natural science arise and with it technology and with it, finally, industrialism.[23]

As Judeo-Christian and monotheistic, *religion is a humanism*, it transpires, so Nietzsche argues, that modern technoscience is only the latest version of this same *humanism*.

Where Heidegger focuses on the human to raise the question of Augustinian immediacy concerning the *who* that I am myself, in order to raise the being question, Anders focuses on the human *qua* human, bracketing the usual concessions human beings claim on their own behalf: an enduring state of exception.

It is common to note that Nietzsche foregrounds the consonance of Western thought with religion, highlighting science as the latest and greatest of "ascetic ideals."[24] Anders takes this insight in a critical direction not towards a "genealogy" of morals but indicative of a "negative ethics," to invoke "*the defect [Manko]* of our 'Western' ethics."[25] We will need to return to the notion of Anders's *negative ethics* but here Anders reminds us that the Western religious tradition is compatible with both theism *and* atheism, uniting the East *and* the West:

> Today, of course, the natural sciences and technology, which would never have existed without theological anthropocentrism, are also rooted in those peoples, such as the Japanese, for example, that did not originally possess the theological presuppositions for them. Yet these presuppositions have also long been forgotten in Judeo-Christian cultural circles. Moreover, the technocratic countries are no longer united by a single faith; to the contrary, what unites them is (rarely as articulated but exercised) atheism that (despite the occasional proclamations of faith on the part of physicists) is the basis of the natural sciences.[26]

Atheistic theology only foregrounds the centrality of the human. Like transhumanism at its core, this is anthropocentrism.

Human, All-Too-Human:
On Becoming a Question to Oneself

The *Who* question is yesterday's news. Today, we do not ask *Who* we are but much rather *What* is the human? To ask a "what" question,[27] as Anders tells us, following Heidegger's cadence, following Scheler's cadence, is to be contrasted with both the that- and the who-question.[28] We are thus returned to the beginning of philosophy and Anders, like Heidegger, is mindful of the conundrum that such questions are rarely posed as *questions*. It does not help matters that we begin with the answer(s). We know, already and in advance, that the human *is* the rational animal, the techno-political animal, a featherless biped, and so on.

In *Being and Time*, Heidegger has recourse to the conventionality of traditional definitions: "*Das Dasein*, that is, the Being of humanity is in common as in philosophical 'definition' comprehended as ζῷον λόγον ἔχον, the living being whose being is essentially determined by the capacity for speech."[29] Heidegger's reference points include Plato and Aristotle, Rousseau but also, so Anders argues, Kant's *What Is Enlightenment?* Indeed, Anders, the son of a famous father, the psychologist William Stern,[30] would also emphasize the challenges of speaking in one's own voice, in accord with Kant's language of *Mündigkeit*.[31]

Inasmuch as Heidegger's definition repeats Aristotelian cliché, ἄνθρωπον hierarchically stands in place of ζῷον. Thus, Aristotle traces the schematism of *plant* nutrition and growth, *animal* perception that is to say, sentient awareness or consciousness, and *human* contemplation: thinking thinking.

Giving ourselves a name for the kind of beings we are, a habitus of naming that we have adopted for ourselves—this is anthropology—we name ourselves *homo sapiens*. Yet the attribution of "wisdom" only describes human aspiration not fact. Today's crisis may be characterized by what is claimed to be a 'virus' (defining such having long been a scandal in biology), claimed to be 'new,' or driven by the economic strategy of lockdown (reset) or "climate change," but all such claims are perforce anthropically engendered, human driven. Less than an expression of "wisdom" we are beset by what Heidegger called *Idiotismus* on the same planetary scale he describes.[32]

Above I recalled Heidegger's claim that Da-Sein in its being for itself is distinctive in its mineness: the "me" in each case is rarely "authentically" mine but characteristically "unowned." Thus Anders repeats the intentionality-driven point Heidegger makes concerning distraction/absorption: "[E]ven in its fullest concretion Dasein can be characterized by inauthenticity."[33] For Heidegger, "inauthenticity" by no means corresponds to a "'lower' degree of Being" (*"niedrigeren" Seinsgrad*) but determines Dasein in its "fullest concretion."[34] Occupied with, or preoccupied by what one is doing, looking forward to a good time, we may note that Heidegger's list reflects the most 'human' ways of being human.

Thus Heidegger reminds us of a perplexing reflex in Augustine's *Confessions*, where the saint asks what could ever be more proximate to me than myself to myself: "*Quid autem propinquius meipso mihi?*"[35] Augustine's answer is well-known *and* poorly read. The challenge remains even as we note the beauty of the formula, confounding as it was for the author himself, for Augustine who sets his text before God: "*mihi quaestio factus sum.*"[36] Augustine's successive reflection concerning time and his understanding of it, likewise including a variation on this questioning after himself, foregrounding the same proximity to himself, compounds the problem ("*ego certe laboro hic et laboro in meipso: factus sum mihi terra difficultatis et sudoris nimii*").

The logical immediacy of mineness is key. This Heidegger seeks to unpack, and many scholars have observed that it is worth reading Heidegger alongside Augustine.[37] In the same way, Augustine's writerly style invites the reader to follow his confessional modality quite to the literalistic extent of ahistorical error,[38] for Heidegger and for others like Nietzsche.[39]

Questioning Da-Sein

Like Heidegger's question concerning technology, the question concerning science as a question assumes the prior question of what is assumed to count as a science. But Heidegger offers no "Question Concerning Science" among his essays. Indeed, it is Nietzsche who claims that he was the first to have raised "the question of science as a question."[40] Like Husserl, Heidegger, with his own focus on questioning,[41] raises the question of the human sciences,[42] observing that these depend for their data, their least interpreted "facts," upon a prior or pregiven "foundational" conception of that science:

> But heretofore our information about primitives has been provided by ethnology. And ethnology operates with definite preliminary conceptions and interpretations of human Dasein in general, even in first "receiving" its material, and in sifting it and working it up. Whether the everyday psychology or even the scientific psychology and sociology which the ethnologist brings with him can provide any scientific assurance that we can have proper access to the phenomena we are studying, and can interpret them and transmit them in the right way, has not yet been established.[43]

To just this extent, "anthropology" was challenged by Gottlob Frege as by Husserl, and Heidegger was able to hear this challenge as presupposing a defining orientation entailing the necessity of hermeneutic phenomenology: "Ethnology itself already presupposes as its clue an adequate analytic of Dasein."[44]

ANTHROPOLOGISM

"Isms" in general, and this holds whether one follows analytic or continental styles of philosophy, do not tend to be good things.[45] In this way the reproof of "anthropologism," like the cognate charge of "psychologism,"[46] follows from Frege's admonition "to sharply separate the psychological from the logical, the subjective from the objective."[47] For his part, Frege is only repeating the rigor of Kant's critical distinction of his own inquiry into practical reason from traditional "anthropology" and not less, because this is part of the critical enterprise, from what belongs to a science "properly," that is, "authentically" said.[48] By contrast, that means, as opposed to an "anthropology," Heidegger emphasizes "the Being question itself as—the task of laying bare that *a priori* basis which must be visible before the question of 'what man is' can be discussed philosophically."[49]

Thus Heidegger follows Kant's refusal of empirical recourse to the ontic affair that is human practice. The critical Kant distinguishes his inquiry into practical reason from "anthropology," emphasizing that what belongs to a science—properly said—requires the calculative advantage afforded by neither anthropology nor psychology but by mathematics. For Kant, and our notion of science "proper" follows this contention to this day: "[A] doctrine of nature can only contain so much science proper as there is in it of applied mathematics."[50] To the same degree, ethnography or anthropology are "sciences" only improperly speaking so, quite as chemistry also remains qualifiedly limited on Kant's account.[51]

In the same way, Heidegger emphasizes the urgency of "the Being question itself as—the task of laying bare that *a priori* basis which must be visible before the question of 'what man is' can be discussed philosophically. The existential analytic of Dasein comes before any psychology or anthropology and certainly before any biology."[52] For Heidegger, the analytic of Da-sein precedes *anthropological* questions along with questions of the proper/improper in general for Kantian reasons just to the extent that the analysis is not limited to the human being per se. Famously, Kant takes his prescription literally, hence as applicable to extraterrestrials[53] and even, supernaturally, to the "holy one of the gospels." Perhaps it is as a result of this tradition that, concerned as we are with AI and robot rights, that we have made little progress when it comes to the question of animal or plant intelligence—or even rock intelligence (Thales ascribes this to the lodestone). Thus we might one day ask the question of the human: the anthropological question concerning ethnography.[54]

Psychologism

For Kant, both anthropologism and psychologism are deficient methodological modes. In this fashion, seemingly justifying Reiner Schürmann's remark that "[n]o modern philosopher has caused more ink to be spilled than Kant,"[55] a Kantianism haunts phenomenology and its animus contra psychologism. As Martin Kusch reports:

> According to Wundt, Husserl had exchanged psychologism for logicism. Wundt defined the two positions as mirror images of one another such that things would not seem to have progressed much since 1884: "Psychologism wants to turn logic into psychology; logicism wants to turn psychology into logic."[56]

Famously, Husserl would accuse Heidegger of both anthropologism and psychologism. To this day many scholars concur: convicting Heidegger of existentialism, subjectivism, and so on. Some respected Heideggerian scholars have maintained that in talking of 'Dasein' Heidegger means to emphasize the human or, as Ingo Farin summarizes in his careful reading of Tom Sheehan's recent reading of Heidegger (and Richardson), "[T]he human is the very site, *Da-sein*, where the clearing comes to pass or is achieved."[57]

Yet Heidegger invokes his Da-sein for different reasons. To this extent, Husserl's rebuke that Heidegger only advances an anthropology cannot but miss Heidegger's project of fundamental ontology. And by the same token, and beyond the question of equating being with meaning or there-being with human being, it will turn out that Heidegger's approach to a philosophy of science is essential for thought even if he does not initiate the question of science as Nietzsche does or put science in question along with technology inasmuch as he traces the order of reflection, articulating perhaps just what it is that a philosophy of science is and can be and, not less, the fundamental dependence of science on philosophy for the sake of reflection. To this extent, Heidegger importantly argues that "neither" the human sciences nor the so-called "positive sciences"

> "can" or should wait for the ontological labours of philosophy to be done, the further course of research will not take the form of an "advance" but will be accomplished by recapitulating what has already been ontically discovered, and by purifying it in a way which is ontologically more transparent.[58]

Referring to human beings in the context of the social or human sciences—*Geisteswissenschaften*—Heidegger invokes the social world, as such, speaking of *das Man*, and not less of the objectively minded concept of a *Menschending*, a human thing.

But "What" Is a *Menschending*?—"Who" Is Da-Sein?

The enduring concern of humanity is with itself. To this extent, philosophical anthropologies typically draw on the claimed distinctiveness and thereby the claimed excellence of the human being as they have done since Aristotle. Thus Daniel O. Dahlstrom points out that for Heidegger "the transcendence that makes up the very being of being-here encompasses a relation to oneself as well as a correlative relatedness to the world at large. Heidegger attempts to capture this distinctive transcendence with the metonym, 'being-in-the-world.' "[59] In addition to Heidegger's critique of anthropologism, Dahlstrom urges that one take Heidegger's repudiation of transcendence with a grain of salt, citing Heidegger: "Dasein's transcendence is the condition of the possibility of the ontological difference."[60]

Above, we noted the traditional distinction between What and Who in the Heideggerian hermeneutic, phenomenological context. To say, as Heidegger does, that Da-sein is "that entity which in its Being has this very Being as an issue,"[61] suggests that Da-sein may not be limited to the human being. But in its Aristotelian context, the reflexive focus is not open but immediately foregrounds the human, suggesting that it is only the human who is "able" to be Da-sein, the "there," once again, as some humanistically minded Heideggerians maintain, of being.[62]

As Heidegger opens the question of the I-myself "self" of Da-sein, this can be related to the famous question of "the friend," the subject of Heidegger's interrogation of the preoccupation of Da-sein with the issue of its own being just as this "may" turn out, in the conceit of the questions Heidegger didactically raises here, to be other than assumed. Who is the friend? Is this parallel reflex *psyche*, that is the soul or some other remnant of the bicameral mind, a psychological optical illusion, or perhaps an emergent phenomenon, generated by the reflex of self-address, doubled, theticizing, as Schürmann argues in his seemingly indefatigable tracking of the dark night of the soul beginning with Parmenides following the leading strings of his maidens to Porphyry and Augustine (and his almost invention of the "I"), to Aquinas and Eckhart and Luther, "grounding the there," as Schürmann argues towards the end of his study, *Broken Hegemonies*?[63] The fluidity opens a range of possibilities. In addition to raising the question of humanism for Heidegger,[64] theology with all its advantages and all its (often confessional) *aporiae*[65] follows on the heels of this thinking. To this extent phenomenology remains ensconced in what Dominique Janicaud suspiciously regarded as a deleterious turn toward the theological.[66]

It was with reference to what Schürmann characterized as the durability of "the existentialist misunderstanding of *Being and Time*," that Schürmann undertook for pedagogical reasons to clarify this same "misunderstanding," attributing it not as Adorno does to Jaspers's *Existenzphilosophie* but to the French existentialist tradition of Jean-Paul Sartre, who selected "some themes from *Being and Time*—being-towards-death, dread, etc.,—developing them into a so-called 'ontology of human existence.' "[67]

By contrast, Schürmann argues, "in *Being and Time*, Heidegger is preoccupied with the question of Being as such—whatever that will turn out to mean—and only therefore with the question of Dasein."[68] To the same extent, reflecting on the signal importance of the *Beiträge*, Schürmann reminds us that to ask the question "*Who?*" takes us to the

> center where, as Heidegger never stops repeating, metaphysical strategies have always been hatched, [a center which] has been and remains "man"—the concept of representable beings endowed with attributes and capable of perfecting themselves (be it by ascending toward the universal, by entering into themselves, or, yet again, by progress).[69]

Schürmann is careful not to claim that Heidegger reserves all his secrets for his *Beiträge* anymore than the current author has argued that he relegates them to his *Black Notebooks*. Instead Schürmann proposes that we might read our Heidegger the way we read Lotze, Aristotle, or Nietzsche, that is to say, mindful of Heidegger's *style*, of the way he writes, including tacit influences on his writing, and not less *what* he writes. As Schürmann explains (I make a related case elsewhere), Heidegger's *Beiträge* has the privilege it has owing to the influence of Nietzsche who spoke "from a site which is already no longer ours" but also because, note Schürmann's tack for establishing his claim, "[T]he Husserl of the *Crisis* did not put the primacy of subjectivity and consciousness into question" and also and not less, for Schürmann, "because Wittgenstein made it a point of honor to neglect history" all the while "all three only got rid of the very question of metaphysics—the question of being—by speaking of an Indo-European language and therefore using the copula 'is' without interpreting it."[70]

Thus Schürmann speaks of the 'monstrous' as he also speaks of the importance of underscoring that Heidegger in the *Beiträge* takes his own point of departure—and this for Schürmann involves the explicit revisiting of *Being and Time*, including the Kant book, but also *Introduction to Metaphysics*, gathered under "the most intense combined influence of Hölderlin and Nietzsche."[71] Schürmann takes care to emphasize, and the distinction matters with reference to Anders, that "the final section of the *Contributions* is entitled 'The Last God.' "[72] The context Schürmann explains, as if with reference to the title of the first section of Nietzsche's *Human, All too Human*, "On First and Last Things," anthropologically, that is to say, *biographically*, recollecting Heidegger's seminars with Rudolf Bultmann on nothing less than "a theology of *eschata* (last things), not in the sense of a denouement at the end of time but in the sense of the plenitude of salvation offered in the instant."[73] Reading the *Beiträge* contra *Sein und Zeit*, underlining the "contingency" of Da-sein, Schürmann argues that the *there* in question (these are Schürmann's italics) "remains still 'to be prepared' (BzP 231) and Da-sein . . . 'the ground of a determinate human-being of the one that is yet to come' (BzP 200)." In this sense, Schürmann goes on to explicate "the surprising contingency of Da-sein. It may, and it may not, come to be."[74]

I began this essay by recalling Anders's "concrete" critique of Heidegger's authenticity as this is articulated, as Heidegger emphasizes, first and foremost and most of the time by way of inauthenticity, i.e., in intimate and immediate concrete distraction/absorption. To answer the challenge of the question on every level, ontic and spiritual, "Who am I?" Schürmann can summarize, not unlike Anders: "Most of the time I am 'they,' doing as 'they' do and living as 'they' live."[75] It is in this sense that it is "clear," as Schürmann says, that the "question clearly veers to the ontic."[76]

The point for Schürmann concerns Heidegger's self-splintering self-critique, but the insight requires that we let go of the common conviction that inscribes Heidegger not only within National Socialism but perhaps as the philosopher of the "movement" par excellence. Schürmann finds this not only untenable but risky to the extent that it can blind us to what else is going on in the *Beiträge* (and, so I would argue, likewise in the *Black Notebooks*). There is for Schürmann an explicitly modern hegemony still in the ascendant. Then, in Heidegger's day, Schürmann gives us the date, 1933, one sought to speak in the name of a certain "phantom" (phantom would be Nietzsche's word), "a new German will." For Schürmann Heidegger is both, on the one hand, a dupe and yet conscious of the same[77]—and on the other hand at odds with himself:

> It is known that Heidegger never shared the biological and racist consequences of this new will. His polemic follows from this: In his rectoral address he had placed his hopes on a renewal of science, but pseudo-biology had disabused him of that; then self-criticism led him to see that essential continuity, grounded in the interest of mastery, between modern science and eugenics.[78]

The issue for Schürmann (and for many of us) remains enmired in Heidegger's conviction that he understood "the Nazis better than they understood themselves."[79] But what is perhaps more problematic is the current circumstance of our own (quite ongoing) antiquatedness, our newly transhuman condition, now and, seemingly, henceforward. This seeming concerns the current pandemic and its medicalization of everyday life at intervals, physically-physiologically, but here it is hard to imagine that we are not still and yet "riveted," to use Schürmann's language,

> to the site of a planetary self-destruction which has become an imminent possibility, the old tragic knowledge has come back within our reach, the knowledge that within every constellation laying down the law, the transgressive pull backwards towards the No pulls us more powerfully toward death than the universalizing and normative Yes pulls us to life.[80]

Schürmann does ask the question we are seeking to ask here, writing, "Toward what then, may man transmute himself? How is one to describe his possible shape, exceeding as it does the epoch of technicity?"[81]

At issue is the question less of existentialism (or humanism) than "anthropology." At issue for Heidegger as for Anders in another "antiquated" sense, is what Schürmann names a fractured hegemony, almost as Husserl would appear to object. This is there from the start in *Being and Time* as Heidegger elaborates a *hermeneutics* of phenomenology. For all the emphasis on Aristotle and given Heidegger's research on scholastic/school logicians, for all the reference that we would be following out with respect to Descartes and Kant, and hence and therefore to Husserl, Heidegger follows this preliminary exposition *contra* anthropology.

The expression "phenomenology," as Heidegger writes, "can be formulated in Greek as λέγειν τὰ φαινόμενα. But λέγειν means ἀποφαίνεσθαι. Hence phenomenology means ἀποφαίνεσθαι τὰ φαινόμενα—to let what shows itself be seen from itself, just as it shows itself from itself."[82] In looking at what shows itself one also considers what is patently concealed, un- or nonevident. This includes ontology. As Heidegger explains: "*Ontology is possible only as phenomenology*" and of course, as already noted at the start, "there are various ways phenomena can be covered up."[83]

For Schürmann what is problematic is the Western world: as *mathesis* "the world rendered uniform makes being-there (Da-sein) difficult and rare, it perverts it into being gone' (*Weg-sein*, BzP 323)."[84] Parallel, as I would argue, to Anders, Schürmann alludes to the Frankfurt School and its reflection on 'the disenchantment of the world,' the work of which he maintains "was already completed in the first half of the twentieth century. Giganticism and operational machination had taken care of it quite effectively."[85]

"Aether" and Care: Other Others

Our protracted focus on ourselves is a preternaturally human thing. This preoccupation includes our transhumanism, which as it transpires corresponds less to the quaint futurism of a Buck Rogers or comic book Superman, but merely and only to being constantly online, AI, and robot rights, vaccines and nanotech adjuvants, manufactured to the latest, eternally to be repeatedly upgraded specifications of the current age of technological productivity and reset. To this extent our new technological "gadgets" resemble the same gadgets that, as Anders reflected in his first book on the outdatedness of the human, inspired our Promethean shame, an anti-idealization of our humanity by comparison or contrast with the things we *have* made or plan forever iteratively to make *in future*.

I noted above, and I cited Schürmann as echoing in a different direction, the point that Anders argues whereby our collective religious legacy justifies planetary destruction, all too humanistically. To the same degree, Anders cites Nietzsche's definition of the human as "the unfinished animal": collectively, those animals who do not take themselves to be animals and thus suppose that the universe itself was either specifically *designed* for them or else, hence the economic idea of a global "reset," that that same universe can be remade in our image by design, via software, or more or less violent geo-engineering (cloud spraying and HF and 4G/5G transmission).

To this extent, despite his numerous attacks on Heidegger, Anders remains closer to Heidegger than to Adorno. But as Anders also argues, "nature" is ontologically ordered to Da-sein for Heidegger, emphasizing on the level of embodiment that Heidegger's analysis in *Being and Time*, in spite of its focus on being in the world, leaves out—rather than brackets—all questions of hunger or of sex. As Anders writes, "All want is wanting."[86]

One can make (scholars have) the contrary argument but here with reference to transhumanism or else to the idea of "hacking" the human, just to the extent that the term "hacking" makes the process seem a casual venture, tech geek style and thereby harmless, despite the dedication to prolonging life by whatever means possible, Ray Kurzweil style, Bill Gates style, via genetic engineering, that is the enterprise Anders already named "Human Engineering" in 1956. A year earlier, on the ten-year anniversary of Hiroshima and Nagasaki, Heidegger had argued that the project of human engineering via biochemistry already made the idea of atomic weapons (to the banning of which Anders would dedicate his life) trivial by comparison.

In *Gelassenheit*, Heidegger cited an "international meeting of Nobel Prize winners," quoting the biochemist and virologist Wendell Stanley on the ability "to synthesise, split, and change living substance at will."[87] Winner of the 1946 Nobel Prize for chemistry for work done on the tobacco mosaic virus in 1938, work that arguably underlies GMO technology to date, including mRNA and viral vector vaccines, Stanley decried the financial stakes of the competition that changed science from the life of ideas and open exchange between scientists, to a then newly closed and newly entrepreneurial science, citing "the story of the poliomyelitis virus and the attempts to find a safe vaccine."[88] Thus Stanley argued that,

> during the race for a polio vaccine, the results of the research were only judged by committees behind closed doors. As a

consequence, there were some serious mistakes made and for some time a vaccine was used, in particular on children, which actually resulted in paralysis.[89]

The problem as Heidegger reflects on science is that we "marvel at the daring of scientific research, without thinking about it." Thus Heidegger can continue:

> We do not stop to consider that an attack with technological means is being prepared upon the life and nature of the human being compared with which the explosion of the hydrogen bomb means little. For precisely *if* the hydrogen bombs do not explode and human life is preserved, an uncanny change in the world moves upon us.[90]

Thoughtless, without thinking, not thinking, this is the language Heidegger uses to speak of science in *What Is Called Thinking?* Earlier, Heidegger had invoked the Sophoclean language of the uncanny—*das Unheimliche*—to epitomize the nature of the human in his *Introduction to Metaphysics*, claiming that the human, as he says again and again, the term he uses is *Mensch*, "is *to deinotaton*, the strangest of the strange."[91]

Here the same Sophocles inspires Alexander Pope's 1734 *Essay on Man*:

> Plac'd on this isthmus of a middle state,
> A being darkly wise, and rudely great.

Following the steps and turns, the rhythm of the lines and tacks of Sophocles's first chorus in *Antigone*, Pope might seem to be predicting today's geo-engineering:

> . . . Go, wond'rous creature! mount where Science guides,
> Go, measure earth, weigh air, and state the tides;
> Instruct the planets in what orbs to run,
> Correct old Time, and regulate the Sun . . .

Clearly, at least we might say just with reference to Pope and his mid-eighteenth-century vision: "Science" is the key.

To be sure, we also know, as students of history as of philosophy of science, that what counts as "science" changes. Heidegger raises his own question regarding humanism in his 1955 lecture concerning "a new ground and foundation" in what can seem to be void—and here we may remember that Heidegger echoes Kant who begins his first *Critique* by reminding us of the hindrance that resistance appears to present, that is the air against which the dove's wings flail and seek to climb,[92] but without which resistance, in the absence of that same elastic air, the dove could not fly at all. The question for Heidegger is whether "humanity [*das Menschenwesen*] and all its works can flourish in a new way even in the atomic age."[93]

Elsewhere I argue that Heidegger would have to have known Kant's allusion to the dove. Earlier, Hölderlin would write that he held to another standard, as he wrote to his brother in 1779, on New Year's Day, given his own "stumbling" efforts to approximate the Greeks,

> these only human beings in the world, and in what I do and say I am often only the more inept and inconsistent because I stand, like geese, with my flat feet in modern water and helplessly beat my wings up to the Greek sky.[94]

το δεινότατον

What is the human?

Sophocles tells us quite to the point Hölderlin repeats, quite as Heidegger does, including as we should note not only the "aether" with all its elemental archaicism, but wind and water:

> There is much that is strange but nothing
> That surpasses man in strangeness.
> He sets sail on the frothing waters
> Amid the south winds of winter. . . .[95]

The Greek begins πολλὰ τὰ δεινὰ and Heidegger repeats the first point to be emphasized[96]—"there is much that is strange"—to describe the *human* as strange or uncanny: κοὐδὲν ἀνθρώπου δεινότερον.

There are conventions and sensibilities, and these vary between linguistic schemes. Thus, Anglophone readers may cite Pope's *Essay* as the *Inbegriff* of every cliché application. On another day one might cite Milton or Byron or Browning or Emerson, and Heidegger had his Hebel along with the Hölderlin (who also translates Sophocles) and Goethe.

Sophocles moves between positive encomium and drastic warning, to and fro in the meter:

> And he has found his way
> to the resonance of the word [φθέγμα],
> And to wind-swift all-understanding [φρόνημα]
> And to the courage of rule over cities [ἀστυνόμους].[97]

I argue that we have to read the Greek, as Heidegger reads the Greek along with Hölderlin and Nietzsche, because Sophocles does all this in chained conjunction: καὶ.

The question of the human is posed contra today's attunement to the transhumanism that reads itself as "über-humanism," rather like Heidegger's parenthetical dismissal—reminding us that "among the Greeks there were no personalities (and for this reason no supra-personality [*Über-Persönliches*])."[98]

Overcoming, *überwinden*, as Anders "varies Nietzsche's word,"[99] turns on even more concrete affairs. At stake today is the medicalized body, qua submitted to constant violating as part of the testing ordeals of the same, cleared and registered as certified, via testing, and thus attested, or with access to air blocked and hindered, but most of all flagged or marked, via masking, and above all: infused on the level of the organs, the tissues, the lymph, the blood itself, via vaccine, into the body. The *attention* to the human, the *urge* to overcome or reengineer the body, is not quite or utterly modern or postmodern as it may be found in what Nietzsche in *The Gay Science* called the "preludes to science" quite as it holds sway in modern technoscience as such, all gene modified and "crispr'd," as we anticipate the results of the new vaccine (and this is meant as a plural, serial, and above all: ongoing affair) meant to change (reset) a world.

Qua prelude, Goethe already has a tale, for Anders, his most influential. This is not the *Zauberlehrling* as this intrigued Anders (and Hollywood) as parable for the age of technoscience, but *Faust*. The story calls up not mops and brooms gone amok but elemental, demonic forces. And Faust's effort succeeds, which is where the problem begins, as Heidegger suggests, just when and just *if* we successfully manage not to bomb the human race to oblivion.

The language in Goethe's German is more fraught, more conflicted than Pope's language as we read his English. As *Erdgeist*, the Spirit of the Earth points out to Faust that he is barred from knowing anything that is not of Faust's own creaturely domain: "*Du gleichst dem Geist, den Du beigreifst.*"¹⁰⁰ In the same way as Pope's *middle* creature that is the human being *is* deiform by nature, that is, made to receive the image, the likeness of its creator which entails that it, middle creature, "darkly wise," cannot know the earth as such despite being formed of the earth: the only thing it can know is that to which it is, *qua* creature, allied.

The exchange between Faust and his conjured Earth Spirit offers the key to Nietzsche's understanding of interpretation, here to speak of Nietzsche's *elective* affinities: one is only able to understand that which is in some fashion related to one¹⁰¹—in addition to more esoteric reflections on Nietzsche's *Übermensch*,¹⁰² just to the extent that Goethe's Earth Spirit is likewise inspired by the second century AD, Lucian of Samosata. Already this tells us that what we think we know of the Greek is more complicated, other than Greek (Lucian is a Syrian by birth and linguistic inheritance), more than Greek. Thus we need to be as Nietzsche was, as Heidegger was inclined to be, a philologist. What is certain is that lacking Lucian's ὑπεράνθρωπος or overhuman, along with the very idea of high and low, above and below, we cannot understand *the human*.

Elsewhere I recall, as others also do, Heidegger's citation of Hyginus's influential allegory or fable of "Cura" or Care, relevant to the extent that *Sorge* informs human life. Heidegger tells us that he takes his account from Konrad Burdach's philological, 1923 exposition of Goethe.¹⁰³ Goethe took his own account from Herder, and Heidegger cites Hyginus in Latin as in German translation,¹⁰⁴ to explain the designation, the name of the human qua human. As Heidegger explains, using the titanic language we may recognize from Hölderlin:

> [T]his pre-ontological document becomes especially significant not only in that "care" is here seen as that to which human Dasein belongs "for its lifetime," but also because this priority of "care" emerges in connection with the familiar way of taking the human as compounded of body (earth) and spirit. . . . It gets the name "homo" not in consideration of its Being but in relation to that of which it consists (*humus*). The decision as to wherein the "primordial" Being of this creature is to be seen, is left to Saturn, "Time."¹⁰⁵

It should be noted that few, among the very many who have written on this, go further than Heidegger's own footnote supplied in *Being and Time*. Thus there has not been extended commentary on the philological detail that Heidegger's text refers not to a Greek nor indeed to an Aramaic genesis but and only a Roman myth, as he cites Seneca's Latin:

> Among the four existent natures (trees, animals, man, and God), the latter two, which alone are endowed with reason, are distinguished in that God is immortal while man is mortal. Now when it comes to these, the good of the one, namely God, is fulfilled by his Nature; but that of the other, man, is fulfilled by care [*die Sorge*] (*cura*): *unius bonum natura perficit, deiscilicet, alterius cura, hominis*.[106]

This has a twofold articulation as Heidegger glosses:

> Man's *perfectio*—his transformation into that which he can be in Being-free-for his ownmost possibilities (projection) [*in seinem Freisein für seine eigensten Möglichkeiten (dem Entwurf)*]—is "accomplished" by "care" [*ist eine "Leistung" der "Sorge"*]. But with equal primordiality "care" determines what is basically specific in this entity, according to which it has been surrendered to the world of its concern (thrownness [*Geworfenheit*]). In the "double meaning" of "care" ["*cura*"], what we have in view is a single basic state in its essentially twofold structure of thrown projection.[107]

The human is fundamentally divided and, although formed of clay or earth, the human is not *of* the earth, not even qua form or inspiration, even as named from clay or humus.

As with Sophocles's ode, Hölderlin's "An den Aether" speaks of the human in its relatedness to the divine. Here we recall Hölderlin's closing lines from his ode, which I cite here in English:

> But while I long to ascend into the twilight distance, Where you embrace foreign shores with your blue-tinted waves, You come whispering down from the fruit trees' blossom'd peak, Father Aether! and soften yourself this my striving heart And I live gladly now, as before, with the flowers of the earth.[108]

The other meaning for the human, *homo sapiens*, "wise human," is as Heidegger never fails to emphasize, the mortal—"the corpse," so Schürmann reminds us, "is never far off"[109]—we human beings are those who *can* die.

In great measure, Heidegger took pains throughout his life to remind his readers of mortality, being unto-death, being all-too-human. It is thus that Heidegger defines the 'possible totalization of the being of Dasein and being towards death' (*Das mögliche Ganzsein des Daseins und das Sein zum Tode*.)

This Anders goes along with, as a matter not quite of Arendtian natality, having been born, but before birth Anders speaks of swimming like a fish, having been engendered, *begotten* not made and thereby distinguished from the deathless gods. Our shame beyond natality is our navel, our sign of this having been begotten. For Anders, this "defect" signifies our shame in our imperfection. Concerned as we are with the human, we seek protection, exposed as we are, as Rilke says, in vulnerability. But as Nietzsche would say, that, too, is human.

On Animal Da-Sein

I tend in writing (and teaching) to underline with some mirth, it is a joke that is no joke, that there is *dolphin* Da-sein, *squirrel* Da-sein, *elephant* Da-sein, *cat* Da-sein, *alien* Da-sein. *Da-sein* is not, *pace* Sheehan, *pace* Aristotle, the human *qua* privileged "there" of Being, dim *imago dei*, created being in the image and likeness of uncreated being.

Much rather—and here our current attention to AI may help to begin to illuminate the question, certainly our attention to animals never did (perhaps it always should have done so, as Nietzsche reminds us that the tiniest insect, *Mücke*, takes itself to be the center of the universe), no more than our attention to mountains or the desert or anything like a land ethic—Da-sein is any being whatever for whom its being is an issue. If we ourselves as we saw above flee the question, as we tend to do, we also vigorously deny the question when it comes to regarding beings like *and* unlike ourselves, human *and* otherwise.

Heidegger claims that the essence of technology is nothing technological, and he also underlines that he ascribes no deviltry, he is very specific, to technology. But Anders (like Schürmann after him, albeit differently) affirms a religious dimension, negative and silenced regarding deity in the factic wake of history, essential to any philosophy meaning to consider the world and the damage wrought by beings such as ourselves. For Anders humanity has less to do with "being" as such, with being the there of being as such, than with its claimed possessions. This will induce a certain parsing of authenticity, or as Anders expresses it: with "having."[110]

Anders argues that our religious legacy would appear to justify global destruction,[111] certainly natural law makes the case for it, whereby our infernally Promethean "capacity"—the language is calculatedly Kantian—appears as *fait accompli*. To this day, we regard climate change in the same way, in the age of apocalypse, a 'happening,' innocent of our actions, complete with the character of revelation:

> That man should be the *goal* and the world *a means*, this anthropocentrism was the common denominator (only rarely interrupted by pantheistic *intermezzos*) of the European philosophies and vulgar worldviews, whose innumerable differences hardly matter in comparison with what they have in common.[112]

If Anders emphasizes animals in a passage memorializing Hannah Arendt (in his *Die Kirschenschlacht*),[113] he is not thereby an advocate, as Adorno was, *for* animals. But we cannot afford such niceties as advocacy: we today need to add the question concerning animality, for thousands of years an unasked and unquestionable question in philosophy as we also had occasion to recall Virilio's reflections (on GMOs) along with Heidegger's reference to Stanley (on vaccines), whereby like the woman question, like the Jewish question, the question of utilizing animal/human body parts has to be adverted to as it is constantly ignored. What is at issue is not intelligence (nearly always disappointingly defined) or moral-political agency (stipulated such that even *human beings* can be excluded, given that the whole point of right turns on wealth and privilege). Much rather, the closest philosophical convention for this concern is minimally Kantian: a matter of respect, as that is all we need to attend to the dignity of animals as other beings.[114]

Thus I have repeatedly sought to underscore Heidegger's discussion of mechanized, industrialized agriculture in its all-too-literal force. Heidegger could not be more accurate. The meat industry *is* "the manufacture of corpses."[115] To do this I emphasize Adorno's attention to the efficacy of inattention.

The *locus* is *Minima Moralia* in an aphorism predating Levinas while encapsulating and extending Levinas's reflections on the look, the regard, the gaze, for Adorno: "*Human beings look at you.*" The context is elliptical as Adorno emphasizes a certain constitutive blindness as key to anti-Semitism. This is our constitutive failure to see "Jews as human beings." For Adorno:

> The ceaselessly recurrent expression that savages, blacks, Japanese resemble animals, or something like apes, already contains the

key to the pogrom. The possibility of pogroms is decided in the moment when the gaze of a fatally-wounded animal falls on a human being. The defiance with which he repels this gaze—"after all, it's only an animal"—reappears irresistibly in cruelties done to human beings, the perpetrators having again and again to reassure themselves that it is "only an animal," because they could never fully believe this even of animals.[116]

Here we should ask, it is an ontic affair and to the point, what do the masks we insist on wearing on our own faces, the masks we insist on having those around us wear as a matter of stipulation, command, mandate, what do these masks "do" to our perception of ourselves and our perception of one another, children and strangers, in a time of crisis?[117]

Anders offers a dialogical reflection on phantastic realism as given to be seen and by the same token unseen or inconspicuous. Anders's language here reminds us of Levinas (no accident perhaps as Levinas was one of Anders first translators into French[118]):

"Your face. Or mine. In mine you know *me*. In yours I see *you*. More or less with all things, as all of them have a face. Animals too. Also machines. Also a house. Even a summer's day."[119]

If Heidegger focuses on the human to proceed from the most proximate to pose the question of Augustinian immediacy concerning the *who* that I am myself in order to raise the question of being qua being, Anders focused on the human qua human *without* the usual concessions human beings tend to grant for themselves, the privilege of exception.

Coda: Heidegger's Da-Sein and Anders's Devil

Heidegger, so I argue, is concerned, quite as he claims, with the being question. And to this the question of the human along with the question of humanism would take a decidedly second place. The discovery is not news, hence Jean Beaufret's question in "The Letter on 'Humanism.'" If Heidegger can be faulted by Anders for excluding the most typically "concrete" elements of the human situation, that is, hunger *and* sex, *and* tooth pain, that is incarnate being, the body with all its needs in his thematization of that same Da-Sein, that There-Being that we are, each one of us, and for whom its own being is an issue, Anders also shows that human cares tend to be self-referred concerns that are not as such at issue for Heidegger. To this extent Heidegger focusses, very much as Aristotle does when it comes to virtues like courage, on mortal stakes, last things, Schürmann's *eschata*, and only those.

What excites our interest in reading Heidegger goes beyond the where, the there, the here of our earthly being, as we guess that Heidegger's concerns are likely to touch the gods in flight. In the same way, Heidegger reads Nietzsche on his "unfinished animal" and Hölderlin speaks of the Syrian (this is Christ) as he also invokes archaic Greek divinities in their passage, calling to them, *Where are you? Wo bist du?*[120]

Nietzsche points out that we cannot see beyond our own shadow. To this extent, Heidegger can seem to bring us a little into what might be a kind of light. And still, we are utterly lost.

If the thinkers of existentialism sought to claim their movement as a "humanism," if the human *face* became the cause of a philosophical generation, we have embarked by mandate and decree in an age now without faces, a masked era, anthrophobic to the core, self-hating humans.

In the midst of the "danger" Heidegger invokes, "not just any danger but danger as such," the human is "endangered from out of destining."[121] Here we can and should add: all other beings, likewise. Thus Anders who thought about the difference between what can be done and the facticity of doing it, reminds us that we are transhuman:

> Although we are unchanged anatomically, our completely changed relation to the cosmos and to ourselves has transformed us into a new species—beings that differ from the previous type of man no less than Nietzsche's superman differed from man. In other words—and this is not meant as a mere metaphor—we are Titans, at least as long as we are omnipotent without making definitive use of this omnipotence of ours.[122]

Anders's point is that, like a number of Goethe's negative (qua ultimately impotent) heroes, we are smaller than we fantasize ourselves to be. We are as modern human beings negative-, quasi-Fausts. "Whereas Faust had infinite inclinations and boundless feelings, and suffered because his finite knowledge and power were unequal to these feelings, we know more and produce greater things than we can imagine or feel."[123]

The tension between capacity and actuality is essential for Anders, because, no matter whether one is an ordinary, a banal, human being of the everyday variety or a Faust conjured by Goethe, there is no challenge involved in having the mind or the power required to destroy a "Gretchen" in and through that same cavalier mindlessness: no sooner is she seduced than she reveals her impurity to the seducer: this is Hegel's (it is also Rée's) debt to Goethe. Such destructions, such revelations of what a man can do to a girl's/a boy's life (this crosses gender lines), a woman's life (this crosses age lines), happens every day.[124] This is the "tragedy" of *Faust I*.

Nietzsche is unsparing as he assesses *The Faust Idea*: "A little seamstress is seduced and made unhappy; a great scholar of all the four faculties is the evil-doer."[125] This is the "fifty-cents and a box-top" summary if ever there was one and Nietzsche is not quite done, as he goes on to mock the poetic conceit, as Goethe writes his *Faust*, that the achievement required the power of hell itself: "the assistance of the Devil in person."[126]

The 'more' we can now do—this is or would be *Faust II*—the more that is done, is the danger of titanism: we are not and cannot be equal to the deed. This is the word we might remember from Nietzsche's madman, "—and yet" (—*und doch*) he found himself musing in his consternated failure to speak to those to whom he had come: distant from the deed: "they have done it themselves" (*haben sie dieselbe gethan*).[127] To this extent, Anders argues, "[t]he Biblical 'They know not what they do' here assumes a new, unexpectedly terrifying meaning: the very monstrousness of the deed makes possible a new, truly infernal innocence."[128]

Where, for Anders, "we are barely able to repent an individual murder"—the guilt would visit our souls, night by night—today, "in our capacity for killing, for producing corpses, we have already entered the proud stage of industrial mass production."[129] The point for Anders is that there is no comprehension: we cannot grasp this. Nor did we ever manage to grasp Hiroshima or Nagasaki any more than Auschwitz or Buchenwald. This inability leaves us as "cosmic parvenus," and it is why Anders argues, contra Bloch, that there is "no hope at all: the actual masters of the infinite are no more imaginatively or emotionally equal to this possession of theirs than their prospective victims, i.e., ourselves."[130]

For Heidegger, and Anders follows Heidegger to this extent, the "danger" is human *qua* "cosmic parvenu," *qua* "usurper of the apocalypse" inasmuch as the human "precisely as the one so threatened, exalts himself to the posture of lord of the earth."[131] Here, silently, the Augustinian retreat is at work: "It seems as if the human everywhere and always encounters only himself." But, Heidegger contends using the term 'precisely' *contra* Heisenberg who here articulates the Copenhagen interpretation of quantum mechanics as the Uncertainty Principle,[132] "precisely nowhere does the human today encounter himself, i.e., his essence."[133]

Perhaps owing to his focus on Da-sein, it is Heidegger who challenges human exceptionalism: "For there is no such thing as a human who, solely of himself, is only human."[134] *Contra* "humanism," Heidegger thinks Hölderlin's reflexive, gnomic word . . . *Dichterisch wohnet der Mensch*. The "questioning that is the piety of thought"[135] is thought in "the presence of the gods, bringing the dialogue of divine and human destinings, to radiance."[136] In this spirit, the final line of "The Turning" reads as a kind of prayer: "May world in its worlding be the nearest of all nearing that nears, as it brings the truth of being near to the essence of the human, and so gives the human to belong to the disclosing bringing to pass that is a bringing into its own."[137]

"Human" are we allied with the divine? Allied to that which, as Browning tells us, *doth provide and not partake*? Image and likeness? Or else, much rather, as Anders contemplated the fact not merely of Auschwitz but also Hiroshima and Nagasaki as of Chernobyl, and the ongoing perpetuation of violence,[138] is there an evil within us?

The tradition that has installed the prince of evil, in the phrase Jacob Taubes uses as title for a collection dedicated to Carl Schmitt, as "prince of the world"[139] seems increasingly relevant to the extent that we seem today more than ever inclined, as Anders mused, to do the devil's work for him.

Notes

1. I here follow Heidegger's direction for translation, quite as Joan Stambaugh attests. It is worth quoting her, as Anglophone readers can forget that the hyphen makes a difference, qua distinction, as Dasein ordinarily means "existence" in German, thus with respect to Da-sein, Stambaugh explains, "It was Heidegger's insight that human being is uncanny: we do not know who, or what, that is, although, or perhaps precisely because, we are it." Joan Stambaugh, translator's preface to Martin Heidegger, *Being and Time* (Albany: State University of New York Press, 1996), xiv. Beyond Stambaugh, the hyphen also indicates the locative (and concrete) dimension in Heidegger's thought. Thus I use Da-sein in what follows (this does not extend to revising printed texts as I cite them).

2. Günther Stern [Anders], "On the Pseudo-concreteness of Heidegger's Philosophy," *Philosophy and Phenomenological Research* 8, no. 3 (1948): 337–71.

3. Martin Heidegger, *Sein und Zeit*, 7th ed. (Tübingen: Niemeyer, 1953), 42. Translations are from Martin Heidegger, *Being and Time*, trans. John Macquarie

and Edward Robinson (New York: Harper and Row, 1962). Page numbers, as given here, can be matched to the H numbering used in the margins of the Macquarie and Robinson translation.

4. Giorgio Agamben, *Where Are We Now? The Epidemic as Politics* (London: Eris, 2021).

5. I discuss these protocols, with further references in Babich, "Pseudo-science and 'Fake' News: 'Inventing' Epidemics and the Police State," in *The Psychology of Global Crises and Crisis Politics Intervention, Resistance, Decolonization*, ed. Irene Strasser and Martin Dege (London: Palgrave/Springer, 2021), 241–72.

6. Günther Anders, *Die Antiquiertheit des Menschen*, vol. 1, *Über die Seele im Zeitalter der zweiten industriellen Revolution* (1956; repr., Munich: Beck, 1980).

7. See Stefan Lorenz Sorgner, "Nietzsche, the Overhuman, and Transhumanism," in *Nietzsche and Transhumanism: Precursor or Enemy?*, ed. Yunus Tuncel (Newcastle upon Tyne: Cambridge Scholars, 2017), 14–26. See also Nick Bostrom, "Transhumanist Values," *Journal of Philosophical Research* 30, suppl. (2005): 3–14; Steve Fuller, *Nietzschean Meditations: Untimely Thoughts at the Dawn of the Transhuman Era* (Basel: Schwabe, 2019); Jeffrey Bishop, "Nietzsche's Power Ontology and Transhumanism: Or Why Christians Cannot Be Transhumanists," in *Christian Perspectives on Transhumanism and the Church: Chips in the Brain, Immortality, and the World of Tomorrow*, ed. Steve Donaldson and Ron Cole-Turner (Frankfurt: Springer, 2018), 117–35. See, for another reading, Babette Babich, "Nietzsche's Post-human Imperative: On the Human, 'All-too-Human' Dream of Transhumanism," in Tuncel, *Nietzsche and Transhumanism*, 101–13, as well as, for additional references and discussion, "Wer ist Zarathustras 'Übermensch'?," in *Nietzsches Antike* (Berlin: Academia, 2020), 111–31.

8. Friedrich Nietzsche, *Jenseits von Gut und Böse: Vorspiel einer Philosophie der Zukunft*, in *Kritische Studienausgabe* (Berlin: De Gruyter, 1980), 5:81 (§62).

9. Nietzsche, *Jenseits von Gut und Böse*, §62.

10. Nietzsche, *Jenseits von Gut und Böse*, §62.

11. See, for example, broadly, Renato Cristin, *Heidegger and Leibniz* (Dordrecht: Kluwer, 1998), as well as, specifically, Erich Hörl, "Die offene Maschine: Heidegger, Günther und Simondon über die technologische Bedingung," in "Selbstregulierung als Provokation," German issue, *MLN* 123, no. 3 (2008): 632–55; Wolf Kittler, "From *Gestalt* to *Ge-stell*: Martin Heidegger Reads Ernst Jünger," in "Radical Conservative Thought in Transition: Martin Heidegger, Ernst Jünger, and Carl Schmitt, 1940–1960," special issue, *Cultural Critique*, no. 69 (2008): 79–97; Søren Riis, "The Ultimate Technology: The End of Technology and the Task of Nature," *Artificial Life* 19, no. 3/4 (2013): 471–85; Babette Babich, "Between Heidegger and Adorno: Airplanes, Radios, and Sloterdijk's Atmoterrorism," *Kronos Philosophical Journal* 6 (2017): 133–58.

12. Martin Heidegger, *The Question concerning Technology*, trans. William Lovitt (San Francisco: Harper Torchbooks, 1977), 23. First published in 1962.

13. Heidegger, *The Question concerning Technology*, 29.
14. Heidegger, *The Question concerning Technology*, 18.
15. ". . . for I should have given myself all the perfections of which I have any idea, and thus I should myself be God." René Descartes, *Meditations on First Philosophy*, trans. John Cottingham (Cambridge: Cambridge University Press, 2017), 38.
16. See, on Nietzsche on the death of the Buddha/death of God, Babette Babich, "Pluralism and the 'Happiness' of the Present," in *Moral Education and the Ethics of Self-Cultivation: Chinese and Western Perspectives*, ed. Michael Peters, Tina Besley, and Huajun Zhang (Singapore: Springer, 2021), 197–218, esp. 198–201.
17. Paul Virilio, *Art and Fear*, trans. Julie Rose (London: Continuum, 2003). For a discussion of Virilio and Anders, see Babette Babich, *Günther Anders' Philosophy of Technology: From Phenomenology to Critical Theory* (London: Bloomsbury, 2021), esp. "From Anders' Sexless Capuchin to Virilio's Chimeras," 123ff.
18. Günther Anders, *Die Antiquiertheit des Menschen*, vol. 2, *Über die Zerstörung des Lebens im Zeitalter der dritten industriellen Revolution* (Munich: Beck, 1980), 26.
19. Anders, *Die Antiquiertheit des Menschen*, 2:22.
20. Anders, *Die Antiquiertheit des Menschen*, 2:22.
21. For a recent discussion regarding today's ethical issues, see Bethany Brookshire, "How Making a COVID-19 Vaccine Confronts Thorny Ethical Issues," *Science News*, July 7, 2020, https://www.sciencenews.org/article/coronavirus-covid19-vaccine-ethical-issues.
22. Martin Heidegger, "Einblick in das was ist," in *Bremer und Freiburger Vorträge*, vol. 79 of *Gesamtausgabe*, ed. P. Jaeger (Frankfurt: Klostermann, 1994), 27.
23. Anders, *Die Antiquiertheit des Menschen*, 2:432–433n8.
24. See Babette Babich, "Nietzsche's *Antichrist*: The Birth of Modern Science out of the Spirit of Religion," *Jahrbuch für Religionsphilosophie*, ed. Markus Enders and Holger Zaborowski (Freiburg: Alber, 2014), 134–54.
25. Anders, *Die Antiquiertheit des Menschen*, 2:433n8.
26. Anders, *Die Antiquiertheit des Menschen*, 2:433. See further Babette Babich, "Adorno on Science and Nihilism, Animals, and Jews," *Symposium* 14, no. 1 (2011): 110–45.
27. Günther Anders, "Wesen und Eigentlichkeit nämlich bei Heidegger (1936)," in *Über Heidegger* (Munich: Beck, 2001), 33.
28. See Heidegger, *Sein und Zeit*, 45. Reiner Schürmann, *Broken Hegemonies*, trans. Reginald Lilly (Bloomington: Indiana University Press, 2003), offers a complex prism of reflections on this from Parmenides to Eckhart and Luther as well as Kant and Heidegger.
29. "Das Dasein, d. h. das Sein des Menschen ist in der vulgären ebenso wie in der philosophischen 'Definition' umgrenzt als ζῷον λόγον ἔχον, das Lebende, dessen Sein wesenhaft durch das Redenkönnen bestimmt ist." Heidegger, *Sein und Zeit*, 25.

30. And a famous mother, Dr. Clara Stern, who coauthored with Anders's father a book on Anders and his siblings. See for further detail, Babich, *Günther Anders' Philosophy of Technology*, 8, and references: 229.

31. Anders, "Wesen und Eigentlichkeit," 37.

32. "Der eigentliche Schrittmacher der Einheit von Planetarismus und Idiotismus, aber auch ihr eigentlich gemäßer Erbe, ist der Amerikanismus, die wohl ödeste Gestalt der 'historischen' Geschichtslosigkeit." Martin Heidegger, "Überlegungen XV," in *Überlegungen XII–XV (Schwarze Hefte 1939–1941)*, vol. 96 of *Gesamtausgabe*, ed. Peter Trawny (Frankfurt: Klostermann, 2014), 266.

33. Anders, "Wesen und Eigentlichkeit," 37.

34. "Die Uneigentlichkeit kann vielmehr das Dasein nach seiner vollsten Konkretion bestimmen in seiner Geschäftigkeit, Angeregtheit, Interessiertheit, Genußfähigkeit." Heidegger, *Sein und Zeit*, 43.

35. Augustine, *Confessions*, vol. 2, trans. Carolyn Hammond, Loeb Classical Library (Cambridge, MA: Harvard University Press, 2016), 10.16.

36. Augustine, *Confessions*, 10.33.

37. This has been done, to be sure, especially with reference to time and generically, but should repay further reflection. See, for example, Jean Grondin, "Heidegger und Augustine: Zur hermeneutischen Wahrheit," in *Die Frage nach der Wahrheit*, ed. Ewald Richter (Frankfurt: Klostermann, 1997), 161–73; as well as Friedrich-Wilhelm von Herrmann, "Die 'Confessiones' des Heiligen Augustinus im Denken Heideggers," *Questio* 1 (2001): 113–46.

38. This is the point of departure for Pierre Hadot's *Philosophy as a Way of Life* as a means used for the sake of setting his own reflective work on Augustine and the Stoic tradition on the path of a science, that is, philology, citing Pierre Courcelle's conventional and literary rather than biographical account, scandalous then, as Hadot emphasized that the scandal would last two decades (Schürmann concedes this influence with his remark that Augustine's dialogue *On Free Will* "is largely Stoic" [*Broken Hegemonies*, 215]), and, perhaps, it continues to date. As Hadot writes, "Alerted by his profound knowledge of Augustine's literary procedures and the traditions of Christian allegory, Courcelle dared to write that the fig tree could well have a purely symbolic value, representing the 'mortal shadow of sin,' and that the child's voice could also have been introduced in a purely literary way to indicate allegorically the divine response to Augustine's questioning." Pierre Hadot, *Philosophy as a Way of Life* (Oxford: Blackwell, 1994), 51.

39. If Nietzsche's style exemplifies the same invitation it also intriguingly, as David Blair Allison shows foregrounding the same personal immediacy, sidesteps some of the same risks if Nietzsche's writerly achievements have hardly prevented misreadings. See the first chapter of David B. Allison, *Reading the New Nietzsche* (Lanham, MD: Rowman and Littlefield, 2001).

40. This claim appears in Nietzsche's late-written and Kantian "Attempt at Self-Critique," appended to his first book on tragedy dedicated to sensible, verita-

bly phenomenological, i.e., "aesthetic science" (*aesthetische Wissenschaft*). Friedrich Nietzsche, *Die Geburt der Tragödie, Kritische Studienausgabe*, 1:25.

41. See Babette Babich, "On Heidegger on Education and Questioning," in *Encyclopedia of Educational Philosophy and Theory*, ed. Michael A. Peters (Singapore: Springer, 2017), 1641–52; "The Essence of Questioning after Technology: *Techne* as Constraint and Saving Power," *British Journal of Phenomenology* 30, no. 1 (1999): 106–24.

42. See, for a discussion, for example, Marco Cavallaro, "Der Beitrag der Phänomenologie Edmund Husserls zur Debatte über die Fundierung der Geisteswissenschaften," *Phänomenologische Forschungen* (2013): 77–93; as well as Dieter Lohmar, "On Some Motives for Husserl's Genetic Turn in His Research on a Foundation of the Geisteswissenschaften," *Studia Phaenomenologica* 18 (2018): 31–48; and, for a different logical take on a theory of everything social, assuming as the author says, that "social theory is not just 'social philosophy for failed philosophers,'" see Frédéric Vandenberghe, "Empathy as the Foundation of the Social Sciences and of Social Life: A Reading of Husserl's Phenomenology of Transcendental Intersubjectivity," *Sociedade e Estado* 17 (2002): 563–85.

43. Heidegger, *Sein und Zeit*, 51.

44. Heidegger, *Sein und Zeit*, 51.

45. Thus in lectures on art styles and aesthetic theory, Adorno reminds us of the ambivalence-suffused suffix: "The painfulness of experimentation finds response in the animosity toward the so called isms: programmatic, self-conscious, and often collective art movements. This rancor is shared by the likes of Hitler, who loved to rail against 'these im- and expressionists,' and by writers who out of a politically avant-garde zealousness are wary of the idea of an aesthetic avant-garde." Theodor W. Adorno, *Aesthetic Theory* (London: Continuum, 1997), 24.

46. See Matthias Rath, *Der Psychologismusstreit in der deutschen Philosophie* (Freiburg: Alber, 1994).

47. Gottlob Frege, *Die Grundlagen der Arithmetik: Eine logisch mathematische Untersuchung über den Begriff der Zahl* (Breslau: Koebner, 1884), x.

48. Thus, as Kant writes, "a doctrine of nature can only contain so much science proper as there is in it of applied mathematics." Immanuel Kant, *Prolegomena and Metaphysical Foundations of Natural Science*, trans. Ernest Belforth Bax (London: Bell, 1883), 141.

49. Heidegger, *Sein und Zeit*, 45.

50. Kant, *Prolegomena and Metaphysical Foundations of Natural Science*, 141.

51. To be sure, chemists and philosophers of chemistry make counter arguments. I discuss some of these arguments, including (instructively) "concretely," Bernadette Bensaud-Vincent, in an overview of so-called other sciences in the schema of the philosophy of science in Babette Babich, "Towards a Critical Philosophy of Science: Continental Beginnings and Bugbears, Whigs, and Waterbears," *International Studies in the Philosophy of Science* 24, no. 4 (2010): 343–91.

52. Heidegger, *Sein und Zeit*, 45.

53. Cited in Friedrich Nietzsche, *Kritische Studienausgabe*, 7:667. The reference is to Kant's *Metaphysical Foundations of Morals* and the precedent set by David Hume. Nietzsche for his part cites Hume's *Dialogues concerning Natural Religion*, part 10, where Hume argues that an alien visitor offered a tour of our earthbound achievements might find it hard to distinguish *positive* cultural features from *negative* ones, a perspectival shift dating back to Lucian's *True History*, the very first instance of science-fiction. See, for discussion, Babette Babich, "Nietzsche's Aesthetic Tension and Hume's Standard of Taste," in *Reading David Hume's "Of the Standard of Taste,"* ed. Babette Babich (Berlin: De Gruyter, 2019), 213–45, esp. 236. See Peter Szendy, *Kant in the Land of Extraterrestrials: Cosmopolitical Philosofictions*, trans. Will Bishop (New York: Fordham University Press, 2013); as well as, earlier, David L. Clark, "Kant's Aliens: The Anthropology and Its Others," *New Centennial Review* 1, no. 2 (2001): 201–89; in addition to Holger Schmid's afterword to a French translation of Immanuel Kant, *Sur les extraterrestres: Théorie du ciel* (Paris: Éditions Manucius, 2019). But see, too, given the current discussion, Tyke Nunez, "Logical Mistakes, Logical Aliens, and the Laws of Kant's Pure General Logic," *Mind* 128, no. 512 (2019): 1149–80.

54. See, for a discussion of the broader European tradition in ethnography, Dennis Johannßen. "Mensch und Dasein in Heideggers *Sein und Zeit*," in *Das Leben im Menschen oder der Mensch im Leben? Deutsch-Französische Genealogien zwischen Anthropologie und Anti-Humanismus*, ed. Thomas Ebke and Caterina Zanfi (Potsdam: Universitätsverlag Potsdam, 2017), 91–104. For another discussion, more precise, perhaps terminologically regarded, see Annette Sell, "Leben führen—Dasein entwurfen: Zur systematischen und gesellschaftspolitischen Bedeutung von Plessners anthropologischem und Heideggers fundamental-ontologischem Konzept des Menschen," in *Vom Wissen um den Menschen: Philosophie, Geschichte, Materialität*, ed. Kevin Liggieri and Julia Gruevska (Freiburg: Alber, 2018), 46–61.

55. Schürmann, *Broken Hegemonies*, 448.

56. Martin Kusch, "The Sociology of Philosophical Knowledge: A Case Study and a Defense," in *The Sociology of Philosophical Knowledge*, ed. Martin Kusch (Dordrecht: Springer, 2000), 15–38. Kusch gives the locus here as "1910, p. 516." See, too, Kusch's valuable discussion in *Psychologism: A Case Study in the Sociology of Philosophical Knowledge* (New York: Routledge, 1995).

57. Ingo Farin, "A Response to Sheehan's Attempted Paradigm Shift in Heidegger Studies," *Parrhesia* 26 (2016): 117–35, here: 130.

58. Heidegger, *Sein und Zeit*, 51. See, for a discussion of Heelan in the context of the social sciences, Babette Babich, "Hermeneutics and Its Discontents in Philosophy of Science," in *Hermeneutic Philosophies of Social Science*, ed. Babette Babich (Berlin: De Gruyter, 2017), 163–88; and, more generally, with reference to technoscience, see Babette Babich, "Material Hermeneutics and Heelan's Philosophy of Technoscience," *AI and Society* (2020), https://philpapers.org/

go.pl?id=BABMHA&proxyId=&u=https%3A%2F%2Fdx.doi.org%2F10.1007%2Fs00146-020-00963-7.

59. Daniel O. Dalhstrom, "Heidegger's Transcendentalism," *Research in Phenomenology* 35, no. 1 (2005): 29–54, esp. 35.

60. Dalhstrom, "Heidegger's Transcendentalism," 49.

61. Heidegger, *Sein und Zeit*, 42.

62. See George A. Schrader, Jr., "Heidegger's Ontology of Human Existence," *Review of Metaphysics* 10, no. 1 (1956): 35–56; and see, too, the contributions to Holger Zaborowski and Alfred Denker, *Heidegger Jahrbuch* 10, particularly Raimon Paez Blanch, "Dasein und Mensch bei Heidegger. Eine Überlegung anlässlich des 'Humanismusbriefes,'" *Heidegger Jahrbuch* 10 (2017): 165–77; Tschasslaw D. Kopriwitza, "Heidegger und der Anthropozentrismus," *Heidegger Jahrbuch* 10 (2017): 178–90; and, especially, Holger Zaborowski, "Bedingungen und Möglichkeiten des Humanismus—heute: Jaspers, Heidegger und Levinas zur Frage nach dem Menschen," *Heidegger Jahrbuch* 10 (2017): 251–64.

63. Schürmann, *Broken Hegemonies*, 571.

64. See my own reflections on the question of the human in Heidegger's "Letter on 'Humanism,'" "Heideggers Brief über 'Humanismus': Über die Technik, das Bösartige des Grimmes—und das Heilen," *Heidegger Jahrbuch* 10 (2017), 237–50; as well as, yet more radically, Matthew Calarco, "'Another Insistence of Man': Prolegomena to the Question of the Animal in Derrida's Reading of Heidegger," *Human Studies* 28, no. 3 (2005): 317–34; as well as, more conventionally, Simon James, "Phenomenology and the Problem of Animal Minds," *Environmental Values* 18, no. 1 (2009): 33–49.

65. It is for this reason that Lawrence Perlman can point to the distinction between speaking of *Mensch* (Perlman writes "man") and Da-Sein between Heidegger and Heschel. See Lawrence Perlman, *The Eclipse of Humanity: Heschel's Critique of Heidegger* (Berlin: De Gruyter, 2016), 29–31ff.

66. See Dominique Janicaud, *Phenomenology and the "Theological Turn": The French Debate* (New York: Fordham University Press, 2000).

67. Reiner Schürmann, *On Heidegger's Being and Time*, ed. Simon Critchley (London: Routledge, 2008), 56.

68. Schürmann, *On Heidegger's Being and Time*, 56.

69. Schürmann, *Broken Hegemonies*, 517.

70. Schürmann, *Broken Hegemonies*, 515.

71. Schürmann, *Broken Hegemonies*, 515.

72. Schürmann, *Broken Hegemonies*, 518.

73. Schürmann, *Broken Hegemonies*, 518.

74. Schürmann, *Broken Hegemonies*, 520.

75. Schürmann, *Broken Hegemonies*, 524.

76. Schürmann, *Broken Hegemonies*, 524.

77. Schürmann, *Broken Hegemonies*, 523.

78. Schürmann, *Broken Hegemonies*, 525.
79. Schürmann, *Broken Hegemonies*, 526.
80. Schürmann, *Broken Hegemonies*, 527.
81. Schürmann, *Broken Hegemonies*, 531.
82. Heidegger, *Sein und Zeit*, 34.
83. Heidegger, *Sein und Zeit*, 35–36.
84. Schürmann, *Broken Hegemonies*, 544.
85. Schürmann, *Broken Hegemonies*, 544.
86. Stern [Anders], "On the Pseudo-concreteness of Heidegger's Philosophy," 346n11.
87. Martin Heidegger, *Discourse on Thinking: A Translation of "Gelassenheit,"* trans. J. M. Anderson and E. H. Freund (New York: Harper and Row, 1966), 52. Translation slightly altered.
88. Anders Bárány commenting on Wendell Stanley, "Viruses" (lecture presented at the Fifth Nobel Laureate Meeting, 1955), https://www.mediatheque.lindau-nobel.org/videos/31538/viruses-1955/meeting-1955.
89. Anders Bárány commenting on Wendell Stanley, "Viruses."
90. Heidegger, *Discourse on Thinking*, 52. Translation slightly altered.
91. Cited in Heidegger, *Introduction to Metaphysics*, trans. Ralph Manheim (New Haven, CT: Yale University Press, 1959), 147.
92. Immanuel Kant, *Critique of Pure Reason*, trans. Paul Guyer and Allen W. Wood (Cambridge: Cambridge University Press, 1999), A5/B9.
93. Heidegger, *Discourse on Thinking*, 53. Translation slightly altered.
94. Friedrich Hölderlin, *Essays and Letters on Theory*, trans. Thomas Pfau (Albany: State University of New York Press, 1988), no. 172, p. 140.
95. Cited in Heidegger, *Introduction to Metaphysics*, 146.
96. Heidegger, *Einführung in die Metaphysik* (1953; repr., Tübingen: Niemeyer, 1976), 113.
97. Cited in Heidegger, *Introduction to Metaphysics*, 146.
98. Heidegger, *Introduction to Metaphysics*, 148.
99. Anders, *Die Antiquiertheit des Menschen*, 1:31
100. See further Babette Babich, "Heidegger and Holderlin on Aether and Life," *Études phénoménologiques/Phenomenological Studies* 2 (2018): 111–33.
101. "Zuletzt kann Niemand aus den Dingen, die Bücher eingerechnet, mehr heraushören, als er bereits weiss. Wofür man vom Erlebnisse her keinen Zugang hat, dafür hat man kein Ohr." Friedrich Nietzsche, *Kritische Studienausgabe*, vol. 6: EH, *Warum ich so gute Bücher schreibe*, 1, 299–300.
102. See, for Lucian's parodic influence on Nietzsche's *Übermensch*, Babette Babich, "Le Zarathoustra de Nietzsche et le style parodique: A propos de l'hyperanthropos de Lucien et du surhomme de Nietzsche," *Diogene* 232, no. 4 (2010): 70–93.

103. The full reference Heidegger gives cites Burdach on Herder and Goethe. See Konrad Burdach, "Faust und die Sorge," *Deutsche Vierteljahrsschrift für Literaturwissenschaft und Geistesgeschichte* 1 (1923): 1–60. For a specific discussion of Heidegger and Goethe on this theme, see Ellis Dye, "*Sorge* in Heidegger and in Goethe's *Faust*," *Goethe Yearbook* 16 (2009): 207–18.

104. See Heidegger, *Sein und Zeit*, 197–98.

105. Heidegger, *Sein und Zeit*, 198.

106. Heidegger, *Sein und Zeit*, 199.

107. Heidegger, *Sein und Zeit*, 198–99.

108. See Babich, "Heidegger and Hölderlin on Aether and Life."

109. Schürmann, *Broken Hegemonies*, 306.

110. Gabriel Marcel explicitly acknowledges his own work as taken up on the basis of Günther Stern [Anders], *Über das Haben: Sieben Kapitel zur Ontologie der Erkenntnis* (Bonn: Cohen, 1928).

111. "With these formulas—which also define our *status religioso*—a fracture in our existence (and for the first time, our current existence) has been described, a disjunction, which surpasses in importance or, more precisely, makes the fracture that once existed between flesh and spirit, or between duty and inclination, or however such differences that were once considered to be so decisive might be denominated, not appear to be so serious. What is our 'capacity' for robbery or adultery or blasphemy or murder compared with our 'capacity' to commit genocide or, even worse (I have to introduce this term), *globicide*?" Anders, *Die Antiquiertheit des Menschen*, 2:410.

112. Anders, *Die Antiquiertheit des Menschen*, 2:433.

113. Günther Anders, *Die Kirschenschlacht: Dialoge mit Hannah Arendt*, ed. Gerhard Oberschlick (Munich: Beck, 2011).

114. There are fellow travelers, with different approaches, such as Matthew Calarco, *Zoographies: The Question of the Animal from Heidegger to Derrida* (New York: Columbia University Press, 2008); or Gary Francione and Anna Charlton, *Eat like You Care: An Examination of the Morality of Eating Animals* (n.p.: Exempla Press, 2013); or Sue Donaldson and Will Kymlicka, *Zoopolis: A Political Theory of Animal Rights* (Oxford: Oxford University Press, 2011); or, indeed, and I tend to note such contributions for personal reasons, as I began as a biologist before turning to philosophy, see Marc Bekoff, *Wild Justice: The Moral Lives of Animals* (Chicago: University Of Chicago Press, 2010); as well as Jeffrey Bussolini, who works on themes of recognition and respect between disciplinary fields and has a valuable reflection, "*Felidae* and Extinction: 'Victim' and 'Cause,'" *Temporal Belongings* (blog), Immortality and Infinitude Presentations, April 20, 2015, https://www.temporalbelongings.org/presentations4/previous/2.

115. As cited, and note the context there, in Babette Babich, "Constellating Technology: Heidegger's Die Gefahr/The Danger," in *The Multidimensionality of*

Hermeneutic Phenomenology, ed. Babette Babich and Dimitri Ginev (Frankfurt: Springer, 2014), 153–82, esp. 172.

116. Theodor Adorno, *Minima Moralia: Reflections from Damaged Life*, trans. E. F. N Jephcott (London: Verso, 2005), §68. Originally published 1951.

117. See for discussion, my essay "Pseudo-science and 'Fake' News," 245, 254.

118. Günther Stern [Anders], "Une interpretation de l'*a posteriori*," *Recherches Philosophiques* 4 (1934–35): 65–80; "Pathologie de la liberté: Essais sur la non-identification," *Recherches Philosophiques* 6 (1936–37): 22–54.

119. Anders, *Antiquiertheit des Menschen*, 2:322. Hannes Bajohr in his review of Anders's posthumous *Die Weltfremdheit des Menschen: Schriften zur philosophischen Anthropologie*, reminds us that drafts of what appears in Anders's *Die Antiquiertheit des Menschen* (both volumes, as we may note) had already appeared in French in 1937–38, an esoteric reference made even more salient given that the succeeding essay "The Pathology of Freedom," is missing the German original, such that our sole English access to Anders's text is via the French. See Hannes Bajohr, "World-Estrangement as Negative Anthropology: Günther Anders's Early Essays," *Thesis Eleven* 153, no. 1 (2019): 141–53.

120. See, for a discussion between Nietzsche and Pindar, Babette Babich, "Between Hölderlin and Heidegger: Nietzsche's Transfiguration of Philosophy," *Nietzsche-Studien* 29 (2000): 267–301.

121. Heidegger, *The Question concerning Technology*, 26.

122. Günther Anders, "Reflections on the H Bomb," *Dissent* 3, no. 2 (1956): 147.

123. Anders, "Reflections on the H Bomb," 152.

124. Indeed, to this day, scholars continue to blame Gretchen, a standard claim in societal judgment. Thus T. K. Seung is only one of many male (and female) scholars who emphasizes that Gretchen can only be seen as innocent if she is innocent: if and if she is a virgin. Thus in an instance of philosophically and philologically well-founded misogyny (Schopenhauer might be one of the first in line), Seung cites Eudo Mason as adducing "ample textual evidence that she was burning with her own erotic passions and cleverly connived in the game of seduction." T. K. Seung, *Goethe, Nietzsche, and Wagner: Their Spinozan Epics of Love and Power* (Lanham, MD: Lexington Books, 2006), 39.

125. Nietzsche, *Menschliches, Allzumenschliches: Der Wanderer und sein Schatten*, in *Kritische Studienausgabe*, 2:606 (§124).

126. Nietzsche, *Kritische Studienausgabe*, 2:606.

127. Nietzsche, *Die fröhliche Wissenschaft*, in *Kritische Studienausgabe*, 3:482 (§125).

128. Anders, "Reflections on the H Bomb," 151.

129. Anders, "Reflections on the H Bomb," 154.

130. Anders, "Reflections on the H Bomb," 147.

131. Heidegger, *The Question concerning Technology*, 27.

132. See, for this articulation, if not explicitly with reference to Heidegger, Patrick Aidan Heelan, *Quantum Mechanics and Objectivity* (The Hague: Nijhoff, 1965).

133. Heidegger, *The Question concerning Technology*, 27.

134. Heidegger, *The Question concerning Technology*, 31.

135. Heidegger, *The Question concerning Technology*, 35.

136. Heidegger, *The Question concerning Technology*, 34.

137. Heidegger, *The Question concerning Technology*, 35.

138. Günther Anders, *Gewalt, Ja oder Nein? Eine notwendige Diskussion*, ed. Manfred Bissinger (Munich: Knaur, 1987).

139. Jacob Taubes, ed., *Der Fürst dieser Welt: Carl Schmitt und die Folgen*, Religionstheorie und Politische Theologie, vol. 1 (Munich: Fink, 1983).

This chapter was composed in ongoing conversation with the late Tracy B. Strong to whom it is also dedicated.

Chapter Three

The Unfought Battle

Heidegger and Plessner

Thomas Schwarz Wentzer

> However, it might also seem as though the essence of divinity is closer to us than what is so alien in other living creatures, closer, namely, in an essential distance that, however distant, is nonetheless more familiar to our ek-sistent essence than is our scarcely conceivable, abysmal bodily kinship with the beast.
>
> —Martin Heidegger, "Letter on 'Humanism'"

> Once one has become convinced of the impossibility of a free-floating dimension of existence, it becomes necessary to find a way to ground it. What might this foundation look like and what power does it have? How strong is its bond with the lived body? This is a justified question, as only embodied being can be in a mood or be afraid. Angels do not know fear.
>
> —Helmuth Plessner, *Levels of Organic Life and the Human*

Among the important philosophical debates that never actually took place, one finds the conversation between Martin Heidegger and Helmuth Plessner. This chapter aims to sketch an agenda for an imaginative dispute between the two. This dispute would have been about the problem of how to approach the human being in the first place—whether via philosophical anthropology, the movement of which Plessner was a chief representative, or via an analysis of the task assigned to the human as Dasein, as Heidegger in different, but compatible, versions kept insisting.

The reasons for the actual lack of communication between the two thinkers are contingent, some of them located in the category of all-too-human psychological dispositions from which comedies or soap operas draw their material. At first glance, Heidegger never took notice of his colleague, who was three years younger than him, and whose masterwork, *Levels of Organic Life and the Human: An Introduction to Philosophical Anthropology*, came out less than one year after his own *Being and Time*, from 1927. The German university system, with its hierarchical structures and the need for reliable strategic alliances for upcomers, prevented a relation as among equals and allowed Heidegger to ignore Plessner. Plessner's ambitions to become recognized as a pioneer of philosophical anthropology were moreover blocked by the presence of Max Scheler, the ordinarius in Cologne, who claimed this endeavor—philosophical anthropology—to be a child of his genius alone. While *Being and Time* made its author instantly famous, confirming the actual truth of what had already been rumored in the years before—Heidegger in Marburg was "the hidden King of German philosophy" (Arendt)—Plessner's *Levels*, a demanding and all too voluminous book by an associate professor from Cologne University, remained largely unnoticed. A second edition came as late as in 1965 (with a new preface unable to hide the enduring bitterness of its author), and only recently (2019!) the book was finally translated into English.[1] If academic philosophy were a sports competition, nobody would deny that Heidegger remained unbeaten by Plessner, precisely because the former refused to get into an argument with the latter. There was no need to do so.

However, due to the edition of Heidegger's lecture courses and other documents, and because of the detective work of several scholars, we are today in a position to qualify and to correct this "official" picture.[2] It is true that Heidegger never mentioned Plessner by name in his publications, public lectures, or lecture courses, not even in the available notebooks. But he nonetheless very likely commented on Plessner anonymously. There is also evidence that he was influenced by Plessner in the years after the publication of *Being and Time*, when he sought to reorient the abandoned project of fundamental ontology toward a stance labeled as "metaphysics of Dasein." It has even been argued that Heidegger's efforts concerning this matter are the result of his uneasiness after having studied Plessner's *Levels*, culminating in the lecture course from 1929–30 known as *Fundamental Concepts of Metaphysics* with references to an agenda seemingly akin to that of Plessner.³

Plessner, on the other hand, commented on Heidegger in the preface to the first edition of his *Levels* and kept arguing against him in every phase of his authorship. In most cases, he relates to Heidegger's early position when he wrote *Being and Time*, comparing Heidegger's project regarding existential fundamental ontology with his own philosophical anthropological approach in various aspects. He never doubts that the two conceptions—existential ontology and philosophical anthropology—in fact were engaged in a true γιγαντομαχία περὶ τῆς οὐσίας, a battle of the giants about being,⁴ even though the situation both before and after World War II did not allow for an unbiased reception of Plessner's work. Back in the late twenties, in a philosophical situation characterized by the decline of a by then sclerotic neo-Kantian paradigm, in revisiting the legacy of both Dilthey and Husserl, Heidegger and Plessner each claimed "creating philosophy anew"⁵ and aimed at providing the guiding philosophical paradigm of their times.

In what follows, I want to deal with the "and" in "Heidegger and Plessner," as if it really indicated a gigantomachia among the two single most powerful approaches of philosophy in the second quarter of the last century, existential ontology and philosophical anthropology, personified by Heidegger and Plessner. I will do so in four steps. After giving a short historical account of the contingent circumstances that apparently prevented any actual open philosophical exchange, I will comment on Heidegger's anonymous rapprochement with Plessner in the Davos debate with Cassirer and related texts from the period also referred to as Heidegger's "anthropological intermezzo."⁶ Provided that Plessner's position and line of argument in his magnum opus for reasons given in the first section are not well known, I will present an outline of his thinking with a view to substantiating the claim that Plessner's *Levels of Organic Life and the Human* provides a foundation of existence via philosophical anthropology and the hermeneutics of organic life, thus developing a program that is the inverse of that of Heidegger concerning any philosophy of the human. As a conclusion, I will briefly present Heidegger's hidden answer to Plessner from the letter that just as well might have been written as a late response to Plessner's project, the "Letter on 'Humanism.'"⁷ The crucial difference between the two conceptions remains the same throughout the different stages in the course of their development: it is about how to approach the human being in its essential character, either from *organic life* (Plessner) or from *existence* (Heidegger), and it is only of minor significance to this chapter if "existence" indicates the projection of being in the course of care, as in *Being and Time*, or—as "ek-sistence"—the place of clearing assigned to the human in the "truth of being," as in Heidegger's later writings.

The issue "Heidegger and Plessner" deserves a book-length treatment in order to deal with it exhaustively and with the necessary reference to the historical as well as the philosophical context. This chapter only points out a selection of topics that such a book would have to dive into.

Rumor Has It

Plessner wrote his habilitation thesis about Kant's third *Critique* in 1920 in Cologne, under the guidance of Hans Driesch.[7] In 1923 he published *The Unity of the Senses*, which provided an "anthropological hermeneutics of the senses,"[8] and only a year later he presented another book to the audience, his *Limits of Community*, in which he defended a liberalist position against communitarianist versions of sociality.[9] In its preface he announced a project with the working title "Plant, animal, human being—a cosmology of the living form," devoted to developing the "principles of anthropology."[10] This project was published in January 1928 as the book *Levels of Organic Life and the Human: An Introduction into Philosophical Anthropology*, Plessner's magnum opus.

When Plessner was about to finish the last chapters, he gave his text to Scheler. Although the two in earlier years had regularly engaged in private as well as philosophical discussions, by 1927 their mutual collegial trust was in fact undermined due to Scheler's suspicion that the younger colleague—who in fact never was a disciple of Scheler's—might have taken his ideas from him. Scheler no doubt invented the *project title* concerning a "philosophical anthropology" and had raised the issue already back in 1915 (in a thoughtful essay entitled *On the Idea of Man*[11]), but now he had to face the risk of becoming outpaced by Plessner in the realization of the indicated project. Obviously due to the fear of being betrayed and outmaneuvered, Scheler started a twofold rumor that would prove to be very efficient in relation to the future reception of Plessner's book and the public perception of the mastermind behind the upcoming conception of philosophical anthropology. He claimed that Plessner's text was a result of intellectual theft, that Plessner had stolen his original thoughts and ideas, and he declared that he was as good as finished with his own "greater anthropology," a book that would provide the last and authoritative version to be published very soon in 1929.[12]

The competition between the two and the shocking insight concerning Plessner's progress induced Scheler to make a quick strategic move. He transformed a lecture manuscript from a series in Darmstadt into the essay called *The Human Place in the Cosmos* as a sort of prerelease of the opus to come, which he announced in its preface.[13] He also managed to publish this text almost simultaneously with Plessner's *Levels*. As a result, Scheler's straightforward programmatic sketch, not Plessner's dense and thorough study, came to be known as the fundamental document of philosophical anthropology. From the point of view of Plessner, this predicament became even worse with the unexpected death of Scheler in May 1928, whose name, to an even greater extent, was linked to the—*his*—legacy of philosophical anthropology.

The Cologne operetta fostered "academic gossip"[14] and did not pass unnoticed by Heidegger. Plessner had actually met with Heidegger back in 1924, when he visited him in Marburg and asked him to join the advisory board of *Der Philosophische Anzeiger*, a newly established journal to be edited by Plessner. The same year in December, Heidegger was invited by Scheler to give a lecture at the Cologne Kant Society.[15] Plessner, whose friend Josef König already enthusiastically had reported about Heidegger's powerful lectures and his auratic appearance in Marburg, was not in doubt that "something is in the making in Marburg which deserves utmost attention."[16] Although Heidegger had not published anything, Plessner and Scheler were nonetheless quite aware of his efforts to reposition Husserl's phenomenological enterprise, which had taken a turn toward an idealism that in the eyes of most contemporaries and fellow phenomenologists (like Scheler)[17] only provided a one-way street back into Cartesianism and to an obsolete rationalistic and cognitivist paradigm of philosophical thinking. Encouraged by the impression of Heidegger's second public lecture at the Kant Society in Cologne in December 1927, Plessner sent one of the first copies of his book to Heidegger in Marburg,[18] who much to Plessner's disappointment never responded, neither in a private letter nor in his publications.

The reason for Heidegger's silence might very well be related to the internal fight about intellectual copyrights and originality between Scheler and Plessner. During his Cologne visit, Heidegger presumably got inoculated by Scheler's lament concerning Plessner's alleged plagiarism.[19] Heidegger took sides. His letter to Georg Misch[20] in March 1928 reveals that Heidegger had read at least the preface of Plessner's book, as he adds a rather mean notice: "The remark, with which Plessner gives me short shrift in his preface, is very foolish. However, with this he cannot cover up that he in quite many respects has spelled out my book in his superficial manner. It is a disgustingly phony sphere, in which one has to move around nowadays."[21] Hence, Plessner was not only accused of having stolen his main ideas from Scheler. Heidegger "doubles" (Fischer) the plagiarism accusation, insinuating that Plessner's book in large parts relies on material taken from Heidegger. Plessner surely had read *Being and Time*, but assured in the preface that it only came to his attention while his own book was going to press—adding nonetheless a couple of sentences in which he accused Heidegger of methodological subjectivism.[22] This was obviously enough to trigger the latter's wrath.

Whether or not Heidegger really did study Plessner's book, and not just the preface, is unclear. But he did not refuse the welcome opportunity that Plessner against his own better will had provided, giving Heidegger and the philosophical community sufficient reason for not engaging seriously with the book. Moreover, Heidegger's general comments on philosophical anthropology in *Being and Time* had already worked like a "barring clause,"[23] making it even more difficult for Plessner to find a receptive audience.

There is another missed opportunity that belongs to the history of the prevented exchange between Heidegger and Plessner. One might ponder whether Scheler, if he were still alive, would have been a natural participant of the famous second Davoser Hochschultage in spring 1929, devoted to the topic "Mensch und Generation," which culminated in the lectures by and the public discussion between Heidegger and Ernst Cassirer. This event gained enormous public attention already back then and certainly in the last decades, almost a century later. It quickly came to be perceived as the event that staged the battle over the future of German, if not Western, philosophy.

The contemporaries compared the symbolic significance of the debate with Thomas Mann's novel *Der Zauberberg*, notably in the dispute between Settembrini (Cassirer) and Naphta (Heidegger).[24] Due to the actual course of this seminar and its prominent participants (not confined to only Cassirer and Heidegger), scholars tend to approach Davos from either Heidegger's or Cassirer's side, sometimes with a view to stressing its importance to analytical philosophy or the Frankfurt School or French philosophy.[25] The position of philosophical anthropology typically remains absent.[26] This seems strange, given the topic of the meeting, "man and generation." For my part at least, I would have wished for Plessner to have occupied the vacant spot and to have been around when Cassirer and Heidegger were discussing the true legacy of Kant. All the more so, as the idea of some version of philosophical anthropology came to provide a common neutral ground for Heidegger's existential ontology and Cassirer's philosophy of culture, although neither of them wholeheartedly endorsed the actual project.

Philosophical anthropology was the elephant in the room, the *"tertium comparationis"*[27]—but Plessner, the author of a book subtitled *Introduction into Philosophical Anthropology*, published only a year before, was not there. Joachim Fischer describes the situation as follows:

> The disputation at Davos is arguably the clearest expression of the so-called "anthropological turn"—but the initiating idea of Philosophical Anthropology evanesces in this constellation. Scheler is dead and Plessner not invited. [. . .] The "anthropological turn" is confirmed, but the critique joins forces against the possibility of Philosophical Anthropology as a specific conception based on philosophy of nature, as it was simultaneously articulated by Scheler and Plessner.[28]

Why did neither Heidegger—who invited Levinas to be among the French delegation[29]—nor Cassirer invite Plessner? Cassirer *had* actually read carefully Plessner's book. Like Heidegger, he received a copy from Plessner in December 1927, while he was working on the third volume of his *Philosophy of Symbolic Forms*. Clearly satisfied with what he had read, he saw his position confirmed by the anthropologists (Scheler and Plessner), acknowledging that philosophical anthropology delivers a critical philosophy of nature that apparently smoothly supported his own findings in the philosophy of symbolic forms. He wrote: "This connection becomes especially apparent in Plessner's account of 'philosophical anthropology,' the result of which touches upon ours most closely, albeit it has been gained via an avenue indeed different from ours."[30] However, the passage just quoted did not make it to the text published as volume 3 in 1929, presumably due to the length of the entire manuscript. Cassirer announced in the preface to volume 3 the instant publication of an appendix book under the title "Life and Spirit: Towards a Critique of Contemporary Philosophy." But his obligations as the rector of the University of Hamburg, followed by the growing hostile political situation leading to his emigration, prevented him from doing so. The chapter was postponed and published posthumously in 1995. Instead, his anthropological turn became manifest in *An Essay on Man* in 1944, the anthropological "Readers Digest" of his *Philosophy of Symbolic Forms* to be published in the US—with no mention of Plessner.

The philosophical situation around 1930 is as follows: The question concerning the human being has gained central attention. There is even a trend toward anthropology in philosophy,[31] as Scheler notices with ostensive satisfaction—and Heidegger counters by saying that this is not only a trend, but a true "plague"[32]—but the most elaborated available position up to 1940, Plessner's *Levels of Organic Life and the Human*, remains unnoticed and does not play any significant role in the anthropological turn in philosophy.

Taking Plessner to Davos: On Borrowing a Concept

In the Davos disputation with Cassirer, Heidegger draws the departure and demarcation line between himself and Cassirer by drawing on Plessner's vocabulary. Cassirer's ultimate focus of concern or terminus ad quem is "the whole of a philosophy of culture" in the sense of the "forms of the shaping consciousness," leaving his point of departure or "*terminus a quo* [. . .] utterly problematical." And Heidegger continues: "My position is the reverse: The *terminus a quo* is my central problematic, the one I develop."[33] Whereas Heidegger's terminus ad quem relies on the question "What in general is called being?" he keeps reinterpreting his terminus a quo again and again, revisiting and deconstructing the origin of his philosophical position, which he in these years and in the debate with Cassirer labeled the "metaphysics of Dasein." One should take Heidegger's own characterization of his central problematic at face value. His thinking remains concerned with questioning over and over again an arsenal of metaphorically related avenues—conceptualized as the "foundation" or the "ground," the "rootedness" or the "soil," the "origin" or the "beginning," the "horizon" and ultimately "the event"—that each serve as the hermeneutical background based on which and *wherefrom* one can articulate in philosophical inquiry what is revealed in the openness or *Da* of Dasein: *understanding of being*. In fact, as Heidegger repeatedly insists, the only and entire purpose of the published parts of *Being and Time* and the systematic function of fundamental ontology is to provide a reliable perspective or terminus a quo, from which the task of ontology can be tackled. The difference between Heidegger and Cassirer is evident: whereas Cassirer already builds his castle, Heidegger keeps digging the soil for a fundament.

Heidegger exhibits the hermeneutical strategy of this way of backward questioning in public in his response to Cassirer, when he gives his account of Kant's famous list of philosophy's basic questions, which conclude with the question "What is man?"[34] Far away from inviting anthropological answers, it demands, Heidegger claims, a "metaphysics of Dasein itself as a possibility of the fundament of a question of metaphysics. In this way, the question of what man is must be answered not so much in the sense of an anthropological system, but instead it must first be properly clarified with regard to *the perspective from within which* it wants to be posed."[35] The perspective from within which the human adequately can be addressed needs to be gained and prepared. At the end of the day, Kant's question leads back to the "finitude in Dasein," which is grounded in the understanding of being.[36] The happening of metaphysics "in" or qua Dasein is the distinctive mark of the human.

It is at this point of his argument that Heidegger chooses yet another conceptuality to explain his position concerning the Kantian legacy, surprisingly granting the necessary profoundness to deal with the problems at issue with an alternative philosophical option—but not Cassirer's:

> It must be shown that: because man is the creature that is transcendent, i.e., who is open to beings in totality and to himself, that through this eccentric character man at the same time also is posited within the totality of beings in general—and that only this way do the question and the idea of Philosophical Anthropology make sense. The question concerning the essence of human beings is not to be understood in the sense that we study human beings empirically as given objects, nor is it to be understood in such a way that I project an anthropology of man. Rather, the question concerning the essence of human beings only makes sense and is only justifiable insofar as it derives its motivation from philosophy's central problematic itself, which leads man back beyond himself and into the totality of beings in order to make manifest to him there, with all his freedom, the nothingness of his Dasein.[37]

The first two lines of this passage might be said to draw anonymously on Scheler's understanding of transcendence as human "world-openness"; lines three and four obviously make use of Plessner's concept of "excentric positionality." Heidegger concedes this concept to provide a feasible way to address the problem of the human. Such an account—and *only* such an account—might even confidently promise to explore the otherwise hopeless project of a philosophical anthropology. This is so because only *this* idea of philosophical anthropology allows questions to be asked about the essence of the human being in a way that is intrinsically linked to the very problematic of philosophy, as it regards the human being as posited in a stance beyond itself in and towards the totality of what there is—that is, "excentrically." As it were, philosophical anthropology based on a conception of the emplacement of the human being in terms of "excentric positionality" leads to "the metaphysics of Dasein." Excentric positionality in fact provides a topological account of human finitude in the Heideggerian sense.

But put forward in this manner, the (Plessnerian) idea of philosophical anthropology actually offers a reliable point of departure or terminus a quo, providing an option that Heidegger typically does not assign to philosophical anthropology. On the contrary, he usually—most extensively so in his Kantbuch, which came out a few months after the Davos seminar in fall 1929—dismisses positions included under this label, as their approach is "not expressly grounded in the essence of philosophy."[38] But the position Heidegger has in mind in the Cassirer dispute is obviously not confined to these "inherent limits" of anthropology; it *does* allow understanding the question concerning the human being in light of the question of metaphysics. Philosophical anthropology based on the excentric character of man would then provide a different way to reach the same result as Heidegger's existential analytics of Dasein in *Being and Time* (or the phenomenological analysis of "profound boredom" in the lecture course 1929–30), namely, to a grounding of metaphysical questioning in the finitude of Dasein. Ironically and presumably without any awareness of Cassirer's private assessment of Plessner's position, Heidegger comes to a similar conclusion about the profoundness and philosophical scope of Plessner's account. Plessner's *Levels of Organic Life and the Human* touches upon Heidegger's project "most closely," "albeit it has been gained via an avenue indeed different" from that of Heidegger.[39]

In his lecture "Philosophical Anthropology and Metaphysics of Dasein,"[40] there is evidence of a similar conclusion. After having presented Scheler as the strongest representative of the anthropological movement in philosophy, Heidegger points out the inherent limits of Scheler's position in its incapability to grasp the intrinsic belongingness of anthropological and metaphysical questioning. This problem—the true "basic problem" or *Grundfrage* of philosophy[41]—cannot be addressed from within the anthropological frame, Heidegger claims. However, there is a way of asking about the essence of the human that is prior to any philosophical anthropology, as it "lays the ground for the inner possibility of philosophy as such and hence of all philosophical questioning," including philosophical anthropology.[42] This way of questioning reveals the human essence as something by virtue of which "man is something more original than man: in so far as the humanity of man is grounded in what we call *Dasein*." Varying the parallel phrasing from the Kantbuch, Heidegger states: "More original than the humanity of man is the primordial happening of Dasein's understanding of being, in which man is thrown in factical existence."[43]

The understanding of being propels the human being beyond the boundaries of human essence. But on the other hand, the understanding of being as the mark of the human qua Dasein is what makes human human. The conclusion of his talk, which would have had to present a conceptual elaboration of these prima facie paradoxical or at least thought-provoking remarks, is not elaborated and only rendered in sketches, pinpointing the cues that Heidegger presented in his oral presentation. The conclusion begins with the following notes:

> Metaphysics of Dasein—man at the center, but not *as man!*— Essence of Dasein, therein man exists, is qua temporality *ecstatic—excentric*. Positing man as Dasein at the center—on the basis of the inner necessity of the basic problem—means simultaneously to be thrown out of the center.[44]

As I will come back to in the next section, the described movement of simultaneously being at the center and out of the center is the key thought in Plessner's account of organic life culminating in the human life form. Hence, Heidegger apparently aligns his position and the claim about the ecstatic temporality of Dasein with Plessner's claim concerning the excentric positionality of the human being. In a similar vein, he explains his position in *On the Essence of Ground*—Heidegger's contribution to the Festschrift on the occasion of Husserl's seventieth birthday—rejecting the accusations of an "anthropocentric standpoint" in *Being and Time*. It is qua the "transcendence of Dasein" that "the human being" comes into the "center" in such a way that his nothingness amid beings as a whole can and must become a problem in the first place. What dangers are entailed, then, by an "anthropocentric standpoint" that precisely puts its entire effort solely into showing that the essence of Dasein that there stands "at the center" is ecstatic, that is, "excentric"?[45] Heidegger adopts the idea of excentricity as a model that allows the articulation of the transcendence of Dasein, adding another topographic register (centered/decentered/excentric) to the account of Dasein's ecstatic temporality. As Dasein, man is both in the center and out of the center, ex-centric.[46] The essence of Dasein is excentricity.

I consider Heidegger's last sentence—excentricity is the essence of Dasein—to provide the point of issue in the unfought battle or the conversation that never occurred between Heidegger and Plessner. *The debate would have had to address the question concerning the sense in which existence is related to life, and, vice versa, how life must be thought of and conceptualized in order to allow for existence.* One might hold that Heidegger's closest approximation to philosophical anthropology—the aforementioned lecture course of 1929–30, *Fundamental Concepts of Metaphysics*—explores the first part of the question, albeit presenting an answer that ultimately excludes existence from the animal kingdom and hence does not allow approaching the human being from a natural conception of life.[47] Plessner's part would have been to discuss the second part of the question,[48] presenting a vocabulary that allows understanding the becoming of Dasein from a bio-philosophical point of view, thus providing a metaphysical underpinning of the claim of human finitude different from Heidegger's existential foundation in the being of Dasein. Not Cassirer, whose preoccupation with the terminus ad quem of a philosophy of culture did not allow for a sufficient philosophical inquiry of *the perspective from within which* this questioning was possible in the first place, but Plessner competes with Heidegger concerning the terminus a quo for a philosophy of the human.

Pushing Nature to Its Boundaries: On Naturalizing Existence

Levels of Organic Life and the Human presents a phenomenology of natural life that unfolds its organizational structures, allowing us to understand the emergence of a life form—human life—that is able to objectify itself and its stance in life while remaining a living organism. The way Plessner introduces the aspect of the human is not anthropocentric. It does not claim humankind being the telos of creation, as in metaphysical humanism and its inherent entelechy. The line of argument is not built on paleontology or evolution theory either. The envisaged levels of organic life do not render metaphysical or evolutionary stages in the course of the genesis of life on Earth.[49] Rather, they sketch ideal-typical (Weber) organizational patterns that organisms display according to the guiding organizational principle, which the human life form displays and actualizes in its reflexive mode. This guiding principle is *positionality*, introduced as the mark of living entities, which term articulates the way organisms are actualizing their environmental emplacement with regard to their *boundaries*.

In "constituting hermeneutics as philosophical anthropology and doing anthropology on the basis of a philosophy of living being and the layers of nature essentially correlated to it,"[50] Plessner seeks to lay the ground for a sufficient understanding of human life in the manifold of its registers. The envisaged philosophical foundation of hermeneutics—ever since Dilthey the methodologically elaborated understanding of the expressions of lived experiences approached in the humanities (*Geisteswissenschaften*)—is not gained via a descriptive psychology (Dilthey) or existential analysis (Heidegger), but in philosophical anthropology, which again is to be based on the living being in its natural horizon.[51]

This way (and firstly), the *concept of life* is disenchanted and regained from the irrationalism of the various lofty versions of philosophy of life in which "life" served as a vague mythologem rather than a well-defined concept. What is more (and secondly), the scope of *hermeneutics* is expanded, covering not only written documents or linguistic utterances, but the entire sphere of human expressivity, including bodily gestures or facial expressions in their "psychophysically neutral" phenomenality.[52] Heidegger too had seen the true significance of hermeneutics, though from the perspective of his encounter with Aristotle and a reorientation of ontology on the basis of human praxis; programmatically so in his project description *Phenomenological Interpretations of Aristotle* from 1923. Plessner's "hermeneutic of life" departs from early Heidegger's (Aristotelian) proto-ethical "hermeneutic of facticity" or "hermeneutic of Dasein" in its natural or organic basis, individualized not in the each-mineness of existence in the course of care, but in the emplacement of one's own lived body.[53]

Plessner's point of departure too requires the refutation of Cartesian dualism, in particular the mechanistic conception of organic bodies as (just another class of) physical bodies or res extensa. Anticipating Merleau-Ponty, Plessner claims human embodiment and the double aspect of lived body (Plessner: *Leib*; Merleau-Ponty: *corps vécu* or *corps propre*) and physical body (*Körper*; *corps*) to be the litmus test for any philosophy aiming at overcoming Cartesianism and its aftermath. This double aspect—having *and* being one's body—provides the experiential basis of Plessner's anthropology.[54] Hence, Plessner's naturalization of hermeneutics remains nonetheless within the scope of possible phenomenological description and original intuition, despite his cautious distance to Husserl's static idealism in *Ideas I*.[55] This version of a philosophy of nature avoids reductive naturalism of any kind—bracketing any claim based on causal explanations—and insists on the methodological requirement to bring its conceptions and conceptual distinctions to an understanding based on "outward intuition," in so far as philosophical anthropology is "only feasible on the basis of a science of the essential forms of living existence and must therefore create its own conceptual framework for the entire sphere, the entire radius, in which the human as a (psychophysically neutral) person is situated."[56] The phenomenological task, then, is to deliver a conceptual framework prior to scientific research that would allow an approach to the essential forms of living existence. Such an agenda implies "creating philosophy anew," which includes the "rediscovery of the problem of ontology."[57]

Provided that life can be grasped from the viewpoint of a body's relation to its boundary, the philosophy of life has to develop forms as organizational structures or patterns that a priori determine how bodies possibly can display "boundary realization." These structures are called "organic modals" and stand in functional analogy to Kant's categories. Like these, they are not concepts derived from (scientific or everyday) experience, but they provide essential characteristics and constitutive forms of life's phenomenal layer of being "that guide both the naïve and the scientific conceptualization of biology."[58] But just as Kant did not "invent" or originally introduce the formal content of his categories, Plessner draws on regressive analysis of contemporary biologists that render elementary functions such as regulation, heredity, metabolism/nutrition, reproduction, growth/development, and so on.[59] Although this list may vary according to the state of the art in actual empirical research, it nonetheless features characteristics that serve as organic modals or (with reference to Dilthey) "categories of life," specifying necessary modes of boundary realization.

One might compare Plessner's hermeneutic of life, which seeks to develop a theory of *organic modals* from the point of view of a body's boundary realization, with Heidegger's existential analytic of Dasein in *Being and Time*, which uncovers the characteristics of the being of Dasein grasped as *existentialia*. Both conceptions are "before any psychology or anthropology and certainly before any biology," allowing (Heidegger) or aiming at (Plessner) the "ontological foundation" of philosophical anthropology.[60] They differ in their choice of where to ground the foundation of the respective hermeneutic enterprise: in factical existence or embodied organic life, respectively.

Plessner's claim that takes a body's relation to its boundary as the mark of animate being deserves to be explained in more detail, in order to understand what is meant by "boundary realization." Intuitable in the visual realm, every discrete physical entity is shaped and has contours. Either this contour is merely the "virtual in-between" of the entity and the medium next to it, in which case the outline remains external to the entity, demarcating only where the body begins or ends and the surrounding medium ends or begins. In this case, the physical body is perceived as an inanimate thing. Or the outline *belongs* to the entity, so that the demarcation between the physical body and its surroundings organizes their relation along the logic of "interior" and "exterior," in which case the body is perceived as a living being. Already in the first case, the contours are recognizable as giving shape or *Gestalt*. But only in the second case, this shape is manifest *as boundary*, which lets the body appear animated. The boundary posits the primordial matrix of orientation, allowing the distinction between movements in the twofold opposite directions inside-out or outside-in in the relation between an entity and its environment.

Heidegger's analysis of the *being-in* distinguishes in a similar fashion between a "garment in the cupboard," specifying spatial relations along the categorically organized region of the present-at-hand, and the being-in of Dasein as an existentiale. Heidegger argues that the "in" here does not refer to locations and their mutual relation in physical space, but to a mode of "dwelling-alongside" that already has transgressed what in the mode of present-at-hand would look like a spatial limitation or demarcation.[61] In Plessner's perspective, the difference is a difference of boundary realization, which in the case of living entities (and not only humans) qualifies them to be posited, that is, to have a place in an environment and not just an area in space.

The mark of animality according to Plessner relies on the capability of a thing to appear as posited. With this simple thought Plessner finds a way to solve the riddle in the contemporary discussions between entelechial vitalism (Hans Driesch) and mechanistic gestalt theory (Wolfgang Köhler, Kurt Koffka) of how to conceptualize living beings in their phenomenal reality:

> The living organic body, then, is distinguished from the inorganic body by its *positional character* or *positionality*. [. . .] Phenomenally, however, living bodies differ from nonliving bodies in that the former claim space while the latter merely occupy it. Every space-occupying entity is at one position. Every space-claiming

entity, on the other hand, has a relationship to the position of "its" being by virtue of the fact that it is out beyond the entity (into the entity) that it is. In addition to its spatiality, it is *into space or spacelike* and accordingly has its natural place.[62]

Living organic bodies are thus space-claiming entities. By virtue of this property they have positionality, transforming physical *space* into their natural *place*. That is, they do not just occupy a particular spot that might allow for physical measurement of its location relative to others in physical space. They claim their place due to their relation to their boundaries. A living body employs not only boundary traffic (in the sense that a membrane allows the ingestion or excretion of nutrients), but preserves its integrity in being beyond itself (in exteriority) and back toward itself (in interiority). Hence a living body does not end with its boundary, as it is always already beyond and within the mere surface of its spatial bound.

Boundary realization, however, is not confined to space and spatiality. It is essentially temporal as well. In unfolding the processual dynamics that are involved in a living body's relation to its boundary, Plessner turns to the temporality of animated being. Given that positionality "constitutes a space-claiming body, it is potential in its actual existence; it is ahead of itself. The space-related essential properties of positionality thus allow us to determine the essential laws of the living body's relation to time."[63] Positionality implies potentiality, which again implies the primacy of future orientation in the temporal dialectics of future actualizations of actual present potential. To animated entities, time is not an external medium that organizes biological events in chronological order. The episodes involving a living being in the course of its life are not linked in time like pearls on a neckless or the chain of causal events. The "not yet" as well as the "not anymore" belong to the "now" of the organic body's presence. The organism performs its being temporally, as the exterior/interior matrix realizes temporal boundaries of an organism in terms of an "ahead of itself" and "back to itself." Any reader of Heidegger's *Being and Time* will find striking resemblances between the analysis of the temporality of the care structure and Plessner's organic modals based on the temporality of organic being, only that Plessner—again—claims already the living organism as such to be essentially characterized by temporality:

> The organic body, as set into the body that it is, is ahead of itself. It *is* inasmuch as it stands in a relation of anticipation

to the body that it is (to itself). Or its being is grounded in a timelike way, determined by the direction "from the future." [. . .] "Being ahead of itself" and living being are one and the same thing. Living being is thus just as much *according to itself* or the fulfilment of itself. This essential trait secures for the living thing something that is not given to any inanimate thing: *presence*.[64]

No translation into English can adequately render the fact that, in these and related passages, Plessner painfully avoids the grammar of reflexivity in his elaboration.[65] The criterion of animality—"claiming" a natural position in space and time via boundary realization—counts for any kind of natural life, including unicellular organisms, fungi, or plants. Plessner does not want to say that these organisms have any awareness of a temporal or spatial "boundary politics." They nonetheless and in various guises phenomenally display dynamic loops in the process of their becoming. Hence, the dialectical modality of the boundary in organic life is not per se employing factual, let alone conscious reflexivity. But the logical or structural possibility of a reflexive position is on the table. The direction toward philosophical anthropology and the distinguishing mark of the human then is obvious.

We have now reached the stage that shows Plessner's attempt to found human existence in organic life and "to do anthropology on the basis of a philosophy of living being":

> As an excentrically organized being, the human must *make himself into what he already is*. It is only thus that he fulfills the way in which his vital form of existence forces him to stand in the center of his positionality and at the same time to know of his being-positioned, rather than simply becoming fully absorbed in it, like the animal that lives out from its center and relates everything to its center. This mode of being of standing in one's being-positioned is only possible as *execution* from out of the center of this being-positioned. Such a way of being can only be carried out as realization. The human lives only insofar as he leads a life.[66]

Plessner's *Levels of Organic Life and the Human* takes the human condition, *conceived as the human position*, to be center stage for the project of philosophical anthropology. Based on "excentric positionality," Plessner captures the human in the three dimensions of "outer world," "inner world" and "shared world,"[67] arguing that to humans "boundary realization" is experienced as an assignment to be executed or realized. It is due to the excentric positionality of human beings that living a life is an issue for every such entity.

Return to Sender: On Reassigning Humanitas

The abbreviated summary through Plessner's opus magnum shows that there would have been something to talk about if Heidegger had met or exchanged letters with Plessner in the aftermath of the publication of Plessner's book. The vocabulary used by Cassirer and Heidegger in Davos indicates that they compete in delivering the ultimate terminus a quo for any philosophical understanding of the human, the alternatives being (organic) *life* vs. *existence* (of Dasein). Heidegger does not share Plessner's intention concerning a foundation of the human being or Dasein's existence in organic life or nature. Even when Heidegger claims—in his 1929–30 lecture course[68]—the human being to be "world-building" in contrast to the animal, which is considered to be "poor-in-world," his comparison aims to show that any attempt to reach the former on the basis of the conceptual frame of the latter must fall short. The human stance is, in principle, incommensurable to any other form of being, requiring an entry different from the one delivered by contemporary biologists (like von Uexküll or Roux) or philosophical anthropologists (like Scheler and Plessner). Regarding Heidegger's alleged approximation to philosophical anthropology, Plessner is right in his later assessment. Due to Heidegger's ignorance of the lived body, "there is no path from Heidegger to philosophical anthropology, either before the Kehre or after it."[69]

In Plessner's view, the fact that there is no turning off to philosophical anthropology on Heidegger's path marks the insufficiency of the existential analysis. Plessner accuses Heidegger's analysis of "free-floating existence" to commit "metaphysical shirking,"[70] in so far as it avoids addressing "the linkage of the human way of being with the human organism."[71] Because of the unwillingness to engage with the natural basis of human existence, Heidegger's position fails to achieve the envisaged neutral and purely formal description. The phenomenological plausibility hinges on the rather Western idea of "authenticity," attested in the "call of conscience."[72]

Plessner's most disturbing evaluation of Heidegger's thinking is found in a piece written for Thomas Mann's exile journal *Maß und Wert* in 1939: "Pre-fascist philosophy, cunning, evil and brave."[73] Plessner nonetheless grants that Heidegger has succeeded in breaking the spell of the dominating positivist or neo-Kantian conceptions that merely presented ghost-like patchwork models of human existence, concluding: "As a paradigm for a new doctrine of the human being, *Being and Time* hasn't finished playing its part yet." This evaluation—although hidden from the authorities under a pseudonym—issues another provocative invitation to Heidegger to join in the discussion concerning philosophical anthropology. In Plessner's perspective, Heidegger's own repeatedly claimed indifference to and disinterest in anthropological questioning obscures the fact that he nonetheless keeps going into philosophical anthropology. To Plessner, Heidegger's thinking *was* assessable as a contribution to the discourse on the human that the project labeled "philosophical anthropology" programmatically pursued. However, Heidegger with his growing stubbornness kept denying this, thereby "blocking *and* in a narrow way pursuing anthropology."[74] Of course—as one is inclined to say—Heidegger never answered Plessner's criticism directly. But what if Heidegger's "Letter on 'Humanism'" actually *also* was an anonymous written reply to Plessner's criticisms and provocations?

Heidegger's text is a letter of reply on various levels, offering his response concerning the matter of a possible discourse on the human being in a straightforward manner: "The history of being is never past but stands ever before us; it sustains and defines every *condition et situation humaine*."[75] On the face of it, Heidegger (1) provides a response to questions asked by the young French scholar Jean Beaufret, in particular on the matter of humanism and the chances or possibilities of a renewal in light of the blackout of humane civilization that mankind just had to experience. But then (2) Heidegger does not *answer* Beaufret's question. Rather, his response carves out the hermeneutical background or the perspective from within which any question concerning the human and the matter of humanism possibly can be asked. As the quoted passage proclaims, only the "history of being" provides this perspective. And (3) thinking about the human condition or position in light of this perspective in fact uncovers a responsive trait at the center of the human condition, as the focus of such a perspective does not point backward to a developmental history, but points forward toward an assignment to be fulfilled. It recognizes the inherent demand and the historical urge in the history of being that characterize the human qua human. In short: Heidegger's response presents *responsiveness to being* as the origin of *humanitas*.

Launching the history of being, Heidegger reclaims the authority regarding the discourse on the human being. Traditional (or, as Heidegger says in 1947, "metaphysical") anthropological thinking does not ask "in what way the essence of the human being belongs to the truth of being." In approaching the human as a living being, it fails to see that it depends on and presupposes the clearing of being that provides the "interpretation of beings as 'ζωή' (life) and 'φύσις' (nature), in which what is living appears." What is more, the forgetfulness of being too hastily posits the essence of the human being in the dimension of *animalitas*. Heidegger concedes to anthropological questioning—with implicit reference to Plessner (and Scheler)—that one as well can address the human as a living being among others "in contrast to plants, beasts and God." This way, one will even be able to state "something correct about the human being." The remark, however, is but a poisoned concession to philosophical anthropology. Heidegger thunders against this way of approaching the matter, claiming that it only leads to "*homo animalis*," leaving the "essence of the human being [. . .] too little heeded and not thought in its origin, the essential provenance that is always the essential future for historical mankind. Metaphysics thinks of the human being on the basis of *animalitas* and does not think in the direction of his *humanitas*."[76]

Mankind has to be dealt with in its historicity and historical fatefulness. Only this way philosophy is able to address the *humanitas* of humankind. Philosophical anthropology—as any other metaphysical or scientific way of questioning—must remain blind to this dimension, as it keeps locating the human being with its basic conceptualities in a domain—natural life—from which the essence and the origin of the human being never can be addressed. Hence, Heidegger unfolds his own position on the matter of the human being as follows:

> Metaphysics closes itself to the simple essential fact that the human being essentially occurs in his essence only where he is claimed by being. Only from that claim "has" he found that wherein his essence dwells. Only from this dwelling does he "have" "language" as the home that preserves the ecstatic for his essence. Such standing in the clearing of being I call the ek-sistence of human beings. This way of being is proper only to the human being.[77]

This passage entails what I claim to be Heidegger's anonymous rejoinder to Plessner concerning the question of the proper perspective from within which the essence of the human being philosophically has to be approached. Not boundary realization of a living organism but *responding to the claim of being* assigns *humanitas*. Heidegger outlines, in his "Letter on 'Humanism,'" a responsive onto-anthropology,[78] understanding human positionality in terms of *dwelling*, which culminates in the famous statement concerning language providing the "house of being." The dimension opened up in the "history of being" is settled to be before any nature-history or nature-culture divide. It recalibrates metaphysics in terms of metaethics or "originary ethics": "The truth of being as the primordial element of the human being, as one who exists, is in itself originary ethics."[79]

Heidegger contrasts his onto-anthropology of historical responsiveness explicitly to traditional anthropological thinking in the lecture course published as *Introduction to Metaphysics*. The traditional, "zoological" formula captures the human being as the animal rationale or the living being that possesses speech ("ἄνθρωπος = ζῷον λόγον ἔχον"). Against this, Heidegger contraposes his own "formula": "φύσις = λόγος ἄνθρωπον ἔχον: Being, the overwhelming appearing, necessitates the gathering that pervades and grounds being-human."[80] This way, *"logos"* does not refer to a quality or specific difference ("language") that humans possess, which would distinguish these from other animals. Rather, *"logos"* replaces *"zoon"* as the generic term, with the human being assigned as the entity under its command or claim. *Logos* "has" the human being, and this "having" demands the onset of historical dwelling conceived of as human existence. All Greek terms at stake—*physis* (nature: being as overwhelming appearing), *logos* (language: gathering), *echein* (possessing: pervading as grounding)—gain different meanings when approached in the light of the history of being. Most certainly so the *anthropos*, which according to Heidegger's humanism cannot be approached sufficiently when thought within the category of living beings. The task remains to understand "existence," in the "Letter on 'Humanism,'" approached as "being claimed by being."

Heidegger keeps insisting on human exceptionalism with regard to existence. There is no possibility of placing the human being in the cosmos or identifying organizational patterns as "levels" in the continuity of organic life. Humans exist; and this way of being cannot be approached philosophically via accounts of organic living. In this respect, Heidegger's humanism remains binary, answering the question posed by Shakespeare's Hamlet by dividing everything that is said to be into what exists and what does not. Accordingly, the inventory list of Heidegger's cosmos reads as follows: "The being that exists is the human being. The human being alone exists. Trees are, but they do not exist. Horses are, but they do not exist. Angels are, but they do not exist. God is, but he does not exist."[81]

Heidegger's imagined anonymous response to Plessner, as provided in the "Letter on 'Humanism,'" rephrases—once again—the terminus a quo, the conceptual frame from within which the question about the human being might properly be asked. The human being as the one who exists exhibits a way of being that intrinsically or "originarily" unfolds as "ethos." It is assigned to and claimed by a primordial normativity that it responds to, thus exhibiting a movement that Heidegger captures as ek-sistence in the history of being. This mode of being cannot be captured from nonhuman life forms or modes of being, be they biological or supranatural (spiritual) in nature. Heidegger's thinking—as hermeneutics of Dasein or hermeneutics of being—keeps refusing any possibility that would allow for an explanatory background that draws on naturalist or biological trajectories.

The debate between Heidegger and Plessner, if it had taken place, would very likely have been a dispute over whether to capture the human being in terms of natural life or in terms of historical existence. Not just a disagreement about some shared philosophical problem or issue, it would have been a clash between two competing paradigms each of which aims to create philosophy anew. The fight would thus have been how—and from where—one is to approach the human being, via excentricity or existence. *Tertium non datur.*

Notes

1. Helmuth Plessner, *Levels of Organic Life and the Human: An Introduction to Philosophical Anthropology*, trans. Millay Hyatt, intro. J. M. Bernstein (New York: Fordham University Press, 2019).

2. Hermann Schmitz, *Husserl und Heidegger* (Bonn: Bouvier, 1996); Joachim Fischer, *Philosophische Anthropologie: Eine Denkrichtung des 20. Jahrhunderts* (Freiburg: Alber, 2008); Michael Großheim, "Inspirierende Irritation: Die Bedeutung der Anthropologie Helmuth Plessners für das Denken Martin Heideggers," *Deutsche Zeitschrift für Philosophie* 66, no. 4 (2018): 507–31; Hans-Peter Krüger, "De-Zentrierungen und Ex-Zentrierungen: Die quasi-transzendentalen Unternehmungen von Heidegger und Plessner heute," in *Homo Absconditus: Helmuth Plessners philosophische Anthropologie im Vergleich* (Berlin: De Gruyter, 2019), 565–89.

3. Schmitz, *Husserl and Heidegger*, has made this point, followed more recently by Großheim, "Inspirierende Irritation."

4. Plato, *Sophist* 246a4–5. See also Gerard Raulet, "Vorwort (1928) und Vorwort (1965) (III–XXIII)," in *Helmuth Plessner: Die Stufen des Organischen und der Mensch*, ed. Hans-Peter Krüger (Berlin: De Gruyter, 2017), 30.

5. Plessner, *Levels of Organic Life and the Human*, 27.

6. Michael Großheim, "Heidegger und die philosophische Anthropologie," in *Heidegger Handbuch: Leben, Werk, Wirkung*, ed. Dieter Thomä (Stuttgart: Metzler, 2003), 333–37.

7. Driesch was the foremost representant of "vitalism," a position philosophically rejected by Plessner in *Levels of Organic Life and the Human*.

8. Helmuth Plessner, "Selbstdarstellung," in *Schriften zur Soziologie und Sozialphilosophie*, vol. 10 of *Gesammelte Schriften*, ed. Günter Dux, et al. (Frankfurt: Suhrkamp, 2003), 320.

9. Notably, in juxtaposition to Ferdinand Tönnies's influential *Gemeinschaft und Gesellschaft*, from 1887 (translated as *Community and Society*, in 1912), and its contemporary political reception.

10. Helmuth Plessner, *The Limits of Community: A Critique of Social Radicalism*, trans. Andrew Wallace (New York: Humanity Books, 1999), 10.

11. Max Scheler, "On the Idea of Man (1915)," *Journal of the British Society for Phenomenology* 9, no. 3 (1978): 184–98. See also Fischer, *Philosophische Anthropologie*, 85.

12. Fischer, *Philosophische Anthropologie*, 90.

13. Max Scheler, *The Human Place in the Cosmos*, Northwestern University Studies in Phenomenology and Existential Philosophy (Evanston, IL: Northwestern University Press, 2009). Originally published 1928. Plessner referred to this text as a "brochure" or "booklet," and, while conceding its public success, also seemed to indicate his view of it as a "minor" work. See Plessner, "Selbstdarstellung," 328.

14. Plessner, *Levels of Organic Life and the Human*, xxiii.

15. The talk entitled "Dasein und Wahrsein (nach Aristoteles)" [Being-there and being-true according to Aristotle], is published in Martin Heidegger, *Vorträge Teil 1: 1915–1932*, vol. 80.1 of *Gesamtausgabe*, ed. Günter Neumann (Frankfurt: Klostermann, 2016), 55ff.

16. Plessner, in a letter to F. Cohen, from October 31, 1924, quoted in Fischer, *Philosophische Anthropologie*, 55.

17. On Scheler, see Keane, this volume; on Husserl, Heidegger, and phenomenology, see Farin, this volume.

18. "On me personally he left a much better impression this time than three years ago. I am pretty curious how he will position himself to my book," Plessner confides in a letter to Georg Misch, from December 7, 1927. Quoted in Fischer, *Philosophische Anthropologie*, 109.

19. Heidegger commemorates this last meeting with Scheler in Cologne a year later in public, reporting that Scheler was "in disquiet" about the inner belongingness of anthropological and metaphysical questioning, a topic they dwelled on,

in intense conversations, "for days." It is unlikely that Scheler, at this occasion and with these topics, did not tell Heidegger about his unease related to his suspicion against Plessner. See Heidegger, *Vorträge Teil 1*, 219.

20. Misch, the addressee of both Plessner's and Heidegger's aforementioned letters, was the son-in-law of Wilhelm Dilthey and editor of his collected works. He wrote a review of *Being and Time* that grew to a systematic and, also today, still valuable comparison between (especially Heideggerian) phenomenology and the Diltheyian project of a philosophy of life, of all places originally published in a series of articles in *Philosophischer Anzeiger*, edited by Plessner: Georg Misch, "Lebensphilosophie und Phänomenologie: Eine Auseinandersetzung mit Heidegger und Husserl," *Philosophischer Anzeiger* 3, no. 3 (1929): 267–368; and Misch, "Lebensphilosophie und Phänomenologie: Eine Auseinandersetzung mit Heidegger und Husserl (Schluss)," *Philosophischer Anzeiger* 4, no. 3–4 (1930): 354–432. In 1931, it was published as a separate monograph: Georg Misch, *Lebensphilosophie und Phänomenologie: Eine Auseinandersetzung der Diltheyschen Richtung mit Heidegger und Husserl*, 3rd ed. (1931; Darmstadt: Wissenschaftliche Buchgesellschaft, 1967).

21. Heidegger, in a letter to Misch, from March 7, 1928. Quoted in Fischer, *Philosophische Anthropologie*, 109–10.

22. Plessner, *Levels of Organic Life and the Human*, xvii.

23. Helmuth Plessner, "Der Aussagewert einer philosophischen Anthropologie," in *Conditio Humana*, vol. 8 of *Gesammelte Schriften*, ed. Günter Dux, et al. (Frankfurt: Suhrkamp, 2003), 381.

24. K. Riezler in the *Neue Zürcher Zeitung* from March 30, 1929. See Deniz Coskun, *Law as Symbolic Form: Ernst Cassirer and the Anthropocentric View of Law* (Dordrecht: Springer, 2007), 59.

25. Apart from Heidegger and Cassirer, Otto Friedrich Bollnow, Léon Brunschvicg, Rudolf Carnap, Jean Cavaillès, Eugen Fink, Maurice de Gandillac, Victor Kraft, Emanuel Levinas, Herbert Marcuse, Joachim Ritter, Alfred Sohn-Rethel, and Leo Strauss were among the participants. From the point of view of Cassirer, see, for instance, Dominic Kaegi and Enno Rudolph, eds., *Cassirer, Heidegger: 70 Jahre Davoser Disputation* (Hamburg: Felix Meiner, 2002); Edward Skidelsky, *Ernst Cassirer: The Last Philosopher of Culture* (Princeton, NJ: Princeton University Press, 2008). From the point of view of Heidegger, see Dieter Sturma, "Die Davoser Disputation zwischen Ernst Cassirer und Martin Heidegger: Kontroverse Transzendenz," in *Heidegger-Handbuch*, ed. Dieter Thomä (Stuttgart: Metzler, 2003), 110–15; Francesca Cecchetto, *Distruggere e costruire: Heidegger e Cassirer a Davos*, Ricerche/ Facoltà di lettere e filosofia dell'Università di Venezia (Padua: Il poligrafo, 2012). For the significance to analytical philosophy, see Michael Friedman, *A Parting of the Ways: Carnap, Cassirer, and Heidegger* (London: Open Court, 2000). For the history of continental philosophy, see Peter Eli Gordon, *Continental Divide: Heidegger, Cassirer, Davos* (Cambridge, MA: Harvard University Press, 2010). For the significance to French philosophy see Ethan Kleinberg, *Generation Existential:*

Heidegger's Philosophy in France, 1927–1961 (Ithaca, NY: Cornell University Press, 2005). A beautiful poetic narration is rendered in Wolfram Eilenberger, *Time of the Magicians: Wittgenstein, Benjamin, Cassirer, Heidegger, and the Decade that Reinvented Philosophy*, trans. Shaun Whiteside (New York: Penguin, 2020).

26. An exception is Vida Pavesich, "Hans Blumenberg's Philosophical Anthropology: After Heidegger and Cassirer," *Journal of the History of Philosophy* 46, no. 3 (2008): 421–48.

27. Hans-Peter Krüger, "Life-Philosophical Anthropology as the Missing Third: On Peter Gordon's *Continental Divide*," *History of European Ideas* 41, no. 4 (2015): 432.

28. Fischer, *Philosophische Anthropologie*, 104–5.

29. See Kleinberg, *Generation Existential*, 40.

30. Ernst Cassirer, *Zur Metaphysik der symbolischen Formen*, ed. John Michael Krois and Oswald Schwemmer, *Nachgelassene Manuskripte und Texte*, vol. 1 (Hamburg: Meiner, 1995), 60. See also Krüger, "Life-Philosophical Anthropology as the Missing Third," 436.

31. See Großheim, "Inspirierende Irritation," 523.

32. See Scheler, *The Human Place in the Cosmos*, 4; Martin Heidegger, *Vom Wesen der menschlichen Freiheit*, vol. 31 of *Gesamtausgabe*, ed. Hartmut Tietjen (Frankfurt: Klostermann, 1994), 122.

33. Martin Heidegger, *Kant and the Problem of Metaphysics*, trans. Richard Taft, 5th ed. (Bloomington: Indiana University Press, 1997), 202.

34. Kant put the task of philosophy into three questions that *in totum* would cover the scope of human questioning: What can I know? What shall I do? What may I hope? This interrogative *trivium*, Kant adds in his lectures on logic, can be expressed in one single question: "What is man?" Immanuel Kant, *Logik*, ed. Gottlob Benjamin Jäsche, in vol. 9 of *Gesammelte Schriften der Preussischen Akademie der Wissenschaften* (Berlin: De Gruyter, 1910), 25.

35. Heidegger, *Kant and the Problem of Metaphysics*, 202.

36. Heidegger, *Kant and the Problem of Metaphysics*, 160.

37. Heidegger, *Kant and the Problem of Metaphysics*, 204. Translation modified.

38. Heidegger, *Kant and the Problem of Metaphysics*, 148. Heidegger declares: "If man is only man *on the grounds of the Dasein in him*, then in principle the question as to what is more original than man cannot be anthropological. All anthropology, even Philosophical Anthropology, has already assumed that man is man. [. . .] No anthropology which understands its own particular questioning and the presuppositions thereof can even claim to develop the problem of a laying of the ground for metaphysics, let alone carry it out. The necessary question for a laying of the ground for metaphysics, namely, that of what man is, is taken over by the metaphysics of Dasein" (161–62). Similar, Heidegger, *Vom Wesen der menschlichen Freiheit*, 122. Kant's question—What is man?—cannot be answered in the discourse of philosophical anthropology, but only by Heidegger's metaphysics of

Dasein. A third option—as indicated in Davos to Cassirer and which, in my reading, Heidegger is aware of as having been put forward by Plessner—is not conceivable.

39. Cassirer, *Zur Metaphysik der symbolischen Formen*, 60.

40. Presented at the Frankfurt Kant Society on January 24, 1929, two months before the seminar in Davos. The not entirely elaborated manuscript is available in Heidegger, *Vorträge Teil 1*.

41. See also Heidegger, *Vom Wesen der menschlichen Freiheit*, 123.

42. Heidegger, *Vorträge Teil 1*, 222.

43. My translation. The entire passage without my omissions reads in German: "Allein, auch diese Idee der Anthropologie als Grunddisziplin muß fallen; dann nämlich, wenn das Seinsverständnis nicht nur zum Wesen des Menschen gehört, sondern sich als dasjenige erweist, in kraft dessen der Mensch etwas Ursprünglicheres ist denn Mensch; wenn das Menschsein des Menschen in dem gründet, was wir *das Dasein nennen*. [. . .] Ursprünglicher als das Menschsein ist dieses Urgeschehen des Seinsverstehens des Daseins, in das der Mensch als faktisch existierender geworfen ist." Heidegger, *Vorträge Teil 1*, 236–37. See also Heidegger, *Kant and the Problem of Metaphysics*, 160–61.

44. Heidegger, *Vorträge Teil 1*, 240ff.

45. Martin Heidegger, "The Essence of Ground," in *Pathmarks*, ed. William McNeill (Cambridge: Cambridge University Press, 1998), 371.

46. On transcendence and the parallel ecstatic temporality/excentric positionality in Heidegger and Plessner, see Thomas Schwarz Wentzer, "Rethinking Transcendence: Heidegger, Plessner and the Problem of Anthropology," *International Journal of Philosophical Studies* 25, no. 3 (2017): 348–62.

47. Early Heidegger's Freiburg lecture courses prominently deal with the concept of life—see his *Ontology: The Hermeneutics of Facticity*, trans. John van Buren (Bloomington: Indiana University Press, 1988)—conceived as "factical life"; but they never really approach the concept in its natural or biological semantic field. Hence, I disagree with Schmitz, who states about Heidegger's position in 1929–30: "He agrees with the anthropological conception of Plessner including his terminology. [. . .] The existential analytic transforms into an anthropology of eccentric positionality in the sense of Plessner's." See Schmitz, *Husserl und Heidegger*, 374, 389.

48. "How must life be thought that it can provide or contain existence?" See Plessner, "Der Aussagewert einer Philosophischen Anthropologie," 388.

49. See also Helmuth Plessner, "Der Mensch als Lebewesen: Adolf Portmann zum 70. Geburtstag," in *Conditio Humana*, vol. 8 of *Gesammelte Schriften*, 314–27.

50. Plessner, *Levels of Organic Life and the Human*, 27.

51. The circumscribed program can be put in a slogan: "Without a philosophy of the human there is no theory of the human experience of life in the humanities. Without a philosophy of nature there is no philosophy of the human." See Plessner, *The Levels of Organic Life and the Human*, 22.

52. Plessner, *Levels of Organic Life and the Human*, 23ff.

53. See Heidegger's *Ontology: The Hermeneutics of Facticity* and *Being and Time*, which explore *hermeneutics* along these lines. Heidegger's attempt, Plessner holds with reference to Misch, is "based on a hermeneutic ontology of existence [and] evades the thought of a hermeneutic of life." See Plessner, "Deutsches Philosophieren in der Epoche der Weltkriege," in *Schriften zur Philosophie*, vol. 9 of *Gesammelte Schriften*, ed. Günter Dux, et al. (Frankfurt: Suhrkamp, 2003), 288.

54. See Plessner, *Levels of Organic Life and the Human*, 31. Apart from here, this claim is most extensively unfolded in his *Laughing and Crying: A Study of the Limits of Human Behavior* (Evanston, IL: Northwestern University Press, 1970). Originally published 1941. On Plessner and Merleau-Ponty, see Maren Wehrle, "Medium und Grenze: Der Leib als Kategorie der Intersubjektivität: Phänomenologie und Anthropologie im Dialog," in *Grenzen der Empathie. Philosophische, psychologische und anthropologische Perspektiven*, ed. T. Breyer (Paderborn: Fink, 2013), 217–238; Jasper van Buuren, *Body and Reality: An Examination of the Relationships Between the Body Proper, Physical Reality, and the Phenomenal World, Starting from Plessner and Merleau-Ponty* (Bielefeld: Transcript, 2018), 137ff.

55. See Plessner, *Levels of Organic Life and the Human*, xxx, 20, 25, 102, 107. See also Hans-Peter Krüger, *Homo Absconditus: Helmuth Plessners philosophische Anthropologie im Vergleich*, 26. Compare also Plessner's obituary on Husserl in *Schriften zur Philosophie*, 122–47. The way Plessner argues for the necessity of philosophical prior to scientific conceptualization in dealing with the question of how to settle the meaning of the concept of "life" and "animality" in the first place recalls late Husserl's corresponding analysis on the origin of geometry in his *Crisis of European Sciences* and the function of the *Lebenswelt* for concept formation. See Plessner, *The Levels of Organic Life and the Human*, xxxi, 107; also "Der Aussagewert einer philosophischen Anthropologie," 391.

56. Plessner, *Levels of Organic Life and the Human*, 24.

57. Plessner, *Levels of Organic Life and the Human*, 27. This phrase entails a hidden objection presumably to Nicolai Hartmann's *Metaphysics of Knowledge* (1921), not to Heidegger.

58. Plessner, *Levels of Organic Life and the Human*, 110, 113, 114. Compare "Der Aussagewert einer Philosophischen Anthropologie," 391.

59. Plessner, *Levels of Organic Life and the Human*, 104.

60. See Martin Heidegger, *Being and Time*, trans. John Macquarie and Edward Robinson (New York: Harper and Row, 1962), 71, 38.

61. See Heidegger, *Being and Time*, 79ff.

62. Plessner, *Levels of Organic Life and the Human*, 121, 123.

63. Plessner, *Levels of Organic Life and the Human*, 165.

64. Plessner, *Levels of Organic Life and the Human*, 167.

65. Explicitly flagged at *Levels of Organic Life and the Human*, 119. The pronominal phrase Plessner uses is "ihm selbst," not "*sich* selbst," which would be the indication of reflexivity, a difference that "itself" cannot capture. See *Die Stufen*

des Organischen und der Mensch, vol. 4 of *Gesammelte Schriften*, ed. Günter Dux, et al. (Frankfurt: Suhrkamp, 2003), 181, 240, and many times elsewhere.

66. Plessner, *Levels of Organic Life and the Human*, 288.

67. Plessner, *Levels of Organic Life and the Human*, 272. Early Heidegger similarly introduces *Selbstwelt* (self-world), *Mitwelt* (with-world or social world), and *Umwelt* (environmental world) as the three equiprimordial and irreducible elements of the *Lebenswelt* (life-world). See Martin Heidegger, *Grundprobleme der Phänomenologie*, vol. 58 of *Gesamtausgabe*, ed. Hans-Helmuth Gander (Frankfurt: Klostermann, 2010), 64; *Phänomenologie der Anschauung und des Ausdrucks*, vol. 59 of *Gesamtausgabe*, ed. Claudius Strube (Frankfurt: Klostermann, 2007), 10.

68. Martin Heidegger, *The Fundamental Concepts of Metaphysics: World, Finitude, Solitude*, trans. William McNeill and Nicholas Walker (Bloomington: Indiana University Press, 1995). See also Ruin, this volume.

69. Plessner, *Levels of Organic Life and the Human*, xxvi.

70. Plessner, "Der Mensch als Lebewesen," 324.

71. Plessner, "Homo Absconditus," in *Conditio Humana*, vol. 8 of *Gesammelte Schriften*, 356. See also Plessner, "Immer noch Philosophische Anthropologie?," in *Conditio Humana*, 245.

72. Plessner, "Macht und menschliche Natur," in *Macht und menschliche Natur*, vol. 5 of *Gesammelte Schriften*, ed. Günter Dux, et al. (Frankfurt: Suhrkamp, 2003), 157.

73. Plessner, "Deutsches Philosophieren in der Epoche der Weltkriege," 280.

74. Plessner, "Selbstdarstellung," 328.

75. Heidegger, "Letter on 'Humanism,'" in *Pathmarks*, 240.

76. Heidegger, "Letter on 'Humanism,'" 246–47.

77. Heidegger, "Letter on 'Humanism,'" 247.

78. The term "onto-anthropology" is borrowed from the much-discussed essay on Heidegger's "Letter on 'Humanism,'" by Peter Sloterdijk, "Regeln für den Menschenpark: Ein Antwortschreiben zu Heideggers Brief über den Humanismus," in *Nicht gerettet: Versuche nach Heidegger* (Frankfurt: Suhrkamp, 2001), 302–37.

79. Heidegger, "Letter on 'Humanism,'" 271. On Heidegger's argument centered on the translation of Greek *êthos* as "abode" and the topological aspects concerning language as the "house of being," see Jeff Malpas, "The House of Being: Poetry, Language, Place," in *Paths in Heidegger's Later Thought*, ed. Günter Figal, Diego D'Angelo, Guang Yang, Tobias Keiling (Bloomington: Indiana University Press, 2020), 15–44.

80. Martin Heidegger, *Introduction to Metaphysics*, trans. Gregory Fried and Richard Polt (New Haven, CT: Yale University Press, 2000), 187.

81. Martin Heidegger, introduction to "What Is Metaphysics?," in *Pathmarks*, 284.

Chapter Four

On the Twofoldness of Human Beings
Husserl's "Reply" to Heidegger's Critical Remarks

Sara Heinämaa

Introduction

At the very beginning of the first part of *Being and Time*, Heidegger distinguishes his own Dasein-analytic and the new phenomenological hermeneutics that it motivates from Husserl's classical phenomenology, which, in Heidegger's reading, is dominated by rationalist epistemological interests and misguided by taken-for-granted concepts. Heidegger attacks Husserl's classical phenomenological account of human existence as an outdated form of philosophical "personalism," hopelessly entangled with ontic theories and pre-phenomenological notions of human life. Thus, he argues that his former teacher falls victim to fundamental mistakes that are analogous to those that strain all nineteenth- and twentieth-century philosophies of life and philosophical anthropology.[1]

The fundamental problem that Heidegger identifies, in all of his contemporary philosophy, is a neglect not only of the question that concerns the meaning of being but also of the crucial and distinctive role that this question plays in our own existence. We are not just one type of being among other types but, more essentially, are beings who question the sense of being (*der Sinn von Sein*) from within unique situations in the historical world, and who ask, in particular, about their own way of being *there*—that is, *Da*-sein, For Heidegger, the realization of our distinctively inquiring relation to being must serve as the transcendental basis for a new philosophical anthropology, as distinct from all traditional philosophies of man as well as from empirical inquiries into human beings and their achievements and possessions, material or mental. As Steven Crowell aptly formulates:

> The [Heideggerian] approach gave philosophical shape to the basic existential insight that thinking about human existence requires new categories not found in ancient or modern thought; human beings can be understood neither as substances with fixed properties nor as subjects interacting with a world of objects.[2]

Heidegger acknowledges that his contemporary philosophies of life and personhood involve implicit tendencies toward posing the question about our human way of being, but he argues that these philosophies never undertake this task properly, since they do not critically investigate the inherited philosophical terminology of subjects, persons, egos, souls, and spirits but take these terms as given. "Thus," Heidegger writes, "we are not being terminologically idiosyncratic when we avoid these terms as well as the expressions 'life' and 'human being' in designating the beings that we ourselves are."[3]

In this context, Heidegger claims that his contemporary philosophy, in all its variations, is still seriously strained and delimited by the influences of Hellenistic philosophy and Christian theology, and most recently by Cartesian subjectivism, pieced together from ancient and medieval concepts: "What obstructs and misleads the basic question of the being of Da-sein is the orientation thoroughly colored by the anthropology of Christianity and the ancient world, whose inadequate ontological foundations also personalism and the philosophy of life ignore."[4] In Heidegger's account, the tradition of anthropology seriously burdens and also delimits Husserl's classical phenomenology. In a similar manner as his philosophical contemporaries and predecessors, Husserl analyzes the existence of human beings by concepts that have roots in Christian teachings and ancient philosophy, roots that, already centuries ago, had lost contact with their original foundations in concrete phenomena and the living experiences of human beings.

But how exactly is this problem manifested in Husserl's phenomenology? What is the seeming self-evidence that classical phenomenology presupposes, despite all of its radicalness and rigor? The aim of this chapter is not only to answer these questions by studying the validity of the critical claims that Heidegger directs against Husserl's discourse of human beings as persons but also to ask to what extent his presentation of the Husserlian alternative holds. Such a comparative inquiry advances the development of contemporary philosophical anthropology by differentiating two influential discourses on human being, both of which are "phenomenological," in the general sense that both describe and analyze conditions of our experiencing, and both of which entail a critique of anthropologism. However, instead of the simple opposition that Heidegger's early critique suggests, we find two alternative approaches that share the phenomenological-transcendental interest in clarifying the conditions of experiencing but that also diverge on crucial matters concerning our experiences of human beings, ourselves, and others.[5]

This chapter offers three considerations. After a summary, in the second section, of Heidegger's early critique of Husserl, the third section proceeds to distinguish between two dimensions of Husserl's discourse on human persons. It argues that Husserl does not put forward one analysis of the being of humans but explicates two different accounts and then critically studies their mutual relation of dependency. On the one hand, there is the naturalistic account of human beings as *layered psychophysical beings*, and, on the other hand, there is the personalistic account of human beings as peculiar kinds of *unified wholes*, in which the mental and the sensuous-bodily are inextricably intertwined. The fourth section of this chapter clarifies Husserl's theory of individuation and its consequences for our discourse on human persons. Finally, the fifth section explicates the conceptual means by which Husserl develops his account of human beings as persons, most importantly, for our purposes, the concepts of expression and expressive whole. The chapter ends by drawing some conclusions for contemporary philosophical anthropology.

Heidegger's Critical Remarks

For Heidegger, the main conceptual weakness of classical Husserlian phenomenology is that it leaves unclarified what the performance (*Vollziehung*) of acts means, how acts are given, and what their being is.[6] More precisely, what remains merely presumed is the way in which performed acts relate to performing subjects, and how the subjects are given to themselves. In the 1925 lectures on the history of the concept of time, Heidegger acknowledges that, while articulating the constitution of time-consciousness, Husserl does provide explications of the structures of the stream of lived experiencing (*erleben*) and of the unity of life, which are supposed to guarantee the continuum of intentional activity and intentional acts. Nonetheless, his crucial objection remains: "But even if the being of acts and the unity of the experiential stream were determined in their being, the question of the being of the full concrete man would still remain."[7]

In Heidegger's account, this fundamental indeterminacy of classical phenomenological concepts is manifest, most clearly, in its ambiguous discourse on persons. For Husserl, Heidegger contends, the human person is essentially a performer of acts, but since the concepts of acts remain indeterminate, Husserl and his followers—for example, Max Scheler and Edith Stein—cannot but proceed negatively and thus argue that the person is not a material thing or a natural organism. In *Being and Time*, Heidegger formulates his objection as follows:

> The person is not a Thing [*Ding*], not a substance, not an object [*Gegenstand*]. [. . .] Essentially the person exists only in the performance of intentional acts, and is therefore essentially *not* an object. [. . .] Acts are performed; the person is a performer of acts. What, however, is the ontological meaning of "performance"? How is the kind of Being which belongs to a person to be ascertained ontologically in a positive way [*positiv*]?[8]

Heidegger's critique emphasizes the fact that classical phenomenological accounts proceed by first stating, negatively, that the being of a person is not like the being of things and natural entities.[9] As a preparatory step, such a characterization would not be a problem, but Heidegger then argues that, in Husserlian phenomenology, this initial negative move is never fully compensated by a proper account of the being of persons in positive terms. In his reading, Husserlians fail to characterize persons positively and proceed merely by distinguishing between different types, products, and parts of persons.

Being and Time does not include an explicit attack on Husserl's theory of subjectivity or his analysis of personhood. Heidegger bypasses Husserl's work on the basis that it is still in a stage of dynamic development, and most of it remains unpublished.[10] Thus, he ends up directing his critical remarks at Scheler's exposition, instead of Husserl's, and attacks Husserlian phenomenology by way of a detour. Despite this manner of proceeding, the main thrust of his critique is intended to work in both directions:

The phenomenological Interpretation of personality is in principle more radical and more transparent [than philosophies of life]; but the question of the Being of Dasein has a dimension which this too fails to enter. No matter how much Husserl and Scheler may differ in their respective inquiries, in their methods of conducting them, and in their orientations towards the world as a whole, they are fully in agreement on the negative side of their Interpretations of personality.[11]

In the 1925 lectures, Heidegger is more explicit in his critique of Husserl. He argues that, if we would ask Husserl what the being of the person is, Husserl would be able to answer merely by pointing out that the being of persons differs from the being of thing-like natural realities. And, if we would insist on receiving a more precise and positive determination of personal being, Husserl would just lead us to reflect on the inner structures and processes of pure consciousness: "At the bottom, we are being led back to the same basis, to the immanent reflection of acts and lived experiences, without these acts on their part being actually defined."[12]

There is another crucial problem in Husserl's "personalism," according to Heidegger, which is connected to its neglect of the ontological preconditions of the ideas of personhood and act-performance.[13] The trouble, Heidegger argues, is that, insofar as classical phenomenological discussions of human beings—their souls, minds, spirits, and bodies—draw conceptual resources from earlier philosophies, they inescapably refer back to the natural attitude that the phenomenological-transcendental reduction is supposed to leave behind through the suspensions of the general thesis of being. The classical phenomenologists, so to say, borrow concepts that belong to the natural attitude and use these concepts to flesh out their supposedly rigorous transcendental accounts of personhood and subjectivity. However, they never pay back this conceptual debt and thus remain bound to supposedly suspended natural notions. In other words, the heroic attempts that Husserl and his followers made for the reinterpretation of the relations between soul, spirit, mind, and body irretrievably repeat ancient and early modern conceptualizations of life and existence, never really breaking new ground for a philosophical anthropology—and even less for a true ontology of ourselves:

> In their turn "body," "soul," and "spirit" may designate phenomenal domains which can be detached as themes for definite

investigations; within certain limits their ontological indefiniteness may not be important. When, however, we come to the questions of man's Being, this is not something we can simply compute by adding together those kinds of Being which body, soul, and spirit respectively possess—kinds of Being whose nature has not as yet been determined. And even if we should attempt such an ontological procedure, some idea of the Being of the whole must be presupposed.[14]

Heidegger thus contends that if we decide to proceed by the methods and concepts of classical Husserlian phenomenology, then we are bound to formulate all philosophical questions that concern our own being by the concepts of person, and, since these concepts are inextricably bound up with pre-transcendental concepts of act, soul, spirit, mind, and body, as well as with naive everyday notions about human agents and their lives, we do not really proceed in any philosophical way. The problematic character of these concepts can properly be illuminated only by fundamental-ontological investigations that lead us to pose the questions of our own way of being in a completely new way.

For systematic reasons, it is important to notice that, in the 1925 lectures, Heidegger also develops a third critical perspective on classical Husserlian phenomenology. This criticism is more specific than his general complaint about the inadequacy of the concepts of persons (as act-performers), and it is also more specific than his consequent remarks about the transcendental indeterminacy of the concepts of act, soul, spirit, mind, and body. In the lectures, Heidegger claims that Husserl's phenomenology is bound to resort to the concepts of body and embodiment in the task of individuating human beings. The point is formulated as follows:

> The *fundamental stratum* is still the *naturally real*, upon which the psychic is built, and upon the psychic the spiritual. Now comes the question of the constitution of the spiritual world. It is true that the genuine naturality of the personalistic attitude is thematically emphasized, but the actual account still gives precedence to the investigation of nature. The being of the person is not as such experienced in a primary way. The matter instead remains in the reflection on acts, in the *inspection sui*. Only now the theme is not the pure consciousness and pure

ego but instead the isolated individual consciousness and ego. *But the isolation is always conditioned by the body.*[15]

Here, Heidegger does not dismiss the fact that Husserl explicitly argues that consciousness has its own internal or immanent manner of individuation, but he contends that this argument cannot help us with the interpretation of the being of human persons, since persons are not pure consciousnesses but are practically engaged and affectively involved with the worldly objects that they intend and with the world as an integrated context of such objects. Essentially, Heidegger's critical remarks suggest that the immanent principle of individuation that Husserl presents can distinguish the reflecting ego or self from everything else but cannot differentiate between separate individuals in the experienced plurality of human life. On purely immanent grounds, we can only keep ourselves distinct from *everything alien*, or from a *general anonymous other*, without ever coming to *You, He, She*, and so forth. Thus, in order to individuate other human beings, and not just himself, a Husserlian phenomenologist would have to resort to the natural distinctness of human bodies, which goes against the method being employed.

In order to be able to evaluate Heidegger's problematization of Husserl's discourse of persons, and to see to what extent it may be justified, we need to clarify three central factors of Husserl's approach: a distinction between two attitudes, the principles of individuation, and the analysis of the structure of expression. These are the tasks of the next three sections.

Psychophysical Complexes vs. Unified Persons

In the second volume of Husserl's *Ideas* (*Ideas II*), we find an analysis of several different but related ways of apprehending human beings. The main distinction is between two attitudes with two different kinds of thematic positings: the naturalistic (dogmatic natural-scientific) attitude, which posits nature as the basis of being, and the personalistic attitude, which posits spiritual units and wholes. In other words, Husserl describes two different ways of understanding and studying human beings, which are possible within two different attitudes.[16] The main methodological aim of *Ideas II* is to carefully distinguish between these two thematizations—and between the two attitudes and interests in which they are formed—and then to explicate their inner structures individually, as well as in their mutual relation of dependency.

The reflective phenomenological attitude is supposed to make this radically critical inquiry possible by suspending all of the positings of being that are operative within the two attitudes under investigation.[17]

More precisely, Husserl argues that, on the one hand, human beings can be apprehended, or grasped, as stratified two-layered complexes or, more precisely, as psychophysical systems. On the other hand, human beings can be grasped as persons—that is, as spiritual-bodily wholes, with spiritual-bodily constituents and spiritual-bodily relations to the environing world. *Ideas II* characterizes the difference between these two modes of apprehension as follows:

> In the [naturalistic attitude], the totality of "objective" physical nature was, or is, there for us, founding, [and] scattered therein, living bodies [*Leiber*], sensitiveness, and physic lives. All men and animals we consider in this attitude are, if we pursue theoretical interests, anthropological or, more generally, zoological objects. We could also say physio-psychic objects, whereby the inversion of the usual expression "psychophysical" indicates quite appropriately the order of the founding. What has been said concerns all our fellow men as well as ourselves, to the extent that we consider ourselves theoretically precisely in this attitude: we then are animated living bodies [*beseelte Leiber*], objects of nature, themes of the relevant natural sciences. But it is quite otherwise, as regards the *personalistic attitude*, the attitude we are always in when we live with one another, talk to one another, shake hands with one another in greeting, or are related to one another in love and aversion, in disposition and action, in discourse and discussion. [. . .] To live as a person is to posit oneself as a person, to find oneself in, and to bring oneself into, conscious relations with a "surrounding world."[18]

This means that, in the naturalistic attitude, we have two types of beings, causally and functionally connected one to the other: the psychic that emerges and operates on a physical substrate, and the physic that supports the psychic and produces it. In the personalistic attitude, we only have one unified being. The spiritual is not a second something emergent on or juxtaposed with a bodily-material "basis" but thoroughly penetrates the body and organizes it according to its own principles. Both attitudes conceive human beings as mental beings with bodily capacities, but whereas the former attitude conceptualizes the mental as an emergent *psychic layer* of being, ontologically dependent on the fundamental layer of the physical, the latter conceives the mental as a formative *spiritual power* that operates on bodily-sensible materials.

Unlike Heidegger, Husserl aims to undermine neither the naturalistic, or natural-scientific, attitude nor its theories of human beings. In his account, this attitude is integral to many of our practices, from traditional medical therapies to modern neurosciences, and thus has both its own justification and its own limits. Rather than rejecting the naturalistic attitude, Husserl aims at demonstrating under which conditions this attitude becomes possible, what interests it serves, and where its limits lie.[19] However, Husserl's radically critical inquiry into the relations between the two attitudes also reveals that the naturalistic attitude—with its objects, the merely material thing and the human being as a psychophysical complex—is not a self-supportive or independent sense-formation. The analyses of *Ideas II* and *The Crisis of European Sciences* disclose this attitude as a highly complex sense-accomplishment that necessarily refers to and presupposes a more fundamental attitude in which we grasp human beings as unified wholes with meaningful, expressive bodies. In *Ideas II*, this argument is summarized as follows:

> Upon closer scrutiny, it will even appear that there are not here two attitudes with equal rights and of the same order, or two perfectly equal apperceptions which at once penetrate one another, but that the naturalistic attitude is in fact subordinated to the personalistic, and that the former only acquires by means of an abstraction or, rather, by means of a kind of self-forgetfulness of the personal ego, a certain autonomy—whereby it proceeds illegitimately to absolutize its world, i.e., nature.[20]

Thus, Husserl questions the supposed self-sufficiency and primacy of the naturalistic attitude and argues that it depends, in its sense, on a more profound attitude, in which we do not apprehend or study human beings—ourselves and others—as psychophysical compounds but experience them as spiritual-bodily persons in comprehensive motivational, significative, and communicative relationships with their surroundings. The reductively purified, reflective attitude of the phenomenologists allows the distinction between these two attitudes and an account of their mutual relations of dependency. The problem that attends on the naturalistic apprehension of human beings is not that it would lack sense or legitimation; rather the problem is that the attitude harbors, in itself, universalizing tendencies that buttress the dogmatic notion that everything is ultimately physical.

A Question of Individuation

Husserl's argument about the primacy of the personalistic attitude, and the human being as a meaningful expressive whole, may seem to undermine the natural scientific research paradigm, according to which our psychic or mental life, however it is organized as such, results from the purely physical processes of the human brain or the neural make-up of the human organism. However, the opposition here is merely apparent, since the relations discussed by Husserl and the natural scientists are different in kind. Whereas Husserl studies constitutive dependency relations between different *senses of being*, the natural scientific conception concerns causal-functional relations between two different types of *real properties*—on the one hand, mental properties (e.g., veracity, aboutness, phenomenality), and, on the other hand, physical properties (e.g., weight, length, intensity, electric charge).[21]

However, on the basis of the natural scientific paradigm of explanation and theorization one can put forward a comprehensive ontological thesis, according to which all being—and consequently also all psychic, mental, and spiritual being—depends on the fundamental being of purely physical entities and processes. This is not a natural scientific theory but is the ontological position of modern materialism and physicalism.[22] In their analysis, the mental is either identical with the material-physical or merely an epiphenomenal and emergent property of the material-physical, without any power to determine the latter.[23]

Against such philosophical programs, Husserl argues that all materialist and physicalistic arguments take for granted the possibility of individuating material-physical being, independently of any reference to individual consciousnesses. This, he contends, is untenable. In his analysis, material-physical individuation, in terms of positions in objective space-time and in terms of causal roles, remains dependent on individuation by the "here" and the "now," and these, in turn, refer back to individual subjects—that is, to experiencing selves that are individuated on other grounds. *Ideas II* conveys this argument as follows:

> What distinguishes two things that are alike is the real-causal nexus, which presupposes the here and the now. And with that

we are led back necessarily to an individual subjectivity, whether solitary or an intersubjective one, with respect to which alone determinateness is constituted in the position of location and of time. *No thing has its individuality in itself*.[24]

And a few pages below, the thesis is formulated even more explicitly:

> Objective thinghood is determined physicalistically but is determined as a this [*als Dies*] only in relation to consciousness and the conscious subject. All determination refers back to a here and now and consequently to some subject or nexus of subjects.[25]

Husserl's treatment, here, rests on his account of the constitution of the unity of the stream of transcendentally purified consciousness and of immanent time as its basic structure. In his account, all individuation of things, events, processes, and other types of realities in objective unified space-time rests on the primary individuation of pure subjects and their acts, and these, in turn, are grounded in the fundamental individuation of streams of consciousness, with their egoic poles.[26] Or, to put it more technically: subjectivity alone is independently individual, and all spatiotemporal individuality is only nonindependently individual; that is, it necessarily presupposes the intrinsic individuality of streams of consciousness.[27]

The main implication of this theory of individuation to philosophical anthropology is the insight that, as conscious subjects, human beings are not originally individuated by their positions in objective space-time, or in causal nexuses, but are individuated by their subjective modes of taking position and responding to what is given in experience, and of yielding to or withstanding from what draws them.[28]

But since each subject only lives, and can live, through his or her own experiences, and not those of others,[29] the situation of individuation is different in one's own case and in the case of others. This is the dilemma that Heidegger identifies in his 1925 lectures when he argues that classical phenomenology cannot avoid resorting to bodily individuation.[30] Even if the reflecting self could individuate itself on grounds that are purely immanent to its stream of conscious experiencing, it cannot proceed in the same manner when distinguishing and identifying other selves, since other streams are inaccessible to it. Two alternatives seem to open up: either one has to conclude that the reflecting self cannot individuate any other egos than itself, or the self has to find in its sphere of ownness grounds for the individuation of others. To see how Husserl handles this dilemma, we need to look more closely into his analysis of the structures of our experiences of persons and their living bodies.

Persons as Expressive Wholes

We have seen that Husserl's *Ideas II* argues that, in experience, we primarily encounter one another as persons, and that the layered notion of human beings is a dependent formation of sense, presupposing the experiential givenness of persons. In *Ideas II*, Husserl introduces the concepts of *expression* and *expressive whole* to characterize and analyze the special type of being that is central to his account of persons.[31] He argues that, when we operate within the personalistic attitude and experience human beings as persons, we grasp them as expressive wholes, comparable to the units of written and spoken languages, such as words, sentences, and texts:

> [T]he imprinted page or the spoken lecture is not a connected duality of word-sound and sense, but rather each word has its sense [. . .]. Exactly the same holds for the unity, man. It is not that the living body is an undifferentiated physical unity, undifferentiated from the standpoint of its "sense," from the standpoint of the spirit. Rather, the physical unity of the living body there [. . .] is multiply *articulated* [. . .]. And the articulation is that of *sense*, which means it is not of a kind that is to be found within the physical attitude [. . .].[32]

A few pages later, Husserl explicates his main insight, according to which the mental life that we capture in the bodily gestures and postures of living beings is not originally given to us as an appendix to physical being but is given as an organizing power:

> [T]he spiritual is not a second something, is not an appendix, but is precisely animating; and the unity is not a connection of two, but on the contrary, one and only one is there. Physical being can be grasped for itself (carrying out the existential thesis), by means of the natural attitude, as natural being, as thingly being [. . .]. But what we have here is not a surplus which would be posited on top of the physical, but rather this is spiritual being

which essentially includes the sensuous but which, once again, does not include it as part, the way one physical thing is part of another.[33]

The main point of Husserl's comparison is to draw attention to the way in which persons and linguistic units are structured in experience. He argues that, in a similar manner as sentences and words, persons appear as thoroughly meaningful wholes. Each part of such an object is a unity of meaning and sensible matter. Even the ultimate parts—phonemes in the case of language, and organs and limbs in the case of persons—have meaning and are able to connect with other meaningful units. So, rather than having the spiritual as a layer or as a causal-functional part in a nonspiritual substratum, these unities are completely permeated by meaning. Each layer, and each part that can be discovered or disclosed by analysis, is filled with meaning, and no nonsignifying ground can be detected. Moreover, each expressive and meaningful whole, and each part of such a whole, has multiple relations of sense to other meaningful units. So, according to Husserl, persons are not only a central theme of our experience, they are originally experienced in *a holistic manner* that does not distinguish a mental layer and a physical layer but presents a unified whole, in which all layers are sensuous-spiritual.

Husserl's *Cartesian Meditations* develops this analysis further. In the "Fifth Meditation," Husserl points out that the other's conscious life and lived experiences are, necessarily, given to me in a manner different to that by which they are given to him. Whereas the other lives through her experiences, and I can capture her as an experiencing being, I cannot participate in her experiencing. When I see the other, or hear her talking, I intend the other's experiences, but this intention of mine remains unfulfilled, since the other's experiences cannot be given to me immediately and originarily (*originär*), but instead remain forever outside of my reach.[34]

To account for this particular mode of givenness, crucial to all our interpersonal relations and all relations that depend on interpersonal relations, the "Fifth Meditation" introduces a specific abstractive suspension that excludes from my experience everything that is alien to me or that has its constitutive origin in the other. Thus, we exclude all object-references that imply alien selves—for example, all reference to communal, historical, and cultural objects. We also exclude all references to intersubjective objective nature and its numerous parts, since this nature, being given equally to all, essentially entails reference to other selves. Husserl calls the reduced experiential realm thus achieved "the primordial sphere of ownness" (*Eigenheitssphäre*).[35] This is not any type of concrete experience but is a constitutive element of all concrete experiences abstractly separated from them.

In the primordial sphere of ownness, the other's body is given to me without an inner life or egoic determinants, as a mere sensory thing. Its thinghood is not the full-fledged thinghood that characterizes intersubjective objective nature, since that nature has been suspended by the abstractive step that isolates the sphere of ownness. The only body that, in this sphere, appears as a sensing and spontaneously moving thing is my own body. The space in which this body moves is not yet part of the objective world. Rather it is a spatial field organized around the body's central perceptual heres and the theres of its surroundings.[36] However, through the specific operation of transferring the senses of sensing, moving, and living in empathetic pairing, I end up experiencing the other body over there as a body that belongs to an *experiencing self* that is not me.[37]

The operation of sense-transference is not any kind of inference or reasoning. Rather than progressing via already constituted senses, it establishes a completely new sense, that of another living body, a body that belongs to another self. The transfer is motivated by the perceptual experience of similarity between my own bodily behavior and the behavior of the other body. In the progression of its movements and postures, as I perceive them, I recognize a stylistic form (*Stilform*) of moving that "is familiar" (*bekannt*) to me from my own relations to and with my own body. A body "over there," distinct from me in the sense that I cannot sense anything in it and cannot move it without first moving my own body (my arms, or my lips, tongue, and throat), moves in the manner similar to mine. It is not merely tossed around by the forces that work on all bodies around us but also spontaneously, and quite unexpectedly, takes distance from me or approaches me, turns to this or that direction, and responds to my movements in a rhythmic manner that leaves time for me to take my turn.[38] The recognition of similarity of movement allows me to grasp the parts of the other body as hands operating in touch*ing* and grasp*ing*, as feet operating in walk*ing*, as eyes operating in see*ing*, and as face operating in orientat*ing*.[39]

In the context of this explication, Husserl emphasizes that the body, thus perceived, *does not indicate* the other to me or *merely* signal his existence. Rather, the body is given to me as *belonging* to the other:

> If we stick to our de facto experience, our experience of someone else as it comes to pass at any time, we find that actually

the *sensuously seen body* is experienced forthwith as the body of someone else and not as merely an indication of someone else.[40]

It seems to me that Husserl's analysis is the following: If the body of another person would be given to me, in my concrete factual experience, merely or primarily as an indication of the other, as a mere signal of his existence, then he and his body would be separate, independent in their existence, and I could not really be perceptually related to him but would only know that he exists. But this is not the case. We touch others when we touch their bodies, we caress them or we molest them, and not just as some things that signal their existence to us.

Thus, the other's body is not given to me primarily in experience as an indicative sign, but is given as an expression and manifestation of him (not yet by him). And this means that these two phenomena—the person and the body of the person—are fused together in my experience with the same kind of intimacy or interdependence that characterizes the relation between verbal expressions and their meanings.[41] We do not have two somethings—a signaling body and a signaled meaning—but rather we have a whole in which meaning thoroughly permeates and informs what is given perceptually, so that no meaningless parts or layers of embodiment can be distinguished. This is why Husserl says that the other's body belongs (*gehören*) to the other, not in the sense of a possession or a property, but in the sense of a dependent moment. Its living form belongs to the wholeness of his life, and this is how I *experience* him.

This means that Heidegger is correct in pointing out that, in Husserl's account, our experience of other persons depends on the givenness of "bodies," in some sense of the term. But the bodies on which the possibility of this experience depends are not the bodies identified or identifiable in the natural attitude, or in the naturalistic or personalistic attitudes that the natural attitude grounds. The transcendental-phenomenological reduction and the reduction to the sphere of ownness have, together, suspended all such objectivities, so that what we are discussing are mere body-phenomena, which are given to a single self that functions independently of any objective or intersubjective sense of being. The spatial determinants of these "bodies" are not positions in natural, objective, or intersubjective space, since that space has been suspended.[42] Rather, these "bodies" are located as being *there*, relative to the central *here* that exclusively characterizes the body of the constituting self.

After the transfer of sense that establishes the sense of another self, this system of one single *here*, with an infinity of *theres*, is transformed into an open-ended system of other *heres* with their relative *theres*.[43] Thus we now have an experiential space that harbors multiple *here*-centers and that belong to several selves. In this intersubjective space, our own *here* is a *there* for all the other selves.

Conclusion

We have seen that, in Husserl's account, we can apprehend human beings in two different ways. We can understand them as layered psychophysical beings, but more fundamentally, we can experience them as comprehensive expressive wholes. Thus, two of Heidegger's critical remarks prove ill-founded. First, for Husserl, the human being is not a composite being but one unified being. Second, the expressive being of humans is a primary experiential fact and not any sort of construct. Even though we cannot live through the experiences of others and can originally grasp only our own experiences, we experience and perceive one another essentially and primarily as expressing beings with expressive living bodies.

Heidegger's third critical remark, the one on individuation, proves imprecise. According to Husserl, we do not individuate human persons on the basis of the positions of their bodies in objective intersubjective space but instead on the basis of the character of their movements. Movement, of course, is a bodily phenomenon, but, in Husserl's analysis, the crucial movements for the individuation of persons are expressive gestures and not physical processes or natural events.

Thus explicated, our experience of other people as bodily persons is a type of experience in its own right, irreducible to experiences of natural realities and equally irreducible to self-experiences—and nonanalyzable in either concept. This implies that Husserlian phenomenology is neither a hopeless confusion of natural and transcendental insights nor useless for the purposes of philosophical anthropology—contrary to what Heidegger's critical remarks may be seen as suggesting. What Husserl offers is a consistent explication of the being of humans as animated sensing-moving bodies, on the one hand, and as bodily persons, on the other hand. Most fundamentally, he argues, humans are given to us as bodily-spiritual wholes, and as such they relate to one another by sensuous-bodily expressions, by directed movements, signifying gestures, speech, and writing. This implies that any research into human beings, be it empirical or philosophical, depends on and is grounded in our experience of such expressive wholes—and of more comprehensive wholes composed of them.

Notes

1. Martin Heidegger, *Sein und Zeit*, 17th ed. (1927; Tübingen: Niemeyer, 1993), 47; in English, *Being and Time*, trans. John Macquarrie and Edward Robinson (Oxford: Blackwell, 1992), 72–73.

2. Steven Crowell, "Existentialism," in *The Stanford Encyclopedia of Philosophy*, ed. E. N. Zalta, Winter 2017 edition, https://plato.stanford.edu/archives/win2017/entries/existentialism/; cf. Kevin Aho, *Heidegger's Neglect of the Body* (New York: State University of New York Press, 2009), 7–10.

3. Heidegger, *Sein und Zeit*, 46; *Being and Time*, 72, translation modified.

4. Heidegger, *Sein und Zeit*, 48; *Being and Time*, 74, translation modified; cf. Heidegger, *Prolegomena zur Geschichte des Zeitbegriffs*, vol. 20 of *Gesamtausgabe*, ed. Petra Jaeger (Frankfurt: Klostermann, 1979), 180–81; in English, *History of the Concept of Time: Prolegomena*, trans. Theodore Kisiel (Bloomington: Indiana University Press, 1985), 129–30.

5. Both philosophers warn about the mistake of basing philosophical-phenomenological analyses on taken for granted categories of human life and existence. Both can also be interpreted as accusing one another of such mistakes. See Edmund Husserl, "Phänomenologie und Anthropologie," in *Aufsätze und Vorträge (1922–1937)*, vol. 27 of *Husserliana: Edmund Husserl Gesammelte Werke*, ed. Thomas Nenon and Hans Reiner Sepp (Dordrecht: Kluwer, 1989), 164–81; Martin Heidegger, "Letter on 'Humanism,'" trans. Frank A. Capuzzi, in *Pathmarks*, ed. William McNeil (Cambridge: Cambridge University Press, 1998), 239–76, esp. 253ff.

6. Heidegger, *Sein und Zeit*, 47–49; *Being and Time*, 73–75; cf. *Prolegomena zur Geschichte des Zeitbegriffs*, 170–75; *History of the Concept of Time*, 123–25. The critique that Heidegger targets against classical Husserlian phenomenology, in *Being and Time* and in his *History* lectures, is motivated by his analysis, according to which Husserl's thinking is seriously delimited by his rationalist epistemological commitments and thus preoccupied with problems of reason, cognition, theory, and science. See, for example, Heidegger, *Prolegomena zur Geschichte des Zeitbegriffs*, 146–48, 164–65, 177–80; *History of the Concept of Time*, 106–7, 119–20, 128–30. More specifically, the whole project is, in Heidegger's insight, led astray and distorted by modern rationalistic ideals of science and scientificity: mathematical preciseness, systematicity, and logicism. See, for example, Martin Heidegger, *Ontology: The Hermeneutics of Facticity*, trans. John van Buren (Bloomington: Indiana University Press, 1999), 56–57. Such preoccupations, Heidegger claims, lead to a distorted definition and partial analysis of intentionality, formulated by the concepts of thetic

acts, act performances, and purely active subjects. He also argues that Husserl's rationalistic preconception of philosophical inquiries entails a dichotomous and falsifying distinction between the transcendental and empirical aspects of existence, one that overlooks or disregards the singularity of Dasein. See, for example, Heidegger, *Prolegomena zur Geschichte des Zeitbegriffs*, 137–38; *History of the Concept of Time*, 100. Cf. Dermot Moran, "Heidegger's Transcendental Phenomenology in the Light of Husserl's Project of First Philosophy," in *Transcendental Heidegger*, ed. Steven Crowell and Jeff Malpas (Stanford, CA: Stanford University Press, 2007), 135–50, esp. 136–37; Eileen Brennan, "Hermeneutics and Phenomenology," in *The Blackwell Companion to Hermeneutics*, ed. Niall Keane and Chris Lawn (Malden, MA: Wiley, 2016), 461–70, esp. 461–63; Olli-Pekka Paananen, *Fenomenologia ja olemiskysymys: Heideggerin varhaisen Husserl-kritiikin vahvuudet ja rajat* [Phenomenology and the Question of Being: The Assets and Limits of Heidegger's Early Critique of Husserl] (Jyväskylä, FI: University of Jyväskylä, 2018), 62. For more comprehensive accounts of Heidegger's critique of Husserl, see the chapters by Niall Keane and Ingo Farin in this volume.

7. Heidegger, *Prolegomena zur Geschichte des Zeitbegriffs*, 173–74; *History of the Concept of Time*, 125. Husserl's early lectures on time-consciousness are published in vols. 10 and 33 of *Husserliana*. Cf. John B. Brough, "Husserl's Phenomenology of Time-Consciousness," in *Husserl's Phenomenology: A Textbook*, ed. William R. McKenna and Jitendra Nath Mohanty (Lanham, MD: University Press of America, 1989), 249–90; John B. Brough, "Time and the One and the Many (in Husserl's Bernauer Manuscripts on Time Consciousness)," *Philosophy Today* 46 (2002): 142–53; Toine Kortooms, *Phenomenology of Time: Edmund Husserl's Analysis of Time-Consciousness* (Dordrecht: Kluwer Academic, 2002); Lanei Rodemeyer, "Developments in the Theory of Time-Consciousness: An Analysis of Protention," in *The New Husserl: A Critical Reader*, ed. Don Welton (Bloomington: Indiana University Press, 2003), 125–56; Dan Zahavi, "Inner Time-Consciousness and Pre-reflective Self-awareness," in *The New Husserl: A Critical Reader*, 157–180; and Dan Zahavi, "Time and Consciousness in the Bernau Manuscripts," *Husserl Studies* 20, no. 2 (2004): 99–118.

8. Heidegger, *Sein und Zeit*, 47–48; *Being and Time*, 73, translation modified.
9. Cf. Olli-Pekka Paananen, *Fenomenologia ja olemiskysymys*, 44.
10. Heidegger, *Sein und Zeit*, 47n1; *Being and Time*, 72–73, 490nii.
11. Heidegger, *Sein und Zeit*, 47; *Being and Time*, 73.
12. Heidegger, *Prolegomena zur Geschichte des Zeitbegriffs*, 167, cf. 170–71; *History of the Concept of Time*, 120, cf. 122–23.
13. For an account of the relations of the Husserlian concepts of person and those of act and ego, see Sara Heinämaa, "Self—a Phenomenological Account: Temporality, Finitude and Intersubjectivity," in *Empathy, Intersubjectivity, and the Social World: The Continued Relevance of Phenomenology; Essays in Honour of Dermot Moran*, ed. Anna Bortolan and Elisa Magri (Berlin: De Gruyter, 2022).
14. Heidegger, *Sein und Zeit*, 48; *Being and Time*, 74.

15. Heidegger, *Prolegomena zur Geschichte des Zeitbegriffs*, 172; *History of the Concept of Time*, 124. Concluding emphasis added. Cf. Jan Patocka, *Body, Community, Language, World*, trans. Erazim Kohák, ed. James Dodd (1995; repr., Chicago: Open Court, 1998), 149, 178; James Dodd, introduction to *Body, Community, Language, World*, xxix.

16. Edmund Husserl, *Ideen zu einer reinen Phänomenologie und phänomenologischen Philosophie*, bk. 2, *Phänomenologische Untersuchungen zur Konstitution*, vol. 4 of *Husserliana: Edmund Husserl Gesammelte Werke*, ed. Marly Bimel (Haag: Martinus Nijhoff, 1952), 139–43, 172–75, 208–11; in English, Husserl, *Ideas Pertaining to a Pure Phenomenology and to a Phenomenological Philosophy*, bk. 2, *Studies in the Phenomenological Constitution*, trans. Richard Rojcewicz and André Schuwer (Dordrecht: Kluwer Academic, 1993), 147–50, 181–84, 219–22. Husserl, *Ideen zu einer reinen Phänomenologie und phänomenologischen Philosophie*, bk. 2, *Phänomenologische Untersuchungen zur Konstitution und Wissenschaftstheorie*, vol. 4/5 of *Husserliana: Edmund Husserl Gesammelte Werke*, ed. Dirk Fonfara (Haag: Springer, forthcoming), A part 2 H-manuscripts, §2, pp. 178–79, 185; §§5–6, pp. 201–17; §§9–10, pp. 226–30. Cf. Sara Heinämaa, "Embodiment and Bodily Becoming," in *The Oxford Handbook of the History of Phenomenology*, ed. Dan Zahavi (Oxford: Oxford University Press, 2018), 533–57; Dieter Lohmar, "Methodological Problems of Lifeworld Phenomenology in *The Crisis*," in *New Phenomenological Perspectives on the Crisis and the Life-World*, ed. Alexander Schnell, Hernán Inverso, and Guillermo Ferrer (Bern: Peter Lang, forthcoming).

17. Husserl, *Ideen*, bk. 2, vol. 4 of *Husserliana*, 173–74, 179–83; *Ideas*, bk. 2, 182–83, 189–93.

18. Husserl, *Ideen*, bk. 2, vol. 4 of *Husserliana*, 182–83; *Ideas*, bk. 2, 192–93.

19. For example, Husserl, *Ideen*, bk. 2, vol. 4 of *Husserliana*, 190–91; *Ideas*, bk. 2, 200–201; Edmund Husserl, *Erfahrung und Urteil: Untersuchung zur Genealogie der Logik*, ed. Ludwig Landgrebe (1939; Hamburg: Meiner, 1999), 29, 157ff.; in English, *Experience and Judgment: Investigations in a Genealogy of Logic*, trans. James Churchhill and Karl Ameriks (Evanston, IL: Northwestern University Press, 1973), 34, 137ff. Cf. Dan Zahavi, "Phenomenology and the Project of Naturalization," *Phenomenology and the Cognitive Sciences* 3 (2004): 331–47, esp. 340–42; Dan Zahavi, "Naturalized Phenomenology," in *Handbook of Phenomenology and Cognitive Science*, ed. Shaun Gallagher and Daniel Schmicking (Dordrecht: Springer, 2010), 3–21, esp. 10–13; Maria Villela-Petit, "Transcendental Theory of Knowledge," in *Naturalizing Phenomenology*, ed. Jean Petitot, Francisco J. Varela, Bernard Pachoud, and Jean-Michel Ray (Stanford, CA: Stanford University Press, 1999), 515ff.

20. Husserl, *Ideen*, bk. 2, vol. 4 of *Husserliana*, 183–84; *Ideas*, bk. 2, 193. Cf. Husserl, *Ideen*, bk. 2, vol. 4/5 of *Husserliana*, ed. Dirk Fonfara, A part 2 H-manuscripts, §9 p. 226; *Erfahrung und Urteil*, 38–45; *Experience and Judgment*, 42–46; *Die Krisis der europäischen Wissenschaften und die transzendentale Phänomenologie: Eine Einleitung in die phänomenologische Philosophie*, vol. 6 of *Husserliana: Edmund*

Husserl Gesammelte Werke, ed. Walter Biemel (Haag: Martinus Nijhoff, 1954), 244–45; in English, *The Crisis of European Sciences and Transcendental Phenomenology: An Introduction to Phenomenological Philosophy*, trans. David Carr (Evanston, IL: Northwestern University Press, 1988), 297. In *Experience and Judgment*, we read: "[F]or this world which is pregiven to us, we accept the following idea as a matter of course on the basis of modern tradition, namely, 'that the infinite totality of what is in general is intrinsically a rational all-encompassing unity that can be mastered, without anything left over, by a corresponding universal science.'" Quoted from Husserl, *Die Krisis der europäischen Wissenschaften*, vol. 6 of *Husserliana*, 20; *The Crisis of European Sciences*, 22. See *Erfahrung und Urteil*, 39–40; *Experience and Judgment*, 42.

21. Recent decades have witnessed the breakthrough of new synthetizing approaches in philosophy of mind that build on contemporary cognitive science, its naturalistic methodology and ontology, but aim at integrating also phenomenological results or, more ambitiously, the whole of phenomenology as a descriptive theory of lived experiences (*Erlebnisse*). See, for example, Jean-Michel Roy, Jean Petitot, Berndard Pachoud, and Francisco J. Varela, "Beyond the Gap: An Introduction to Naturalizing Phenomenology," in *Naturalizing Phenomenology*, 1–83. The ambitious aim of such programs is to naturalize not only the explanatory-predictive theories of behavior that operate by mental concepts—such as the concepts of belief, desire, emotion, action, agent, and person (i.e., human scientific concepts in Husserl's sense)—but also the results of phenomenological investigations into constitutive consciousness.

Husserl has two different types of arguments against such global approaches of naturalization. One argument concerns the possibility of naturalizing the sciences of the mind (psychology and the human-social sciences in general, for him). In this respect, he argues that what is properly intentional or mental ("spiritual," in his terms) cannot be mathematized. The problem is not merely about the limits and advances of the techniques of mathematization (formalization, axiomatization, or morphodynamical modeling) but, more fundamentally, about conceptualization and individuation: the unities and types thematized by these sciences cannot be defined or described by exact concepts. See, for example, Husserl, *Ideen zu einer reinen Phänomenologie und phänomenologischen Philosophie*, bk. 1, *Allgemeine Einführung in die reine Phänomenologie*, vol. 3 of *Husserliana: Edmund Husserl Gesammelte Werke*, ed. Walter Biemel (Haag: Martinus Nijhoff, 1913), 132–41; in English, *Ideas: General Introduction to Pure Phenomenology*, trans. W. R. Boyce Gibson (New York: Collier Macmillan, 1962), 184–93; *Ideen zu einer reinen Phänomenologie und phänomenologischen Philosophie*, bk. 3, *Die Phänomenologie und die Fundamente der Wissenschaft*, vol. 5 of *Husserliana: Edmund Husserl Gesammelte Werke*, ed. Marly Bimel (Haag: Martinus Nijhoff, 1952) 12–14, 20; *Ideen*, bk. 2, vol. 4/5 of *Husserliana*, ed. Dirk Fonfara, B, no. 7–8, pp. 430–41, 614–15. Cf. *Cartesianische Meditationen und Pariser Vorträge*, vol. 1 of *Husserliana: Edmund Husserl Gesammelte Werke*, ed. Stephan

Strasser (Haag: Martinus Nijhoff, 1950), 63–64; in English, *Cartesian Meditations*, trans. Dorion Cairns (Dordrecht: Martinus Nijhoff, 1960), 24–25.

The other argument concerns the possibility of naturalizing phenomenology itself. Here, the crucial point is that phenomenology is not just a descriptive eidetic science of consciousness or experiences but is, more fundamentally, a radically critical science that deals with the constitutive foundations of all sciences—human-social sciences and mathematized natural sciences—but also with pure grammar, pure mathematics and logics. In other words, Husserl argues that the defining tasks of phenomenology are transcendental and concern the constitution of sense (sense of being, value, goal). In this respect, any attempt at incorporating phenomenology into an explanatory-predictive science of the real or into a formal science of the ideal, or a set of such sciences, betrays a misunderstanding about its critical epistemological and ontological aims. See, for example, Husserl, *Cartesianische Meditationen und Pariser Vorträge*, vol. 1 of *Husserliana*, 65ff.; *Cartesian Meditations*, 26ff.; *Einleitung in die Logik und Erkenntnisstheorie, Vorlesungen, 1906/07*, vol. 24 of *Husserliana: Edmund Husserl Gesammelte Werke*, ed. Ulrich Melle (Dordrecht: Martinus Nijhoff, 1984), 409–411. Cf. Zahavi, "Phenomenology and the Project of Naturalization," 335ff.; "Naturalized Phenomenology," 5ff.

22. Cf. Husserl, *Ideen*, bk. 1, vol. 3 of *Husserliana*, 38; *Ideas*, 78.

23. For example, Husserl, *Ideen*, bk. 3, vol. 5 of *Husserliana*, 17–19. For explications of such positions, see, for example, Paul M. Churchland, *Matter and Consciousness*, rev. ed. (Cambridge, MA: MIT Press, 1988); Patricia S. Churchland, *Neurophilosophy: Toward a Unified Science of the Mind/Brain* (Cambridge, MA: MIT Press, 1986); Steven Stich, *From Folk Psychology to Cognitive Science: The Case against Belief* (Cambridge: Cambridge University Press, 1983); David Armstrong, *A Materialist Theory of the Mind* (London: Routledge, 1968); Herbert Feigl, *The "Mental" and the "Physical": The Essay and the Postscript* (Minneapolis: University of Minnesota Press, 1967). Cf. Roy, Petitot, Pachoud, and Varela, "Beyond the Gap," 63–72.

24. Husserl, *Ideen*, bk. 2, vol. 4 of *Husserliana*, 299; *Ideas*, bk. 2, 313.

25. Husserl, *Ideen*, bk. 2, vol. 4 of *Husserliana*, 301; *Ideas*, bk. 2, 315. Cf. *Ideen*, bk. 2, vol. 4/5 of *Husserliana*, ed. Dirk Fonfara, A part 2 H-manuscripts, §10 p. 229, app. 14, pp. 258–59; *Die Krisis der europäischen Wissenschaften*, vol. 6 of *Husserliana*, 222, 633; *The Crisis of European Sciences*, 218, 230; *Zur Phänomenologie der Intersubjektivität, Texte aus dem Nachlass, Dritter Teil 1929–35*, vol. 15 of *Husserliana: Edmund Husserl Gesammelte Werke*, ed. Iso Kern (Haag: Martinus Nijhoff, 1973), 99, 150.

26. In Husserl's account, the phenomenological epoché discloses the being of the transcendental self as a *transcendental fact* (*Cartesianische Meditationen und Pariser Vorträge*, vol. 1 of *Husserliana*, 104; *Cartesian Meditations*, 70). More precisely, the epoché, which suspends all worldly being, and the subsequent transcendental reduction, which focuses on the constitutive life of the disclosed self, both leave

our philosophical inquiries bound to one fact, the fact of our own transcendental self and its stream of purified experiences. These methods cannot, as such, liberate us from this one facticity. The fact of the disclosed self is, of course, not a worldly fact or any real fact about the world (which needs to be and remains suspended), but it is a transcendental fact. Despite its purity from worldly being, it is a contingent fact all the same (*Cartesianische Meditationen und Pariser Vorträge*, vol. 1 of *Husserliana*, 104–5; *Cartesian Meditations*, 70–71).

On this basis, Husserl argues that if phenomenology is to have universal value, it necessarily needs additional methodological tools that allow us to move forward from descriptions of the transcendentally purified experiences of one singular self. The needed additional method is that of *eidetic variation*. See *Cartesianische Meditationen und Pariser Vorträge*, vol. 1 of *Husserliana*, 103–6; *Cartesian Meditations*, 69–72. Cf. Maurice Merleau-Ponty, *Phénoménologie de la perception* (1945; Paris: Gallimard, 1993), ix, 430n1; in English, *Phenomenology of Perception*, trans. Collin Smith (London: Routledge, 1995), xiii–xiv, 336n1; Merleau-Ponty, *Le visible et l'invisible* (Paris: Gallimard 1964), 70–71; in English, *Visible and Invisible*, trans. Alphonso Lingis (Evanston, IL: Northwestern University Press, 1968), 45–46.

This means that Husserl does not light-heartedly, or due to his regional interest in the sciences of logic or mathematics, proceed to eidetic inquiries of consciousness, but is forced to develop the eidetic methods of pure phenomenology, since the epoché and the transcendental reduction, alone, cannot help produce any objectively valid general claims about the structures of experience or consciousness. The issuing eidetics of consciousness and experience is very different from the eidetics of mathematics or logic. It is material and not formal as the eidetics of logic and mathematics; and it does not deal with exact or ideal objectivities, as logic and mathematics do, but deals with the open manifolds of experience and the developing life of consciousness. See Husserl, *Ideen*, bk. 1, vol. 3 of *Husserliana*, 170–74; *Ideas*, 190–93.

27. Cf. Edmund Husserl, *Erfahrung und Urteil*, 313–14, 318–20; *Experience and Judgment*, 260–61, 265–66.

28. Husserl developed a concept of the *transcendental person* and defined it by the habituation of position-taking acts and commitments in immanent time. See, for example, Husserl, *Cartesianische Meditationen und Pariser Vorträge*, vol. 1 of *Husserliana*, 100ff.; *Cartesian Meditations*, 66ff.; *Ideen*, bk. 2, vol. 4 of *Husserliana*, 111–12; *Ideas*, bk. 2, 118–19; *Ideen*, bk. 2, vol. 4/5 of *Husserliana*, ed. Dirk Fonfara, B, no. 1, pp. 349–56. Cf. Sebastian Luft, "Husserl's Concept of the 'Transcendental Person': Another Look at the Husserl-Heidegger Relationship," *International Journal of Philosophical Studies* 13, no. 2 (2005): 141–77; Heinämaa, "Self—a Phenomenological Account."

29. For example, Husserl, *Ideen*, bk. 2, vol. 4 of *Husserliana*, 200; *Ideas*, bk. 2, 210. Cf. *Cartesianische Meditationen und Pariser Vorträge*, vol. 1 of *Husserliana*, 121ff.; *Cartesian Meditations*, 89ff.

30. Heidegger, *Prolegomena zur Geschichte des Zeitbegriffs*, 172; *History of the Concept of Time*, 124.

31. Husserl, *Ideen*, bk. 2, vol. 4 of *Husserliana*, 235–47, 320; *Ideas*, bk. 2, 248–57, 333. Cf. *Ideen*, bk. 2, vol. 4/5 of *Husserliana*, ed. Dirk Fonfara, A part 2 H-manuscripts, §6, p. 209; §7, pp. 220–21; B no. 3, pp. 361–62. Cf. also Sara Heinämaa, "Embodiment and Expressivity in Husserl's Phenomenology: From *Logical Investigations* to *Cartesian Meditations*," SATS–Northern European Journal of Philosophy 11, no. 1 (2010): 1–15.

32. Husserl, *Ideen*, bk. 2, vol. 4 of *Husserliana*, 240–41; *Ideas*, bk. 2, 253.

33. Husserl, *Ideen*, bk. 2, vol. 4 of *Husserliana*, 239; *Ideas*, bk. 2, 251. Cf. *Ideen*, bk. 3, vol. 5 of *Husserliana*, 18; *Zur Phänomenologie der Intersubjektivität*, vol. 15 of *Husserliana*, 86–88.

34. Husserl, *Cartesianische Meditationen und Pariser Vorträge*, vol. 1 of *Husserliana*, 143; *Cartesian Meditations*, 114. The basic idea is already explained in *Logical Investigations* as follows: "The hearer perceives the speaker as manifesting certain inner experiences, and to that extent he also perceives these experiences themselves; he does not, however, himself experience them, he has not an 'inner' but an 'outer' percept of them." See Husserl, *Logische Untersuchungen*, part 2, *Untersuchungen zur Phänomenologie und Theorie der Erkenntnis*, vol. 19 of *Husserliana: Edmund Husserl Gesammelte Werke*, ed. Ursula Panzer (Haag: Martinus Nijhoff, 1984), 41; in English, *Logical Investigations*, trans. J. N. Findlay, 2 vols. (London: Routledge and Kegan Paul, 1970), 190.

35. Husserl, *Cartesianische Meditationen und Pariser Vorträge*, vol. 1 of *Husserliana*, 124ff.; *Cartesian Meditations*, 92ff.

36. The heres and the theres of our original bodily organization come to operate as parts of objective space (cf. Malpas, *Place and Experience*, [Cambridge: Cambridge University Press, 2018], ch. two), but in Husserl's account, they can become such part only through the operation of intersubjective constitution. Before this, there is no objectivity in the sense "equally given for everyone," and thus there is no objective space either. So, our concrete fully constituted world-experience encompasses, as a constitutive element, a system of heres and theres that, prior to being taken up in intersubjective constitution, are not parts of any form of objectivity. As a constitutive element, this system can be abstractly distinguished from full-fledged worldly experience, but it is not an alternative world-relation.

37. Husserl, *Cartesianische Meditationen und Pariser Vorträge*, vol. 1 of *Husserliana*, 140ff.; *Cartesian Meditations*, 110ff.

38. Cf. Merleau-Ponty, *Phénoménologie de la perception*, 404; *Phenomenology of Perception*, 352.

39. Husserl, *Cartesianische Meditationen und Pariser Vorträge*, vol. 1 of *Husserliana*, 148; *Cartesian Meditations*, 119. Already in his *Logical Investigations*, in the seventh paragraph of the "First Investigation," Husserl emphasizes that the origin of

the expressive linguistic function is in the *relation between two persons*. He writes: "Expressions were *originally* framed to fulfil the communicative function. The articulate sound-complex [. . .] first becomes a spoken word [. . .] when the speaker produces it with the intention [*Absicht*] of 'uttering his thoughts about something' through its means. [. . .] Such a sharing becomes a possibility if the auditor also understands the speaker's intention [*Intention*]. And he does this inasmuch as he takes the speaker to be a person, who is not merely producing sounds but speaking to him." See Husserl, *Logische Untersuchungen*, part 2, vol. 19 of *Husserliana*, 39; *Logical Investigations*, 189. Translation modified, my emphasis. The point here is that we enter into verbal interchange only if we are able to see the other in a special way, that is, as a *person* with communicative interests, capacities, and potentialities. In other words, verbal communication and intimation about one's lived experiences is possible only on the condition that we take the other as a person, that is, as a being capable of experiencing and intending. Such an understanding, as Husserl explains it, "consists simply in the fact that the hearer intuitively takes the speaker to be a person who is expressing this or that, or as we certainly can say, perceives him as such." See *Logische Untersuchungen*, part 2, vol. 19 of *Husserliana*, 40; *Logical Investigations*, 189.

40. Husserl, *Cartesianische Meditationen und Pariser Vorträge*, vol. 1 of *Husserliana*, 150, cf. 151; *Cartesian Meditations*, 121, cf. 124.

41. Cf. Heinämaa, "Embodiment and Expressivity in Husserl's Phenomenology."

42. In Elisabeth Ströker, *Philosophische Untersuchungen zur Raum* (Frankfurt: Klostermann, 1965), 93, Ströker emphasizes a crucial aspect of Husserl's account of embodiment and spatiality: for Husserl, the constitutive grounding of all spatiality is sensory-intuitive and, ultimately, tactile kinaesthetic. See, for example, Husserl, *Ideen*, bk. 2, vol. 4 of *Husserliana*, 157–61; *Ideas*, bk. 2, 165–69; *Ideen*, bk. 2, vol. 4/5 of *Husserliana*, ed. Dirk Fonfara, A part 1 pencil manuscript, §50–54, pp. 364–68. Cf. Heinämaa, "Embodiment and Expressivity in Husserl's Phenomenology." Against this, Heidegger argues that our bodily-spatial being is fundamentally practical. See, for example, David Cerbone, "Heidegger and Dasein's 'Bodily Nature': What Is the Hidden Problematic?," *International Journal of Philosophical Studies* 8, no. 2 (2000): 209–30; Cristian Ciocan, "Heidegger's Phenomenology of Embodiment in the Zollikon Seminars," *Continental Philosophy Review* 48, no. 4 (2015): 463–78; Søren Overgaard, "Heidegger on Embodiment," *Journal of the British Society for Phenomenology* 35, no. 2 (2004): 116–31. Cf. Jeff Malpas, *Heidegger's Topology: Being, Place, World* (Cambridge, MA: MIT Press, 2006); Kevin Aho, *Heidegger's Neglect of the Body*; Steven Crowell, *Normativity and Phenomenology in Husserl and Heidegger* (Cambridge: Cambridge University Press, 2013).

43. Cf. Husserl, *Ideen*, bk. 2, vol. 4/5 of *Husserliana*, ed. Dirk Fonfara, A part 2 H-manuscripts, §4, p. 198.

Part II
Human Being, Otherness, and World

Chapter Five

Returning to Place
Retrieving the Human from "Humanism"

JEFF MALPAS

"It ought to be somewhat clearer now," writes Heidegger in the "Letter on 'Humanism,'" "that opposition to 'humanism' in no way implies a defence of the inhuman but rather opens other vistas."[1] But what are the other "vistas" that are opened by this opposition to humanism? In what does this opposition to humanism itself consist? And, to what extent might the opposition to humanism be a way of retrieving the human—a way that also looks to retrieve the proper place of the human and, in doing so, turn back to place itself?

The Place of the "Letter" in Heidegger's Thinking

Responding to a letter from Jean Beaufret, dated November 10, 1946, the "Letter on 'Humanism'" was published in 1947 in a partial French version,[2] as well as in German.[3] It was written in the December immediately following Beaufret's missive (also being revised prior to publication in 1947) and thus came after the de-Nazification proceedings against Heidegger and just before Heidegger's breakdown and subsequent convalescence.[4] Beaufret had put to Heidegger a series of questions provoked by Jean Paul Sartre's

1945 lecture "Existentialism Is a Humanism."[5] Heidegger hoped to be able to rehabilitate himself, and his thought, through an engagement with the great figure of French existentialism. Having failed in the attempt to communicate with Sartre directly, Heidegger's response to Beaufret provided an alternative path to the same end.

Robert Denoon Cumming provides a lengthy analysis of the circumstances of the writing of the "Letter," emphasizing the way the "Letter" is tied to the particularities of Heidegger's personal political and philosophical context.[6] Cumming talks about his own approach as a "localizing" of the work,[7] making reference to the idea of an *Erörterung* (which can itself mean "placing," but also "discussion"—Cumming translates it as "localizing discussion"). The focus on place and placing is reinforced by the way Heidegger himself orients the "Letter," taking the cue from Beaufret's question regarding "ethics" to focus on *ethos*—which Heidegger tells us means "sojourn, dwelling-place" (*Aufenthalt*). Cumming, who also draws attention to this topological focus, connects it with Heidegger's greeting to Jaspers on the latter's eightieth birthday in 1963: "May you be able to arrive at [*gelangen*] and abide there [*verweilen*], where your thinking has established a sojourn [*Aufenthalt*] for meditation."[8] Despite the attention he gives to these matters, however, Cumming says little about the thematization of place as that occurs in the "Letter." Yet it is quite clear that place plays an important role that goes well beyond its significance for any mere historical contextualization.

For all that it can indeed be read as against the background of Heidegger's own attempt to rehabilitate himself in the wider philosophical world, the "Letter on 'Humanism' " is also part of the rehabilitation of Heidegger's thinking *for its own sake* as it emerges out of the difficulties of the previous decade or more—out of the difficulties that stem, in no small part, from *Being and Time* and from both the success and the failure of that work. This "rehabilitation" is also a "re-habitation," which can be understood as the finding again of, or a returning to, the proper place or *habitus* to which Heidegger's thinking belongs—a process that can perhaps be seen as having already begun in the *Contributions*, in 1936, and the continuation of which is evident in the *Black Notebooks*. In this respect, Cumming's invocation of the notion of *Aufenthalt*, in the context of the 1946 "Letter," seems entirely correct and highly relevant, even though Cummings does not read it in quite the way suggested here. It is in the period from the "Letter" onwards that it becomes evident just how important place is for Heidegger, not only to his thinking of and with Hölderlin, or to his thinking of poetry and art, but to his thinking of being itself, and in a way that is no longer tied to the national-historical (as was the case for much of the 1930s and earlier 1940s). Moreover, as Heidegger's thinking becomes more explicitly topological, so Heidegger comes more clearly to reject, or at least significantly to modify, some of the concepts and modes of approach of his earlier thinking—and not only those of *Being and Time*.

Returning to Place

The "Letter on 'Humanism'" clearly represents a watershed in Heidegger's thinking. It is one of the key markers along the path of his thinking—hence its appearance in the volume *Pathmarks* (*Wegmarken*). The "Letter" represents, in fact, a key point in the shift that had been underway in Heidegger's thinking since at least the early to mid-1930s, and that has its origins in the failure of *Being and Time* (and not only in the failure of the shift within that work from division 2 to division 3, but the failure that consists in the work's own inability adequately to make the shift to the topological to which it is nevertheless already committed⁹). It is this shift—which is no mere reversal, but rather a turning back, a *returning*, to the very place of thinking, and so it is also a *reorienting*—that is part of what is at issue in the so-called *Kehre*, the "turn" or "reversal," that Heidegger himself refers to in the "Letter." As he puts it there, the turn at issue is "not a change of standpoint from *Being and Time*, but in it the thinking that was sought first arrives at the locality of that dimension [*die Ortschaft der Dimension*] out of which *Being and Time* is experienced [. . .]."¹⁰

Kehre is an equivocal term in Heidegger's thought and its meaning can neither be captured in any single, unique specification nor in any single systematic framework.¹¹ There is no single "turn" in Heidegger, but several, and many of them overlap with and shade into one another. Even the turn that occurs in the form of the shift in Heidegger's thinking from the 1930s to the 1940s does not take the form of a single "reversal" but an extended movement whose course can be mapped across several important points, from "The Essence of Truth," to the *Contributions*, to the "Letter on 'Humanism'" itself. Moreover, the fact of such a turning in Heidegger's thinking is not some contingent feature of his intellectual biography. It corresponds to Heidegger's own attempt to follow the turning of being itself. And that turning is a turning that belongs to thinking no less than to being, and to the thinking of the thinker no less than to the thinking of the tradition or of thinking as such. It is no accident that this idea of "turning" has a spatial sense to it—a sense of turning round or back. The turning is, as Joseph Fell points out,[12] a turning that belongs to place—to *topos* or *Ort*—and so a turning of and in place, as well as a turning back to that place.

The shift in Heidegger's thinking that is at issue in the "Letter" is a turn toward the explicit focus on and explication of what he calls *die Topologie des Seyns*—the "topology of being." The place or *topos* at issue here is the place that belongs to thinking as well as the place that belongs to being.[13] Indeed, on my account—and, I would say, on Heidegger's—being and place belong essentially together. The phrase "topology of being" does not appear in the "Letter" itself. But it does appear in a line from one of the poems in *Aus der Erfahrung des Denkens* from 1947 (not published until 1954): "[T]he poetry that thinks is in truth the topology of being,"[14] and it also appears several times in the pages of the *Black Notebooks* from the same year (where it occurs along with other key phrases such as "place of beyng"—*Ortschaft des Seyns*). The phrase is thus contemporaneous with the "Letter" and directly connected to the thinking the "Letter" attempts.

Heidegger's concern with the place of thinking—and so with topology—must not be read as if it were simply a way of speaking of the contextual situatedness of thought or of the situatedness of any interpretive engagement with thinking. The notions of context and of interpretive situation themselves carry a topological significance. Not only is that significance routinely overlooked or ignored, however, but in this case to treat what is at issue as primarily about such notions is to step back from the more fundamental topology to which Heidegger's language here directs us. The place of thinking is indeed the very place of being—and this is necessarily so given that the inquiry into being can proceed only by means of an inquiry that also attends to that which thinking itself *is*. The question of being already contains the question of thinking within it just as the question of thinking carries within it the question of being. The intimate connection between the question of the place of thinking and the place of being is made quite explicit by Heidegger himself, and no more so than in the *Black Notebooks*. There he writes: "How should we attend to the carrying forward of the condition of thinking [*des Standes der Denkenden*], if we don't know the place [*die Ortschaft dieses Standes*] of this condition? This place is the truth of being [*Wahrheit des Seyns*]"—and he asks: "Who today are still wandering [*auf die Wanderschaft*] in this place?"[15]

Place and the Human

Once place is seen as a central concept, and the turning is understood as a turning to place, then one can more clearly see why it might indeed be that the human (which is never in Heidegger a merely *biological* notion but always *ontological*[16]) cannot be given primacy here. The human is essentially placed—stands in an essential relation to the *Da* (it is this relation that is constitutive of the human)—and yet the being-placed of the human, being placed as such, is not identical with place as such. This point was already evident, although differently put, in *Being and Time* and, especially, in the *Kantbuch* of 1929. In the latter work Heidegger makes the claim that "[m]ore original than man is the finitude of Dasein in him,"[17] and already this can be seen to prefigure the argument of the "Letter" even though it makes no explicit reference to humanism as such. It is this claim, and together with it, Heidegger's rejection of the Kantian claim for the priority of philosophical anthropology that was the focus for Martin Buber's critique of Heidegger in *Between Man and Man*[18] (and one can find sympathy for Buber's position at the same time as one can also understand the point of Heidegger's[19]). Similarly, in the *Contributions*, Heidegger again emphasizes the priority of Da-sein (the hyphenation reinforcing its topological character) over the human, rejecting any reading that would prioritize the human as *subject*:

> If *Being and Time* says that what first becomes determinable through the "existential analytic" is the being of non-human being, then this does not mean the human being would be what is given primarily and first of all and would be the measure according to which all other beings receive the stamp of their being. Such an "interpretation" assumes that the human being is *still* to be understood as understood by Descartes and by all his followers and mere opponents (even Nietzsche is one of the latter), namely, as a subject.[20]

And he goes on in a way that both echoes his earlier discussions as well as presaging what is to come in the "Letter"—including the turn toward place here expressed both in terms of the focus on Da-sein and the "realm" [*Bereich*] that is the "clearing of beyng":

> The very first task, however, is precisely to discontinue postulating the human being as a subject and to grasp this being

> primarily and exclusively on the basis of the question of being. If, despite everything, Da-sein does gain the priority, then that means humans, grasped in terms of Da-sein, grasp their essence and their proprietorship [*Eigentumschaft*] of their essence on the projection of being and thereby, in all comportment and restraint, keep themselves to the realm of the clearing of beyng. This realm is nevertheless utterly non-human [*unmenschlich*], i.e., it cannot be determined and borne by the *animal rationale* and just as little by the *subjectum*. This realm is not at all a being; instead, it belongs to the essential occurrence of beyng. [. . .] The priority of Da-sein is not merely contrary to every sort of anthropologizing of the human being; it even grounds a completely different history of the essence of the human being, a history that could never be grasped by metaphysics or, consequently, by anthropology. This does not exclude, but rather includes, the fact that the human being now becomes even *more* essential for beyng though at the same time less important with respect to "beings."[21]

In summary terms, one might say that although the question of being is only *approached* through the question of the human (since it always implicates the question of the being of the one who questions), the question of being cannot be *reduced* to the question of the human: *being, even the being of the human, is not self-identical with the human*. Moreover, once the nature of the question of being is recognized, and so also the proper relation of human being to that question, then one is forced to recognize that what comes first here is the clearing of being, the "there" of being, in which even human being comes first to find itself.

Rather than thinking "the human" as if it were indeed some primal phenomenon—as if it were that from which all other phenomena flow—we must think *the place* of the human, but that means first thinking *place* itself. Thinking the essence of the human means thinking place, because the being of the human is essentially placed being—it is a being given over to the "there," to the place, as Heidegger emphasizes almost from the very start.[22] This place is not merely to be identified with the place *of* the human as if it were a place already determined *as* human. To take such an approach would indeed be to retain the commitment to a prior conception of the human when not only is the human that which is itself open to question, but such questionability always remains central to the human. It is thus that humanism must already appear as problematic from the start inasmuch as it depends on assuming that which remains obscure, namely, the human itself, as if the human were something already settled. Moreover, in doing this, it effectively takes place, which must include the place that belongs to the human, as itself determined by the human and only in relation to the human. In contrast, the human must be understood as determined *from place* and not place *from the human*—and this is so even though understanding can only approach place from and through the human and the place of the human. The focus on the human is not lost in this turning back to the prior question of the being—or the place—of the human (since the human does not stand apart from its own being even though it is not simply identical with it). Instead, the question of the human is thereby given greater clarity and precision.

From Truth to Ethics

I have emphasized the continuity of the "Letter" with Heidegger's earlier thinking, and so also the continuity of Heidegger's concern with the human, even as I have also singled out the "Letter" as marking a key point in the shift in Heidegger's thinking toward a more explicitly topological orientation. In this respect, what occurs in the "Letter" is a certain sort of recapitulation, as well as a clarification and explication, of Heidegger's previous thinking as much as it also points toward, and may even be said to set the framework for, what comes after. The "Letter" stands in a particularly important relation to the essay from 1940 (which itself goes back to a lecture course of 1931), "Plato's Doctrine of Truth,"[23] and the relation is especially illuminating since it helps to illuminate the continuity that is at issue here.

"Plato's Doctrine of Truth" concerns itself with a theme that is already presaged in *Being and Time*, the question of truth. The essay ends, however, with a brief discussion of humanism and the assertion of the identity of the beginning of metaphysics with the beginning of humanism—both have their origin in the movement of human beings to a central place among beings. Yet "Plato's Doctrine of Truth" also takes as its focus an examination of what Plato presents to us as "the place of our dwelling which (in an everyday way) is revealed to us as we look around."[24] Not only is this place shown to be a place of illusion—so that our place turns out to be a place of imprisonment in which we are already cut off from what is real, cut off, one might say, from being—but that place allows access to the real through understanding it as being that which is only secondarily real. Truth is dependent, on this account, on our relatedness to what lies beyond and outside of the place in which we immediately find ourselves. Heidegger's own thinking of truth can be interpreted as a thinking that attends, no less than does Plato, to the "place of our dwelling," but unlike Plato, Heidegger takes truth to belong to this very place.

As is evident from his discussions of truth elsewhere, understood as *aletheia*, truth is not some relation to what lies beyond or outside, instead it arises in the play of hiddenness and unhiddenenss to which we are already given over—in the play of that place in which we already find ourselves. Once again, however, it is important to emphasize that this place, even though it is grasped only in and through our human being in place, is not a place that is derived from the human nor is it reducible to the human. It stands apart from the human even though it also belongs with it.

The relation between human being and the place of being is one that Heidegger describes, in the "Letter" and elsewhere, in terms of the idea of *Wohnen*, usually (if inadequately) translated as "dwelling." *Wohnen* is a term that already appears in *Being and Time* (as Heidegger points out in the "Letter"),[25] and *Wohnen* is also a term that has to be read as already implicated with the thinking of place. To be "in" a place is not, as Heidegger argues in *Being and Time*, a matter of mere spatial containment—the human being is not in place like one Russian doll inside another—and neither is place itself identical with simple location. *Wohnen* implies place, since "to dwell" is precisely to stand in a certain relation to place. It is a relation of the sort that is partly what Heidegger refers to in *Being and Time* as *Care* (*Sorge*). Consequently, even though this is not all that is at issue, we can say that "to dwell" is to attend and respond to place.

However, the relation that arises in dwelling is not merely one that requires a certain response or responsiveness on the part of human beings nor does it consist in such responsiveness. Fundamentally, dwelling is to be understood as encompassing the character of human being as indeed already standing in a relation to place—as essentially *placed*. Our own "care" in respect of place is derivative of this. This prior relatedness to place can be understood in terms of the dependence of human being on place: not merely in the sense that human lives are shaped by the places in which they are lived, but in the sense that it is only in and through place that human lives take on any shape at all—that they appear as human.

Such dependence is not diminished by the fact that place itself, the clearing of being, emerges only in relation to language, and so in relation to human being—the being of human being is inextricably bound to language. The primary event here, however, is not the appearing *of human* being, but *of being*, which is then only grasped in relation to human being. *Wohnen* is thus the term Heidegger comes to use to describe the mode of being that is human and that emerges in the event of being itself—it is also Heidegger's response, one might say, to the difficult question of the relation of being to human being. Human being, mortal being, plays a necessary role in the event of being, and yet it is not that in which the event of being is itself founded.

Towards the end of the "Letter" the question of human being is raised directly in relation to the question concerning the possibility of a fundamental *ethics* that might correlate with a fundamental *ontology*. Heidegger responds by asserting that

> [*e*]*thos* means abode, dwelling place. The word names the open region in which the human being dwells. The open region of his abode allows what pertains to the essence of human being, and what in thus arriving resides in nearness to him, to appear. [. . .] If the name "ethics," in keeping with the basic meaning of the word *ethos*, should now say that ethics ponders the abode of the human being, then that thinking which thinks the truth of being as the primordial element of the human being, as one who eksists, is in itself originary ethics.[26]

Ethics here is not treated as the realm of prescriptive principle, but rather concerns a recognition of our own prior belonging. Such a view leads on to a very different concept of the ethical than is usually the case—one that brings us closer to the later thinking of *Gelassenheit*—though not in the sense of a mere quietism so much as of an *attentive responsiveness*. Exactly what such a topological "ethics" might entail requires much more elaboration, but it certainly cannot be taken to simply converge with any form of reactionary politics or with any refusal of ethical concerns.[27]

The Critique of "Humanism"

Heidegger's critique of humanism, no less than his topology, is not some later intrusion into his thinking, but has its origins in the very nature of that thinking—in its very focus on the question of being. The critique of humanism is thus almost as central to Heidegger's thinking as is the question of being itself. Moreover, as the latter question increasingly comes to be understood as a question concerning the *place* of being, so what also emerges is the question concerning the place of the human—of that wherein humans "dwell." That the critique of humanism is indeed close to the center of Heidegger's thought is particularly important given the way in which that critique might otherwise be seen as suggesting some connection back to Heidegger's entanglement in Nazism. In fact, Heidegger's anti-humanism predates that, and, one might argue, is itself incompatible with the "German political humanism" that Alfred Rosenberg, as Karsten Harries reports matters, took to be associated with Nazism.[28]

In this latter respect, however, even though Heidegger's anti-humanism is a feature of his early as well as later work, the way the critique of humanism is developed in the 1946 "Letter" can be seen as containing within it an implicit critique of some of Heidegger's own earlier ideas—including ideas bound up with his own espousal of Nazism. If Heidegger's own seduction by ideology is one of the concerns to which the *Black Notebooks* may be thought to give rise, then far from being some continuation of any such ideological seduction, Heidegger's critique of humanism is implicitly a critique and rejection of ideology itself—and this remains so even though we also need to beware of the limitations of Heidegger's capacity to carry this critique through to his own self-understanding. The critique of humanism is thus a critique of those "-isms," those "ideologies," of which "humanism" is perhaps the most significant and encompassing, that bedevil thought.

The sense of "humanism" at issue here can be said to include not only most of the traditional "humanisms" with which we are familiar (although Grassi, for one, would contest whether it properly applies to the humanism of Renaissance thought[29]), but also those "subjectivisms" that, one way or another, take the human or the realm of the human as primary—that, as Heidegger puts it, make the human "the measure." Of these, perhaps the most pervasive contemporary examples are "constructionism," which takes all phenomena, inasmuch as they are taken up by the human, as essentially *produced* by the "human" (the human as given in terms of the social and political) and also "scientism" or "objectivism," which reassert the primacy of the human through their very neglect, even refusal, of it and of that to which the question of the human itself points.

Perhaps even more noteworthy, however, is the widespread currency of the notion of the Anthropocene (a notion that now seems uncritically accepted across much of contemporary academia), since it demonstrates how humanism may remain as an element even in what might otherwise be viewed as a form of anti-humanism. The idea of the Anthropocene reinforces the core idea of modern humanism, namely, that the world *is subject to the human*—so much so in this case that the age of the world comes to be *named in terms of the human*. To take issue with the idea of the Anthropocene in this way is to take issue, not with the cataclysmic environmental impact of human activity to which it supposedly draws attention, but rather to the very subjectification of the world of which environmental catastrophe is itself a consequence.

For some, of course, the claim that humanism might be in any significant way problematic, that it might even be an ideology that can be connected to Nazism itself, will appear to be a dangerous and reactionary idea, and, so far as Heidegger is concerned, even to obscure the real extent of Heidegger's own political culpability.[30] Yet to be a critic of humanism is not to be a Nazi, just as to be a critic of liberalism is not, by that very fact, to be a fascist—or even a conservative. Moreover, neither humanism nor liberalism (nor either constructionism or scientism) offer an unequivocally benign face. Indeed, one of the lessons of the twentieth-century, and of the nineteenth before it as of the twenty-first after it, is that both humanism and liberalism can have anti-human and even anti-liberal consequences, may even take on anti-human and anti-liberal forms. From the perspective of the analysis offered in the "Letter," it is precisely the metaphysical character of humanism, which also means its subjectivism, that underlies the equivocal character of humanism—and that one might argue underpins all ideologies, all "-isms." The critique of humanism is thus itself directly tied to both the practice of and the inquiry into thinking—Heidegger's own thinking no less than thinking itself. The critique of humanism is an attempt more clearly to think what thinking *is*, and therefore, necessarily, to think the *place* of thinking—a task carried on, most obviously perhaps, in *What Is Called Thinking?* in which similar themes take center stage, and in which, even if humanism is not so directly taken up, there is also a clear focus on the problems of subjectivism and the prioritization of the human.

Place and Its Forgetting

Why, given that the topological character of Heidegger's thinking by the time of the "Letter" is so self-evident, has this character been so consistently and continually overlooked or ignored? That it is overlooked and ignored seems clear. Within the existing Heidegger scholarship only a handful of thinkers have taken seriously the role of topology in Heidegger's thinking, and even fewer have attended to the topology present in the "Letter on 'Humanism.'" Even when the topological language Heidegger employs is pointed out or noticed, the tendency is invariably to treat it as "metaphorical" or "figurative." Yet such a response is to disregard Heidegger's own explicit warnings against such an approach—in the "Letter" and elsewhere. As Heidegger comments in relation to the famous claim that "language is the house of being":

> Thinking builds upon the house of being, the house in which the jointure of being, in its destinal unfolding, enjoins the essence of the human being in each case to dwell in the truth of being. This dwelling is the essence of "being-in-the-world." The reference in *Being and Time* (p. 54) to "being-in" as "dwelling" is not some etymological play. The same reference in the 1936 essay on Hölderlin's word, "Full of merit yet poetically, man dwells upon this earth," is not the adornment of a thinking that rescues itself from science by means of poetry. The talk about the house of being is not the transfer of the image "house" onto being. But one day, we will, by thinking the essence of being in a way appropriate to its matter, more readily be able to think what "house" and "dwelling" are.[31]

This passage not only draws attention to the topological elements in Heidegger's thinking—and reinforces the claim that those elements are already present in *Being and Time*—but it also makes explicit the point that this topology is not to be passed off as peripheral, merely "playful," or indeed as metaphorical (as the explicit rejection of the idea of the "transfer" of the image of "house" indicates).

The tendency, when it is not simply overlooked, to treat Heidegger's topological language as metaphorical is symptomatic of a widespread and deeply rooted tendency on the part of philosophers to disregard the placed character of thinking, even of their own thinking, and to view place, if it is attended to at all, as a secondary, derivative, and largely irrelevant concept whose ubiquity is simply a consequence of the ubiquity of topological and spatial metaphors more generally. Philosophical thinking thus draws constantly on the language of place and yet equally constantly disregards it. It is characteristic of Heidegger's thinking—even though it might be thought to rely centrally on a range of metaphors (and especially those of space and place), that it refuses any metaphoric readings. As such, it insists that we pay attention to the way in which the topographic itself, and the images and ideas associated with it, is at work; it requires that we do indeed "listen to language,"[32] and so attend what is given in the very Saying of language.

The refusal of metaphor—or, at least, of metaphor as it is conventionally contrasted with the literal, and so of metaphor as that which takes us away from the immediately given—does not entail the insistence on some simple linguistic univocity or determinacy. Heidegger's language is not metaphorical in this sense, and yet it always retains an essential multivocity. In Heideggerian terms, one might say that is part of the very essence of language *as* language. If there is a problem that attaches to language—a lack, neediness, or distress of language (*Sprachnot*)—then it is a lack or neediness that arises from the tendency to forget the character of language as Saying, and so also to reduce language to a mere "instrument," to a system of symbols, or even to a "calculus." This is an ever-present danger in the contemporary world in which language is always in danger of being emptied out, and so of being removed from the proper place in which the Saying of language sounds and resounds. In his lectures on Hölderlin's *Remembrance*, Heidegger writes: "It is enough here to consider just this: 'things themselves,' before any so-called 'symbols,' are already poetized."[33] If we fail to attend to the way place appears in the "Letter," not as a metaphor, but as an originary phenomenon in itself, then we will fail to understand what is at issue in the critique of humanism, and in the insistence of looking beyond the human alone.

To talk of "vistas" is already to speak in a way that envisions a landscape that is opened before one. The "Letter on 'Humanism'" opens just such a landscape. It is, moreover, a landscape that belongs to thinking—it is the landscape of thinking, thinking's very place—and so it is the landscape that belongs to the explicit topology of Heidegger's later thinking (but which can be read back into the earlier). It is this landscape that opens before us when we move beyond the narrow thinking of traditional humanism and the subjectivism of metaphysics. Yet the opening of this landscape is not the opening of a landscape that bypasses or transcends the human. It is rather the landscape in which the human belongs, the landscape of dwelling, and so is the landscape in which the human first appears properly *as human* (as Heidegger says in the Kantbuch of 1929, "[M]an is man only on the grounds of the Dasein in him" or, as it might be rephrased, the human is human only on the grounds of its being-placed). What is essential to the thinking of place is the thinking of appearance as arising only in bounded openness, and this is what surely also lies at the heart of human being. To be human is to find oneself always and only in the "there." It is not the power of the human, but the fragility and finitude of human being, and this is directly connected to the topological character of the human. It is thus through the turn back to place that a turn back to the human is possible. If this is not always fully recognized in Heidegger (and to what extent it is so recognized is arguable on both sides), then this only shows how much all thinkers remain to some extent blind to the full implications of their thought.

The Retrieval of the Human

The critique of "humanism" appears in its most explicit form in the "Letter," and there is no similarly developed critique nor any extended discussion of the term elsewhere in Heidegger's published writings.[34] Yet what is at issue in the critique of "humanism" is clearly at work in Heidegger's early and later thinking. The critique of "humanism" is directly tied to Heidegger's concern to find a way back to the question of being that he also comes to understand as a question about the place of being. That question of being and of place is seen to come prior to the question of the human, even though it is approached through the human, and even though it returns us back to the question of human.

The critique of "humanism" is closely tied to the critique of technological modernity that is also present in the early work but develops in more refined form in the later. That critique is one in which, once again, topological elements are central—the nature of modern technology is most evident in the way it seemingly brings about a change in the character of the near and the far, in the character of space, of time, and of place. This follows necessarily from the fundamental nature of the connection between being and place—to understand technological modernity in ontological terms, it must also be understood in topological terms, since the topology of being is what ontology becomes once the relation of being and place is acknowledged. Humanism plays a central role in the development of technological modernity, and yet it does so in a complex fashion. Part of this complexity resides in the fact that technological modernity seems to set the human at the center and yet at the same time it subjugates even the human, reduces the human to that which is inhuman. The loss of the human, which occurs even in and through humanism itself, is a large part of what preoccupies Heidegger in the "Letter" and elsewhere—and especially in the late essays in which place is so directly taken up.

To what extent does Heidegger's anti-humanism tend Heidegger's thinking toward a reactionary politics? In spite of the claims that are regularly made asserting such a connection (as they also assert a connection between such a politics and the focus on place), it seems to me doubtful whether any real sense can be attached to this question. The connections between ideas are more complex than such a claim seems to presuppose, and the fact that certain ideas may, in some contexts, be taken to lead to one set of outcomes, but elsewhere to another, is indicative of both the indeterminacy that is characteristic of thought, and the uncertain and serendipitous character of human lives. In an important sense, Heidegger's anti-humanism ought to imply a rejection of the politics that has traditionally been associated with both the left and the right. It certainly ought to force us to a more critical examination of "humanism" and its contemporary perpetuations.

Notes

1. Martin Heidegger, "Letter on 'Humanism,'" trans. Frank A. Capuzzi, in *Pathmarks*, ed. William McNeill (Cambridge: Cambridge University Press, 1998), 265.

2. The first, but incomplete, French version appeared in Heidegger, "Lettre a Jean Beaufret (Fragment)," *Fontaine* 63 (November 1947): 786–804. The complete version was not published in French until 1953, when it appeared in *Cahiers du Sud*, no. 319 (1953): 385–406; and *Cahiers du Sud*, no. 320 (1953): 68–88. The first version in English is Heidegger, "Letter on 'Humanism,'" trans. Edgar Lohner, in *Philosophy in the Twentieth Century*, ed. William Barrett and Henry D. Aiken, vol. 3 (New York: Random House, 1962), 270–302.

3. Martin Heidegger, *Platons Lehre von der Wahrheit; mit einem Brief über den "Humanismus"* (Bern: Francke, 1947).

4. See Andrew J. Mitchell, "Heidegger's Breakdown: Health and Healing under the Care of Dr. V. E. von Gebsattel," *Research in Phenomenology* 46, no. 1 (2016): 70–97.

5. Presented October 29, 1945, and first published as Jean-Paul Sartre, *L'Existentialisme est un humanisme* (Paris: Nagel, 1946).

6. See Robert Denoon Cumming, *Phenomenology and Deconstruction*, vol. 4, *Solitude* (Chicago: University of Chicago Press, 2001).

7. Cumming, *Phenomenology and Deconstruction*, vol. 4, *Solitude*, 72.

8. Martin Heidegger and Karl Jaspers, *Briefwechsel, 1920–1963*, ed. Walter Biemel and Hans Saner (Frankfurt: Klostermann, 1990), 216. Quoted in Cumming, *Phenomenology and Deconstruction*, vol. 4, *Solitude*, 82.

9. See Jeff Malpas, *Heidegger's Topology: Being, Place, World* (Cambridge, MA: MIT Press, 2006), ch. 2.

10. Heidegger, "Letter on 'Humanism,'" 249–50. See also Heidegger, "Brief über den 'Humanismus,'" in *Wegmarken*, vol. 9 of *Gesamtausgabe*, ed. Friedrich-Wilhelm von Herrmann (Frankfurt: Klostermann, 1976), 328.

11. Thomas Sheehan's criticism of the standard reading of the "turn," as referring to the shift from early to later Heidegger, and his own attempt to supply a systematic account of the multiple senses of "turn," or *Kehre*, as it figures in Heidegger—see Sheehan, *Making Sense of Heidegger: A New Paradigm* (London: Rowman and Littlefield, 2015), 238–45—seems misconceived from the very start. That *Kehre* is a complex and equivocal term is not something that most commentators have ever denied or ignored. Certainly, William J. Richardson's treatment even of the *Kehre*, as it figures in the shift from the early to late thinking (and in whose work the idea of a turn or reversal between early and later Heidegger—between "Heidegger I" and "Heidegger II," as Richardson has it—is first addressed in an English commentary), is in no way dependent on some univocal meaning attaching to the term. See William J. Richardson, *Through Phenomenology to Thought* (The Hague: Martinus Nijhoff, 1963), 623–41. See also Richardson's references to the "reversal" that appears in Rilke, in *Through Phenomenology to Thought*, 396–99. Moreover, the manner of Sheehan's own approach means that he is unable to encompass the way the term belongs to the larger topological context of Heidegger's thought overall, at the same time as Sheehan's own systematized approach effectively threatens to impose an analytic unity onto the idea that is antithetical to the very character of Heidegger's approach. Sheehan's *Making Sense of Heidegger* is certainly an impressive undertaking, and it is a valuable resource for the detailed investigation of the Heideggerian texts, but whether it delivers any genuinely new or significant insight into Heidegger's thinking and the matters with which it engages is arguable at best.

12. See Joseph Fell, *Heidegger and Sartre: An Essay on Being and Place* (New York: Columbia University Press, 1979), 200–204. Note also Fell's comment that "the *Kehre* is perhaps best understood as a continuing event, a protracted process of 'remembering' the place displaced" (208).

13. On this, see my discussion in Jeff Malpas, "The Anthropology of the World," ch. 2 in *In the Brightness of Place* (Albany: State University of New York Press, 2023).

14. Martin Heidegger, *Aus der Erfahrung des Denkens*, vol. 13 of *Gesamtausgabe*, ed. Hermann Heidegger (Frankfurt: Klostermann, 1983), 84. Originally published in 1954 by Neske (Pfullingen). Published in English as "The Thinker

as Poet," in *Poetry, Language, Thought*, trans. Albert Hofstadter (New York: Harper and Row, 1971), 12.

15. Martin Heidegger, *Anmerkungen I–V (Schwarze Hefte 1942–1948)*, vol. 97 of *Gesamtausgabe*, ed. Peter Trawny (Frankfurt: Klostermann, 2015), §115, p. 184.

16. This means that the human (*das Menschliche*) is not to be identified simply with the domain of modern humans as a biological species. Yet Heidegger is sometimes read as if he did indeed understand the human in just that way. Such a reading founders not only because of the lack of any genuine textual support for it, but also because of the inconsistency between such an identification and other elements in Heidegger's thinking (especially his steadfast opposition to biologism or anthropologism—something also explored by Farin in chapter 1 of this volume).

17. Martin Heidegger, *Kant and the Problem of Metaphysics*, trans. Richard Taft, 5th enl. ed. (Bloomington: Indiana University Press, 1997), 160.

18. Martin Buber, *Between Man and Man*, trans. Ronald Gregor Smith (London: Routledge, 2002), 193–214.

19. See Jeff Malpas, "In the Vicinity of the Human," *International Journal of Philosophical Studies* 25, no. 3 (2017): 423–36.

20. Martin Heidegger, *Contributions to Philosophy (of the Event)*, trans. Richard Rojcewicz and Daniela Vallega-Neu (Bloomington: Indiana University Press, 2012), §271, p. 385.

21. Heidegger, *Contributions to Philosophy*, §271, p. 385.

22. Although Heidegger nowhere makes the point directly, the way the notion of the "essential" continues to operate in his thinking (notwithstanding Heidegger's eschewal of the traditional language of "essence") is such that it names precisely that original placing that belongs to things and from out of which they come to presence.

23. Two other important essays from the same period are "The Saying of Anaximander" (*Der Spruch der Anaximander*), from 1946, which appears as "The Anaximander Fragment," in Martin Heidegger, *Early Greek Thinking*, trans. David Farrell Krell and Frank A. Capuzzi (New York: Harper and Row, 1975), 13–58; and, from 1945, "On Poverty," in *Heidegger, Translation, and the Task of Thinking: Essays in Honor of Parvis Emad*, ed. Frank Schalow (Dordrecht: Springer, 2011), 3–10.

24. Martin Heidegger, "Plato's Doctrine of Truth," in *Pathmarks*, 164.

25. Although its appearance there is somewhat occluded in the original Macquarrie and Robinson edition of *Being and Time* through the inconsistency in the translation of *Wohnen* and its cognates—a problem to some extent rectified in the Stambaugh and Schmidt edition.

26. Heidegger, "Letter on 'Humanism,'" 269, 271.

27. Dennis Schmidt takes Heidegger's comments as the starting point for his exploration of a "hermeneutic ethics," in "Hermeneutic as Original Ethics," in *Hermeneutic Rationality*, ed. Maria Luísa Portocarrero, Luis António Umbelino, and Andrzej Wierciński (Münster: LIT Verlag, 2012), 31–42.

28. For a discussion of Nazism's rejection of "universal humanism" and its replacement by a "biological humanism," see also Wolfgang Bialas, "Nazi Ethics and Morality: Ideas, Problems, and Unanswered Questions," in *Nazi Ideology and Ethics*, ed. Wolfgang Bialas and Lothar Fritze (Newcastle: Cambridge Scholars, 2014), 23–27. Philippe Lacoue-Labarthe goes so far as to claim that "Nazism is a humanism" inasmuch "as it rests upon a determination of *humanitas*, which is, in its view, more powerful—i.e., more effective—than any other." See Philippe Lacoue-Labarthe, *Heidegger, Art and Politics: The Fiction of the Political*, trans. Chris Turner (Oxford: Blackwell, 1990), 95.

29. See Ernesto Grassi, *Heidegger and the Question of Renaissance Humanism*, trans. Ulrich Hemel and John Michael Krois (New York: State University of New York Press, 1983). Grassi's engagement with Heidegger on this question is especially important. Not only was it Grassi who first published the "Letter" in German, but Grassi's own defense of Renaissance humanism is based in its engagement with the question of the poetic and the way that engagement prefigures key elements in Heidegger's approach. There is a further complication in Grassi's account that relates not to humanism as such, but to *metaphor* (which he takes to be tied up with the poetic, but with respect to which Heidegger has a more critical attitude); however, this itself opens up a further question as to how metaphor, no less than humanism, should be understood in the Renaissance context. On the question of metaphor, see Jeff Malpas, "The Refusal of Metaphor," in *In the Brightness of Place*, ch. 6.

30. Tom Rockmore, *Heidegger and French Philosophy: Humanism, Antihumanism, and Being* (London: Routledge, 1995), esp. 160–61. Rockmore takes issue with Lacoue-Labarthe in particular.

31. Heidegger, "Letter on 'Humanism,'" 272.

32. Martin Heidegger, "Art and Space," in *The Heidegger Reader*, ed. Günter Figal, trans. Jerome Veith (Bloomington: Indiana University Press, 2009), 307.

33. Martin Heidegger, *Hölderlins Hymne "Andenken,"* vol. 52 of *Gesamtausgabe*, ed. Curd Ochtwadt (Frankfurt: Klostermann, 1982), 40. "Es genügt hier, nur dies Eine zu bedenken: Auch die 'Dinge selbst' sind shon, bevor sie zu sogennanten 'Symbolen' werden, jedesmal gedichtet."

34. Heidegger discusses the anthropologizing tendency at work in humanism in other works, and "humanism" is mentioned in many of Heidegger's writings—as readily demonstrated in Francois Jaran and Christophe Perrin, *The Heidegger Concordance* (London: Bloomsbury, 2013)—but nowhere outside the "Letter" is humanism given the same sort of specific and sustained consideration.

Chapter Six

Being Human and Being Open
Heidegger's Radicalization of the Transcendental after Husserl

Niall Keane

Heidegger's Critique of Psychologism

Heidegger was well aware of the importance of separating thematically the world of human experience from the conditions of its manifestation. Yet as phenomenologist he also recognized that the way of being of the human is itself constitutive of such manifestation. Because of this insight, he identified the inconsistency, naturalistic misconception, and reductionist approach of psychologism in its attempts to give an epistemological account of experience by appealing not to the givenness of things in experience but rather to the factual psychological connections by which one apprehends these things. Whereas Husserl's rejection of psychologism hinges on his concern with protecting the ideal from being reduced to the factual or causal empirical, as well as his resistance to forms of all-encompassing naturalism, Heidegger's concern is with the human being's practical, worldly and historical situatedness. Yet, in many ways, Heidegger endorses Husserl's critique of psychologism. For instance, in 1925, he writes that "[t]he meaning of the principle of contradiction is not at all related to the framework of mental events. That is, its validity is completely independent of a possible change in the mental nature of human beings."[1] In this move to ensure that logical validity is kept distinct from the factual structures of psychological life, there is to be found an attempt to protect truth from becoming a mere psychological achievement and subsequently to conceive anew the human being and its relation to truth. The critique of psychologism thus paves the way for rethinking the grounds of human rationality, which, according to Heidegger, had been "locked off from various regions of being [. . .] blind to them, cut off from them and locked up in one specific area of being, that of the empirical nature of the physical and mental."[2]

Psychologism, for Husserl and Heidegger, is possible only because of a blindness to ideal being, and its fundamental misstep is to be found in its reduction of the ideal and eidetic being of logical laws to the factual being of the psychical. In a word, by failing to distinguish between empirical and eidetic-descriptive psychology, the all-important distinction between "sense" and "object" is missed.[3] However, unlike Husserl, Heidegger saw this important technical discussion as provisional and in need of deepening with respect to the human being and its relation to the meaning of being. And this obviously has consequences for Heidegger's reception of Husserl's concept of intentionality. If intentionality, for Husserl, refers to the structural directedness of consciousness toward its object, in Heidegger's hands it takes on the sense of the human being's opening and sustaining of a relation to the world and to itself as being-in-the-world, without this being reducible to the directness of consciousness. In this sense, the human being is constitutive of the phenomenon of world, yet without the world being reducible to the human being. What this means is that the being of the world is not a static container of context-based meaning relations, but is instead an a priori living structure that belongs together with the continual emergence, expansion, and possible disappearance of such meaning relations.[4] From this perspective, distinguishing between two spheres of being, real and ideal, is a necessary preliminary stage, and this insight was, for Heidegger, one of the many great merits of Husserl. But what Heidegger was after, with Husserl and yet beyond him, was the unitary root of these two spheres of being and what it tells us about being human and being worldly. He writes:

> Philosophy will be forced to confront the question about what really is the case with this "mental." Can we simply brush off the act of judging, its enactment, or the statement, as something empirical and mental, as contrasted with a so-called ideal sense? Or does an entirely different dimension of being finally press to

the fore here, one that can certainly be very dangerous once we glimpse it and expound it as something fundamental?[5]

In the above passage one can see clearly both Heidegger's dependence on and his emerging distance from the letter of Husserlian phenomenology. When it comes to his critique of psychologism, the entirety of the early Husserl's philosophical energy was focused on analyzing two distinct regions of experience: the psychical and the logical. Heidegger instead was focused on interrogating the openness that both precedes and makes possible the differentiation between atemporal being and temporal being, what is thought and the activity of thinking. What interested Heidegger, however, is not simply the critique of psychologism, but that "a new kind of research is introduced: *phenomenology*."[6] The radicality of this new methodological approach is to be found not in its thematizing of these two spheres of being, but rather in its search for a unitary ground. Heidegger writes:

> Basically, we are in a situation where we have to see these two separate orders or fields or spheres or regions as coming together in unity: that which has being and that which has validity, the sensible and the non-sensible, the real and the ideal, the historical and the transhistorical. We have not yet apprehended an original kind of being in terms of which we could understand these two fields as possible and as belonging *to* that of being. Philosophers do not even ask about such being.[7]

It is precisely here, however, where Heidegger points to the limits of Husserlian phenomenology. In his critique of psychologism, Husserl thematized two distinct regions of being and searched for a unitary foundation. But in doing so, he remained bound to the framework of examining the fundamental structures of consciousness, later on transcendentally purified consciousness, insofar as they bridge the gap between these two regions. What Husserl misses, Heidegger claims, is a true understanding of what it means to be human, which is not reducible to the transcendental structures of consciousness, but instead to being the kind of entity that does not so much "cast a bridge over the gap between these two regions, but instead renders possible these two regions of being in their original unity."[8] The point here is that Husserl remains locked firmly within a philosophy of consciousness, with the essence of the human all too restrictively circumscribed and determined. Consequently, his concept of intentionality, notwithstanding his attempts to demonstrate that all consciousness is consciousness "about" something that is always distinguishable from the acts themselves, operates within a theoretical framework of mental life and act structures. Heidegger's point is that with Husserl's interest focused on the intentional structures of transcendentally purified consciousness, he overlooks the particular being of the human being, its worldliness, and with that he misses the being of the intentional relation as well as the being of the intentional "subject."[9]

The Being of the Intentional and Human Experience

While Husserl's position in the first volume of the *Logical Investigations*, *Prolegomena to Pure Logic* of 1900, is openly critical of the psychologistic interpretation and its conflation of the logical and epistemological with the psychological, in his later writings he becomes more fully absorbed in an analysis of lived experience, embodiment, and the temporal position-taking structures of consciousness. Most Husserl scholars have interpreted the earlier critique of psychologism as a preliminary phase in the development of a richer and more full-blown transcendental phenomenology that sets out to characterize the essential structures of consciousness as such and not simply of this or that actually existing consciousness.[10] It is this approach by Husserl that is seen to immunize him against the specter of psychologism in his own work.[11] Heidegger's work throughout the 1920s seems to be of a piece with Husserl's critique of psychologism, albeit pointing away from Husserl's focus on transcendental consciousness and its accomplishments to the particular being of intentional life in relation to world and meaning manifestation. However, in a 1963 retrospective on the issue, Heidegger is more critical of his teacher:

> Husserl falls back with his phenomenological description of the phenomena of consciousness into the position of psychologism which he had just refuted. But if such a gross error cannot be attributed to Husserl's work, then what is the phenomenological description of the acts of consciousness? Wherein does what is peculiar to phenomenology consist if it is neither logic nor psychology?[12]

The early Heidegger, while clearly cagey about criticizing his teacher, at least openly, responds to the above questions by seeking to transform and radicalize Husserlian phenomenology by way of his reading of Aristotle on the finitude and temporalizing movedness of human life. Heidegger's principal claim, broadly conceived, is that the particular movedness of the human being is best understood as disclosing the phenomenon of world and simultaneously opening up a new philosophical perspective on what it means to *be* in the world and what this tells us about the being of the human being. However, even if Heidegger takes a distance from the Husserl of *Ideas I*, this does not mean he was committed to a form of realism. This was the case, however, for the early students of Husserl who rejected the move to the transcendental precisely because it endangered the very thing that phenomenological method was supposed to describe, namely, a sphere of being independent of the human through which it is manifest.

Heidegger's difficulty with the transcendental, as espoused by Husserl, has little in common with the concerns of phenomenological realists such as Reinach, Meinong, Conrad-Martius, and Ingarden.[13] In fact, Heidegger's version of phenomenological analysis is deeply consonant with Husserl's and is analogously interested in bringing about a modification of and in intentional life that brings with it a new understanding of the various modes of givenness as well as of the region that enables such givenness. But the aim and experience of this modification are distinct for teacher and student, with Heidegger focused on radicalizing phenomenological method so that the being of what manifests itself in experience can be brought into an essential relationship with our being human, prior to our being conscious subjects or rational agents. I do not want to suggest, however, that Heidegger is rejecting outright notions of rational subjectivity and agency. That said, for Heidegger, remaining within the discourse of subjectivity and objectivity always carries the risk of sliding back in the modern metaphysical bias toward interiority or immanence and in so doing forgetting the nature of the human being's disclosive openness toward the world that has always already been opened. And with this focus comes Heidegger's transformation of intentionality, examining instead the way of being of the human: care, transcendence, and being-in-the-world with others. Therefore, rather than looking at the correlation between psychic acts and the ideal objects of logic or mathematics as a way of bridging the previously mentioned two spheres of being, real and ideal, Heidegger looks to locate the original unity of the two in the manner of the being of human life, or the mode of being of the Dasein *in* the human. Again, he alludes to the limits of the concept of intentionality and to his break with Husserl's brand of transcendental phenomenology precisely on the issue of what it means to be human, why the human must not be understood in subjective or egoic terms, and how the Dasein *in* the human being is central to the question of manifestation and meaning.[14] He writes:

> With an adequate interpretation of intentionality, the traditional concept of the subject and of subjectivity becomes questionable. [. . .] We cannot decide anything about intentionality starting from a concept of the subject because intentionality is the essential though not the most original structure of the subject itself.[15]

Intentional Correlation and the Critique of Sense-Conferring

But what exactly does Heidegger mean above by the "original structure of the subject itself"? Husserl's definition of transcendental subjectivity, which engages in acts of positing and judging, cannot be equated with individuality pure and simple, because as an individual I find myself living and thinking within an open region of experience that constitutes who I am as an empirical being, altogether different from ideal objects. Therefore, transcendental, for Heidegger, means the kind of dynamic open region of possibility that establishes the two poles of the intentional relation, ideal and real, in the first place. But in addition to this, Heidegger's emphasis on the kind of unique being that one is and *has* to be (*zu sein*), his attempt to outline what it means to shed light on the essence of this ontologically distinct being needs to incorporate the element of genuine historicality into its analysis. So, when Heidegger talks about Husserl overlooking "the mode of being of intentionality,"[16] he also infers that Husserl's concept of transcendental consciousness carries with it a theoretical bias, with the pure subject eclipsing, by putting out of play, historical existence altogether. It is the historicality of existence and one's *having-to-be* the being one *is* that Heidegger will see as the most "original structure of the subject itself," and by historicality he means the ontological problematic of the temporal nature of beings and the unique happening of Dasein, seeking to understand their ontological underpinnings. Accordingly, he does not want human existence to be turned into an *object* of historical scientific study, because this would necessarily occlude the particularity and significance of the having-to-be of the human being, as well as every access to the fundamental phenomenon of historicality. While Husserl sees that there is a correlation between certain types of acts and certain objectivities, Heidegger seeks to explore how such correlations emerge and the historical conditions of such emergence. For instance, if I am a defined by intentional directedness and receptivity, absent of which objects and state of affairs would never appear, it is altogether legitimate to ask how and under what conditions are such structures possible.

Heidegger thus follows a path opened up by Husserl, yet radicalizes it by looking at the transcendental problematic in terms of the conditions of appearance as such, including the appearance of a psychical subject and a physical object, and reflecting on those conditions historically, existentially and ontologically. Yet in 1911, Husserl had already criticized Dilthey's historicism because of what he saw as the specter of historical relativism, indicating the need to distinguish between a science of historical consciousness, a factual science, and science of objective validity. In the name of scientific "rigor," this leads Husserl to contrast "science as a cultural phenomenon and science as a valid systematic theory."[17]

It is around these issues that Heidegger parts company with his teacher, and, in his Marburg lecture course from 1923–24, he examines in great detail the rapport between historicism and phenomenology, as well as Husserl's critique of Dilthey, claiming that the pursuit of absolute and universally binding validity is itself an expression of "anxiety in the face" of the historicality of human existence.[18] In other words, even though Husserl discovered something radically new, his drive for certainty and absolute validity is, Heidegger writes, a "sedation of the being of knowing."[19] It is a sedation of the existential-ontological modality of human existence, namely, Dasein, which amounts to claiming that the constitutively situated uncertainty of life sedates itself against uncertainty.[20] Husserlian phenomenology sedates itself with certainty and at that very moment, Heidegger tells us, "the tendency to get a grip on human existence is severed."[21] What this amounts to, for Heidegger, is that Husserl overlooks or neglects the historical roots of his own philosophical questioning and misses the fact that his demand for clarity, distinctness, and absolute scientific status is itself borne out of the human being's openness to itself and the world.[22]

As Heidegger puts it, "In the critique of historicism it is evident that the care and what it is concerned about—absolute validity in the interest of shaping the idea of humanity—put the existence of the human being and genuine interrogation of it out of play."[23] With Heidegger's reference to something being put "out of play," he is obviously pointing to what must necessarily be suspended in the name of the neutralizing phenomenological abstention, and as suspended it becomes surplus to phenomenological analysis. This is the case because Husserl, fearing that historicism will lead to skepticism, does not fully examine how the contrast between factual and absolute validity comes into being in the first place. And when he does, he is forced to choose between two grounds: the concrete and factual or the intellectual and rational. According to Heidegger, Husserl does not give an account of how the contrast between these two spheres, "absolute validity" and "holding something to be valid,"[24] is itself possible, with only "a squinting glance at [anxiety-inducing and uncertain] existence" being offered.[25] The point is that the contrast between validity and factuality is itself derived from a historical openness to which we are always already disposed and limiting the analysis to these two spheres is tantamount, he tells us, to the analysis becoming "unfree."[26]

Distancing himself significantly from the letter of Husserlian phenomenology thanks to indications provided by Dilthey, doing phenomenology, for Heidegger, means examining the historical openness that makes theory and analysis first possible. In pursuing the question of historical openness that renders the two spheres of being, factual and ideal, possible, he both remains faithful to Husserl's efforts to ensure that meaning, truth, and logic are neither reduced to the psychological sphere nor banished to an unworldly region. Yet he redirects Husserl's energies in claiming that meaning, truth, and logic are valid for everyone because one move within an openness, established by historical being-in-the-world, that is not simply a product of human being and doing, while nonetheless having the character of the human as a meaningful whole.

For Heidegger, intentionality is shifted from the centrifugal sphere of conscious experience and its constitutive structures, its directedness at the world, and redirected toward the opened and open space of appearances that are disclosed by the mode of being of the human as standing out toward the world and holding a horizon in front of itself. Everything that exists as disclosed and uncovered is taken as stemming from this radicalized notion of intentionality, which is reframed in terms of the moved standing-out care-structure of human existence as constitutive of the meaning of being that is sharpened further in the late 1920s through the concept of transcendence.[27] Accordingly, Heidegger refashions Husserl's theory of intentionality because he thinks Husserl remains beholden to a modern conception of subjectivity and by extension is trapped within a certain modern understanding of objectivity.

Now even if Heidegger's analysis of Husserl is arguably beholden to an excessively Cartesian picture, and has little to say about Husserl's more ontological, personalistic, practical, and teleologically-oriented approach, I would nonetheless like to explore what is driving his analysis. I do not want to give the impression, however, that the appearance of things or the appearance of objective sense is, for Husserl, simply the result of an intellectual synthesis. Husserl rejected such a move and saw it as the hallmark of a neo-Kantian approach. Instead of a heterogenous bundle of sensations that need ordering, for Husserl, one perceives objects in an orderly way both because the object, taken ontically, is one and the same object, independent of individual and collective acts, and because being conscious involves conferring meaning on an already orderly experience so as to arrive at the sense of the world. Moreover, it should be said that Husserl's theory of intentionality, as it develops from early to late, does not just concern the acts in which we intend logical and mathematical objects. Rather it includes all acts of intending, including more concrete personal and practical objects, nonideal objects, emotive objects, axiological objects, and intellective objects.[28]

This notwithstanding, it is the understanding of the human being as a sense-bestowing or sense-conferring being, as transcendental and volitional agent, that Heidegger finds the most difficult pill to swallow when it comes to understanding the humanity of the human being. Therefore, while Husserl does not view intentionality as a psychic event, he does see it as the mode of being of consciousness, and it is for this reason that Heidegger problematizes it, confessing in 1921–22, "What always disturbed me: Did intentionality come down from heaven?"[29]

Oddly enough, while Heidegger grappled with the concept of intentionality throughout the 1920s, the account of intentionality he provides in his summer semester 1927 Marburg lecture course, *The Basic Problems of Phenomenology*, is not altogether dissimilar to Husserl's. This lecture course opens with the surprising claim that "it is precisely intentionality and nothing else in which transcendence consists,"[30] transforming this claim quite significantly a year later, and moving to the more radicalized conception of intentionality found in the summer semester 1928 Marburg lecture course. This course, *The Metaphysical Foundations of Logic*, concludes with the claim that "transcendence, being-in-the-world, is never to be identified and equated with intentionality."[31] This marks a fundamental shift in Heidegger's position, with the concept of intentionality taken up and transformed into the problematic of transcendence as Dasein's mode of being open to the world, Dasein conceived as that which "goes beyond" or "exceeds" (*das Übersteigende*) and world, that which is transcended, conceived as "beings as a whole" (*das Seiende im Ganzen*).[32] Clearly dissatisfied with fundamental misunderstandings of the care structure of Dasein and being-in-the-world as nothing more than a warmed-over existential take on Husserl's concept of intentionality, he states, "Dasein itself is the passage across. [. . .] Transcendence is the fundamental constitution of its being."[33]

What this means is that the world is no longer seen as arising from Dasein's mode of being, pure and simple, even if the essential correlation between Dasein and world is still maintained. World, after *Being and Time*, comes to be defined as "the wholeness of the constitution of being" (*das Ganze der Seinsverfassung*), or as "the how of beings as a whole" (*das Wie des Seienden im Ganzen*), indicating that the transcendence that constitutes Dasein's mode of being must be read in tandem with the distinct domain of "beings as a whole" (*das Seiende im Ganzen*).[34] It is only when these corresponding moments are taken together in their unity, in their mutual alliance in distinctness, that we can understand what Heidegger terms "the inner organization of the wholeness of being" (*die innere Organisation dieser Seinsganzheit*) as defining the being of the human.[35] What emerges after *Being and Time* is a concept of the human coming into its own not only in its being world-open, but more fundamentally by its being-opened by the world. In this sense, it is brought into itself by being placed into the world, and in the process confronted by "beings as a whole."[36] One should thus not simply understand Dasein as projectively and understandingly disclosing the world, as being open *to* the world, or the world as having the being or form of existence as Dasein, or as a totality of relational significance.

This internal developmental tension notwithstanding, Heidegger continues to affirm that Husserl was insufficiently radical in questioning the presuppositions of the modern conception of subjectivity when developing his theory of intentionality. And if one is to get to the essence of the intentional, one needs to move, or so Heidegger claims in the winter semester 1928–29 course, cited above, from subjectivity to world as the "original play of transcendence"[37] so as to examine the appearance of meaning and its historical lineage. Clearly, meaning is not to be understood here in terms of its having been bestowed on the world by a transcendental subject, or even intergenerational collective or intersubjective constitution. It is to be understood rather in terms of the totality of human practices and practical contexts of meaning that make up the human world stemming from Dasein's exposure to the world, and not the result of what Dasein does, but rather how Dasein is. What Heidegger is trying to bring together, as opposed to "put out of play," is the "play character of life as transcendence," "beings as a whole," and "the wholeness of world."[38] Dasein is thus not a subject that playfully confers meaning on encountered factual objects or states of affairs, but is rather the site through which openness can show up, the site through which beings and the world can appear as always having been disclosed and understood, though never as an object of knowledge.

What Heidegger brings to the fore is that the world puts meaning into the human as much as the human puts meaning into the world. The world is that element that Dasein is given over to and that it allows itself to be given over to. The human thus becomes most fully human by actively surrendering itself to the world as the site of meaning emergence. Naturally enough, our unique and discrete frames of reference set the terms in which meaning can show up, but one remains significantly participative and receptive to what is given by the world. To arrive at this insight, it was necessary for Heidegger to overhaul the concepts of intentionality and sense-bestowal and to center it around the kind of being that both understands and occupies itself with what it means when one says something *is*. For Heidegger, no form of subjectivity, be it empirical or transcendental, can account for this sufficiently, because "subjectivity" itself is an "arbitrary" and "phantom construction" of something more original, existing prior to the construction and yet occluded by it.[39]

From Husserl and through Scheler: Heidegger's Breakthrough

It goes without saying that even if Heidegger is looking for "something more original," occluded by the "arbitrary" and "phantom construction" of subjectivity, he does not start from scratch or look for a presuppositionless starting point. This is mainly because such an original "something" is itself historical and worldly and Heidegger's historical sensibility would not have allowed him to countenance anything like starting afresh. While Husserl clearly "opened [his] eyes"[40] methodologically, and Dilthey provided the impetus with his analysis of historical life—with Aristotle's practical philosophy and his *Physics* offering him a way of reconceiving the structure of worldly human existence—it is the influence of Max Scheler that is perhaps underprized in the reception of Heidegger's breakthrough analysis of human life, world, and the meaning of being.[41]

Heidegger connects with Scheler on the following: both problematize the neo-Kantian assumption that the sensibly given is a disordered and heterogenous continuum that is ordered and apprehended as an abiding object of experience as a result of the synthetizing activity of cognition.[42] For Scheler, it is not possible to give an account of our experience of entities within the world and their relations by appealing to disordered sensations and their cognitive synthesis. Moreover, Scheler claims, one experiences the sense of the world personally in its immediate and direct givenness. In this way, Scheler, too, distances himself from Husserl's post *Logical Investigations* account of transcendental subjectivity through which worldly appearances are accounted for by way of the specific intentional operations of consciousness and its accomplishments. For Husserl, at least according to Scheler, one finds oneself in a field of sensuous experience. And thanks to his transcendental constitutive analysis, a sense of transcendent worldly objects of experience can be established. What goes missing, for Scheler, in Husserl's transcendental turn, and specifically the Cartesian approach of *Ideas I*, is the phenomenological status of the object that was central to Husserl in the *Logical Investigations*. With this move, Husserl's phenomenology becomes transcendental idealism, with the sense of the world, though not things in the world,[43] existing only as long as there are continual subjective sense-bestowals and intersubjective verifications there to ensure it. It is thus Husserl's focus on the transcendental ego as a position-taking subject giving identity and unity to the world of experience that causes difficulty for Scheler.[44]

It is impossible in this essay to do justice to the complexity of Scheler's thought and his analysis of the person and material axiology, but suffice it to say that he goes in a different direction than Husserl's perceived intellectualism. For Scheler, when I perceive a table, for instance, what I have before me is immediately and directly evident, with the concept of table becoming thematic only due to a subsequent procedural reflection. With this, reflective analysis becomes a derivative moment and secondary to the human being's immediate rapport with the world of affects, emotions, and relations. Thus, descriptive phenomenological analysis should not begin from the constitutive structures of consciousness accessed through immanent perception. Instead, Scheler claims, it should begin with a description of the original and prereflective experience of the phenomena, the intuitively given, that constitutes the genuine sense of phenomenology. Consequently, it is an abstract and "mythical assumption"[45] to claim that the given is, in essence, a "chaos of sensations" that due to certain "synthetic functions"[46] becomes orderly. As Scheler puts it:

> Phenomenological experience, in contrast to this, contains *no* separation between what is "meant" and what is "given." Taking our *departure*, so to speak, from non-phenomenological experience, we can also express this in the following fashion: In phenomenological experience nothing is *meant* that is not *given*, and nothing is

> given that is not meant. It is precisely *in* this *coincidence* of the "meant" and the "given" that the *content* of phenomenological experience alone *becomes* manifest [kundwerden].[47]

For this reason, Scheler believes it makes little sense to ask how it is possible to know something, because things are by nature both immediately meant and given. One is thus never a "subject" without an "object." When I open my eyes and perceive, I do not see the simulacra of a table or chair, but rather the table or chair *itself*. Hence, when one asks how objects are known, how it is possible to transcend one's subjective states and get to those objects, one ends up misconstruing the very content of human experience, insofar as human experience is necessarily and inextricably bound up with the experience of things and objects in which one is always already in relation.

Here one can already see what Heidegger takes from Scheler's critique of Husserl: our encounter with meaning is immediate, worldly, and not the result of a subjective or intersubjective achievement. Rejecting the either/or of realism and idealism, both Heidegger and Scheler take their start from Husserl's concept of intentionality in an attempt to transform it. Of course, while Scheler believed he had found a solution to the problem of ontology by way of philosophical anthropology,[48] Heidegger claims that intentionality is not a name for a solution to a "problem," functioning like a key that opens "all doors."[49] It is rather the name for a "problem"[50] from which one is only just beginning: the necessity of a radically new ontological interpretation of what it means to be human and worldly.

Consequently, while Scheler remains at the more "objective" level, staying with the phenomena and their givenness to the person, with the person understood as nonobjective and nonsubstantial,[51] Heidegger goes further in examining the openness that permits the phenomena to show up as meaningful in the first place. It is thus that Heidegger remains a transcendental philosopher in a very particular sense. Still, for Heidegger, Scheler's critique of Husserl goes too far in the other direction. Scheler defines our relation to things, with the world defined as a structural totality of things, in terms of their being unearthed or uncovered by the person and not constituted or encountered *as* things in their historical and practical referential context. From Heidegger's perspective, this does not provide an adequate account of the condition of their manifestation, the "ontological foundations" of the human being, or a genuine understanding of the "being of the whole,"[52] and thus fails to provide a properly transcendental analysis relative to the conditions of possibility of the phenomena.

Scheler reproaches Husserl's *Ideas I* for having put forward an "epistemological idealism," focusing excessively on the "structures of consciousness" and for subsequently having made those structures the "condition of the objects of experience."[53] Heidegger, no doubt sympathetic to the general thrust of Scheler's critique and often blind to Husserl's so-called ontological way, refuses to follow Husserl's account of transcendental subjectivity, developing the Schelerian idea according to which the human being's rapport with things is given because of the phenomenon of world. Though for Heidegger, unlike Scheler, this is not definable in terms of a totality of things or goods experienced by the person,[54] but rather as a dynamic and historical totality of meaningful references that emerge historically against the backdrop of world openness. Consequently, even if Heidegger called Scheler "the strongest philosophical force in contemporary philosophy,"[55] with an "irrepressible drive always to think out and interpret things as a whole,"[56] he nonetheless resists the phenomenological "objectivism," "intuitionism," "anthropologism," and "absolutism" of Scheler's thought. In a nutshell, Scheler's thought provided insufficient analysis of the constitutive interconnectedness of being-in-the-world and the phenomenon of world.[57] What Heidegger is looking for, and what Scheler's work does not offer him, is an understanding of the world as "the how of beings as a whole,"[58] the necessary correlation between historical human existence, that is, transcendence as belonging to the finite being of human Dasein,[59] and the phenomenon of world as the structural totality of meaning. Again, it will be Heidegger's account of finite being-in-the-world as both opened up and self-opening that makes the difference when it comes to his disagreement with Scheler. As he puts it, "Scheler did not see what was meant by transcendence."[60] And since transcendence is understood in the winter semester 1928–29 lecture course as the ground of "philosophizing"[61] itself, it is reasonable to assume that Heidegger believed both Husserl and Scheler did not philosophize in a sufficiently radical way.

It is hence Heidegger's commitment to rethinking the original structure of transcendence in transcendental terms, distinct from transcendental subjectivity or intersubjectivity, that plays out in terms of our transcendence shaping the world of meaningful references and relations, as well as exposing us to the nothingness and groundlessness of our being.[62] It is his concern with the historical and finite groundlessness of transcendence and its opening of the world that forms his critical rejoinder to both Husserl and Scheler.

Heidegger's Polemic with Philosophies of Consciousness and Subjectivity

Their differences notwithstanding, both Scheler and Heidegger draw attention to a stubborn theoretical bias: the assumption that there are psychophysical states and corresponding external objects or states of affairs, and the treatment of intentionality as itself a special relation between such states and their corresponding external objects or states of affairs. According to Heidegger, and following Scheler, this is an altogether artificial and speculative construction that runs counter to phenomenological experience. If one examines one's perceptual experiences in a more unbiased way, one quickly sees that when one encounters an object—say, a table—one does not perceive or see sensations. Sensations, which are interpreted in a transcendent sense, are not given in experience. Heidegger puts it thus:

> It is not the case that at first only a psychic process occurs as a nonintentional state (complex of sensations, memory relations, mental image and thought processes through which an image is evoked, where one then asks whether something corresponds to it) and subsequently becomes intentional in certain instances. Rather, the very being of comporting is a directing-itself-toward.[63]

If one encounters an object and is then asked to explain what one sees, surely no one would reply that they have seen sensations of color and form. One would surely reply that one has seen something made in this or that way and with this or that function. When Heidegger claims to be radicalizing the Husserlian concept of intentionality and thinking it more originally, he means it precisely in this way: intentionality becomes the relational meaning of things as opened up by Dasein's world-openness. Things, for Heidegger, show up as meaning-objects and meaning-relations and not as bare objects of sense data. And to be human means to be the discloser and sustainer of such meaningfulness, yet with such meaningfulness having a life of its own beyond the disclosing. While Husserl situates the sense of the world and its bestowal firmly within the noetic realm of subjective and intersubjective life, Heidegger appears to account for both the noetic and noematic sense, *intentio* and *intentum*, with the interrelatedness of Dasein's disclosiveness and the meaningfulness of the world kept distinct, separable, though not separate. Heidegger will later term this relation "Inständigkeit in der Lichtung."[64]

Again, Heidegger is inspired by Husserl, but takes it in a direction other than the one outlined by Husserl in *Ideas I*, where intentionality is defined as a "fundamental property of consciousness,"[65] as well as the universal and unified "stream of mental processes."[66] For this reason, Heidegger claims, Husserl does not develop the consequences of his intentional analysis more originally. His problem with Husserl's theory of intentionality, and by extension with his uncritical endorsement of the language of subjectivity, is explained further in Heidegger's 1973 Zähringen seminar. He writes: "If one adds intentionality to consciousness, then the intended object still has its place in the immanence of consciousness. In *Being and Time*, on the contrary, the 'thing' has its place no longer in consciousness, but *in the world* (which again is itself not immanent to consciousness)."[67] Therefore, while fully aware that Husserl's theory of intentionality, and his reflections on the intentional subject, object, and relation, was conceived to resist the more pernicious forms of immanence and absolute idealism, by starting from consciousness and the intentional unities of experience as the seat of meaning, the specter of subjective immanence will always insinuate itself back into the discourse. Or, as Heidegger articulates, in his 1966 *Zollikon Seminar*:

> In his *Logical Investigations* of 1900–1901, Husserl speaks about meaning bestowing acts [*Bedeutung verleihende Akte*]. According to Husserl, the constitution of an object of consciousness occurs in such a way that the hyletic data, pure sensations, are given as primary and then receive a meaning as *noemata* [intentional objects of consciousness]. In other words, a meaning [*noema*] is ascribed to the [sensory] stimulus by a psychical [noetic] act. Nevertheless, the whole is a pure construct.[68]

Starting from here one can see the real polemic of Heidegger's reflections: the idea that there are initially formless sensations that only in a second moment receive meaning thanks to subjective and intersubjective bestowal and verification. However, this polemic is already front and center in *Being and Time*, where he writes:

> It requires a very artificial and complicated frame of mind to "hear" a "pure noise." The fact that motor-cycles and wagons are what we proximally hear is the phenomenal evidence that in every case Dasein as Being-in-the-world, already dwells alongside what is ready-to-hand within-the-world; it certainly

does not dwell proximally alongside "sensations"; nor would it first have to give shape to the swirl of sensations to provide the springboard from which the subject leaps off and finally arrives at a "world." Dasein, as essentially understanding, is proximally alongside what is understood.[69]

That the human being primarily hears a motorcycle and a wagon attests to the fact that Dasein, insofar as it is constitutively being-in-the-world and exists understandingly, is always already engaged with its referential contexts of meaning involvement, of which pure sensation is derivative.

The Appropriation of Apriority and Categoriality

Before one can talk about what Heidegger means by openness as the very essence of the human being, one needs to get clear on what he means by experience and its relation to the a priori. Taking his start from Husserl's notion of categorial intuition, in Heidegger's *Prolegomena* lectures from 1925, he understands that the givenness of something *as* something, while founded on sensory intuition or perception, is not itself sensuously given. However, Heidegger refuses to locate the a priori in either subjective immanence or in reality. Rejecting both the transcendent world of objects and the immanence of subjective life as the site of the a priori, he defines the original sense of the a priori as "a *title for being*," or "*a feature of the structural sequence in the being of entities, in the ontological structure of being*."[70] Here he does not limit himself to the Husserlian account of categorial intuition and apriority, however, and is most certainly not claiming that intellective acts owe everything to perceptual acts, or that there is a stratification at work. For Heidegger, the important discovery is that the categorial is given, without being contained in the sensory. As he understands it, the categorial is an excess through which the sensuously given manifests itself *as* something, and not just as random perceptual *Gestalten*. He writes: "[W]hen I see this book, I do see a substantial thing, without however seeing the substantiality as I see the book. But it is the substantiality that, in its non-appearance, enables what appears to appear."[71]

What this illustrates is that categorial intuition, as a founded act, is not given sensibly, but is given analogously to the sensible, making possible the givenness and comprehension of something *as* something. For Heidegger, it is the a priori ontological structure of being itself that makes possible the givenness and comprehension of something *as* something. Yet his reconceiving of categorial intuition brings with it a significant modification in the notion of the givenness of the phenomena that one finds analyzed and described in Husserl's transcendental phenomenology. Again, here Scheler is an underprized influence, with Scheler defining the a priori as

> ideal units of meaning and those propositions that are self-given by way of an *immediate intuitive* content in the absence of any kind of positing [*Setzung*] of subjects that think them and of the real nature of those subjects, and in the absence of any kind of positing of objects to which such units of meaning are applicable. The point, therefore, is to leave aside all kinds of *positing*, including the positing of "real" or "non-real," "illusion" or "real," etc.[72]

The a priori is thus reconceived as what precedes any account of reality as posited, rendering judgment and predication possible before it can be taken as true or false, real or unreal. The condition of the possibility of experiencing something *as* something is given in and through the categorial. This entails that our experience, including our experience of being human, is rendered possible by the givenness of the categorial in directly intuitive "phenomenological experience,"[73] absent of which nothing could show up as meaningful, including our relation to ourselves as human.

It is such a discovery that enables Heidegger to develop a new orientation toward the question of the meaning of being and with it to reconceive what it means to be human. As he writes, "There is no ontology *alongside* a phenomenology. Rather, *scientific ontology is nothing but phenomenology*."[74] It is patently clear that Heidegger is not interested in examining why things are as they are in some larger cosmological sense, and that his focus is on how things are given from the transcendental perspective. He is intent on assessing how things are given, what enables their givenness, and its bearing on what it means to be human.[75]

Here, I believe he is taking up Scheler's notion of the "material a priori,"[76] which means he is searching for the conditions of meaning manifestation in the being of things that manifest themselves in the world. Or more precisely, he is looking for the conditions of meaning manifestation in the worldly openness that allows something to be given *as it is*. This means again reflecting on the conditions of manifestation without locating such conditions in subjectivity, but rather in the openness of worldly appearance and its ontological underpinnings. Thus, Heidegger's analysis is not simply beholden to a revamped notion of the subject, rebranded Dasein, but is instead in search of an openness through which, as Chad Engelland puts it, "transcendence is possible in the first place."[77] With the notion of the a priori, Heidegger's analysis attempts to side-step the tradition of modernity that insisted on analyzing the a priori structures of subjectivity that precede experience and make it possible. The nucleus of this refashioning of Husserlian phenomenology, taking its cue from Scheler, is to be found in his affirmation of the material a priori. As Heidegger puts it in 1925:

> Phenomenology has shown that the apriori is not limited to subjectivity, indeed that in the first instance it has primarily nothing at all to do with subjectivity. The characterization of ideation as a categorial intuition has made it clear that something like the highlighting of ideas occurs both in the field of the ideal, hence of the categories, and in the field of the real.[78]

Therefore, it is not the case that something appears *as* something because the subject operates some sort of formal and productive synthesizing activity. Rather, in the givenness of things in the world, things exhibit a given categorial structure, absent of which they would not appear as meaningful and nothing could be predicated of them. The categorial is thus the basis of meaning and of the meaning-relations through which something can appear as something, both specifically and generally.

Consequently, the a priori, for Heidegger, belongs to the phenomena of world as such, although he does not stop here with his analysis. If Husserl determines being as objectivity, as an ideality corresponding to the accomplishments of subjectivity and intersubjectivity, for Heidegger, being is instead the a priori worldly openness through which things appear as what they are. Accordingly, something can appear *as* something, can be identified *as* something in particular, only within the a priori open region of meaningful references that defines the identity and function of the encountered thing.

Apriority, History, Openness

Again, the openness that Heidegger refers to is neither determined by subjectivity nor founded in a theory of the subject. Put otherwise, one does not have subjectivity on the one side and temporal ideality on the other.

Instead, the historical and worldly openness of meaning makes possible the psychical and the logical, an openness that allows thinking (as the structure of consciousness) and thought (as the object of consciousness) to come into their own. In this way, the being of things, their meaning, is determined differently from Husserl. For Husserl, the being of a thing is its givenness to subjective consciousness in lived experience, as the intentional object of the intentional act. For Heidegger, the meaning of a thing does not emerge because it offers itself to consciousness as an intentional object, but stems from its belonging to a referential context of historical worldly meaning. What this amounts to is that the being of something, its specific meaning, can only be grasped by a being who understands the totality of meaningful references and for a being who is caught up in the task of understanding what one means when one says something *is*. As is made abundantly clear in *Being and Time*, "letting something be" what it *is* does not mean making or producing something. Instead, it means "that something which is already an 'entity' must be discovered in its readiness-to-hand, and that we must thus let the entity which has this being be encountered."[79] Thus, while "world is the designation for human Dasein in the core of its essence,"[80] the holding-open of the a priori open domain of being is the work or task of Dasein in its practico-transcendental involvement with the world.

In this way, Heidegger reinterprets Husserl's notion of categorial intuition, which means the structure and content of perceptual directedness, seeking to understand in what the identity of an object consists. His solution to this is to be found not in the perception of an object as given, but rather in the totality of its practical involvements and worldly referential meaning contexts as understood. Hence, it is only by starting from the practical dimension of a thing's worldly involvement that one can understand the being or meaning of the thing as given. And yet, equally, such a totality of meaningful references or referential totality can only be understood by a being that has understanding as its constitutive mode of being.

Accordingly, Heidegger returns to Husserl's concept of intentionality, but only as a starting point, writing: "The insight into intentionality does not go far enough to see that grasping this structure as the essential structure of Dasein must revolutionize the whole concept of the human being."[81] Yet Heidegger is not only looking to revolutionize our understanding of what it means to be human. He is also trying to revolutionize how one understands the world and the relationality of things in the world. What he is getting at is that, taken together, the two poles of the correlation, subject and object traditionally conceived, emerge out of the openness of the world as a space for the possibility of understanding and its temporal unfolding. The poles and their relation only appear because of the unity of this structural openness,[82] working in tandem with the disclosive and meaning-establishing activity of human understanding.

However, the previously mentioned categorial structure, understood as the condition of the possibility of meaning manifestation and judgment, is not something given once and for all, something contained immutably within the structure of perceptual experience, as Husserl believed, but rather as a structure tied to human life and world, historically determined. One is not here dealing with conceptual schemes and their contents, and for this very reason, Heidegger is able to overcome the traditional opposition between experience and thought, life, and logic. In effect, Dilthey had already noted that the categories of life, such as meaning, values, and goals, are not applied a priori to life from without, but rather "emerge from life itself."[83] Taking up this point in his 1923 Freiburg lecture, Heidegger writes:

> The categories are not inventions or a group of logical schemata as such, "lattices"; on the contrary, they are *alive in life itself* in an original way: alive in order to "form" life on themselves. They have their own modes of access, which are not foreign to life itself, as if they pounced down upon life from the outside, but instead are precisely the preeminent way in which *life comes to itself.*[84]

Conclusion

It should be said that even if there is a clearly anti-subjectivist and anti-psychologist streak in Heidegger's work, he is not simply promoting an anti-subjectivistic or anti-psychologistic thought-model as a good in itself. Instead, he is trying to reconceive the human being from the ground up, and with that to reconceive our relation to the world as an open whole that is surpassive or always in excess of this or that disclosure. In this sense, he is radicalizing the very notion of the transcendental by problematizing an understanding of it purely in terms of the subjective conditions of the possibility of knowledge and objective reality. In his early phenomenological lectures, and especially after *Being and Time*, one finds a concept of world that is distinct from Dasein's mode of being, an excess that is always more than the transcendence that brings it into view. This is Heidegger's attempt to depsychologize or dementalize understanding by making it constitutively worldly, without, however, reducing the world as such to projective understanding or to the ecstatic-horizonal movement of transcendence. The later Heidegger, however, found his earlier account insufficiently radical and saw anthropologistic and subjectivistic undertones to it.[85] As the story goes, in the middle of the 1920s and up to and including *Being and Time*, the world is understood as of a piece with the being-thrown and projective understanding of human existence, with the world having the character of Dasein or being "Dasein-ish" (*daseinsmäßig*),[86] and yet always in excess of Dasein. Heidegger later came to the conclusion that the task of his earlier fundamental ontology still contained the vestige of subjectivity, with the disclosive and uncovering movement of the human being toward entities remaining perhaps too central. So, if there is a modification in this thinking, it consists in understanding Dasein, no longer in terms of care structure, projective understanding, or "transcendence on the basis of ecstatic temporality,"[87] but rather as the open region of being that allows beings to be, with human existence interpreted as the previously mentioned "Inständigkeit in der Lichtung."[88]

Heidegger later rethinks openness not as shaped or established by the human being, but openness as the element that pulls the human being out into its worldliness, allowing it to stand- or dwell-in the truth of being. These later shifts of emphasis notwithstanding, in the mid- and late 1920s, Heidegger held that the transcendental element remained vital for reflecting on the human for at least two reasons: (1) one can encounter things or states of affairs as meaningful because of one's prior disclosiveness; and (2) one can encounter meaning due to the historical and temporal particularity of the referential context. That the shift to his later reflections entails the "quasi-disappearance of man,"[89] as Michel Haar worried, is perhaps an overstated concern. What is clear, however, is that this later move is already contained in his analysis from the 1920s and any shift in his position is one of reemphasis or rephrasing as opposed to overhaul or the abandoning of earlier positions. The later Heidegger is thus not so much concerned with the renunciation of theoretical and practical concerns, or with the renunciation of entities metaphysically construed, but more with the task of reflecting on the *topos* of the human being as the space for reflecting on its own essence as constitutive of manifestation, while thinking manifestation as always being in excess of such constitutiveness.

However, unlike Husserl, this means that our concrete being-in-the-world is reconcilable with its transcendental character. What I mean by this is that in anxiety, for instance, one encounters one's deepest and most human self, but one simultaneously encounters the worldhood of the world as it makes itself felt, emptied of innerworldly meaning. Reconciling a separability that is never separate is something that Husserl struggled with, and I think the same is true of Heidegger. Up until the late 1920s, Heidegger was trying to find different ways of harmonizing the pre-phenomenological and worldly with the phenomenological and transcendental, and reflecting on the conditions of the manifestness of the correlation between real and ideal, subject and object, though not "in a one-sidedly subjectivistic manner."[90]

This I take to be Heidegger's *palintropos harmoniê*, his analysis of the discordant harmony between human and world that constitutes all possible human experience. It is his attempt to expose philosophy to such a discordant harmony without collapsing one into the other. But to expose philosophy to it, he continually seeks to analyze the experience of a dislocating modification from a captivity with objects in the world to a being captivated or oriented by the openness of the world that first allows objects and contexts to appear as meaningful. Therefore, it is a question of how openness is understood. Is it synonymous with the nonanthropologistic interrogated and self-interrogating Dasein analysis of *Being and Time*, or the slightly later transcending question of "the metaphysics of Dasein" or the "Dasein im Mensch,"[91] without remainder? Or was Heidegger always pointing to an a priori openness that pulls human existence out into the open, making it a "Weltwesen Mensch"?[92]

Whether it is Heidegger's early nonsubjectivistic transcendental understanding of the human being as *eksistent* Dasein, or the later, more radically nonsubjective understanding of the human being as *insistent* and assigned to the task of becoming its Da-sein as an essence still to come,[93] what remains constant is his concern with analyzing the structures of temporal and historical openness that make manifestation first possible. Such structures are, however, continually tied to the question of what it means to be a finite human being, to what it means to *do* philosophy starting from finitude, and of challenging the traditional concept of the human when asking such questions.[94] That said, what is clear is that the human being, for Heidegger, while being the disclosive space of manifestation, has never been the measure of all things.

Notes

1. Martin Heidegger, *Logik: Die Frage nach der Wahrheit*, vol. 21 of *Gesamtausgabe*, ed. E. Biemel (Frankfurt: Klostermann, 1976), 49; or Heidegger, *Logic:*

The Question of Truth, trans. Thomas Sheehan (Bloomington: Indiana University Press, 2010), 42.

2. Heidegger, *Logik*, 53; or *Logic*, 44.

3. See Rudolf Bernet, "Different Concepts of Logic and Their Relation to Subjectivity," in *One Hundred Years of Phenomenology*, ed. Dan Zahavi and Frederik Stjernfelt (Dordrecht: Kluwer Academic, 2002), 19–29.

4. See Niall Keane, "Dasein and World: Heidegger's Reconceiving of the Transcendental after Husserl," *Journal of Transcendental Philosophy* 1, no. 3 (2020): 265–87.

5. Heidegger, *Logik*, 51–52; or *Logic*, 43–44.

6. Heidegger, *Logik*, 51–52; or *Logic*, 43–44.

7. Heidegger, *Logik*, 92–93; or *Logic*, 77.

8. Heidegger, *Logik*, 93; or *Logic*, 77.

9. See Rudolf Bernet, "Husserl and Heidegger on Intentionality and Being," *Journal of the British Society for Phenomenology* 21, no. 2 (1990): 143–47.

10. See Donn Welton, *The Other Husserl: Horizons of Transcendental Phenomenology* (Bloomington: Indiana University Press, 2000), 259–85. See also Andrea Staiti, *Husserl's Transcendental Phenomenology: Nature, Spirit, and Life* (Cambridge: Cambridge University Press, 2014); Sebastian Luft, *Subjectivity and Lifeworld in Transcendental Phenomenology* (Evanston, IL: Northwestern University Press, 2011); Dan Zahavi, *Husserl's Legacy: Phenomenology, Metaphysics, and Transcendental Philosophy* (Oxford: Oxford University Press 2017).

11. See John J. Drummond, "The Transcendental and the Psychological," *Husserl Studies* 24, no. 3 (2008): 193–204; Drummond, "The Logical Investigations: Paving the Way to a Transcendental Logic," in *One Hundred Years of Phenomenology*, ed. Dan Zahavi and Frederik Stjernfelt (Dordrecht: Kluwer Academic, 2002), 31–40. See also Dan Zahavi, "Constitution and Ontology: Some Remarks on Husserl's Ontological Position in the 'Logical Investigations,'" *Husserl Studies* 9, no. 2 (1991): 111–24.

12. Martin Heidegger, "Mein Weg in die Phänomenologie," *Zur Sache des Denkens* (Tubingen: Niemeyer, 1969), 83–84; Heidegger, "My Way into Phenomenology," in *Time and Being* (Chicago: University of Chicago Press, 2002), 76.

13. The so-called phenomenological realists at Göttingen and Munich were initially drawn to Husserl's *Logical Investigations* and believed that his descriptive phenomenological method could be applied to concrete philosophical problems as they understood them. However, they saw Husserl's move to transcendental phenomenology and transcendental subjectivity, announced around 1906–7, as a move away from descriptive phenomenology and the empirical analysis of conscious states such as memory, imagination, and perception. The realist students of Husserl saw this move as surrendering the richness of descriptive phenomenology to more pernicious forms of transcendental idealism.

14. Martin Heidegger, *Einleitung in die Philosophie*, vol. 27 of *Gesamtausgabe*, ed. Otto Saame and Ina Saame-Speidel (Frankfurt: Klostermann, 1996), 324.

15. Martin Heidegger, *Die Grundprobleme der Phänomenologie*, vol. 24 of *Gesamtausgabe*, ed. Friedrich-Wilhelm von Herrmann (Frankfurt: Klostermann, 1975), 91–92; or Heidegger, *The Basic Problems of Phenomenology*, trans. Albert Hofstadter (Bloomington: Indiana University Press, 1982), 65.

16. Heidegger, *Die Grundprobleme der Phänomenologie*, 83; or *The Basic Problems of Phenomenology*, 60.

17. Edmund Husserl, "Philosophy as Rigorous Science," in *Phenomenology and the Crisis of Philosophy* (New York: Harper and Row, 1965), 125.

18. Martin Heidegger, *Einführung in die phänomenologische Forschung*, vol. 17 of *Gesamtausgabe*, ed. Friedrich-Wilhelm von Herrmann (Frankfurt: Klostermann, 1994), 95; or Heidegger, *Introduction to Phenomenological Research*, trans. Daniel O. Dahlstrom (Bloomington: Indiana University Press, 2005), 70.

19. Heidegger, *Einführung in die phänomenologische Forschung*, 289; or *Introduction to Phenomenological Research*, 221.

20. On this very issue, see the excellent chapter in this collection by Ingo Farin, "Heidegger's Engagement with and Critique of Philosophical Anthropology."

21. Heidegger, *Einführung in die phänomenologische Forschung*, 94; or *Introduction to Phenomenological Research*, 68.

22. It could and should be mentioned that Husserl's *Crisis* and his later genetic phenomenology have plenty to say about historical life when it comes to the formal and general structures of the lifeworld and of lived-experience. Thus, when Heidegger says that "Husserl neglects the historical roots of his own philosophical questioning," he means historical in a very specific manner, distinct from Husserl's later "transcendental-historical analysis" of meaning and validity establishment and intergenerational accomplishment. It has little to do with Husserl's more enigmatic claim in the *Crisis* regarding "the hidden unity of intentional inwardness which alone constitutes the unity of history." See Husserl, *The Crisis of European Sciences and Transcendental Phenomenology*, trans. David Carr (Evanston, IL: Northwestern University Press, 1970), 73. With history or historicality, Heidegger has in mind the specific manner of being-thrown into a world and projecting meaning in order to hold open the world. In this sense, for Heidegger historicality is a constitutive element of our being as both authentically and inauthentically historical, which is rooted in our being self-temporalizing beings. While there might appear to be analogous issues at stake for Husserl and Heidegger, the manner in which they approach them, via subjectivity and intersubjectivity, or by way of the moved care structure of existence and then transcendence, is not only a manner of different emphases, but also suggests different philosophical commitments. Speaking more personally, as phenomenologists reflecting our Husserl's and Heidegger's distinct ways of approaching the issues of being human and being worldly, we can either commit to the concept of subjectivity and intersubjectivity as containing enough flexibility and richness so as to include the entirety of what Heidegger sees as necessary, even if for him the language of subjectivity has buried what is necessary, or we follow

Heidegger's path and do so in manner as phenomenologically careful as possible. I have chosen the latter route.

23. Heidegger, *Einführung in die phänomenologische Forschung*, 95; or *Introduction to Phenomenological Research*, 69.

24. Heidegger, *Einführung in die phänomenologische Forschung*, 95; or *Introduction to Phenomenological Research*, 70.

25. Heidegger, *Einführung in die phänomenologische Forschung*, 95; or *Introduction to Phenomenological Research*, 70.

26. Heidegger, *Einführung in die phänomenologische Forschung*, 95; or *Introduction to Phenomenological Research*, 70.

27. See Chad Engelland, *Heidegger's Shadow: Kant, Husserl, and the Transcendental Turn* (London: Routledge, 2017), 53.

28. See the chapter in this collection by Sara Heinämaa, "On the Twofoldness of Human Beings: Husserl's 'Reply' to Heidegger's Critical Remarks."

29. Martin Heidegger, *Phänomenologische Interpretationen zu Aristoteles: Einführung in die phänomenologische Forschung*, vol. 61 of *Gesamtausgabe*, ed. Walter Bröcker and Käte Bröcker-Oltmanns (Frankfurt: Klostermann, 1985), 131; or Heidegger, *Phenomenological Interpretations of Aristotle: Initiation into Phenomenological Research*, trans. Richard Rojcewicz (Bloomington: Indiana University Press, 2001), 98.

30. Heidegger, *Die Grundprobleme der Phänomenologie*, 89; or *The Basic Problems of Phenomenology*, 63.

31. Heidegger, *Die Grundprobleme der Phänomenologie*, 215; or *The Basic Problems of Phenomenology*, 168.

32. Heidegger, *Einleitung in die Philosophie*, 309.

33. Heidegger, *Die Grundprobleme der Phänomenologie*, 211; or *The Basic Problems of Phenomenology*, 165.

34. Heidegger, *Einleitung in die Philosophie*, 240.

35. Heidegger, *Einleitung in die Philosophie*, 309.

36. Heidegger, *Einleitung in die Philosophie*, 328.

37. Heidegger, *Einleitung in die Philosophie*, 310–11.

38. Heidegger, *Einleitung in die Philosophie*, 310–11.

39. Heidegger, *Einleitung in die Philosophie*, 115.

40. Martin Heidegger, *Ontologie: Hermeneutik der Faktizität*, vol. 63 of *Gesamtausgabe*, ed. Käte Bröcker-Oltmanns (Frankfurt: Klostermann, 1988), 5; or Heidegger, *Ontology: The Hermeneutics of Facticity*, trans. John van Buren (Bloomington: Indiana University Press, 1999), 4.

41. For notable exceptions to this trend, see Parvis Emad, *Heidegger and the Phenomenology of Values: His Critique of Intentionality* (Glen Ellyn, IL: Torey, 1981); Frank Schalow, "The Anomaly of World: From Scheler to Heidegger," *Continental Philosophy Review* 24, no. 1 (1991): 75–87; Manfred S. Frings, "Heidegger and Scheler," *Philosophy Today* 12, no. 1 (1968): 21–30; Steven Crowell, "The Middle

Heidegger's Phenomenological Metaphysics," in *The Oxford Handbook of the History of Phenomenology*, ed. Dan Zahavi (Oxford: Oxford University Press, 2018), 229–50.

42. Max Scheler, *Die deutsche Philosophie der Gegenwart*, vol. 7 of *Gesammelte Werke* (Bern: Francke, 1973), 310.

43. It must be said, for Husserl of *Ideas I*, such acts, always executed on the basis of intuitive fulfillment, are considered true or authentic only insofar as they correspond to objects and states of affairs that are experienced as *existing*.

44. Max Scheler, *Formalism in Ethics and Non-formal Ethics of Values* (Evanston, IL: Northwestern University Press, 1973), 374.

45. Scheler, *Formalism in Ethics and Non-formal Ethics of Values*, 52.

46. Scheler, *Formalism in Ethics and Non-formal Ethics of Values*, 52.

47. Scheler, *Formalism in Ethics and Non-formal Ethics of Values*, 51. The emphasis on "becoming" is given in the original German through Scheler's italicization of *werden* in *kundwerden*.

48. Martin Heidegger, *Metaphysische Anfangsgründe der Logik im Ausgang von Leibniz*, vol. 26 of Gesamtausgabe, ed. Klaus Held (Frankfurt: Klostermann, 1978), 63; or Heidegger, *The Metaphysical Foundations of Logic*, trans. Michael Heim (Bloomington: Indiana University Press, 1984), 51.

49. Heidegger, *Metaphysische Anfangsgründe der Logik im Ausgang von Leibniz*, 166; or *The Metaphysical Foundations of Logic*, 132. See also Heidegger, *Einleitung in die Philosophie*, 235.

50. Heidegger, *Metaphysische Anfangsgründe der Logik im Ausgang von Leibniz*, 166; or *The Metaphysical Foundations of Logic*, 132.

51. Martin Heidegger, *Sein und Zeit*, 17th ed. (Tubingen: Niemeyer, 1993), 47–48; or Heidegger, *Being and Time*, trans. John Macquarie and Edward Robinson (New York: Harper and Row, 1962), 73–74.

52. Heidegger, *Sein und Zeit*, 48; or *Being and Time*, 74.

53. Scheler, *Die deutsche Philosophie der Gegenwart*, 311.

54. Scheler, *Formalism in Ethics and Non-formal Ethics of Values*, 393.

55. Heidegger, *Metaphysische Anfangsgründe der Logik im Ausgang von Leibniz*, 62; or *The Metaphysical Foundations of Logic*, 50.

56. Heidegger, *Metaphysische Anfangsgründe der Logik im Ausgang von Leibniz*, 62; or *The Metaphysical Foundations of Logic*, 51.

57. On this very issue, see Steven Crowell, "The Middle Heidegger's Phenomenological Metaphysics," 234.

58. Heidegger, *Einleitung in die Philosophie*, 240.

59. Heidegger, *Einleitung in die Philosophie*, 214–16.

60. Heidegger, *Metaphysische Anfangsgründe der Logik im Ausgang von Leibniz*, 215; or *The Metaphysical Foundations of Logic*, 168.

61. Heidegger, *Einleitung in die Philosophie*, 214.

62. Heidegger, *Einleitung in die Philosophie*, 353.

63. Martin Heidegger, *Prolegomena zur Geschichte des Zeitbegriffs*, vol. 20 of *Gesamtausgabe*, ed. Petra Jaeger (Frankfurt: Klostermann, 1979), 40; or Heidegger, *History of the Concept of Time: Prolegomena*, trans. Theodore Kisiel (Bloomington: Indiana University Press, 1985), 31.

64. Martin Heidegger, *Seminare*, vol. 15 of *Gesamtausgabe*, ed. Curd Ochwadt (Frankfurt: Klostermann, 1986), 384; or Heidegger, *Four Seminars*, trans. Andrew Mitchell and François Raffoul (Bloomington: Indiana University Press, 2003), 71.

65. Edmund Husserl, *Ideas Pertaining to a Pure Phenomenology and to a Phenomenological Philosophy*, bk. 1, *General Introduction to a Pure Phenomenology*, trans. F. Kersten (Dordrecht: Kluwer Academic, 1983), 349.

66. Husserl, *Ideas*, bk. 1, 199.

67. Heidegger, *Seminare*, 382; or *Four Seminars*, 70.

68. Martin Heidegger, *Zollikoner Seminare*, vol. 89 of *Gesamtausgabe*, ed. Peter Trawny (Frankfurt: Klostermann, 2017), 261; or Heidegger, *Zollikon Seminars*, ed. Medard Boss, trans. Franz K. Mayr and Richard R. Askay (Evanston, IL: Northwestern University Press, 2001), 208.

69. Heidegger, *Sein und Zeit*, 164; or *Being and Time*, 207.

70. Heidegger, *Prolegomena zur Geschichte des Zeitbegriffs*, 101; or *History of the Concept of Time*, 74.

71. Heidegger, *Seminare*, 377; or *Four Seminars*, 67.

72. Scheler, *Formalism in Ethics and Non-formal Ethics of Values*, 48.

73. Heidegger, *Seminare*, 377; or *Four Seminars*, 67.

74. Heidegger, *Prolegomena zur Geschichte des Zeitbegriffs*, 98; or *History of the Concept of Time*, 72.

75. The relationship between fundamental ontological analysis and what Heidegger terms, in 1928, as "metontological analysis" takes on significance here. What Heidegger is trying to think together in 1928 is the joint-task of reconceiving what it means to be a thing and reconceiving our relationship to things as such, which is precisely what he refers to as "metontology," understood as the "reversal" or "overturning [*Umschlag*] of ontology" (*Metaphysische Anfangsgründe der Logik im Ausgang von Leibniz*, 199; or *The Metaphysical Foundations of Logic*, 157). This is Heidegger's attempt to avoid both idealism and realism and to challenge the naturalistic understanding of the world as a manifold of splintered sensations, so that another sense of the world and our being-in-the-world is both conceivable and retrievable as a "metaphysical ontic" science (*Metaphysische Anfangsgründe der Logik im Ausgang von Leibniz*, 201). On foot of this, Heidegger claims that our relationship to the world is one of "intimate familiarity with the entity" (*Prolegomena zur Geschichte des Zeitbegriffs*, 158; or *History of the Concept of Time*, 152), and because of this forgotten familiarity—forgotten because it is so intimate—he sets out examine the world, both on its own terms and in terms of disclosedness. For a critical assessment of Heidegger's use of "metontology," see Steven Crowell, "The Middle Heidegger's Phenomenological Metaphysics," 229–50.

76. Scheler, *Formalism in Ethics and Non-formal Ethics of Values*, 53.
77. Engelland, *Heidegger's Shadow*, 172.
78. Heidegger, *Prolegomena zur Geschichte des Zeitbegriffs*, 101; or *History of the Concept of Time*, 74.
79. Martin Heidegger, *Sein und Zeit*, 85; or *Being and Time*, 117.
80. Martin Heidegger, *Wegmarken*, vol. 9 of *Gesamtausgabe*, ed. Friedrich-Wilhelm von Herrmann (Frankfurt: Klostermann, 1976), 154; or Heidegger, *Pathmarks*, ed. William McNeill (Cambridge: Cambridge University Press, 1998), 120.
81. Heidegger, *Metaphysische Anfangsgründe der Logik im Ausgang von Leibniz*, 168; or *The Metaphysical Foundations of Logic*, 134.
82. Heidegger, *Sein und Zeit*, 365–366; or *Being and Time*, 417.
83. Wilhelm Dilthey, *The Formation of the Historical World in the Human Sciences* (Princeton, NJ: Princeton University Press, 2002), 216.
84. Heidegger, *Phänomenologische Interpretationen zu Aristoteles*, 88; or *Phenomenological Interpretations of Aristotle*, 66.
85. See chapter in this collection by Ingo Farin, "Heidegger's Engagement with and Critique of Philosophical Anthropology."
86. Heidegger, *Die Grundprobleme der Phänomenologie*, 237; or *The Basic Problems of Phenomenology*, 166.
87. Martin Heidegger, *Das Ereignis*, vol. 71 of *Gesamtausgabe*, ed. Friedrich-Wilhelm von Herrmann (Frankfurt: Klostermann, 2009), 131; or Heidegger, *The Event*, trans. Richard Rojcewicz (Bloomington: Indiana University Press, 2013), 112.
88. Heidegger, *Seminare*, 384; or *Four Seminars*, 71.
89. Michel Haar, *Heidegger and the Essence of Man* (Albany: State University of New York Press, 1993), 141.
90. Heidegger, *Die Grundprobleme der Phänomenologie*, 220; or *The Basic Problems of Phenomenology*, 155.
91. Martin Heidegger, *Kant und das Problem der Metaphysik*, vol. 3 of *Gesamtausgabe*, ed. Friedrich-Wilhelm von Herrmann (Frankfurt: Klostermann, 1991), 229–30, 234, 283; or Heidegger, *Kant and the Problem of Metaphysics*, trans. Richard Taft, 5th enl. ed. (Bloomington: Indiana University Press, 1997), 161, 164, 199.
92. Martin Heidegger, *Vom Wesen der menschlichen Freiheit: Einleitung in die Philosophie*, vol. 31 of *Gesamtausgabe*, ed. Hartmut Tietjen (Frankfurt: Klostermann, 1982), 264.
93. Martin Heidegger, *Die Metaphysik des deutschen Idealismus: Zur erneuten Auslegung von Schelling: Philosophische Untersuchungen über das Wesen der menschlichen Freiheit und die damit zusammenhängenden Gegenstände (1809)*, vol. 49 of *Gesamtausgabe*, ed. Günter Seubold (Frankfurt: Klostermann, 1991), 61–62. Although the hyphenated form of Dasein does appear in some earlier passages, it becomes almost standard in the later work.
94. Heidegger, *Einleitung in die Philosophie*, 3.

Chapter Seven

Play, World, and the Human

Bruce Janz

Play and the Human

Of the options to describe or account for the humanness of the human that have been proffered, play is surely one of the most common. Schiller posits a "play drive" (*Spieltrieb*) in his letters on aesthetic education, which rationalize and bring into balance our capacity of sensation and our rational impulse to impose order. Nietzsche, in *Beyond Good and Evil*, tells us that "[a] man's maturity—consists in having found again the seriousness one had as a child, at play." Johan Huizinga foregrounds play in seeing humans as "homo ludens."

Heidegger, too, appeals to play, as we shall see, but in a far more limited fashion than even some of his interlocutors and students such as Eugen Fink, Kostas Axelos, and Hans-Georg Gadamer (each of whom writes extensively about play). We do not get the sense of playfulness in his writing, an embodiment of play as a mode of philosophizing, as we see later in writers such as Derrida. Is play for him, then, merely a minor note, a moment in his vast oeuvre that bears little weight, and that gives little insight into how he thinks about the human?

I want to argue here that, despite the fact that play is rarely foregrounded for Heidegger the way it is for other writers, it is nevertheless important to understand the humanness of the human. It is crucial to the way he thinks about "world," for instance. His approach to play changes at different times in his writing and develops differently than we see in some of these other writers, but always in the service of investigating how we might question Being. I will also argue that another candidate for understanding the human that he rightly argues against, humanism, might be recovered to some extent through the use of play, and we can see this path taken in the work of Sylvia Wynter.

Heidegger on Play

Michael Haar points out that, for Heidegger, "the unfolding of being is 'play'; that is, it is impossible to decipher any program in it, any raison d'etre or any foundation."[1] Heidegger sees play as something that constitutes our ontology, as opposed to theories of play that simply counterpose play to work, or that connect it to pleasure. But the path we see Heidegger take on the question of play is different from many of those around him, despite the fact that many of them are influenced by him. For Heidegger, the concept of play deepens and changes as Heidegger explores the implications of Being. We can, in particular, see a shift from his early thinking about play, which is directly linked to the human and uses human play as a metonym for the way that play is the basis for our most human activity, to his later work, in which the human seems sidelined from the cosmic or transcendental nature of play.

We first see play discussed in the *Einleitung in die Philosophie* (Introduction to Philosophy), his lectures in Freiburg in 1928–29. Play begins from the point of view of the subject or being who plays.[2] His approach here is a revision of Kant's "play of life." At this point he is already connecting play with world, although what he means by that is that the act of engaging in game-playing creates its own world. There is an order internal to game-play, which one must take seriously if the game is to be played at all. To play the game is to engage with other players and with the materiality of the game with a particular mood (and, in this sense, Heidegger comes close to Wittgenstein's account of language games here).

Linked to play is transcendence; indeed, "we take transcendence as a game."[3] The act of playing is what Heidegger calls "being-in-the-world." In other words, the act of play creates a world, and the world is sustained through the actions performed in it, under the rules or practices that structure the game. Heidegger summarizes his sense of how play works:

1. Play is a free making that has its own unanimity, as long as it forms within play.

2. Although play is free making, it is just the bond and not a separate structure. It forms its connections in the playing.

3. Playing is therefore never a behavior towards an object, not a mere behavior at all . . . , rather, the playing of the game and the game of playing are inherently inseparable events.

4. We call play in this sense the Being-in-the-World, the Transcendence that we always characterized as the transcendence of beings. Being-in-the-World has always played over and played around Being; in this play, it first of all constitutes the space, even in the true sense, within which we find beings.[4]

At this point, then, play is a familiar human activity that has ontological implications. Opening up the question of what it means to be human means to move from this familiar activity to its ontological and transcendental grounding. Heidegger's phenomenology at this point is rooted in the world of human practice and experience and is directed at showing the fundamental meaningfulness of play in a manner that goes beyond the objectives of a particular game or, indeed, beyond psychological analysis about the motivations for action within games or the usefulness of games to human development, sociality, or personality development.

We next see some attention to play in *Beiträge zur Philosophie (Vom Ereignis)* (Contributions to Philosophy [of the Event]),[5] from 1936–38, along with other volumes in what Daniela Vallega-Neu calls Heidegger's "poietic writings."[6] The focus here is not on play but interplay (indeed, one section of that work is titled "The Interplay") and the "temporal-spatial playing field." And, more importantly, the writings from this time resituate play. There is no talk of familiar acts of play here, no digging into various experiences of game-play to find a phenomenological basis, and therefore no attempt to ground transcendental questioning in familiar human activity. This is a common Heideggerian move, when thinking about Being, to see it as a unity rather than a multiplicity. The actual human experience of play complicates that—if the ontology of play looks anything like the human acts of play, it would have to face the possibility that the game itself might change, and that there could be fundamentally different ways to play that emerge over time. Heidegger is, of course, very interested in the diversity of human experience, but the move from the kind of play that we see in the *Einleitung* to that which is in these poietic works is a move away from anything that most people would recognize as the experience of play except in the most abstract of terms. We can see this, in fact, in that this sense of play, in the temporal-spatial playing field, is only experienced by very few and is "alien to everything 'close to life' ":

> Humans—a few, unknown to one another—will prepare themselves in the temporal-spatial playing field of Da-sein and will gather themselves into a nearness to beyng, a nearness which must remain alien to everything "close to life."[7]

Play is not, at this point, a universally experienced phenomenon, but something experienced only by a few, as the space in which the truth of beyng opens up. The playing field is the preparation for the leap, which is an exploration of the truth that the temporal-spatial playing field makes possible.

This version of play appears throughout these poietic works. Another of them, *The History of Beyng*, connects beyng to play:

> Beyng is event of appropriation, propriates itself. "How" the event of appropriation "is"—as though it were a being—is a question that cannot be posed. For beyng *is*—authentically, that is, out of being appropriated and as such being appropriated.
>
> "*When*" the event of appropriation is and "where" it is always remains an inappropriate question, for "time" and "space" in the original sense (of the clearing of time-play-space in the sustaining counter-play), and especially in the greatly derivative sense, spring forth from the event of appropriation, *are* together with it. So beyng, then, is "supra-temporal" and "supra-spatial"—no! Rather, as abyssal ground it is the most temporal and spatial—*the time-space dimension of clearing* as site, indeed as sustained in sustainment, *the abyssal ground of the in-between:* abyssally temporalizing-spacing as appropriative event.[8]

In other words, play is the event that lies between time and space, and that is part of the "event of appropriation." The picture we get here is of the establishment of a version of beyng that is disrupted in play. Earth and World are part of this also. Immediately before the passage just cited, he says this:

Every earth closes itself off and thus belongs to a world; closing itself off is its *earth-like* character, but earth is, furthermore, historical and already historical. An error to think that one could say something about "nature" or comprehend it independently of history; the impossibility of such in-itself comprehending does not signify any "subjectivism."

Every world opens itself and remains configured to an earth. Every world and every earth is thus historical in the entirety of what belongs to it. This history, however, in keeping with the history of beyng, is seldom and simple and, as that of the Western world, already configured from out of the essence of beyng.[9]

We have a significant shift in how play is thought, compared to the earlier lecture course. It is not a familiar trope with transcendental or ontological implications in Heidegger's poietic works, which creates a world through enacting the potentialities inherent in a game. Instead, play takes on a different character, the temporal-spatial playing field, the counter-play. It is the space that makes creativity possible. Play is part of the "event of appropriation." The earth closes itself off, while the world opens itself because of time-space-play.

By the time of *Der Satz vom Grund* (The Principle of Reason), his lecture course from 1955–56, play looks different yet again.[10] At the end of the thirteenth lecture, he returns to play. He has been analyzing the principle that for everything that happens there is a reason ("Nothing is without reason"), and not surprisingly finds that the *Grund* diverges into the grounds for something and the reason for something. He traces this back through the Latin *ratio* to the Greek λόγος or *logos*, transforming the question from the one common throughout the nineteenth century, of whether we could in principle access and understand the causes of all things and states of being that existed, to the question of how being shows itself. Being and its reason are not separate; *logos* "names in one breath being and ground/reason."[11] Play, then, in *The Principle of Reason*, follows the leap; it does not prepare the way for it:

If we hear the principle of reason in the other tonality and think about all we hear, then this thinking-about is a leap, indeed a far-reaching leap that brings thinking into a play with that wherein being qua being finds its repose; that wherein being finds its repose is not the sort of thing upon which it depends for its ground/reason. Through this leap, thinking enters into the breadth and depth of that play upon which our human nature is staked. Humans are truly capable of playing and of remaining in play only insofar as they are engaged in this play and thereby at stake in the play. In which play? So far we have barely experienced this play and have not yet considered its nature, which means, what the play plays and who plays it, and how the playing is to be thought here.[12]

"So far we have barely experienced this play," Heidegger says. It is as far from the obvious and familiar sense of play as we could get, and far from the Heidegger of the *Einleitung in die Philosophie*. It is no longer even the temporal spatial playing field. And yet, here we also return to the human. It is play between the two senses of ground and reason; it is play between freedom and necessity:

> [T]he manner of our thinking until now does not suffice to think this, for as soon as we attempt to think the play, which means to think it according to its mode of representation, we take this play as something that is. So just as a ground/reason belongs to the being of a being, so it belongs to the play. Thus the nature of the play is determined as it is everywhere determined, namely as the dialectic of freedom and necessity within the horizon of ground/reason, of ratio, of rules, of rules of play, of calculus.[13]

Heidegger concludes this thought as follows: "When God plays, a world comes to be." And with that, we also have the world making its appearance, in connection with play and with the human. But that play is not just God's play (whatever that might mean for Heidegger). It remains the play of being, and indeed it is the most serious play, because it faces death, "the most elevated play in which humans are engaged in on earth, a play in which they are at stake."[14] Elsewhere this is reinforced—in *Identität und Differenz*, he says:

> Dies sei durch ein Beispiel versucht, wobei im voraus zu beachten ist, daß es für das Wesen des Seins nirgends im Seienden ein Beispiel gibt, vermutlich deshalb, weil das Wesen des Seins das Spiel selber ist.[15]

The last part of this sentence is rendered in the English translation as "because the nature of Being is itself the unprecedented exemplar."[16] While that translation might be understandable given the similarity in the sentence of the words *Beispiel* and *Spiel*, a more accurate translation would be "because the essence of Being is Play in itself." This is, to be sure, merely a side comment of his (that is, he does not develop any view on play in that work), but at least it is in line with the picture we get in *The Principle of Reason*.

It is tempting to see play in Heidegger, across all these different texts, less as a concept and more as a useful image, pressed into service when needed for different things. And yet, Heidegger does not use it randomly. There is a sense in each case that play is what allows the new to present itself. What changes is its relation to the human. Play ceases to have much connection to what we might think of in human experience as the act of playing, and becomes inter-play, the space in which the new can emerge. It moves away from a phenomenological view, and toward an ontological one.

A Connecting Thread: Heraclitus Fragment B52

Lecture 13 in *The Principle of Reason* ends with a fragment from Heraclitus about play. It is not just any sort of play, but the play of a child that "plays, because it plays." Heidegger does not directly translate the fragment from Greek, but rather extemporizes on it:

> The *Geschick* of being, a child that plays, shifting the pawns: the royalty of a child—that means, the ἀρχή [arche], that which governs by instituting grounds, the being of beings. The *Geschick* of being: a child that plays. In addition, there are also great children. By the gentleness of its play, the greatest royal child is that mystery of the play in which humans are engaged throughout their life, that play in which their essence is at stake. Why does it play, the great child of the world-play Heraclitus brought into view in the αἰών [aeon]? It plays, because it plays. The "because" withers away in the play. The play is without "why." It plays since it plays. It simply remains a play: the most elevated and the most profound. But this "simply" is everything, the one, the only. Nothing is without ground/reason. Being and ground/reason: the same. Being, as what grounds, has no ground; as the abyss it plays the play that, as *Geschick*, passes

being and ground/reason to us. The question remains whether and how we, hearing the movements of this play, play along and accommodate ourselves to the play.[17]

This is Heidegger's final answer to the problem of the principle of reason, and it lies in the play of a child that is without why (reminiscent of Angelus Silesius's statement: "The rose is without why"). On the one hand, it seems to move back to Heidegger's earliest version of play, which is connected to acts of play rather than the ontology in which Being can question itself; on the other hand, it is not an extrapolation of the imaginative world of a child at play. The play is, to use religious terminology, the site of creation *ex nihilo*, not the site of *thaumazein*, or the wonder of unfolding.

We see the same fragment used in two other thinkers, more commonly identified as theorists of play: Eugen Fink and Kostas Axelos. Stuart Elden tracks the use of this Heraclitus fragment in both figures.[18] It is worth noting that Heidegger, Fink, Axelos, as well as Elden and Krell[19] all understand αἰών (*aeon*) as something like the time of the world. One Heraclitus scholar, though, argues that Heraclitus's own sense of the term is "the single concrete life-time of an individual human being,"[20] and the interpretation of aeon as a generation, age, or period starts only in the later Greek and the Jewish and Christian time. Plato's *Timaeus* is the first time that aeon "acquires the technical sense of timeless 'eternity' as contrasted with temporal duration."[21] "Heraclitus himself can only have meant to say something not about divinity or about universal principles but instead about the concrete life-time belonging to real, individual humans."[22]

Why should this matter? It matters precisely because of the question about the relationship the question of Being and the life of the human. The interpretation becomes very different if aeon is a single human life. As Most says, "Heraclitus is saying that whatever it is that human beings are during the course of their whole life, they are really nothing more than children playing games: and even if they win the game and become king, they do so only as children, not as thinking, responsible adults."[23]

Raising the possibility that the interpretation by Heidegger and others is anachronistic does not suggest that he or anyone else is philosophically wrong, or that getting Heraclitus right clears up ambiguity (making matters worse, this fragment is regarded by Heraclitus scholars as one of the least clear). The problem with interpreting Heraclitus's fragments is that they are fragments. They do not come with intrinsic explanatory text or argumentation. Their interpretation is extrinsic, in the history of engagement and use of the fragments. And so, Heidegger's use is one trajectory.

But there is another trajectory, one in which play looks very different. If play is simply a human life, the time when a person has vitality, then playing a game in which there is at least some element of chance speaks less to human involvement in world-building and more to our limited ability to apprehend the world. Further, it suggests an incremental approach—each step in a person's life is lived in the moment, and each moment makes available or brings into focus a range of subsequent possible steps. Play does not construct a world in the sense that someone could model that world, write a rule book for it, and market the game to others who want to play it (this is why "game" is a very different concept from "play," despite the fact that they are sometimes interchanged). Another analyst[24] points out that aeon has a long history in Homer of being connected with a duration of vitality in a person's life.

If aeon is something like an age or an epoch, or, more than that, something like timelessness or the eternal, that sense of the incremental and contingent nature of play is lost. It is more amenable to Heidegger's sense that Being is a gathering, and less open to the contingencies and contradictions of one life. We can come to imagine that we can stand both in the position of the child, being absorbed in play, and above that position, seeing the play as constructing a world and seeing that world as an articulable, understandable thing.

If play is the same as a game, even the game of building a world, we run the risk of that game being mastered at a nonhuman level. There are few if any games now that humans still play better than computers. The game of Go used to be held out as the last game too complex for a computer to beat a world-class player, but that too has fallen. Even in a game that holds forth as many possibilities at every stage as Go does (and, the range of possibilities exceeds the number of atoms in the universe), the pattern-recognition capacity of computers, along with their superior memory for past games, makes it impossible that humans can create a world through play. If play is poiesis, computers seem to do it better than we can.

Of course, this line of thinking cannot be right, not for Heidegger nor for Fink or Axelos. The play of computers does not, as of yet, at least, create anything like the world of potentiality and actuality that is the space of human Being. That cannot be what we mean by poiesis, by the ability to create a world. It cannot be through play, if that is what we mean by play. And indeed, it is not what we mean, but the only way we can avoid that version of play is by taking the path of immanence, of recognizing that the life lived is one of stumbling through, playing a game in which there is not only chance along with skill, but also changing conditions that render skill of the past fractured and fragmented. And, more than that, like a child we play foolishly. This is one of the ambiguities of the Heraclitus fragment—what does he mean by including a child? Heidegger and others assume that it is about innocence and purity and intuitiveness, much like the Romantics did. Heraclitus scholars, though, are split on this. They point to other uses of children as figures in ancient texts, including in Heraclitus's. They are often figures of incompetence, "unworthy, immature, and foolish, and generally inferior to adults."[25] The game, too, is ambiguous—Was this a game that solely involved skill, or did it also involve chance, and if so, how much?

Eugen Fink renders the fragment as follows: "Der Weltlauf ist ein spielendes Kind, Brettsteine setzend—eine Königsherrschaft des Kindes,"[26] translated into English as "The course of the world is a playing child, moving pieces on a board—a king's power belongs to the child."[27] Kostas Axelos translates the fragment this way: "Die Weltzeit ist ein spielendes Kind—ein Kind beim Brettspiel: das Königtum eines Kindes."[28] This was rendered in the English translation as "Worldly time is a child at play—a child with a board game: the kingdom of a child."[29] In his earlier work on Heraclitus[30] he translates the same fragment into French: "Le Temps est un enfant qui joue, en déplaçant des pions; la royauté d'un enfant," which might be rendered in English as something like "Time is a child playing, moving pawns; the royalty of a child."

Fink's and Axelos's versions suggest a tension or contradiction, between the child as a limited being, an individual, and the child as king, lord over a kingdom. Indeed, Axelos goes on in his work on Heraclitus to describe time as a child who constantly builds and destroys, who has both a royal face and a childish one. Heidegger's extemporization gives us less of that tension—the child *is* royalty, he does not just pretend to be royalty. As he indicated in earlier remarks on play, it is not every human who can play, but the very rare one who can.

It is perhaps surprising that even though this aphorism plays a part in both Heidegger and Fink, it does not show up in the seminar on Heraclitus that they conducted in 1966–67 and published together[31] (or for that matter in Heidegger's lecture courses on Heraclitus[32]). Both Stuart Elden and David Farrell Krell note this and point out that even though the fragment is not mentioned, all the components are present. While that is generally true, play does not explicitly make an appearance either. The world, and related concepts like world-formation and world order, on the other hand, can be found throughout that seminar.

The direction Fink takes the concept of play throughout his writing resembles the Heidegger of the *Einleitung* much more than the versions of play Heidegger deploys later. The model of play is rooted in actual human game-playing. For Fink, the relationship between play and the world is that (as he says in the title of his major work on play) play is a "symbol of the world." What does this mean? It means that play partakes in the two features of the symbol, which are its fragmentation and its completion.[33] "*Symbolon*," he says, "comes from *symballein*, "coinciding," and signifies a coinciding of the fragment with what completes it." Fink connects play and world through symbol:

> A completely different perspective on play opens up for us when we understand the "non-actuality" of its playworld not as a "reproduction," not as an imagistic rendering and portrayal of an original being, but rather as a "symbol"—and thus think the essence of the symbol from the world-relation. A being, a finite thing, becomes a symbol when it experiences "completion" by the world-whole, when the totality shines forth and gleams in it, when it becomes representative of the universe—when the finite is translucent in its intraworldliness, sets the gaze free, as it were, into the prevailing force that flows through the finite, brings it about, and annihilates it. Each thing in the vicinity of the human being can become a symbol, can wrench us from the fixed limitation of our gaze that sees for the most part only beings: finished, fixed things and finished, fixed events in and with things, but not Being itself, which structures and destroys, which only "sojourns" in the thing, so to speak, and which ultimately conditions all things.[34]

Fink's perspective, then, is distinct from Heidegger's. Play is not that which very few humans have ever truly experienced, but rather that through which the world-whole shines forth. The concern here is to show the worldliness of human play, that is, the way that human action in general and play in particular show the fragmentation of being human while also completing that fragmentation. It is different than other forms of human action:

> For us, play is not an arbitrary theme of philosophy, which can occupy itself with anything and everything. Play has an extraordinary status in its being an existential basic phenomenon, just as primordial as mortality, love, work, and struggle. But in love, work, and struggle there is the appearance that the human being involves himself exclusively with another being—as though he were relating to a nature that is to be transformed, to his fellow human beings, whom he needs for mating as well as for ruling. [. . .] It is otherwise with play. Play is not a human enactment of life in which he involves himself with the other beings in his surroundings.[35]

We see, then, that Fink is working toward a similar existential sense of play as Heidegger is but continues to link it to human activity.

Kostas Axelos's version of play is as the "system of systems."[36] He is interested in the "large system of elementary forces which link man's play to the world's play."[37] What does he mean by the world's play? It is not just play within the world, but "world's play 'itself,' world as play, the unfurling of play in which man's play and world's play encounter each other perhaps to become one. [. . .] The world no longer obeys—even though still obeying—given or assumed rules. It swallows up these rules along with all their possible combinations."[38] He is, in other words, more explicit about not only the difference between human play and the play of the world, but also the exponential variations possible when those two are seen as intersecting and underlying each other.

We have three models of play, then: Heidegger's, in which play becomes increasingly disconnected from human play; Fink's, in which play remains strongly tethered to human modes of play; and Axelos's, in which both of these modes of play exist, and the creative space happens when they interact. Each represents a way of seeing play as fundamental to being human.

Humans and Humanism

Thinking about Heidegger and the human is a far less clear task than it might be for some other philosophers. While we might think of him as describing the human way of being in the world, we start running into barriers of his own making if we think he will be drawing on the most obvious philosophical approaches to accomplish that description. The human is not equivalent to humanism, of either the Roman, Renaissance, or any later variety. Man is not the measure of all things, nor have humans replaced God as the source of meaning. We see him make this case most clearly in the "Letter on 'Humanism'":

> Every humanism is either grounded in a metaphysics or is itself made to be the ground of one. Every determination of the essence of man that already presupposes an interpretation of beings without asking about the truth of Being, whether knowingly or not, is metaphysical. The result is that what is peculiar to all metaphysics, specifically with respect to the way the essence of man is determined, is that it is "humanistic." Accordingly, every humanism remains metaphysical. In defining the humanity of man humanism not only does not ask about the relation of Being to the essence of man; because of its metaphysical origin humanism even impedes the question by neither recognizing nor understanding it. On the contrary, the necessity and proper form of the question concerning the truth of Being, forgotten in and through metaphysics, can come to light only if the question "What is metaphysics?" is posed in the midst of metaphysics' domination. Indeed every inquiry into Being, even the one into the truth of Being, must at first introduce its inquiry as a "metaphysical" one.[39]

Just as we cannot find a humanist Heidegger, at least in the classic sense, we cannot find a Romantic Heidegger. There is no version of the cosmic human, the one in which we can see the microcosm in the macrocosm and vice versa. There is no version of the evolutionary human, the one who is the summation of historical species development. Human existence, the point of Heidegger's investigations, will not be found in individual, cultural, or biological aspirations or definitions we arrive at, from whatever source they come.

The human is everywhere in Heidegger's work, but it does not take these forms. It is further not addressed by thinking about alternatives to the human—what is it to be human as opposed to something else, such as animal, God, matter, technology, creation, and so on. And yet, as we have seen in the discussion of play, for Heidegger the human is also not simply a transcendental extension of an innocent child at play. The human is the one who can ask the question about the truth of Being, and so, no metaphysical frame for humans will ever enable a human to live as a human, but only as something else, something less.

Heidegger's turn against humanism is entirely understandable, given his project of accessing the truth of Being. And yet, the relatively minor role for play in his work suggests an opening for understanding the human that he did not pursue. He could not pursue play in the manner others had, for that would just be another metaphysical frame. It would be a metaphor, however disguised, of the innocence of the child as the telos of the adult. So, he moves play into another space, the space of inter-play, of the temporal-spatial playing field, which cannot be mistaken for a disguised analogy to the play of a child. The child in Heraclitus's fragment B52, for Heidegger, plays because he plays, and no more than that.

The alternative I want to consider here does not primarily come from Fink or Axelos, or even Gadamer,[40] even though those ways of integrating play with the human have much to commend themselves. Instead, I want to think about Sylvia Wynter's reconfiguration of humanism. She writes as a Black Jamaican-American woman, one whose people were left out of Renaissance humanism. If anyone should have cause to reject humanism even more than Heidegger, it should be someone like her.

And yet, she has been on a decades-long quest to rethink humanism, to make it into something that does not stand for the metaphysical certainty about what "Man" is supposed to be like, and the rhetorical certainties about which narratives of human achievement are supposed to be taken as determinative. And, aiding her in this question for a new humanism is none other than Heidegger, among many others.

Sylvia Wynter and the Play of Humanism

Wynter's project, in reconstituting humanism, was to show how it could have been an engine of creativity, but it was in fact captured by a limited imagination. The engine of creativity was turned into a factory that simply produced commodities that we called Humans (or, in her terms, "Man1"), instead of releasing us to be human. She looks back to Heidegger's "Letter on 'Humanism'" in this paragraph:

> The larger issue is, then, the incorporation of all forms of human being into a single homogenized descriptive statement that is based on the figure of the West's liberal monohumanist *Man*.

And this conception of being, because ostensibly natural-scientific, is biocentric. So when Fanon says, "I take my narcissism in both hands and I say that the human is not a mere [biological] mechanism," he overturns this biocentric conception. That doesn't mean that this ethno-class natural organism model of the human doesn't bring you knowledge—as Heidegger points out, it brings you all kinds of knowledge. But it is *not* the knowledge of the human reconceptualized in the direction of a hybridly, both *mythoi* and *bios*, being. We therefore now need to initiate the exploration of the new reconceptualized form of knowledge that would be called for by Fanon's redefinition of being human as that of skins (phylogeny/ontogeny) *and* masks (sociogeny). Therefore *bios* and *mythoi*. And notice! One major implication here: *humanness* is no longer a *noun. Being human is a praxis.*[41]

We will not be able to unpack all the conceptual moves she is making in this interview excerpt, but the key is to notice that Wynter, like Heidegger, is trying to move away from a metaphysical frame that would establish what humans are or could be. Her ostensible reasons for doing this differ from his. For Heidegger, we are unable to truly ask the question of Being if we have these frames, whereas for Wynter, we always have an implicit model for humanity, even when we ask about being human as a universal category, that limits its creative potential. That model left out non-Europeans, women, and many others. The result of that model was not play, but its opposite—a rigid deduction of the human from an essence that privileged Europeans, males, and so forth. Not only did it lead away from play, it also led away from creativity. In "The Ceremony Found," Wynter charts what she calls the "genre-specific modes of knowledge production,"[42] that is, the modes of writing the human experience that start from what amount to genre conventions or restrictions on what kinds of narratives are possible. She makes use of language that biologist Humberto Matarana and cognitive scientist Francisco Varela introduce: the "autopoietic turn/overturn," that is, the self-organizing ability of complex systems, which in the end resist the essentializing that Renaissance humanism introduced for our understanding of humans.

Although she never explicitly uses the word, Wynter is introducing play back into the human experience. She is, in other words, recovering humanism for the human experience. She points out that "neither Fanon nor Césaire want to abandon humanism. They want to correct its vision and fulfil its promise."[43] That correction, as she calls it, is more than simply a strategy of inclusion of previously excluded people. The negative argument she makes, against Renaissance humanism as a way of understanding the human, is close to what we see in Heidegger and indeed implied less directly in Fink and Axelos as well. Her goal is to reenchant humanism. She wants to make it possible to ask the question of what it means to be human, something that has not been possible since the metaphysical program of Renaissance humanism was instituted.

Wynter looks for a ceremony,[44] in other words, not just a theoretical position but a process and an event. She operationalizes something that Heidegger leaves abstract, that is, the way that play can link us back to the temporal-spatial playing field and make it so that the counter-play is not just a Hegelian dialectic or some other teleological form of emergence but a truly creative event that allows the human to be truly human. She posits a "Third Event,"[45] after the first event of the emergence of physical life and the second of biological emergence. The third event comes with the creation of fictitious worlds. But this is more than just narrating human potentialities. It is the location of play, the interaction we have with the future, that makes our stories inherently uncertain but forms the basis of creation.

Heidegger tended to prefer to leave the questioning of the human open. Any models or examples will fundamentally taint the real questioning of Being by predetermining the kinds of answers that are appropriate. Wynter's recovery of humanism might be superficially understood simply as an act of inclusion for those previously excluded, but she is trying to do something more profound than that.

Conclusion

Heidegger's concern with the human runs deep, and is tied to play, but in a manner different from those around him, even those inspired by him such as Eugen Fink and Kostas Axelos. We can see the human not because it is different for him than other ways of being, nor through a phenomenology that locates that which is human in the specific kind of play we see in children, but in our ability to create through Dasein's ability to question within a temporal-spatial playing field, and through counter-play. It is for this reason that Heidegger resists humanism as a strategy for explicating the human—it fails to engage that field of play, but instead starts by defining who we are, thus limiting that field. Sylvia Wynter's recovery of humanism is directed at the recovery of the creativity, and thus the playing field, of the human, and so, perhaps surprisingly, stands in a line of descent from Heidegger's concerns about the human as that which comes out of the questioning that arises from the field of play. Like Heidegger, but unlike Fink and Axelos, she does not engage in a phenomenology of play based on familiar examples, but instead asks how the interrogation of the human might be possible.

Notes

1. Michael Haar, *Heidegger and the Essence of Man* (Albany: State University of New York Press, 1993), 114.

2. Martin Heidegger, *Einleitung in die Philosophie*, vol. 27 of *Gesamtausgabe*, ed. Otto Saame and Ida Saame-Speidel (Frankfurt: Klostermann, 1996), 309ff.

3. Heidegger, *Einleitung in die Philosophie*, 315.

4. Author's translation and reformatting of the following text, from Heidegger, *Einleitung in die Philosophie*, 316:

> 1. Spielen ist ein freies Bilden, das je seine eigene Einstimmigkeit hat, sofern es sich im Spielen bildet. 2. Spielen ist damit, obzwar freies Bilden, gerade die Bindung, aber nicht ein abgelöstes Gebilde, sondern das bildende Sichbinden an und in das spielende Bilden selbst. 3. Spielen ist daher nie ein Verhalten zu einem Gegenstand, überhaupt kein bloßes Verhalten zu . . . , sondern das Spielen des Spiels und Spiel des Spielens zumal ein ursprünglich in sich unzertrennliches Geschehen. 4. Spielen in diesem Sinne nennen wir das In-der-Welt-Sem, die Transzendenz, die wir zunächst immer kennzeichneten als Überstieg über das Seiende. Das In-der-Welt-sein hat immer schon zuvor das Seiende überspielt und umspielt; in diesem Spielen bildet es allererst den Raum, sogar im wirklichen Sinne, innerhalb dessen wir Seiendes antreffen.

5. Martin Heidegger, *Contributions to Philosophy (of the Event)*, trans. Richard Rojcewicz and Daniela Vallega-Neu (Bloomington: Indiana University Press, 2012).

6. Daniela Vallega-Neu, *Heidegger's Poietic Writings: From "Contributions to Philosophy" to "The Event,"* Studies in Continental Thought (Bloomington: Indiana University Press, 2018).

7. Heidegger, *Contributions to Philosophy (of the Event)*, 179.

8. Martin Heidegger, *The History of Beyng (1938–40)*, in *The History of Beyng*, trans. William McNeill and Jeffrey Powell (Bloomington: Indiana University Press, 2015), 92.

9. Heidegger, *The History of Beyng (1938–40)*, 91.
10. Martin Heidegger, *The Principle of Reason*, trans. Reginald Lilly (Bloomington: Indiana University Press, 1991).
11. Heidegger, *The Principle of Reason*, 107.
12. Heidegger, *The Principle of Reason*, 111.
13. Heidegger, *The Principle of Reason*, 112.
14. Heidegger, *The Principle of Reason*, 112.
15. Martin Heidegger, *Identität und Differenz*, vol. 11 of *Gesamtausgabe*, ed. Friedrich-Wilhelm von Herrmann, 2nd ed. (Frankfurt: Klostermann, 2006), 72.
16. Martin Heidegger, *Identity and Difference*, trans. Joan Stambaugh (New York: Harper and Row, 1969), 66.
17. Heidegger, *The Principle of Reason*, 113.
18. Stuart Elden, "Eugen Fink and the Question of the World," *Parrhesia*, no. 5 (2008): 48–59.
19. David Farrell Krell, "Towards an Ontology of Play: Eugen Fink's Notion of Spiel," *Research in Phenomenology* 2 (1972): 63–93.
20. Glenn Most, "Heraclitus Fragment B 52 DK (on OF 242)," in *Tracing Orpheus: Studies of Orphic Fragments: In Honour of Alberto Bernabe*, ed. Miguel Herrero de Jauregui, et al. (Berlin: De Gruyter, 2011).
21. Charles Kahn, *The Art and Thought of Heraclitus: An Edition of the Fragments with Translation and Commentary* (Cambridge: Cambridge University Press, 1979), 228.
22. Most, "Heraclitus Fragment B 52 DK," 106.
23. Most, "Heraclitus Fragment B 52 DK," 107.
24. Sandra Šćepanović, "Heraclitus' Fragment B 52 DK Re-examined," *Rhizomata* 3, no. 1 (2015): 34.
25. Šćepanović, "Heraclitus' Fragment B 52 DK Re-examined," 37.
26. Eugen Fink, *Oase des Glücks: Gedanken zu einer Ontologie des Spiels* (Freiburg: Alber, 1957), 50–51.
27. Eugen Fink, *Play as Symbol of the World and Other Writings*, trans. Ian Alexander Moore and Christopher Turner (Bloomington: Indiana University Press, 2016), 30.
28. Kostas Axelos, *Einführung in ein künftiges Denken: Über Marx und Heidegger* (Tübingen: Niemeyer, 1966).
29. Kostas Axelos, *Introduction to a Future Way of Thought: On Marx and Heidegger* (Lüneburg: Meson, 2015), 144.
30. Kostas Axelos, *Héraclite et la philosophie: La première saisie de l'être en devenir de la totalité* (Paris: Éditions de Minuit, 1962), 54.
31. Martin Heidegger and Eugen Fink, *Heraclitus Seminar, 1966/67*, trans. Charles H. Seibert (Alabama: University of Alabama Press, 1979).
32. Martin Heidegger, *Heraclitus: The Inception of Occidental Thinking Logic; Heraclitus's Doctrine of the Logos* (London: Bloomsbury Academic, 2018).

33. Fink, *Play as Symbol of the World*, 120.
34. Fink, *Play as Symbol of the World*, 135.
35. Fink, *Play as Symbol of the World*, 204–5.
36. Kostas Axelos, "Play as the System of Systems," *SubStance* 8, no. 4 (1980): 20–24.
37. Axelos, "Play as the System of Systems," 21.
38. Axelos, "Play as the System of Systems," 22.
39. Martin Heidegger, "Letter on 'Humanism,'" in *Basic Writings*, trans. David Farrell Krell, rev. and exp. ed. (San Francisco: HarperCollins, 1993), 225–26.
40. Hans-Georg Gadamer, *Truth and Method*, 2nd rev. ed. (New York: Crossroad, 1989), 101ff.
41. Sylvia Wynter and Katherine McKittrick, "Unparalleled Catastrophe for Our Species? Or, to Give Humanness a Different Future: Conversations," *Sylvia Wynter: On Being Human as Praxis*, ed. Katherine McKittrick (Durham: Duke University Press, 2015), 23.
42. Sylvia Wynter, "The Ceremony Found: Towards the Autopoetic Turn/Overturn, Its Autonomy of Human Agency and Extraterritoriality of (Self-)Cognition," in *Black Knowledges/Black Struggles: Essays in Critical Epistemologies*, ed. Jason Ambroise and Sabine Broeck (Liverpool: Liverpool University Press, 2015), 212ff.
43. David Scott and Sylvia Wynter, "The Re-enchantment of Humanism: An Interview with Sylvia Wynter," *Small Axe* 8 (2000): 119.
44. Wynter, "The Ceremony Found."
45. Wynter, "The Ceremony Found," 217.

Chapter Eight

Bio-logies of Being

Human and Animal Life in Heidegger and Beyond

Hans Ruin

Introduction

In his "Letter on 'Humanism,'" Heidegger writes that, "if man is to find his way once again into the nearness of Being, he must first learn to exist in the nameless."[1] With this enigmatic suggestion, he called for a measure of philosophical self-forgetting and self-displacement for the sake of a deeper and possibly transformative understanding of humanism and the ethical. In the same passage, he spoke of the need to, instead, let oneself be "claimed" by being. Thus, the whole treatise moves in the direction of its famous conclusion, that, as we try to think the *humanitas* of the human, we should recognize that man is "not the lord of beings" but "the shepherd of Being."[2] Following this and similar expressions in the "Letter," Heidegger was seen by many postwar philosophers as both a controversial and visionary proponent of a new kind of anti-metaphysical post-humanism, beyond Cartesian dualism and subject-philosophy. Articulated in the aftermath of the Second World War, with its exceptional display of human cruelty and disrespect for basic human rights, the position was of course provocative, particularly in view of his own earlier complicity with the National Socialist regime. Thus, in the "Letter," he also stressed that his kind of anti-humanism should by no means be understood as a "glorification of barbaric brutality," "inhumanity," "atheism," or "nihilism," nor as a simple refusal of "transcendence."[3] Instead, his aspiration was to rephrase the very practice of philosophy, moving it closer to a poetic articulation of being. The famous final and enchanting chord resounded: "The thinking that is to come is no longer philosophy, because it thinks more originally than metaphysics."[4]

Among many of his readers, this aspiration to move beyond traditional anthropocentric humanism was celebrated, by many, as a radical adventure in thought—from Arendt to Foucault and Derrida, and notably in the latter's seminal lecture of May 1968, "The Ends of Man," which, in the spirit of the "Letter," presented the criticism of humanism and anthropologism as one of the "dominant and guiding motifs of current French thought."[5] But in recent decades, the tone has shifted markedly. In an article by Spanish-Italian philosopher Antonino Firenze, from 2017, we read: "Heidegger's philosophy of animality could be fully inscribed in a still humanistic attitude," since he "tries to definitely destroy—by removing the idea of a kinship, albeit remote, with the animal—all risks of a deforming naturalization of the *humanitas* and of the unicity of the human being's essence as a being that is spiritual precisely because it is mortal."[6] The same author states that the post-metaphysical critique of humanism, as articulated in the "Letter," remains a halfway gesture, since it fails to think the anthropological impulse toward the "domestication of otherness."

The type of criticism voiced in Firenze's article has its principal inspiration in a series of seminars on the question of the animal, organized by Derrida from the early 1990s onward.[7] It culminated in the long text that he put together, in 1997, for the Cerisy-la-Salle Conference. Entitled "The Autobiographical Animal," it and other materials form the posthumous publication *The Animal That Therefore I Am*.[8] There, Derrida takes Heidegger to task for having reinstated the anthropocentrist human-animal distinction with his claim that the animal, unlike man, is "poor in world," notably made in his 1929–30 lecture course "The Fundamental Concepts of Metaphysics: World, Finitude, Solitude."[9] Actually, its analysis had been addressed already in Derrida's book *De l'esprit* (*Of Spirit*) from 1987. While noting a certain "humanist teleology," he also suggested, there, that the sharp separation of human and animal life was perhaps a "price to be paid for the ethico-political denunciation of biologism, racism, naturalism, etc.," which was part of the context for Heidegger's position at the time.[10]

In the wake of Derrida's critical interventions, Giorgio Agamben published a small book in 2002, *L'aperto: L'uomo e l'animale* (later, in English, *The*

Open: Man and Animal), wherein he, too, returned to the 1929–30 lecture course for a discussion of the ontological, metaphysical, and ethicopolitical implications of its description of the animal as "poor in world."[11] There, he situates Heidegger's gesture in the context of a larger, culturally constitutive process, which he refers to as "anthropogenesis," and as the "anthropological machine" through which humanity, throughout history, has generated its essence by distinguishing itself from the animal, indeed from its "capture and suspension."[12] In the modern predicament, however, this operation has been gradually inversed, having reached a state where the previous stories of a unique human destiny are replaced by a biopolitical paradigm, and where politics is reduced to caring for the bodily-animal human nature: "[F]or a humanity that has become animal again, there is nothing left but the depolitization of human societies by means of the unconditional unfolding of the *oikonomia*, or the taking on of biological life itself as the supreme political (or rather impolitical) task."[13] On the other hand, toward the end of the fragmentary text, he also suggests, in vague messianic terms and through mythological imagery, how, beyond this machinery, there is a possible higher redemptive fusion of human and animal existence. Agamben does not connect the issue of animality to the political implications of the different life-philosophies in the 1930s, but his biopolitical reading of the whole constellation ultimately points in such a direction. He explicitly says that, as animals are humanized, politics becomes biopolitics as a management of bodies. The political and metaphysical implications of his critical confrontation with Heidegger on animality therefore remain ambiguous. He criticizes Heidegger's attempts to dissociate human from animal existence, yet his own critique of the biopolitical paradigm very much recalls the latter's own analysis of the political consequences of a completed animalization of man.

The political stakes involved in the question of the human-animal distinction remains an important and philosophically challenging aspect of Heidegger's standing today. The humanism and anthropocentrism of which he is now accused was partly motivated by his own precautions against then current biologistic-vitalist ideologies. Yet today, it is critically questioned within a field of animal-studies that generally identifies with emancipatory goals from a liberal standpoint. If traditional humanist thinking leads to a species-centrism that we today need to think beyond, the question becomes even more pressing: What can and should we still salvage from its earlier articulation in order to avoid the ideological pitfalls that may be hiding in the guise of a contemporary progressive critique? In other words, how can we correctly measure the full range of implications in current aspirations to think the world in a post-species-centered manner? Derrida's and Agamben's critical interrogations do not conclude the question of Heidegger's purported entrapment in anthropocentrist discourse. Instead, they highlight the stakes of the debate and the relevance of his early interventions.

How we conceptualize the essence of the human in relation to animal life is a philosophical choice with metaphysical, ethical, and political implications. On the last lines of his critical rehearsal of Heidegger's analysis of animality, quoted above, Firenze writes: "Heidegger failed to understand the link between humanity and animality, precisely because he failed to consider this link in terms of a deeper bond between natural life and human existence—a bond that represents one of the most pressing milestones in contemporary philosophical thinking."[14] I believe Firenze is correct to stress that the philosophical articulation of this bond is indeed a central challenge for our time and situation. Still, exactly where we should locate Heidegger and his contribution along this trajectory is not as clear as Firenze suggests. Heidegger's position is actually more ambiguous than Firenze and many of his later critics suggest. By opening a philosophical dialogue between existential ontology and biology, he demonstrated an early awareness of the philosophical stakes involved. And, even though his conceptual distinctions suggest a reinstated humanist hierarchy, they also served to destabilize its conventional parameters. Through his secular and stated nonevaluative approach, he invited a more encompassing view of the phenomenon of life and the living. But by stressing, at the same time, a remaining distinction between human and nonhuman life-forms in terms of having a world, he was not only complying with a traditional humanist axiology but also responding to a risk—the ethical, political, and also ontological risk—implied by the full biologization of human existence. This risk, and its philosophical challenge, is no less relevant today.

In what follows, I shall rehearse Heidegger's changing approach, throughout the 1920s, to the topic of "life." At first, he comes forth as a strong proponent of a transformative *life*-philosophy, only to change gradually into one of its critics, in a trajectory that culminates in the 1929–30 lecture course on human and animal existence. The interpretation of this development is carried out with a view to the stated dilemma and its repercussions in our contemporary situation and its controversies, as will become clear in a concluding section. As we aspire today to grasp the deeper bond between human and animal existence, and to fathom the scope of its implications, there are still things to learn and keep in mind from Heidegger's early interventions.

Life and the Human Sciences

In Dilthey's pioneering work *Einleitung in die Geisteswissenschaften*, from 1883, life—*Leben*—occupies the center of his endeavor to found the specificity of the human sciences in relation to the natural sciences. Whereas in the natural sciences we confront what is other to ourselves, in the human sciences it is *life that studies life*.[15] Here, the knower and known is of the same nature, and *life* becomes the name for the mode of expressive and interpretive being, that which both generates and apprehends meaning. A similar use of "life," as a hermeneutic platform for the interpretation of human expression at large, is suggested by Nietzsche, who in the famous self-critical preface, from 1886, to his earlier *Die Geburt der Tragödie*, summarizes his own interpretative endeavors with the formula: "to look at science in the perspective of the artist, but at art in that of life."[16] In *Wahrheit und Methode*, written almost a century later, Hans-Georg Gadamer, stresses the significance of this understanding of life in hermeneutic thought as a self-reflexive movement toward an increased self-knowledge and awareness.[17] Among the key thinkers in this vein, he mentions Nietzsche, Dilthey, and his interlocutor Yorck von Wartenburg, but also Husserl, whose idea of transcendental *Leben*, and later of a *Lebenswelt* as the fundamental generative matrix for meaning and expression, situated the concept of life at the center of the phenomenological enterprise. There are many other parallel sources for the rise of "life" as a conceptual focus of intellectual debates of the first decades of the twentieth century, including Bergson, Scheler, Simmel, Jaspers, and others, whose different approaches I shall not try to rehearse here. Suffice it to say that, at least within the hermeneutic and phenomenological circles at the time, *life* captured and held the dual significance of a name for the pretheoretical origin of meaning and theory, as well as its expression and practice in judgment and understanding.[18]

It is in the lecture course given in Freiburg in 1919—during the so-called *Kriegsnotsemester*—that Heidegger first comes forth as an independent thinker in his own right, speaking in favor of phenomenology as an "original science," an *Urwissenschaft*. Polemicizing against what he takes to be a tendency among the neo-Kantians to favor conceptual construction and to get stuck in the subject-object dichotomy, he points precisely to *life* as the most original level of experience, and as a name for givenness or phenomenality as such. As the original unity of temporal experience and expression, life is presented as that which unites Husserlian phenomenology and Dilthey's hermeneutics, and as the basic operative concept for a philosophy with foundational aspirations.[19]

In 1920, Heinrich Rickert—Heidegger's *Doktorvater*—published a critical study of the contemporary life-philosophers, *Die Philosophie des Lebens*, a book that Heidegger first criticized in his lectures the following year.[20] But only shortly after that, something happens and he, too, begins to distance himself from "life" as a foundational philosophical concept. First, he moves from "life" to "factical life," but eventually he opts instead for "Dasein" as a name for that being for which Being is at stake. It is this transformation and conceptual reorientation that we need to rehearse and understand if we are to make sense of what happens, philosophically, in the seminal lecture course on animals and animality, ten years later.

The introductory sections of *Sein und Zeit*,[21] composed some five years after the lecture course, summarize his reservations vis-à-vis *Leben* as a founding philosophical concept as developed in the meantime. In §10, he outlines how "the analytic of Dasein is to be distinguished from anthropology, psychology, and biology"; in other words, from the established life sciences. The principal reason why these disciplines will not suffice as a foundation is that they fail to take into account the "ontological problematic"; in other words, the question of the meaning of Being. Every idea of a "subject," he continues, brings with it a sense of the *subiectum* or *hypokeimenon*, and thus of something "thingly," even when all due precautions have been taken not to "objectify" the subjective. We need to take a different route, he argues, and reach for the ontological possibility of thing-ness as such—of the Being of reality—because, as long as this question is not raised, the Being of the subject will not appear either. When people use traditional terms such as "soul, consciousness, spirit, person," he writes, they always display a "remarkable failure" to inquire about the Being of the beings so designated. And for this reason, "we are not being terminologically idiosyncratic when we avoid these terms as well as the expressions 'life' and 'human being' in designating the beings that we ourselves are."[22]

Yet, immediately after having thus disparaged the traditional attempts to name and capture the being of human existence, he recognizes that a genuinely "scientifically minded 'philosophy of life,'" does contain a tendency toward the "understanding of the being of Dasein." This is followed by a celebration of Dilthey's efforts at having pointed toward the question of life as such. But just as he is said not to have reached all the way in the conceptualization of existence, neither have Husserl or Scheler, or Bergson for that matter, in their different attempts to develop a philosophy of personality. It is noteworthy that, in a marginal note from the so called

Hüttenexemplar (a "cabin-copy" of *Sein und Zeit*, with Heidegger's own critical notes that he, late in life, gave to his assistant von Herrmann for publication), Heidegger explicitly comments on the sentence, just quoted, as to how the life-philosophers at least "tended" toward the true question of the being of Dasein. In the margin he has jotted down an emphatic "no!" indicating that at some later stage (not dated) he did not even recognize such a tendency toward clarification of Dasein in Dilthey's life-philosophy.[23] And, in an adjacent note, he adds: "[N]ot only that, but the question of truth is totally and essentially inadequate." In other words, he sees the question of truth, in the sense of the openness of Dasein, as integral to its mode of existing and as something that has not been worked out adequately in Dilthey and the other life-philosophers. In this sense, *Sein und Zeit* constitutes a step in a trajectory that leads from an initial affirmation of "life"—as a foundational concept in and for phenomenology, over its critical re-elaboration into Dasein—toward an outright rejection of its ontological potential in the later writings.

The reason for distancing himself from life-philosophy is repeatedly articulated in terms of how it fails to raise what he here calls the Being, or the ontological meaning of human existence. Furthermore, the traditional attempts of philosophical anthropology to capture the core of human existence fail to do so by being either ontologically undetermined or by referring to something already *given*, be it *zoon logon echon* (the rational animal), the *ens creatum imago dei* (created in the image of God) in Christian theology, or the modern philosophical-scientific idea of a *res cogitans* or "consciousness." In short, "the anthropological problematic remains undetermined in its decisive ontological foundation."[24] And, despite the positive findings of anthropology, psychology, and biology, their foundations remain philosophically obscure.

To these critical remarks, he also adds a short and somewhat curious passage that addresses the phenomenon of life from a more psychological and biological perspective, anticipating the problems with which he will wrestle a few years later, in the 1929 lecture. He writes that, as "a science of life" biology is rooted (*fundiert*) in the ontology of Dasein, although "not exclusively in it," the reason is that life is said to "have its own kind of being," only accessible (*zugänglich*) in Dasein. The standard definition of life constitutes a "privative" interpretation of what is required for something "just-being-alive" (*Nur-noch-leben*). But life is never merely being present, nor is Dasein just life with some other capacity added to it, be it consciousness, language, or reason.[25] What he seems to imply, in this dense and somewhat obscure passage, is that Dasein both is and yet is not just life. It is not life to the extent that life is understood as disentangled from all relations and reduced to a processual living-prevailing entity.

From this remark, it is clear that the question of Dasein, and thus of the ontological meaning of existence, is staged at the intersection of life as Dasein and life as bare life, to use Agamben's later expression. Dasein is life, it is living, but when life is understood only as a bio-logical process, separated from the ontological question of what it means to be in the first place, this livingness of Dasein will not clarify its mode of being but instead obscure it. And the standard solution, of either adding something to life—a secondary quality, such as consciousness or reason—will not solve this problem. Nor will it be clarified by stressing its nonnatural nature. Instead, the whole conceptual order of the problematic has to be reworked, so as to place the question of the meaning and possibility of being at the heart of what human existence is. But in order to perform and secure such a conceptual reversal, *life* must somehow be turned inside out, transformed from life-process to epistemic condition, without losing its connection to facticity and finitude. For the existential analytic, *life* is thus destined to become a battleground for its own meaning and possibility.

Within the science of biology itself, from Aristotle onward, the struggle for the proper conceptualization of life has shifted from teleological to causal-mechanical models. Today, most biologists reject the cruder seventeenth-century reductionist machine-like models of life, insisting that it is a distinct type of natural-chemical phenomenon that cannot be understood without accepting what is today often referred to as *teleonomy*—in other words, goal-oriented or *functional* processes.[26] Thus biologists see life as a self-nourishing, sensory, finite process with a replicative capacity.[27] One standard definition of life (NASA's) states that it is "a self-sustained chemical system capable of undergoing Darwinian evolution." But as long as we remain within biology proper, the question of the definition of life will not engage the larger context of how this same life can also be the foundation and possibility for its own conceptualization, including biology itself. In other words, it does not address the ontological question. When the issue of the biological possibility of cognition is raised in cognitive science, it is conceptualized in terms of the emergence and functioning of the *brain*, as the most complex biological artifact we know, with the ontological question remaining absent here, too (alternatively framed as the so called "hard problem," how nature can be conscious).

What exactly is missing from the picture? Why will life not be understood properly if it is only understood as a self-sustaining, biochemical process of self-nourishing and self-replicating? How is it that life can occlude life? Or to put it differently: Why do we need to move beyond the concept and traditional (biological) understanding of life in order to make life fully appear? Somehow, it has to do with how we conceptualize its relational nature, the way in which it is connected to a *world*, as both exposed to, acting upon, and also enabling the very phenomenon of world as such. It is to this challenge, which is at the center of Heidegger's intervention in his 1929 lectures, that we now turn.

Life-Worlds of the Living

For the Freiburg winter semester 1929–30, Heidegger gave a course under the heading "The Fundamental Concepts of Metaphysics: World, Finitude, Solitude."[28] The overarching question for the seminar was precisely how to understand the human being as a being *in* a world, and how to understand what it means that we exist both within and outside or beyond a world, as something that we belong to while also being able to contemplate and conceptualize it, as if from a distance. Under normal circumstances, we do not necessarily think about the world as such, it is just there as our all-encompassing reality. Moreover, the life-scientist will take his own life-world for granted in this sense, as he proceeds to explore the chemistry of life in his laboratory. The initial philosophical challenge is therefore to *reawaken* a deeper sense of this predicament, of not just occupying a place in objective space-time, but of actually being-*there in* and *before* a world. It is essentially the same task as the one Heidegger had already explored and articulated in *Sein und Zeit* a few years earlier, but here he tries a different avenue. To begin with, the principal affective mood that he investigates is not that of *anxiety* (*Angst*) but *boredom* (*Langeweile*), as the name for the general all-encompassing mood where existence simply presses upon us. The point here is to bring this indifferent everyday mood to explicit awareness precisely *as* a mood, in order to expose the situatedness of Dasein.

Just as in *Sein und Zeit*, a basic mood of Dasein is here explored for the purpose of awakening the listener and reader to an ontological awareness. A more important difference in relation to *Sein und Zeit*, however, has to do with how Heidegger activates the comparison between humans and (other) animals, to expose the presumably unique way in which Dasein is *in* the world. Whereas in *Sein und Zeit* the biological understanding of life was simply set aside—with reference to the inability of biology to conceptualize its domain ontologically—here, the ontological difference is highlighted and inscribed as a difference within life and the living themselves, in terms of different ways of *having a world*, in an explicit dialogue with contemporary biology and zoology.

This move does not imply that Heidegger had now become more favorable to life-philosophy than he was in *Sein und Zeit*. On the contrary, he makes it clear from the outset that he sees his own trajectory as a challenge against the dominant contemporary life-philosophies, be it in the form of Spengler, Klages, or Scheler. In a sharp critique of vitalist thinkers who posit life and soul in opposition to spirit, he writes of how spirit is now "seen as a sickness that has to be exorcized in order to liberate the soul. Freedom from spirit here means: let's return to life! Life, however, is now taken in the sense of the obscure simmering of drives, which is simultaneously grasped as the breeding ground of the mythical."[29] He enlists a number of ways in which popular intellectuals are mobilizing a concept of *life* meant to serve as a liberating critique of spirit, culture, and rationality, and which he traces back to a Nietzschean inspiration.[30] When we interpret his philosophical dialogue with biology, this critical position, and the cultural context of which it is a symptom, must be kept in mind. The strategy is both ambiguous and precarious, as it seeks to challenge the contemporary life-philosophies by reaching for a philosophically more qualified concept of life, indeed for the "essence of life in general."[31]

The strategy is laid out at the outset of chapter 2 (§42ff.), where he states that he has chosen to follow a path of "comparative examination." Since man is not just a part of the world, but also both its master and servant, he lives in the sense of *having* a world. But what does it mean to *have* a world? And how is it with other entities, other inanimate and animate beings? Do they also *have* a world? It is at this point that he turns to a dialogue with the contemporary work of biologist Jakob von Uexküll, whose nonreductionist approach sought to describe life-processes precisely as ways of relating to and inhabiting a *world*.[32] Uexküll's research was mostly focused on simple creatures, such as worms and ticks. Philosophically, it was Kantian in its basic orientation and in its argument that a life-form can be understood only when seen and analyzed as a teleological and purposeful process within its biological context. Even the tick, with its very limited sensory reach and life cycle, was not seen as a biological machine but as an elementary subjectivity, and as a system of motivation and purpose within a world.[33] In the standard physicalist-mechanistic world-view, there is room only for one subject, the human, for whom all other creatures are mechanisms within a unitary world. But, according to Uexküll, "this belief in the existence of one and only one world, in which all living being are encased" is illusory.[34] In his descriptions of different life-forms, he shows how they construct their world through their specific organs and ways of orienting themselves in space.

On one level, Heidegger follows Uexküll, when stressing that all living creatures must be understood in terms of how they inhabit a world. The animal—even in simplest form, and unlike the stone—essentially *has* a world in relation to which it lives. But then he departs from this relativizing approach by inserting a principal distinction when it comes to the mode in which a world is inhabited. Excusing himself for the preliminary "crudeness" of his distinction, he suggests the following schema: "[1] The stone (material object) is *worldless* [*weltlos*]; [2] The animal is *poor in world* [*weltarm*]; [3] Man is *world-forming* [*weltbildend*]."[35] His point is that, even though the animal has a world and a way of inhabiting this world, it will always be restricted to a limited repertoire of behavior. This is presumably different from that of humans:

> [T]he world of man is a rich one, greater in range, far more extensive in its penetrability, constantly extendable not only in its range [. . .] but also in respect to the manner in which we can penetrate ever more deeply in this penetrability. Consequently, we can characterize the relation man possesses to the world by referring to the extendibility of everything that he relates to. This is why we speak of man as world-forming.[36]

He is quick to point out that this hierarchical ordering should not be taken as carrying an evaluation in terms of higher or superior. He notes that, when it comes to every individual sense-capacity, there are of course animals that are superior to humans (in their ability to see, hear, smell, etc.). It is also singularly characteristic of man to be able to sink to depravity, lower than any animal. In short, the point is not to reestablish an axiological ladder of creation. "Every animal and every species of animal as such is just as perfect and complete as any other."[37]

Yet, there is something that the inanimate and the animal does not have, or that they have only in a restricted and inhibited way. And this is *access* (*Zugang*). The lizard, lying on the warm rock, obviously occupies a life-world of its own, but it does not have it *as* rock, or *as* world. It occupies it, but not in the propositional sense of an *as such*. This turns out to be the key formulation in the overall argument. To have a world is to have *access* to the surroundings as such. Seen from one perspective there is obviously something that the lizard, as well as the tick has, but not in the same way as humans, who can adopt a *stance* toward it as such. The animal, he writes, "thus reveals itself as a being which both has and does not have world."[38]

This basic observation is then repeated at some length, but not really deepened or secured. It is as if Heidegger himself, throughout this argument, is displeased with some of its consequences, not just because of the implied evaluative hierarchy among the living, but also because it just seems to postpone a more genuinely *positive* definition. In a new detour, he therefore turns to the concept of the *organism*, referring to both Uexküll and Driesch, stressing that the animal is not *equipped* with organs as tools or instruments. The animal does not see because it has eyes. Rather it has eyes because it sees. Its sensory organs are not its tools of survival, but its way of having a world. The capacity is not in the organ, but in the organism as a whole. Living beings are not mechanisms, nor are they species of a more general life-force, as in vitalist theories.

In his attempts to encircle the phenomenality of the organism, Heidegger comes close to what modern biologists would also point to as an elementary *teleonomy*, characterized on its most basic level by a self-nourishing and self-replicating capacity. But through this long detour, he ends up returning to the peculiar way in which the animal lives this capacity in and in response to its world. And here he adds another set of terms to his philosophical-biological vocabulary: that of being "absorbed" (*eingenommen*),[39] and of behaving in a way that is both claimed and compelled, which he designates as "captivation" (*Benommenheit*). In contrast to this conditioned mode of behavior, human action is described as "comportment" (*Verhalten*). Within the limited sphere of world-access of the animal, it is open to a range of possibilities, a range that is described as its "disinhibiting ring" (*Enthemmungsring*).[40] It is as if the animal both has the world before it and yet does not fully have it, since it lives *claimed* by the world that it has, unable to free itself from its given and compelling condition. This explains why it is, he writes, that beings are not manifest to the behavior of the animal in its captivation, they are not "disclosed" or "open" to it (*offenbar, aufgeschlossen*).[41] Animality is thus said to be characterized by an "open absorption" (*geöffnete Eingenommensein*). And yet, he adds, being captivated is not the opposite of being open to, rather it is a version of it, a way of "attending" to beings (*beseitigen*). The animal is inhibited from simply "letting" the world and things be (*Sein-lassen*).[42] This remark is noteworthy for how it anticipates what he much later will refer to as *Gelassenheit*, a comportment of "letting-be" or "releasement." Here, it is the animal that, from its very way of being in the world, is unable to reach into this qualified comportment.

Toward the very end of the comparative discussion, he turns to the question of mortality, in an analysis that despite its brevity, has received much commentary, in both Derrida and Agamben, and in others. From *Sein und Zeit*, Heidegger's readers would be familiar with the definition of life as a peculiar kind of "happening" and "event" (*Geschehen*), the outer limits of which are birth and death.[43] When this topic is raised in *Sein und Zeit*, it is as the starting point for a discussion of the *historicity* of human existence. It is also at this point in the lecture course that he first—and very briefly—mentions the problem of history and of heritage (*Vererbung*). He writes: "Birth, maturing, aging, and death all too obviously remind us of the being of man, which we recognize as being historical [*geschichtliches*]."[44] He discards the idea, proposed by some, of seeing the organism as historical just in virtue of the fact that every species has its historical development. It is clear that this is not history in a lived and existential sense. Without exploring it further, he simply notes that the kind of movement and happening of animal life (*Geschehenscharakter*) must be placed on a new ontological foundation.

It is also in this context that we come across the problem of mortality and death, as something belonging to "the innermost essence of life." Only if we are able to properly grasp the question of death can we reach into life. But we do not reach it simply by declaring that they belong together—that life comes from death and death from life. Something more is needed. And here we are aided by death, as the apparent negativity of life that nevertheless helps us—as he writes—to "illuminate the essence of life." In a striking comparison with the question of history and death in the case of human existence, he states: "Just as it remains questionable whether we can speak of the organism as a historical or even historical being, so too it is questionable whether death and death are the same in the case of man and animal, even if we can identify a physico-chemical and physiological equivalence between the two."[45] The way in which life is captivated also prefigures certain ways of dying and of approaching death. He asks: "Is the death of the animal a dying (*Sterben*) or a way of coming to an end (*Verenden*)?" And he responds immediately: "Because captivation belongs to the essence of the animal, the animal cannot die in the sense in which dying is ascribed to human beings but can only come to an end." This is basically all that he has to say about the question of death, while signaling its role as a defining issue in the overall topology of existence. It is in virtue of its qualified experience of mortality and finitude that human existence presumably also stands in a fuller openness than the animal vis-à-vis its world.

In a concluding section to the long discussion of animal captivation—which displays an unusually self-critical tone—Heidegger poses the question as to what extent his phenomenological description has indeed managed to capture the essence of animal-being. In particular, he stresses that it should not be interpreted to say that animal existence is somehow a mode of deprivation.[46] And he repeatedly notes that we must be careful not to insert hierarchies into the world of the living. The animal life that we want to understand is not "inferior" to the human life. On the contrary, it is a domain "which possesses a wealth of openness with which the human world may have nothing to compare."[47] In view of the way the previous analysis has progressed, by listing a sequence of comparisons that all appear to demonstrate precisely such a hierarchy, the reservation is noteworthy.

In the end, it is only with the full clarification of the way of having a world of human existence, as "world-forming," that it is possible to state if the animal is indeed "poor in world." Thus, the conclusion is left pending as he turns, in the last chapter of the long lecture course, to explore the possibility of world. There, he discusses the emergence of world from within Dasein's pre-predicative having of something *as* something. It is developed through a detailed analysis of the gradual emergence of a fully propositional attitude from the ground of a pre-predicative comportment, which largely recapitulates work from earlier writings on the emergence of the so called apophantic attitude.[48] It involves a discussion of language and of truth, as *logos* and *aletheia*, as well as a description of Dasein as finite and as free.

What drives Heidegger in all these pursuits is a desire to explore, again and again, the emergence of the Being of beings as the *having* of a world. In *Sein und Zeit*, he "solved" it by stressing that the whole problem of how the human intellect has access to the world, or comes out into it, is wrongly stated. It was enough to show how Dasein is always already *there*, in the world as a being-*with* others. But through the comparison to the animal, the problem is made more difficult, as it recognizes that the having of a world is something that Dasein partly shares with all living creatures. Together with ticks, and bees, and birds of prey, humans share an elementary teleological or teleonomical existence. Yet there is something in the human way of being that presumably makes is possible for us to *access* our world more fully, and to break the bond of the disinhibiting circle, so as to reach into the open of manifestation and being as such. This is as far as he gets in this largely experimenting and nonconclusive course.

Difficult Delimitations

The introduction summarized the somewhat confused contemporary state of the discussion concerning Heidegger and the human-animal distinction. Whereas certain critics disparage him for having failed to think "the deeper bond" between life, in general, and human existence, it was recalled that, even in Agamben's influential analysis, the actual outcome of the critique is much more ambiguous. Through the so-called anthropological machine, humans have shaped and defined their essence in contrast to other living creatures throughout the ages. But what would it mean to collapse this distinction? And what kind of reality would be opened up on the other side of this divide when humans no longer understand themselves through the *logos* that once defined them, beyond both reason and rights? What does it mean to think life as such from a species-neutral perspective?

From a biological perspective, humans are of course a species of animality or life in general. But biology does not address the ontological question of what it means to have a world, since it takes it for granted, and thus also its own privileged access to it. Nor does it address the ethical, political, and juridical consequences of collapsing the distinction. The real difficulties only begin when we address, as Heidegger does, the question of the distinction from within the question of what it means to have a world in the first place. The same argument is applicable to the question of "rights." If we take it for granted that there is something like human rights or human ethical obligations, we can move innocently to expand these rights also to other sentient beings, arguing that they have been excluded and that they should also be included within its range. But just as in the case of biology, this generalizing way of thinking neglects the difficulty of actually understanding and accounting for the more specific nature and emergence of rights and obligations, through recognition of the other, from within a domain of being characterized by the ability to act freely, and the type of agonistic reciprocity that comes with it.

Simply abolishing the distinction between human and animal is not automatically conducive to a more enlightened mode of thought and action.

It opens the door, not only to a more tolerant and horizontal approach to animal existence, but also to an animalization of man, with troubling political implications. With the collapse of this distinction, we also undermine the specific responsibility that attaches to the human as opposed to the animal (since we have no demands or expectations that they will display reciprocal ethical or political responsibility). Ultimately, we risk undermining the philosophical foundation for raising the question of animal rights in the first place.

Through the critique of the traditional foundations of humanism, be it in divine creation or a metaphysical doctrine of absolute rights and rationality, we find ourselves in a philosophical situation that is both challenging and precarious. We need to find ways of understanding and articulating the ontology of life in view of the ontological difference. Within the growing field of critical animal studies, important questions are being asked and new ways of thinking about sentient life and human-animal interaction are being explored. But in the often-standardized depiction of Heidegger as an example of an outdated Cartesian humanism, the deeper philosophical stakes of the debate are often covered over in favor of a theoretically comfortable rejection of tradition.

As recalled above, both Derrida and Agamben were aware of the ambiguity of Heidegger's position, more so than what is usually recognized in second-order commentaries to the debate. They were, in different degrees, also aware of their own indebtedness to his basic approach, while drawing different critical conclusions. Derrida stressed how Heidegger, despite his sensitivity to the inner lacunae of metaphysical thinking, was unable to break free from the traditional hierarchical metaphysical matrix in his conceptualization of the human-animal relation. The most challenging point in his critical remarks concerned the question of death and dying. In his rather brief remarks on this topic, Heidegger repeats what he takes to be the decisive distinction, but he does not develop it, nor does he explore the rationale of the suggested definitive distinction between dying and simply perishing. This particular issue points to a deeper question concerning the temporality and historicity of human and animal life as different modes of inhabiting finitude. Derrida is more attentive to the problem, but beyond raising it, he does not develop it further.

Agamben's reading is more grandiose in its gestures, but less clear in its conclusions. He anticipates a messianic event, in and through which the anthropological machine and its production of naked animal life somehow ceases and gives way to something new and different. It is quite unclear, however, what this would amount to, beyond the dramatic thought experiment. As noted above, his more concrete philosophical agenda is actually closer to Heidegger's than he admits. He, too, seeks to expose the emergence of a biopolitical paradigm that reduces the living to an object of care and control, rather than seeing it as a source of transcendence, truth, and political responsibility. The most original dimension of his conclusions is the proximity that he traces between the analysis of boredom and animal captivity. From inside Heidegger's own argument, he displays just how difficult it is to secure, conceptually and philosophically, the precarious distinction between how humans and other animals respectively inhabit their worlds. His analysis thus reveals the uncertainty that Heidegger himself expresses toward the end of his lectures in even more acute terms.

Within contemporary animal-studies the ontological question raised and explored by Heidegger is usually not thematized or even recognized as a valid concern. The guiding framework is either a post-humanist vitalism that neglects the problem altogether, or a liberal-enlightenment human rights–agenda that seeks to include nonhuman animals in ways that simultaneously tend to undermine the axiological matrix that it naively takes for granted. What gives Heidegger's analyses their prevailing interest, despite the tentative nature of his conclusions, is how they point toward the uncertain intersection of these different positions. Even when he reproduces a conventional framework, according to which the human being is essentially distinct from the animal, he has once and for all opened up the conventional mode of addressing what is at issue. By formulating the question in terms, not of rationality, rights, or even subjectivity or self-awareness, but in terms of world, of access to world, and of *openness*, he has outlined a framework for the exploration of precisely the "deeper bond between animal life and human existence" that the current philosophical situation is calling for.

Conclusion

In the contemporary theoretical landscape of animal studies, it has become a conventional gesture to disparage Heidegger as a typical representative of Cartesian humanism or anthropocentrism that this new theoretical frontier claims to have left behind. But as I have tried to show here, this is a misguided maneuver. Heidegger approaches this domain with an aspiration to move beyond a Cartesian matrix, by questioning conventional concepts of subjectivity and human essence, in favor of the problem of world-access. The ultimate purpose of the analysis is not to secure the uniqueness of human existence, but to explore the ontology of being-in-the-world through comparisons of different modalities. Saying this does not imply that his analyses should be raised beyond critique. Instead, we should pay attention to their inconclusiveness, taking seriously the aporetic nature of these meandering attempts to secure a conceptual grasp of world as access and openness. We should also do so in awareness of the potential ethical and political consequences of a general biologization of life. It is Heidegger himself who repeatedly remarks on the lack of "positive" results of his own analyses, and who warns against drawing definitive hierarchical conclusions. In this respect, his discussion of the human-animal distinction is best read not as part of the archive of outdated humanisms, but as the starting point of an evolving discourse and a theoretical challenge in the midst of which we still stand.

Notes

1. Martin Heidegger, "Letter on 'Humanism,'" trans. Frank A. Capuzzi, in *Pathmarks*, ed. William McNeill (Cambridge: Cambridge University Press), 243.
2. Heidegger, "Letter on 'Humanism,'" 260.
3. Heidegger, "Letter on 'Humanism,'" 263–64.
4. Heidegger, "Letter on 'Humanism,'" 276.
5. First published in English as Jacques Derrida, "The Ends of Man," trans. Hubert Dreyfus et al., *Philosophy and Phenomenological Research* 30, no. 1 (1969): 31–57, esp. 38; later in French as Derrida, "Les fins de l'homme," in *Marges de la philosophie*, Collection Critique (Paris: Éditions de Minuit, 1972); and again in English as Derrida, "The Ends of Man," in *Margins of Philosophy*, trans. Alan Bass (Chicago: University of Chicago Press, 1982), 109–36.
6. Antonino Firenze, "'A Dog Does Not Exist but Merely Lives': The Question of Animality in Heidegger's Philosophy," *Philosophy Today* 61, no. 1 (2017): 135–54.
7. For a good survey of work in this vein, see Lynn Turner, ed., *The Animal Question in Deconstruction* (Edinburgh: Edinburgh University Press, 2013)—notably, the contributions by Kelly Oliver and Stephen Morton, which both address the critical assessments of Heidegger, in terms of his ambition to set aside humans from animals in virtue of both language and grasping, and in relation to death. In Margo DeMello's encompassing *Animals and Society: An Introduction to Human-Animal Studies* (New York: Columbia University Press, 2012), Heidegger is mentioned, in passing, as a modern philosopher who insisted in a reductive mode on the clear-cut distinction between human and animal (39). The same point is also stressed from early on in Carrie Rohman, *Stalking the Subject: Modernism and the Animal* (New York: Columbia University Press, 2009), 16ff.

8. Derrida, *The Animal That Therefore I Am*, trans. David Willis (New York: Fordham University Press, 2008); first published in French as Derrida, *L'animal que donc je suis* (Paris: Galilée, 2006).

9. First published, later and posthumously, as Martin Heidegger, *Die Grundbegriffe der Metaphysik: Welt, Endlichkeit, Einsamkeit*, vols. 29/30 of the *Gesamtausgabe*, ed. Friedrich-Wilhelm von Herrmann (Frankfurt: Klostermann, 1983). The problematic position of animality in Heidegger had in fact been raised earlier by Derrida, in his first major critical analysis of Heidegger—*De l'esprit* [*Of Spirit*], from 1987—wherein he detected the operation of a "humanist teleology" precisely in the analysis of how the animal is "poor in world." See Jacques Derrida, *Of Spirit: Heidegger and the Question*, trans. Geoffrey Bennington and Rachel Bowlby (Chicago: University of Chicago Press, 1989), esp. ch. 6; or as originally published in French, Derrida, *De l'esprit* (Paris: Éditions Galilée, 1987). In some sense, this point was suggested already in the "The Ends of Man" lecture, which does not address the human-animal distinction but does suggest that Heidegger, for all his radicalness, was still inclined to reinstate humanist values of proximity and a presence to oneself, and to resist the thought of a deeper exteriority. See Derrida, "The Ends of Man," *Philosophy and Phenomenological Research*, 54ff. Another early and important intervention in this debate, closely aligned to Derrida's work, is found in David Farrell Krell, *Daimon Life: Heidegger and Life-Philosophy* (Bloomington: Indiana University Press, 1992).

10. Derrida, *Of Spirit*, 56; *De l'esprit*, 87.

11. Giorgio Agamben, *The Open: Man and Animal*, trans. Kevin Attell (Stanford: Stanford University Press, 2004). First published in Italian as Agamben, *L'aperto: L'uomo e l'animale* (Torino: Bollati Boringhieri, 2002). From Heidegger's perspective, in Agamben's version, there are two alternatives: either the post-humanist animal becomes the technical caretaker of itself in a biopolitical order, or, as a "shepherd of being," it appropriates its own animality, not to master, but as an experience of pure abandonment" (80). But in a Benjaminian gesture, he holds the door open toward a new fusion of human and animal, where "living beings can sit at the messianic banquet." This vaguely indicated political utopia through the suspension of the human-animal distinction is of course outside the scope of Heidegger. But for all its critique, he nevertheless comes close to the latter in his conclusions, where the humanization of the animal points to the animalization of the human, and thereby the completion of the biopolitical reign in which politics becomes the organization of physiology as humanity's "last, impolitical mandate" (77).

12. Agamben, *The Open: Man and Animal*, 80.

13. Agamben, *The Open: Man and Animal*, 76.

14. Firenze, "'A Dog Does Not Exist but Merely Lives,'" 153.

15. Wilhelm Dilthey, *Die Geistige Welt: Einleitung in die Philosophie des Lebens*, vol. 5 of *Gesammelte Schriften*, ed. Georg Misch (Leipzig: Teubner, 1957), 4.

16. Friedrich Nietzsche, *Birth of Tragedy*, trans. Walter Kaufmann (New York: Vintage, 1967), 19.

17. See Hans-Georg Gadamer, "Der Begriff des Lebens bei Husserl und Graf Yorck," in *Wahrheit und Methode: Gundzüge einer philosophischen Hermeneutik*, 2nd ed. (Tübingen: Mohr, 1965), 229–50; or, in English, Gadamer, "The Concept of Life in Husserl and Count Yorck," *Truth and Method*, trans. Joel Weinsheimer and Donald Marshall, rev. ed. (New York: Crossroad, 1992), 242–52.

18. As pointed out to me by Ingo Farin, it should be noted that most of the above-mentioned life-philosophically inclined philosophers primarily start from human life, not life in a broader biological sense. Dilthey, for example, acknowledges the biological base in human life, but abstracts from it in his hermeneutic use of the concept.

19. See Martin Heidegger, *Zur Bestimmung der Philosophie*, vol. 56/57 of *Gesamtausgabe*, ed. Bernd Heimbüchel (Frankfurt: Klostermann, 1987), esp. part 2, *Phänomenologie und transzendentale Wertphilosophie*. Here, he also describes phenomenology as the fulfillment of "the secret longing of Dilthey" (167).

20. See Martin Heidegger, *Phänomenologische Interpretationen zu Aristoteles: Einführung in die phänomenologische Forschung*, vol. 61 of Gesamtausgabe, ed. Walter Bröcker and Käte Bröcker-Oltmanns (Frankfurt: Klostermann, 1985), 80.

21. Martin Heidegger, *Sein und Zeit*, vol. 2 of *Gesamtausgabe*, ed. Friedrich-Wilhelm von Herrmann (Frankfurt: Klostermann, 1977).

22. Heidegger, *Sein und Zeit*, 46.

23. Heidegger's later handwritten notes were inserted in the editions of *Sein und Zeit* from 1976 onward—as in the *Gesamtausgabe* edition.

24. Heidegger, *Sein und Zeit*, 48.

25. See the entire discussion, Heidegger, *Sein und Zeit*, 48–50.

26. For this term, see Addy Pross, *What Is Life? How Chemistry Becomes Biology* (Oxford: Oxford University Press, 2012), 9, also 17, where he writes of how "the living world screams out teleonomy no matter where you look." Ernst Mayr, in *This Is Biology: The Science of the Living World* (Cambridge, MA: Harvard University Press, 1997), argues that we have reached a balance between the two fractions of mechanists and vitalists that have been debating for four hundred years. Even though the older versions of vitalism are scientifically obsolete through the advances of biochemical accounts, we cannot do without some concept of "teleonomy" in the ability to nourish, regulate, and procreate that is characteristic of life-processes.

27. Some might dispute the applicability of talk of the "sensory" to plants and fungi and so might also dispute its applicability in any characterization of life in general. However, recent developments in biological science have led to a revised understanding of plant life, in particular, that makes such a characterization uncontroversial in contemporary discussions. Even a paper such as Jon Mallatt, Michael R. Blatt, Andreas Draguhn, David G. Robinson, and Lincoln Taiz, "Debunking a myth: plant consciousness," *Protoplasma* 258 (2021): 459–76, which is critical of contemporary talk of plant consciousness and cognition, nevertheless uses the

language of sensing in relation to plant life. Most contemporary biological scientists would have no difficulty in talking about fungi in similar fashion

28. Heidegger, *Die Grundbegriffe der Metaphysik*, here (and in the discussion following) quoted from the English edition, *The Fundamental Concepts of Metaphysics: World, Finitude, Solitude*, trans. William McNeill and Nicholas Walker (Bloomington: Indiana University Press, 1995).

29. Heidegger, *The Fundamental Concepts of Metaphysics*, 70.

30. Here, I do not address the (partly questionable) content of his understanding, interpretation, and assessment of Nietzsche, and how it then develops over the course of his extensive lecture courses from the mid-1930s into the early 1940s.

31. Heidegger, *The Fundamental Concepts of Metaphysics*, 201.

32. See, in particular, Jakob von Uexküll, *A Foray into the Worlds of Animals and Humans*, trans. Joseph O'Neil (Minneapolis: Minnesota University Press, 2010). Originally published in German as *Umwelt und Innenwelt der Tiere* in 1909, and in a revised edition in 1921.

33. See Uexküll, *A Foray into the Worlds of Animals and Humans*, 46—where he writes: "[A] stimulus has to be noticed by the subject and does not appear at all in objects."

34. Uexküll, *A Foray into the Worlds of Animals and Humans*, 54.

35. Heidegger, *The Fundamental Concepts of Metaphysics*, 177.

36. Heidegger, *The Fundamental Concepts of Metaphysics*, 177.

37. Heidegger, *The Fundamental Concepts of Metaphysics*, 194.

38. Heidegger, *The Fundamental Concepts of Metaphysics*, 199.

39. Heidegger, *The Fundamental Concepts of Metaphysics*, 233.

40. Heidegger, *The Fundamental Concepts of Metaphysics*, 249.

41. Heidegger, *The Fundamental Concepts of Metaphysics*, 248.

42. Heidegger, *The Fundamental Concepts of Metaphysics*, 253.

43. Heidegger, *Sein und Zeit*, §72.

44. Heidegger, *Fundamental Concepts*, 265.

45. Heidegger, *Fundamental Concepts*, 267.

46. Heidegger, *Fundamental Concepts*, 271.

47. Heidegger, *Fundamental Concepts*, 255.

48. Notably, in Heidegger, *Sein und Zeit*, §31–34. Heidegger distinguishes between two forms of "having something as something"—the apophatic and the hermeneutic. The first is tied to linguistically expressible judgments; the second is not. How and to what extent the second of these (the hermeneutic "as") is applicable in the case of nonhuman animals is an interesting question, the clarification of which would undoubtedly add to the understanding of the difference between having a world and being poor in world. Such clarification would, however, take us beyond the space available here.

Chapter Nine

Heidegger's Race

Laurence Paul Hemming

Heidegger and the Question of Race

What was Heidegger's understanding of race? This question is usually asked of Heidegger personally: To what extent is Heidegger himself racist? To ask the question in this way presupposes that we already understand what "race" is and means, and yet, even as race has become an element of contemporary discourse, it is far from clear that we have an answer to this question. To what extent does "race" explain the being of being human? If we answer, "hardly at all," then we explain only with difficulty, not only a certain preoccupation of the West with race (at least since the seventeenth century), but also the ways in which the contemporary discourses of race call for our attention. To refuse the discourses around race—race itself, indigeneity, colonial rule and postcolonialism, the demand for racial justice and the recognition of race—risks being, or being defined as, a gesture concerned with race.

If, however, we answer that race is, or is part of, the being of human being, we are left only with further questions: To what extent and in what ways? The current discourses of race can seem confused and refuse to run in straight lines. Is this because they are so new, or because they are emerging from places of dispossession or silence? If it is taken for granted, for instance, that colonialism as a historical phenomenon is immoral (as most commentators seem to agree), how are we to understand or explain that the establishment of what we now recognize as Europe was itself achieved through practices of colonization (Greek, Hellenic, Roman), or that the last North African colonizers of much of the Iberian Peninsula departed Spain only in 1492, while Turkish and Ottoman occupations and "threat" to Europe long persisted beyond this date? Is the colonialism that we have in question a consequence of race, or is the emergence of the discourse of race only an effect of colonial rule—or is neither of these the case? Is there indeed a "long history of racism," of which "Europe's oldest racisms [are] anti-Semitism and Islamophobia,"[1] or does the current drive to conflate religious identity with race conceal far older continuities and affinities? Have we forgotten that the origins of anti-Semitism lie, not in any doctrine of race, but in differences in theological doctrine among proselytizing groups who (disputatiously) shared a religious outlook—one full of divisions even before the arrival of Christianity? Have we even yet understood the extent to which the Islamic schools of Baghdad, and later Granada and Cordoba, preserved an advanced religious reading of Aristotle, bequeathing it to Latin Christianity in translations not from Greek, but Arabic? Have we even begun to comprehend the extent to which Christianity absorbed an understanding of God from Islam, in, for instance, the form of those "divine attributes" of God that were reworked from Qur'anic names of Allah? What Heidegger named as the "Christianisation of philosophy" was, as he himself knew, better understood as philosophy's transformation by three, and not just one, traditions that claimed roots in the patriarchs Adam and Abraham.[2]

Heidegger's own discussions of race as a formal topic are few and scattered, mainly found in those *Nachlaß* volumes of his *Collected Works* (or *Gesamtausgabe*), which contain material not published in his lifetime. Aside from the now many considerations of Heidegger's anti-Semitism, three studies in particular have paid attention to Heidegger's understanding of race: all began as article-length contributions. Robert Bernasconi's "Heidegger's Alleged Challenge to the Nazi Conceptions of Race" appeared first,[3] followed by Sonia Sikka's "Heidegger and Race" (later expanded into a book chapter).[4] Finally, Jeffrey Barash published "Heidegger and the Question of Race" in French.[5] They gather a breadth of scholarly enquiry, coincident with the developments in the issue of race underway in the last decades. Barash undertakes meticulous research into the racial ideologues who based themselves in Freiburg during the Nazi period, and to whom Heidegger had access, concluding that Heidegger had little truck with Nazi racist ideology. All three studies focus to a greater or lesser degree on the question that Sikka foregrounded as a chapter-heading when revising her initial study for her later monograph: "Was Heidegger racist?"[6]

How we deal with issues of race is often a question concerning intellectual hygiene. This issue also marks Emmanuel Faye's research: To what extent do—or even, can—we read Heidegger without "contamination," either by his own Nazism, or the racism and crimes perpetrated in Nazism's name? Is there a Nazi taint to his thought? This is the title of Faye's major work—*The Introduction of Nazism into Philosophy*—and drives his readings of Heidegger.[7] Witness the panic at the appearance of the supposedly loaded word *das Volk* (twice, no less, in the whole book!) in *Being and Time*, a full six years before the Nazis take power.[8] The presupposition of almost everyone is that the only possible answer to the question whether Heidegger is racist is "yes." To read Heidegger seriously forces us to take up the position of accuser or rescuer, of the man or his thought, without, therefore, having had to address the question *as a question* of the origins and meaning of race, first in the West and only then in the specificities of Heidegger's writing. This contribution offers to take a step in the direction of answering that question, not as a question about Heidegger's personal racism, but Heidegger's understanding of the historical category of race, its possibilities and effects (and so its being), and its significance for the being of human being. In a study of this length, it will not be possible to give a full answer, but perhaps we can at least open the door to show from where, and how, the question can be addressed. It will, as it must, reach beyond Heidegger himself.

Establishing that someone is racist is often a process of pursuing and justifying an act of devaluation. If we can show that someone is racist, we can forever after suggest that everything they say is suspect until proven otherwise. Heidegger's involvement with Nazism opens him immediately to such a devaluation, especially in anything he has to say concerning race. It is for this reason that different commentators have come to Heidegger either (as with Faye) to claim that everything Heidegger has to say is tainted or to attempt to adjudicate the degree and the particularities of the taint: to claim, in other words, that Heidegger was racist, but just not very racist (pressing, for instance, the distinction between "biological" and "cultural" racism), or, as Julian Young and others have attempted, to define racism in such a way ("biological") that an opponent of "the biological" such as

Heidegger could (by definition, therefore) not have been racist. Young (and he is not alone) attempts to rescue Heidegger as, not so much a racist, but rather a German "chauvinist," as if that made anything better or the man more palatable.[9] None of these, from Faye to Young, nor from Bernasconi to Sikka, address what Heidegger himself understands by the category of race. Few, with the exception of Bernasconi, address directly the question of the meaning of race in itself.

A basic insight of the thinking of race, especially in the contemporary situation, is that we always begin in an unthinking relation to race, even when we cannot see it. It is only when race becomes a question—when we are able to move from an unthinking to a thoughtful relation with it—that the questions concerning judgment and culpability can even become clear.

I do not propose in this contribution to summarize the arguments that previous authors have made. Bernasconi's, Sikka's, and even Barash's work is not difficult to find, and each is a master of her or his material. I do want to take one text of Heidegger's that is common to each of them (and mentioned by many others, Faye not least), and ask whether interpreting it rather differently than they and others have might yield insight, not only into Heidegger's own thought, but into the question of the category of race and its origins as a mode of thinking of human being.

It is, I propose, only when we have understood how the category of race arises in Western thought, and so have brought ourselves into a thoughtful relation with it, that we are in a position to understand what race and racism mean. What follows is an attempt to show how Heidegger himself undertook this passage of thinking, so that we might also think through the meaning of race and its place in the history of Western thought. This is the question of real importance in addressing race and its part in Heidegger and the human. Is race only a thought that arises in the West? Let me turn this thought on its head: let me address myself and all those who think already as Westerners, and as ones who think in a way that the West in its global reach has defined in advance of itself. Wherever "the West" has established itself as the dominant mode of enquiry is where we need to begin: thus we begin where we ourselves are thoughtlessly already rooted ("thrown"). We begin by undertaking a formally historical enquiry and so seek to understand race as it has been thought historically in the West. Such a beginning may entail that we will come to leave the Western thought of race behind and assign it to belonging only to a certain point in Western history, but that is not my concern here.

The Logic Lectures of 1934: Human Beings Without History

How, then, to begin? Concerning the question of race itself (rather than of anti-Semitism), reference to one text of Heidegger's runs as a thread through all discussions of Heidegger and race. The text has been well known among Heidegger scholars, even before its appearance in the Heidegger *Gesamtausgabe*, from one of the many typescripts of his lectures made by, and circulating among, his students.[10] In 1934, shortly after resigning as rector of Freiburg University, Heidegger was scheduled to lecture on the subject of politics and the Nazi state. He instead went to the lectern and announced (to the consternation of the student Nazi lackeys present) "I'm teaching *Logic*."[11] In the Spiegel interview, Heidegger cited these lectures, together with those on Hölderlin and Nietzsche in these years, as one of the places where "everyone, who could hear, heard that this was a confrontation with National Socialism."[12] This claim is often written off by commentators as among Heidegger's more self-serving statements, especially in the area of race, and so its significance is overlooked. For Heidegger is making explicit that these lectures, in their confrontation with National Socialism, were delivered in a code for those "who could hear." We, who have come in the present climate to fear the accusation that we are, *I am*, wittingly or unwittingly, racist, perhaps have little comprehension of what it means to speak and write in a context where at any point one can be denounced for not being racist enough. Such were the times. Public language concerned with race is often coded (What else is "dog whistle" speech?). This is also true of Heidegger's discussion and critique of race. To read without attention to the irony, the code, the *tone* of Heidegger's lecture, is to risk not being among those who could, and can, hear what is being said.

As these lectures on *Logic* proceed, Heidegger says, "[I]f we now take up the question concerning the essence of history, one could think that we have arbitrarily decided what history is: namely, history is what is distinctive for the being of humanity. One could, on the other hand, object that there are human beings, and human groups (blacks, in particular, southern African blacks), that have no history, of whom we say, they are without history."[13] These remarks have often been received with incendiary effect, and, taken at face value, well they might be. The discourse of race has had a remarkable effect in reshaping language itself. Terms at one time common have been erased, made objectionable or problematized (to be reclaimed only in certain contexts or by those against whom they were once negatively used—I think, in this context and in my own life, of the word "queer"), and often with good reason. Yet, in historical texts, we can encounter these terms used in good faith, and because we would now never use them ourselves, they shock us, or our most immediate and unthinking reaction is to presume that they were, or are only ever, deployed with purpose, to negative or pejorative effect. This is not always the case.

Bernasconi, commenting on this passage, is excoriating of Heidegger's use of language: "Heidegger repeated the longstanding idea that the Negro has no history," which he says is a "familiar trope of European racism."[14] He argues that Heidegger repeats this slur "when, the following semester, Heidegger drew the consequence that 'only an historical people is truly a people.'"[15] It is therefore important for us to note that "to be historical" has quite different senses across Heidegger's work, and, as we shall see, especially around the issue of race. If Bernasconi's instinct is correct, that what it means to be historical is the issue here, as I will make clear, the quick inference he draws between two quite disconnected texts is not. Indeed, it is because Heidegger rejects the *historical* basis on which the statement that there is anyone who "has no history" is made, that he then attempts to develop further and elucidate what the historical basis of being human actually is.[16]

If we look more closely, we see that not only one position is stated ("blacks, particularly southern African blacks, have no history"), but that this is a second claim, distinguished from a prior (and more important) one, which actually *is* that "history is what is distinctive for the being of humanity." The real question at issue (which Bernasconi correctly identifies) is, *How* is history distinctive for the being of humanity? Heidegger is therefore disagreeing with what "is said" (generally) because *to be*, to be human, and *to have a history* cannot be taken apart. It should be stressed that Heidegger's procedure here is exactly in line with his understanding of language in *Being and Time*: we move from "inauthentic" "idle chatter" ("one says") to authentic understanding, in order to uncover the *being* in question. Who is it, then, if it is not Heidegger, that says that there are those who "are," but have no history? With whom did this general assertion begin?

The phrase "we might say" refers to a passage from Hegel. Heidegger is dealing with an authoritative source, familiar to most of those present, whose interpretation has become generally ("inauthentically") accepted, and with whom he disagrees: Hegel. Heidegger takes up a term deployed by Hegel at the end of a long discussion of Africa and its inhabitants from the compilation of material based on Hegel's plan for a volume on the *Philosophy of History*.[17] Africa, Hegel says (in the version that Heidegger knew) is *geschichtslos*, "history-less," and so Africa, and Africans, are without history.[18] Heidegger's reported phrase "Neger wie z.B. Kaffern" draws attention to a distinction that was important *for Hegel*.[19] Hegel specifically distinguishes between the different parts of Africa: North Africans, Muslims especially, according to Hegel, do have history, but Africans "proper" are different entirely. Heidegger's use of the term *Kaffern* draws attention to Hegel's specification of the black Africans of the south, who inhabit what Hegel calls "Africa proper," the place, Hegel says, that has been, "as far as history goes back," a "child-land."[20]

To explore Hegel's thoughts on Africa in full would require a much fuller study. Let me, however, show how it is proper to challenge the assumption that Heidegger, in 1934, uses the notion of history and the history-less in a racist sense. The word *geschichtslos* and its accompanying phrase "ohne Geschichte" (without history) can be found quite frequently across Heidegger's works, not always in connection with Hegel, or matters of race,[21] but often enough to make clear that Heidegger was well aware of what was being claimed—and that it troubled him.[22] Heidegger discusses what *geschichtslos* means twice: once in 1920, and again in a text that cannot be dated exactly but that makes explicit reference to the *Logic* lectures of 1934, and that was most likely written in the late 1930s.

In lectures delivered in the summer semester of 1920, Heidegger considers "six meanings of history." Heidegger compares his initial definitions of history with "the talk about 'history-less tribes and peoples,'" whether justified or not," noting that "history-less" here has nothing to do with the notions of history he has already dealt with as the lectures have progressed. Heidegger is clearly alive, in 1920, to the complexity of this term, *geschichtslos*, and assumes its wide reception in his audience. Moreover, the qualification "whether justified or not" indicates that, already in 1920, Hegel's claim is far from unchallengeable. Heidegger speaks of Zulus (by example) and notes that while tribespeoples without a written culture therefore hold no records or public documents, "this does not therefore mean these tribes lack a developed knowledge of history," even if they have no formal tradition (in the sense, he says, that the Middle Ages had a tradition). Heidegger is trying to illustrate different relations to time in real, lived contexts, in which history as such is at work, beyond a mere "sense of the past," where the meaning of the past is understood and preserved, even if it lacks a formal record ("a tradition").

Heidegger speaks not as an anthropologist, nor even as a historian, but as a philosopher: his characterizations are, we might say, somewhat clumsy. Nevertheless, they are neither disrespectful nor negative, let alone formally racist. Heidegger seems ignorant of what contemporary anthropology now understands as the preserving power of the oral and storytelling traditions of many Indigenous and First Nations peoples, even if his point is to draw a distinction between the sense of history as it has been developed in modern Western philosophy and those who do not, in the same way, "cultivate the past." The one statement that appears to run in this direction is the claim Heidegger makes, in the lecture, that those who do not have history in the Western sense therefore have "no future and no tasks,"[23] but the point that is being made here is the opposite of what we might at first assume.[24]

These lectures are preoccupied (as was much of Heidegger's thinking at the time) with delineating philosophy not as a scientific practice that grounds the facticality of everyday life but the other way about. Rather than grounding everyday facticity in prior structures of reason, his aim is to demonstrate that philosophy must set out by being grounded in the facticity of bare life itself. The assignment of a future and tasks to humanity is a feature of German idealism and what followed it. Idealism *does* assign a future, and tasks, to historical humanity, as humanity's "work" overall: as we shall see, Hegel's understanding of race flowed directly from this. For Hegel the southern Africans' *lack* of a sense of historical destiny—of a universal future that is to be striven toward, and of "tasks"—is the source of his judgements about race, and the reason that he places Africans outside history, and even, as we shall see, outside humanity as a whole. There is no negative aspect, no pejorative element, to Heidegger's observation that the Zulu tribe holds before itself no future tasks. Indeed, quite the reverse, the implication from the text is that to live within the day is itself a perfectly adequate mode of Dasein. Pindar, no less, had said the same.[25]

The second text is from Heidegger's background and preparatory notes *Concerning Eventual Thinking*. This material, as with so much of Heidegger's vast *Nachlaß* of private notes, is cryptic and difficult to interpret. The remark comprises just a few words, naming the 1934 *Logic* course, and says: "*people*—never historyless—no more than [they are] speechless."[26] To be capable of speech is to have history. To be capable of speech, for Heidegger—to be ζῷον λόγον ἔχον, the animal having and held by speaking—is the definition of what it is to be human. To understand what follows we must make a distinction that many of the commentators have simply refused to make: in history itself. For Heidegger, especially by the time this second passage was written, all history is the history of being. But the history of being is not the *necessary* course of the history of humanity toward an absolute goal (the "end" of history). The history of being is not programmatic: quite the reverse, it is itself a danger, and fraught with risk. History puts before historical humanity the question of destiny, but does not define the content of that destiny. *Every* people, to be genuinely a people, is confronted with the question of destiny *as a question*. This destiny is not, however, a collective pinnacle over against every *other* people (as Nazism and Stalinism, in ways that had been put before everyone in Germany, right in 1934, both claimed). To live from one's destiny is not to live a "mission," either of civilizing others or lording it over them. It is to live, not merely from the present moment (what in *Being and Time* is called the "they"-self), but with *immediate* resolve, as an understanding that time is always, and immediately, a coming-toward us, as presen*cing*.

Heidegger's Rejection of Hegel's Concept of History

What is the basis for Heidegger's rejection of Hegel's understanding of history? It is grounded in the difference between Hegel's and Heidegger's understandings of the phenomenon of time. Hegel's discussions of time are often confused, even contradictory, so that Kojève, for instance, claimed (as he—wrongly—thought Heidegger had himself) that Hegel had privileged the future over the present and the past.[27] Heidegger rejected that view from the outset, stressing that what he had actually emphasized is "not: the essence of the present is the future, but: the meaning of timeliness (*Zeitlichkeit*) is the future. [. . .] The meaning of the thesis that I hold is, therefore, diametrically opposed to what Hegel [. . .] says."[28]

What is this diametric opposition? The reason for the confusion in Hegel's understanding of time and, therefore (for Heidegger), his confused understanding of history, lies precisely here. In his 1924 lecture on time, Heidegger made a simple point about history, the significance of which has barely been grasped: "*The possibility of access to history lies in the possibility by which any specific present understands itself to be futural.*"[29] For Heidegger, time is a singular, constantly arriving, which the being of human being both "expects" (*gewärtigt*) and "makes present" (*gegenwärtigt*), in denotative speaking, λόγος. It is neither subjective, nor objective: for the later Heidegger, this is the basis of eventuality, *das Ereignis*. History, for Heidegger, is the factical appropriation of the future's ever-arriving, at the highest: it necessitates not just individuality, as *one* who makes the advancing future present, but community as such, as a "wherein," where the experience of making-present is shared across individuals and across time itself, and is formally and fundamentally an event of language (λόγος). At its most basic, this making-present occurs in "community" (*Gemeinschaft*), but at its highest, within a "people" (*Volk*). A people is not an aggregation of individuals, and certainly not a "race" or aggregation of races, but has a (historical) sense of itself, a "from where" and a "whither." Indeed, it is not so much that "a people has a history" as that "history is disclosed *as* the specificity of being-a-people."[30] This is as true in the most generalized sense for a First Nation people as it is for a contemporary European nation (comprised, perhaps, of many different peoples), but the factical experience of it will manifest itself, and *be*, entirely different from one to the other: it will be "proper" for each. Above all, we *need* make no valuation of one factical manifestation over another—that this one is "better" than that one, as a way of distinguishing the relative "value" of nations, tribes, or races. This does not mean that some moments, some historical periods, will not be greater than others: but the greatness has nothing to do with "race."

For Hegel, however, time, as the sequence of nows, is necessarily subjective. In this, as Heidegger explained, Hegel's understanding of time is entirely in accord with Aristotle's claim that without soul there would be no time, since soul does the counting,[31] and so Hegel retains the understanding of time as subjective time that runs through the entire philosophical tradition in the West from Aristotle forward. Simply put, time is "in the mind" (is a function of *spirit*). However, Hegel's understanding of subjectivity is not merely as the subjectivity of the "I think," but at the same time of absolute subjectivity (sublated time, eternity, is the time of *absolute* spirit). It is this that secures time *and history* both as subjective and as absolute (and why, for Hegel, the subjective is formally-absolutely privileged over the objective, even as objectivity's "negation"). For Hegel every present "now" is secured against absolute time, which is eternity. Individual moments of time are (negatively) coeval with absolute time, which is the temporality of absolute *Geist*, or absolute subjectivity. The coevality is necessary because eternity does not come "after" time, indeed, is not a moment of time at all, "since were eternity to follow time, it would thereby be made a moment of time."[32] Time has the same character as the contiguity of space, indeed space *is* this contiguity, or as Heidegger puts it, Hegel "determines the being of space not *from* time but *as* time."[33] For Hegel, history culminates in its end as the absolute, realizing itself. History, thought like this, is (oddly) "outside" time, and only properly understood as the absolutization of time. Fulfilled history *is* (is the realization, the making-present, of) eternity.

It is this that secures the metaphysical ground of Hegel's understanding of race. How else would we understand a text of Hegel's (to which it is unlikely Heidegger had access) that says "the shapes which we see in world-history through the succession in time we also see standing perennially next to one another in space. That these forms subsist next one another and have their necessity in the concept, is essential for us to take note of, and we must convince ourselves of this."[34]

Sikka recognizes that Heidegger's use of *geschichtslos* "recalls" remarks of Hegel's,[35] but seems unwilling to recognize that Heidegger is making the connection explicit—as explicit as it is possible to be in the racist context of the Nazi lecture room. What is the connection that Heidegger makes with Hegel? In lectures from 1925 at Marburg, and at an adult education institute at Kassel on Dilthey's "struggle for a historical worldview," Heidegger had discussed Dilthey's method of enquiry: "the task to view 'life itself' in its structures as the basic reality of history."[36] This description is remarkably close to the task he sets himself of exhibiting what he was to call in *Being and Time* "the structural analytic of *Dasein*." Heidegger had distinguished in these lectures the difference between a "natural worldview" of human being and the "scientific" one that had grown up, in philosophy especially, with Kant.

Heidegger's engagement with Dilthey, and what has been called the "crisis of historicism" was an engagement with the failure of what the early nineteenth century thinkers of the West had meant by "world-development." We could almost say that the nineteenth century—if we also include Kant—is par excellence the century of *theories* of world-development: Heidegger makes plain in 1925 that what is at issue is the bringing-together of a "natural worldview" of human being with a "scientific" one, but inasmuch as it is scientific, he insists that not only theoretical knowledge (*theoretische Kenntnis*), but practical disposition (*praktische Stellungnahme*), what we will direct ourselves to do, will be in question. The "historical" understanding that Heidegger suggests is the struggle for a historical worldview is a composite of just the way we ordinarily or "naturally" take ourselves to be *together* with the way a "scientific" or theoretical understanding takes the world to be. In the course of this development of a new "historical" viewpoint, Heidegger comments that "primitive peoples live, and we ourselves have lived, for a long time without history."[37] Heidegger is wryly mocking the understanding of history as a finality, a goal, an absolute.

Heidegger adds that neither a knowledge of change, nor even a "national consciousness" constitutes historical consciousness, nor, indeed, does the development of humanism, nor the Reformation in its confrontation with Catholicism (another sideswipe at Hegel, among others), and he concludes that an awakening and wakened historical consciousness is more like a task to advance toward (*zu entwickeln*) than anything else. The task is to understand history as universal history: in this context Heidegger now refers directly to Kant, Herder, Humboldt, and Hegel. The culmination of the modern understanding of history is, however, to be found in Hegel, for whom "the humanity of European cultures [is] embodied in the state."[38] The essential movement of history becoming world history, the task to be developed in this understanding, is the movement in German idealism from dependency and limitation to freedom, but this is embodied in the state. With Hegel, freedom is subjectivity becoming absolute subjectivity. Absolute subjectivity finds its embodiment in the state as such, and in God. Eduard Gans reports Hegel as saying that the state is none other than "the path of God through the world":[39] the state, therefore, is the realization of the absolute concept in the world: the embodiment of absolute subjectivity as such.

The remarks about "primitive people" are a reference to race, but Heidegger is being ironic. Bernasconi has asked the question "[W]ho invented the scientific concept of race?,"[40] and clarified this question to specify "the one who gave the concept sufficient definition for subsequent users to believe that they were addressing something whose scientific status could at least be debated"—he points, more than anyone else, to Kant. He adds, "[I]t is usually agreed that the term 'race' was first used in something like its contemporary meaning at the end of the seventeenth century."[41] In fact the development of the "scientific" definition of race is coincident, and necessarily so, with the development of the idea of history as a task. It is only with the development of history as a *universal* task for humanity, for humanity's self-realization, that any concept of the universal essence of humanity could form the unifying concept behind the different expressions of the human race. We must ask: What presents itself in the concept of the human race, of humanity as comprising "races"? Why might this also be a question about "human" history?

How is it that both Western humanity and so-called "primitive peoples" lived so long without "history"? We are already aware of the answer from the texts of Heidegger's I have cited: because there are here entirely different conceptions of history at work. Emmanuel Faye attempts to drive a wedge between the remarks of 1934 and those in Kassel in 1925:[42] on the contrary, we may be certain (from the context itself) that the remarks in Kassel from the Dilthey lectures make the same reference to Hegel as those of 1934, and indeed to the same argument that Hegel makes, but in 1925 Heidegger was less sure of their consequences, which is why he reports them somewhat equivocally, as if our own living without history for a long time could qualify Hegel's argument. What has changed? By early 1934 (when these lectures were delivered), the Nazis were well on the way to seizing total power in Germany: they would do so only in the autumn of that year. Heidegger had by then resigned as rector of Freiburg University—in part rejecting the Nazi program, and in part feeling himself to be forced out of the office. Heidegger does not tell us what of the Nazi worldview he abandoned (certainly he remained sympathetic to the movement behind it). If, as Heidegger had noted, the state is the ground of (European) culture, it has now become clear what kind of state this can result in: a state determined on the basis of a claim about race. This is what he rejects.[43]

By 1934 Heidegger is patently and unequivocally rejecting Hegel's understanding of a "scientific" (*wissenschaftlich*) understanding of history, and most importantly because he rejects how it had come to be embodied by the Nazi state. A few months after the *Logic* lectures, Heidegger would say that in "1933 it was said Hegel was dead: on the contrary, he has only just begun to live."[44] This was a flat put-down to the Nazi jurist Carl Schmitt who had claimed in 1933 that, when Hitler came to power, "Hegel died."[45]

Hegel represents the absolute pinnacle of that development of the understanding of history and the state that coincides with what Robert Bernasconi has identified as the European concept of race, which begins at the end of the seventeenth century. Hegel planned, but never prepared, the published version of his lectures on the philosophy of world-history: that task fell to his son, Karl Hegel, and to Eduard Gans. Nevertheless, as Heidegger claimed, Hegel was the first to introduce a systematic, metaphysical, understanding of history into Western philosophy, such that philosophy itself is understood, and only can be understood, as a historical thinking driven by a force of necessity. Never mind that it has at its center a claim about freedom: the freedom in question is of a strange kind.

At the center is the thought of the human being as a historical being. Commenting on Hegel's understanding of history in 1958, Heidegger argued: "Therefore for Hegel philosophy as the self-production of spirit toward absolute knowledge and the history of philosophy are identical. No philosopher *before* Hegel had achieved such a fundamental position, one which enabled and required that philosophizing itself and at the same time move within its history and that this movement is itself philosophy."[46]

If, in Hegel, this question of history came to be answered through the question of race, in Heidegger the understanding of history is carried out in opposition to Hegel, and in part as an attack on Hegel's understanding of race. This became clear to Heidegger only in the crucible of the formation of a state built on an understanding of race that was not intended by Hegel, but took its justification from the claim to universality, and universal acceptance, of what he had said. It is almost impossible to speak of Nazi ideology: Nazism was a fractious amalgam of warring factions—in a divisiveness encouraged by Hitler himself—who built their state on a terror of devastating criminality, and deployed race as pretext and weapon in that terror. Heidegger took the view that Hegel's metaphysics laid the foundations for such a terror: it is the way in which the Nazis constructed their terror-state on those foundations that constituted Heidegger's view that Nazism was a form of liberalism. I suggest that he came to this view around 1934, at the time the *Logic* lectures were delivered.

As early as 1924, however, Heidegger had distinguished his own historical understanding from Hegel's. He noted that his early concept of historicality, *Geschichtlichkeit*, "should be *understood* not as history (world-history). Historicality indicates *being*-historical of that, which is as history."[47] *Geschichtlichkeit* is factical history, of what actually is and is present, not the history of the absolute, of (absent, negated) absolute subjectivity realizing itself in time. Heidegger's understanding of history is neither subjective in the sense of securing time as an intuition of the "I think" of the subjectivity of the subject, nor on an understanding of the necessity of the unfolding of the eternal-absolute in time.

Hegel argues the contrary. His lectures on world-history are intended to show "that world history has been given as the necessarily rational course of world-spirit:—and world-spirit is *Geist* as such, as the substance of history, the one *Geist* whose nature [is] one and the same and that explicates its one nature through the existence of the world [*Weltdaseyn*]."[48] World history is universal, it is absolute *Geist*, realizing itself. For Hegel, German Protestantism represents the end and goal of history from the land, race, political state, and religion within which humanity, the "human essence," is fully realized as free and capable for subjectivity realizing its absolute form.

The extreme position on race that Hegel describes in his final lectures on world-history, delivered in the last year of his life and so within the full development of his system, has a direct bearing on the underlying motivation for the volume for which this essay is a part. These lectures were among the better-known of Hegel's texts not least because of their more accessible content, when compared, for instance, with the *Logic* or even the *Rechtsphilosophie*. They were the basis of the Lasson edition already referred to, because they were primarily based on Hegel's son Karl's transcript. Karl had been present at these lectures in 1830–31. From the first edition of the lectures in 1837, and in a passage that Heidegger and many among his academic audiences would have known, Hegel comes close to saying (if indeed he does not actually say) that the southern African stands outside what it means to be human. The African persists in an existence that is marked by immediacy, with no "knowledge of an absolute being," neither in the form of God nor, therefore for Hegel, as absolute Subject. In this sense the southern African stands outside the meaning of being as such. Such a form of immediate, and so *un*mediated, life does not, Hegel argues, even achieve the formal stance of finding itself in opposition to the nature that surrounds it. The consequence for the southern African is that "there is nothing of the human to be found in such a character."[49] This position is intelligible only if it is understood metaphysically: Hegel believed himself to have described in his system how particular being is taken up into absolute being through a movement, the movement of being-as-spirit from individual to absolute subjectivity. In one sense Hegel shows how human being is to be taken up into highest (divine) being, but far more fundamentally, Hegel bases what it is to be human as, in advancing toward highest being, itself securing the entirety of being in its being such that to be human is to uncover the human as the ground of the being of everything that is (including the divine).[50] Hegel defines humanity itself as being capable for absolute being, and so makes being in its most universal form an entirely human affair (this is the very basis for Marx's fundamental metaphysical position).

At the same time, Hegel excludes those not capable for absolute being as therefore merely animal, and so not human. Heidegger in contrast, insists that being, even Dasein, is *in itself* nothing human. This means that humanity, either in particular or in general, even if it belongs to being, is not represented or defined by being (which is nothing human) and so does not cease to be human, or is not less than human, in relation to its capability for being.[51] In each case belonging to being means belonging to language. This is why for Heidegger the phrase ζῷον λόγον ἔχον can never be understood or translated as *animal rationale*. The southern African, as much as every other human, has and is held by language, by speaking. Once again it is possible to see to what extent and how Hegel's position is diametrically opposed to Heidegger's.

Hegel, Race, and Metaphysics

We are still very far from a comprehensive understanding of Heidegger's reading of Hegel, and his engagement with German idealism. If it is true that Heidegger added a paragraph to the end of his habilitation thesis to the effect that what was really required in philosophy was a confrontation (*Auseinandersetzung*) "with Hegel," and was capable of describing Hegel in the most elevated terms, he also said that Hegel's dialectic lives off a "fundamental sophistry." More seriously, Heidegger argues that Hegel "kills off" (*totschlägt*) the relation between point, line, and plane that is the hallmark of Aristotle's discussions of space and time (the implication is that there is much Hegel does not know or understand, despite what is claimed), and concludes: "Hegel can say everything about anything, and there are people who discover deep meaning in confusion of such a kind."[52]

Numerous authors have assembled Hegel's scattered, often extraordinary, remarks on the relationship between world-history and race (Alison Stone has made two fine summaries of them),[53] and so I propose to make only the briefest survey of Hegel's points. Hegel represents the pinnacle of the understanding of history that coincides with what Robert Bernasconi identified in Kant as the European concept of race. Hegel's philosophy of world-history is coincident with his observations on race (and religion) across the geography of the entire globe, through the Americas and its First Nations, through China and the other lands of Asia, India, Persia, Egypt, and finally reaching a nadir in Africa. In ways that are regressive even for his time, Hegel in several places justifies the practice of slavery. If in his last lectures of 1830–31 Hegel says "if slavery were unlawful, then [Europeans] would give them their freedom,"[54] the British fleet, as Hegel knew, by contrast had since 1807 been blockading the transport of slaves across the Atlantic (and Britain abolished slavery within two years of Hegel's death). Hegel's views were neither uncontroversial nor universally held.

Hegel's metaphysical position on race is indicated in all three editions of his *Encyclopaedia* from 1817 to 1830. In §393 of his 1830 edition of the *Encyclopaedia* (sometimes known as the *Philosophy of Subjective Spirit*) we find: "the universal planetary life of natural spirit (*Naturgeist*) particularizes itself through the concrete divisions of the earth and disaggregates itself as particular natural spirits (*Naturgeister*), manifesting within the whole the nature of the geographical continents, determining the differentiation of the races."[55] It was from the sections of the *Encyclopaedia* that Hegel based his most important lectures in Berlin from 1816 to 1830.[56] In 1845, Hegel's student, Ludwig Boumann, added considerable additional material from lecture transcripts, as the "remarks," or *Zusätze*, to the *Encyclopaedia*—material well-known to Heidegger. Other manuscripts have come to light, as recently as 1994. The remarks do not carry the authority of the *Encyclopaedia* text (and so have a not dissimilar authority to the versions and edited manuscripts of the *Philosophy of World-History*), but what emerges is a consistent account of *Geist*, race, and history across all the texts and manuscripts. If at times Hegel rejects the "science" of physiognomy, at others he speculates on the meaning of the shapes of faces, colors of skin, and other physical attributes as he sees fit, even at one point parroting the nonsense of the Dutch anatomist Pieter Camper assessing the relative status of races historically and geographically by the angle of the nose in proportion to the forehead.[57] The pseudoscience of Nazis like Rosenberg had precedent in the nineteenth century, with Hegel lending authority to at least some of it.

Hegel regards the physiological aspects of racial difference as subordinate to their metaphysical implications. When discussing the "Camper angles" of "Negro" skulls, Hegel is reported as adding, "[W]hat is of greater concern is how far this corresponds with the relation to spirit,"[58] adding that physiology has *geistige* (spiritual) significance and that the connection is "essential" (*wesentlich*). A transcript of Hegel's lectures of 1825 draws out the significance of this connection with spirit: "The question of racial variety bears upon the rights one ought to accord to people; when there are various races, one will be nobler and the other has to serve it. The relationship between peoples determines itself in accordance with their reason."[59]

None of the contemporary commentators on Hegel's understanding of race relate his remarks to his understanding of absolute spirit, or to its place within German idealism, and yet it is clear, even from this briefest of surveys, that Hegel's fundamental position on race is in consequence of the metaphysics of spirit as absolute spirit. Anything like the physiological or "biological," and history itself, is posited on the metaphysics of absolute spirit and the infinite. Heidegger grasps the significance of this when he argues that "Hegel and German Idealism as a whole can grasp the totality of the being of present being from out of I-hood as infinity." This is because "the subject, the I, is primarily constituted as 'I think.' "[60]

We come up against the peculiarity of Hegel's metaphysics that will explain exactly Hegel's position on race, and so his ability to privilege one race over all the others: Hegel's privileging of one race over any other is a metaphysical position before it is either a historical or even a "biological" one.[61] Hegel's philosophy is above all a philosophy of the present and the immediate. What is most present and most immediate at every given moment is the *in*determinate universal, making itself manifest through its *actual* determinations, through what mediates it. Every actual being *actuates* (makes manifest) the universal at each moment, but the universal is only insofar as that actual being is capable of realizing it.[62] Every actual being is therefore marked by a finitude, a "notness" or negativity that simultaneously makes present the universal and makes present its own finite relation *to* the universal. Inward conceptualizing, intending, or inward tending toward, is only in order to press oneself *out* to make manifest the universal that one both *is* and at the same time *should be* (this is Hegel's understanding of freedom).

This character of Hegel's metaphysics is often the hardest to grasp in its most abstract form.[63] Hegel draws our attention to how we already take the materiality of the world as a whole in a particular way, simultaneously providing both for a public and a private appropriation of it that can be at odds with each other, and yet seemingly confront us with no recognizable contradiction. We take everything present for us *unthinkingly*, as a self-evidence, and we do so, in the manner that we do, in consequence of the attainment of German metaphysics. What is meant by this? If we can think that the attainment of German idealism, and of Hegel's thought in particular, is the relentless assertion and realization of the overcoming and abolition of any supersensible (*Übersinnliche*) realm, then it becomes clear that absolute thinking requires that everything we think, we think in terms of its immediate *and* total presence, at one and the same time and together, because there is nowhere else, no other container, nor place, at which, or within which, it can be thought. We no longer think publicly from out of Plato's "beyond," or preexistent sphere, nor from out of the creative will of God, nor from any ideal or higher realm. We take the world as we now know it out of its most immediate *and* its total presence. Negativity, the "notness" I have named, is the essential corollary of this thought, since, in order to understand each specific and particular actualization of presence, requires that we grant simultaneity to the *absent* presence that each *present* presence indicates: both in being present as it is now, and having been present before in a different way, and needing to be present in some other way in the future. This is to say no more than that it exists and can change in time. Each presence is therefore in a determinable relation to everything else with which it simultaneously is present, even at the moment when it itself "is not." To think in this way arises in a thoughtful tradition that has existed at least since Aristotle, and Plato before him. It is to think, as Heidegger elsewhere had suggested, on the basis of a certain "notness" (*Nichthafte*) or negativity that arose out of Aristotle's (and Plato's) confrontation with Parmenides, "inasmuch as the aspect of negation itself had now to be included within the essence of being."[64]

We see in Hegel's extraordinary intellectual effort, through geography, religion, race, and national identity, but actually through a metaphysics of the present *as* a conception of history and historical development, the attempt to grasp and seize the planet as a whole. Hegel does not lay the conditions for this: the conditions already exist and have taken hold. Hegel systematizes the conditions such that they appear both as order, and as—in his own word—system. The different races in the world are distinguished from each other to the extent that they are more or less (more negatively or less negatively) the realization of the absolute. The African is without history because the African people is (historically) furthest from—even, Hegel suggests, incapable of—realizing the European (Germanic) state. This is the African relation to the absolute, the most negative realization of the absolute: making here-present (by indicating its absence, its negation) the *absent* presence of what is *there* (in the European state) presently-present. The different "races" are the different degrees of negative realization of the absolute. This is the metaphysics of race, as the metaphysics of history.

Heidegger's Rejection of Race

If Julian Young is correct, that "the Heidegger literature contains, unfortunately, a great deal of unhelpful and confusing talk about Heidegger's alleged 'metaphysical' [. . .] racism," Heidegger himself does not agree that "there is no such thing," nor can we concur when Young says, "biological racism is the only kind there is."[65] It is easy to see now that Heidegger can reject anything like a biological understanding of race, because not even Hegel bases his understanding of race on "biology." However, Heidegger also insists that "the biological" is, in fact, a metaphysical designation.[66] For "the biological," as it is applied to the human, has become a way of determining the human "rational animal" in the facticity of its life, thus through categories like "the anthropological," which take the human being as an object of study in the sciences that demark the way those studies are to be carried out: anthropology, sociology, and, as we shall see, above all historiography. For Heidegger, "the biological," like all these scientific designations, is a way of taking the human as object to the subject of (human) subjectivity. As a discourse, especially a scientific one, it depends on the objectivity that already arises on the basis of a metaphysics of subjectivity. This is how Heidegger comes to secure the discussion of race: "[R]ace is a power-concept [which] presupposes *subjectivity*." Speaking of the situation of the present (Nazi) state, Heidegger says, "[T]he cultivation of race is a necessary measure, to which the end of modernity is driven . . . a 'cultural politics' which itself persists only as a means of empowering power." This occurs in "the age of the fulfilment of metaphysics." Heidegger adds that the connection of race with power prevails in the being of what is present in "a veiled and uncomprehended way."[67]

Heidegger developed this position, not accidentally, around 1940, at the height of the powers of the racist Nazi state. Here Heidegger mentions not only the end of modernity, but also the way in which the discussion of race appears in Ernst Jünger, and in Jünger's essay *The Worker*, and Heidegger's own consideration of that text. In this rare consideration (rather than mere mention) of race, Heidegger connects Jünger's figure of the worker as the bearer and representative of a new race with those two thinkers whom he argued are themselves the thinkers of the end of modernity and the consummation of metaphysics: Hegel and Nietzsche, while naming neither. This passage appears as supplement to the *History of Beyng*, but there is also a discussion of race in the body of this text. Here Heidegger is even more explicit: "[T]he metaphysical ground of racial thinking is not biologism, but the metaphysically thought subjectivity of the being of all that is present."[68] What Heidegger means by this formula "metaphysically thought subjectivity" is what he often refers to as "Ich-heit," I-ness, or the securing of the being of everything on the (prior) basis of Kant's "I think," which began with Descartes, and reaches its culmination in Hegel and Nietzsche.

Heidegger provides one further insight into the connection between power and race in this text. Rarely does Heidegger explain what power is—indeed, quite the reverse, especially in connection with Jünger, Heidegger asks (several times in the marginal notes he wrote in his copy of *The Worker*): "[W]hat is power?" because he thinks Jünger's is a romantic, dream-like understanding of power. Power, as will to power, therefore as an expression of the will itself, has "its basis only in the I, which, from itself out, wills spontaneity. Here is its connection with 'freedom.' "[69] What does power seek to represent and order itself toward? Heidegger cites Nietzsche: the inner, victorious will, with which to create "God and the world."[70] The unconditioned will is, however, none other than the absolute will. The will to create God and the world is the will to attain *through* the productive will of the human being the realization of the absolute in the world. Here, in other words, Nietzsche is indistinguishable from Hegel, from Hegel's metaphysics of absolute subjectivity, secured on the *I*, the willing self.

What has this to do with race? Heidegger speaks at this point in the text of *Rassenpflege*, a Nazi term meaning the cultivation and "hygiene" of race, but we would now say the racialization of everyday life through bureaucratic means and through understanding social life as constituted by race (which infected every aspect of life under the Nazis). Thus "racialization is a measure in keeping with the measure of power. It can as soon be deployed as it can be held back."[71] Race, the interpretation of everything through race, is both a means of the exercise of power and a display of power's arbitrariness. Its decisions and effects have no reason, no predictable ground, but become the basis for the manifestation of the spontaneity of freedom as such. Heidegger speaks with no approval: quite to the contrary. He is attempting to describe how in the hands of the Nazi, racialized, state, race has become a weapon. In Heidegger's own text of the 1934 *Logic* lectures, Heidegger mentions and dismisses what had already become a term of Nazi propaganda, *Rassezüchtung* or "selection (and improvement) through breeding" (a precursor of *Rassenpflege* and related to it), a term still used in animal farming, but which was being applied to human populations, in a sentence that does not appear in the Hallwachs transcript of the lectures.[72] We can only presume that the relevant section was not delivered to the audience, and that Heidegger thought already in 1934 that such a clear rejection of Nazi terminology was too dangerous a provocation.[73]

Anyone who takes the trouble to read beyond the notorious *geschichtslos* passage in the volume of the 1934 *Logic* lectures discovers in nearly one hundred pages following, an excoriating critique of Hegel's view of history, coupled with an only thinly disguised attack on the Nazi view of the state. Heidegger's claim, made around this time, that "the state is the being of the people" is as close as Heidegger ever came to Hegel's thought,[74] and yet it is a statement made in confrontation with Hegel. At the end of 1934 Heidegger even took up the language of "future tasks" (although even here, he quotes Hölderlin), only to drop it almost immediately: returning to his more authentic thought that destiny is what is *sent*, is what addresses and befalls us, and is not what anyone, any "people," tribe or nation, produce for themselves.[75] Heidegger's principal aim, especially in unfolding his understanding of the history of beyng, is to free every understanding of beyng, and of the being of the human being, and above all every understanding of history itself, from the force of necessity or determinations of (historical) causality: in particular, from every understanding of history as the necessary realization of a finality or "end" for human life as the fulfilment of humanity's appropriation of the planet as a whole. This is the source of

Heidegger's criticism of liberalism, and his rejection of Nazism as a form of liberalism, and the source of his critique of race. To free history from the force of necessity is not to deny the question of destiny—quite the contrary. It opens a way for the possibility of conversation between places, rather than a racialized discourse of superiority of one body, nation, or one group of humanity over another. We should recall that when, in the *Spiegel* interview, Heidegger is challenged about his German nationalism and his claims for the superiority of the German language, he immediately speaks, not of Germany and nationalism, but of Hölderlin.[76] In the poet, not the nation or the race, is the voice of superiority to be heard.

Was Heidegger racist? We should rather say that Heidegger shows both how the metaphysics of race appear in the history of being (and to what baleful effect), and how in this history nothing like race has any place at all.

Notes

Note that all translations of works cited are the author's own, unless expressly noted to the contrary. Details of English translations are provided where they exist, but these are quoted or cited in the text only when expressly indicated.

1. Sonia Sikka cites Tariq Modood in making this claim. See Sonia Sikka, "Was Heidegger Racist?," in *Heidegger, Morality and Politics: Questioning the Shepherd of Being* (Cambridge: Cambridge University Press, 2017), 156.

2. See Martin Heidegger's comments on the modern anthropological determination of humanity as a "Christian Hellenistic-Jewish" affair in the *Black Notebooks*. Martin Heidegger, *Überlegungen VII–XI (Schwarze Hefte 1938–1939)*, vol. 95 of *Gesamtausgabe*, ed. Peter Trawny (Frankfurt: Klostermann, 2014), 322; as well as his remarks on "Arabic-Jewish and Christian philosophy," in *Sein und Wahrheit*, vol. 36/37 of *Gesamtausgabe*, ed. Hartmut Tietjen (Frankfurt: Klostermann, 2001), 60.

3. Robert Bernasconi, "Heidegger's Alleged Challenge to the Nazi Conceptions of Race," in *Appropriating Heidegger*, ed. James E. Faulconer and Mark A. Wrathall (Cambridge: Cambridge University Press, 2000), 50–67.

4. Sonia Sikka, "Heidegger and Race," in *Race and Racism in Continental Philosophy*, ed. Robert Bernasconi and Sybol Cook (Bloomington: Indiana University Press, 2003), 74–97. The chapter was the basis for "Was Heidegger Rascist?," in *Heidegger, Morality, and Politics: Questioning the Shepherd of Being* (Cambridge: Cambridge University Press, 2018, 156–84.

5. Jeffrey Barash, "Heidegger et la question de la race," *Les Temps Modernes*, no. 650 (July–October 2008): 290–305.

6. Sikka's question parallels that of Rüdiger Safranski "is Heidegger anti-Semitic?," which Safranski also uses as a chapter title in *Martin Heidegger: Between*

Heidegger's Race | 249

Good and Evil, by Rüdiger Safranski, trans. Ewald Osers (Cambridge MA: Harvard University Press, 1998), 248–63. I cannot address, here, the question of Heidegger's anti-Semitism, but see my "Heidegger's Hegel, the Christian Jew: 'Europe' as 'Planetary Criminality and Machination,' " in *Heidegger and the Global Age*, ed. Antonio Cerella and Louiza Odysseos (London: Rowman and Littlefield International, 2017), 187–212. I do not provide summaries of Sikka's, Barash's, and Bernasconi's wide-ranging surveys of the literature on Heidegger and race, but taken together they provide an appraisal of the state of the question to date.

    7. See Emmanuel Faye, *Heidegger: The Introduction of Nazism into Philosophy in the Light the Unpublished Seminars of 1933–1935*, trans. Michael B. Smith (New Haven, CT: Yale University Press, 2009); from the French, *Heidegger: L'introduction du nazisme dans la philosophie: Autour des séminaires inédits de 1933–1935* (Paris: Éditions Albin Michel, 2005).

    8. For a discussion of this topic, see James Phillips, *Heidegger's Volk: Between National Socialism and Poetry* (Stanford, CA: Stanford University Press, 2005), esp. 1–53. *Das Volk* (people, nation) is an everyday German term, no closer in political inference than the English "nation" is to "nationalist." The Nazi term was *völkisch*, "the people's," "popular" (in the populist sense), a kitsch, folksy term implying kin, hearth, and home, and supposedly everything dear to the loyal Aryan heart.

    9. Julian Young, *Heidegger, Philosophy, Nazism* (Cambridge: Cambridge University Press, 1997), 36–7, 44–6, 215ff.

    10. It was from one of these transcripts that I first became aware of the passage. The typescript that long circulated was primarily material from one present at the lectures, Wilhelm Hallwachs. It is likely that Heidegger not only had a copy of it but even suggested corrections before it was typed up. The 1998 text of these lectures published in the Heidegger *Gesamtausgabe* was based on this transcript, while including material and references from four others. See Martin Heidegger, *Logik als die Frage nach dem Wesen der Sprache*, vol. 38 of *Gesamtausgabe*, ed. Günter Seubold (Frankfurt: Klostermann, 1998). The original handwritten text, prepared by Heidegger as the basis of the lectures, was believed to have been lost: an explanation of the history of the published text is given in the *Nachwort* or postscript to the volume. Very often, the volumes of the *Gesamtausgabe* that cover Heidegger's lecture courses combine Heidegger's prepared script with material from at least one (sometimes multiple) student transcript(s), following a well-established German convention—Hegel's and Kant's lectures, for instance, have, even recently, been prepared posthumously in this way, although often providing detail of variations between the scripts, which the *Gesamtausgabe* does not do. In 2020, quite unannounced, a supplementary volume, edited by Peter Trawny and containing Heidegger's lost script, appeared in print. Martin Heidegger, *Logik als die Frage nach dem Wesen der Sprache*, vol. 38A of *Gesamtausgabe*, ed. Peter Trawny (Frankfurt: Klostermann, 2020). The two texts are very close, frequently identical, but the original script in *Gesamtausgabe* 38A contains material that was not delivered (or at least not reported)

by the transcripts in *Gesamtausgabe* 38, whereas the transcripts report numerous asides and developments of themes that are absent from the original script. Which is the more authentic text? Formally we must say both are authentic, assuming the Hallwachs and other transcripts are accurate (which the verbatim closeness would appear to confirm), inasmuch as both are utterances of Heidegger, one from the pen, the other verbally. Far more important, however, is that both repeat positions that can be found, and are consistent with, and in many places are even common, elsewhere in Heidegger's work. What is most remarkable about the original script is that it seems to contain few, if any, surprises.

11. "Ich lese *Logik*" (emphasis in original). See "Editor's Postscript," in Heidegger, *Logik als die Frage nach dem Wesen der Sprache*, vol. 38 of *Gesamtausgabe*, 172.

12. "Alle, die hören könnten, hörten daß dies eine Auseinandersetzung mit dem Nationalsozialismus war." See Martin Heidegger, "Spiegel-Gespräch mit Martin Heidegger, 23 September 1966," in *Reden und andere Zeugnisse eines Lebens, 1910–1976*, vol. 16 of *Gesamtausgabe*, ed. Hermann Heidegger (Frankfurt: Klostermann, 2000), 664.

13. "Wenn wir jetzt die Frage nach dem Wesen der Geschichte aufnehmen, könnte man denken, wir haben willkürlich entschieden, was Geschichte sei, nämlich Geschichte sei das Auszeichnende für das Sein des Menschen. Man könnte einerseits einwenden, daß es Menschen und Menschengruppen (Neger wie z.B. Kaffern) gibt, die keine Geschichte haben, von denen wir sagen, sie seien geschichtslos." See Heidegger, *Logik als die Frage nach dem Wesen der Sprache*, vol. 38 of *Gesamtausgabe*, 81.

14. Bernasconi, "Heidegger's Alleged Challenge to the Nazi Conceptions of Race," 51. Bernasconi and others (see below, note 19) are sniffy about Heidegger's use of the term *Negern*, but only because they insist on translating it with the loaded, often derogatory "negroes." In German there need be no loaded meaning (nor was there at the time): the term just as accurately means black people.

15. Bernasconi, "Heidegger's Alleged Challenge to the Nazi Conceptions of Race," 51. The remark from the following semester is from the first of Heidegger's lecture courses on Hölderlin, published as Martin Heidegger, *Hölderlins Hymnen "Germanien" und "Der Rhein,"* vol. 39 of *Gesamtausgabe*, ed. Susanne Ziegler, 2nd ed. (Frankfurt: Klostermann, 1989), 284.

16. It could plausibly be argued that Heidegger's turn to Hölderlin (that very year) reflected the beginning of the attempt.

17. The first version of this volume, appearing in 1837 (updated in 1840), was edited by Eduard Gans and Karl Hegel as part of the collected edition of Hegel's works published shortly after his death, based on transcripts of Hegel's lectures on the subject from 1822 and thereafter every two years until Hegel's death. Gans, the main editor, seems to have based them at least partly on the transcript of Adolf Heimann (itself published as a single volume in 2005), and partly on a transcript of Karl Hegel's. George Lasson revised and expanded the material from one to four volumes between 1917 and 1920, using Hegel's notes and various lecture

transcripts from 1822–30. The first volume, *Reason in History*, was revised again by Johannes Hoffmeister in 1955. The editors of the Academy Edition, *Gesammelte Werke* (Hamburg: Felix Meiner Verlag, 1957–), have taken a different approach, reissuing the various extant manuscripts and transcripts of Hegel's Berlin lectures, both in the *Gesammelte Werke* (with the various introductory texts from *Gesammelte Werke* vol. 18, and in five volumes of transcripts, *Gesammelte Werke* vol. 27.1–5, of which the last, at the time of writing, is still to appear) and one volume in the series *Ausgewählte Nachschriften und Manuskripte* (Hamburg: Meiner, 1983–). See *Ausgewählte Nachschriften und Manuskripte*, vol. 12.

18. "Was wir eigentlich unter Afrika verstehen, das ist das Geschichtslose." See G. W. F. Hegel, *Vorlesungen über die Philosophie der Weltgeschichte*, vol. 1, *Vorlesungen über die Philosophie der Weltgeschichte: Erster Band, Die Vernunft in der Geschichte*, ed. Georg Lasson (Leipzig: Felix Meiner, 1917), 224. This (Lasson's) edition was the one that Heidegger used. The section on Africa can be found at pp. 203–24.

19. The word *Kaffer* in German has not always had exclusively negative connotations and has a complex etymology from different sources. One of these is its use by anthropologists of the eighteenth century and later (Blumenthal, Buffon, etc.) to designate both the land (*Kaffraria*) and inhabitants of a region of southern Africa, and this is contextually the sense in which Heidegger deploys it. Sikka, in "Was Heidegger Racist?," 159, translates the term as Xhosa, which is not wrong, although the reference is wider than a single people, and Heidegger himself at one time speaks of *Zulukaffern*. The term is not used by Hegel. Sikka also objects to Heidegger's use of the term *Negern*, but see note 14 above.

20. "Das eigentliche Afrika . . . soweit die die Geschichte zurückgeht . . . das Kinderland." See Hegel, *Vorlesungen über die Philosophie der Weltgeschichte: Erster Band, Die Vernunft in der Geschichte*, ed. Georg Lasson (Leipzig: Felix Meiner, 1917), 204–5.

21. The term appears already in Heidegger's first lecture course in 1919. See Martin Heidegger, *Zur Bestimmung der Philosophie*, vol. 56/57 of *Gesamtausgabe*, ed. Bernd Heimbüchel (1987; repr., Frankfurt: Klostermann, 1999), 130, in a discussion of the concept of culture in the nineteenth century. Despite the importance of the arguments constructed on the term *geschichtslos*, and its frequency of occurrence, the term is not listed in *The Heidegger Concordance*, although the term *Geschichtslosigkeit* (which does not figure in these discussions of race) is. See François Jaran and Christophe Perrin, *The Heidegger Concordance*, 3 vols. (London: Bloomsbury, 2013).

22. The term appears again in a lecture from the end of 1934, "The Present Situation and Future Tasks of German Philosophy." See Martin Heidegger, "Die Gegenwärtige Lage und die künftige Aufgabe der deutschen Philosophie," in *Reden und andere Zeugnisse eines Lebens 1910–1976*, vol. 16 of *Gesamtausgabe*, ed. Hermann Heidegger (Frankfurt: Klostermann, 2000), esp. 328.

23. "Die Rede von 'geschichtslosen Stämmen und Völkern,' mag sie berechtigt sein oder nicht, meint wieder etwas anderes mit dem Wort 'Geschichte.' [. . .] Damit

ist nicht gemeint, diesen Stämmen fehlte es an einer ausgebildeten Geschichtswissenschaft [. . .] sie pflegen nicht die Vergangenheit [. . .] Sie haben auch keine Zukunft, keine Aufgaben." See Martin Heidegger, *Phänomenologie der Anschauung und des Ausdrucks: Theorie der philosophischen Begriffsbildung*, vol. 59 of *Gesamtausgabe*, ed. Claudius Strube (Frankfurt: Klostermann, 1993), 45–46.

24. The same must be said for Bernasconi's reference, aimed at buttressing the claim for Heidegger's racist use of *geschichtslos* and discrediting his claim that the Nietzsche lectures were a confrontation with Nazism, when contrasting "historical Western man" with what is "spared an African tribe." See Bernasconi, "Heidegger's Alleged Challenge to the Nazi Conceptions of Race," 51, citing the English translation of Martin Heidegger, *Nietzsche I*, vol. 6.1 of *Gesamtausgabe*, ed. Brigitte Schillbach (Frankfurt: Klostermann, 1996), 498; also Martin Heidegger, *Nietzsches Lehre vom Willen zur Macht als Erkenntnis*, vol. 47 of *Gesamtausgabe*, ed. Eberhard Hanser (Frankfurt: Klostermann, 1989), 134. In fact, the distinction that Heidegger makes in this text has nothing to do with having no history: Heidegger is merely making a passing contrast between Western humanity and the mode of being of life in a tribe. He is precisely acknowledging the validity and reality of difference. To understand what is really being said, Bernasconi would do well to contemplate the second *Zusatz* to the "Age of the World Picture," written almost certainly around the same time, where the relations between a constellation of terms—*Besinnung, geschichtslos*, and Hegelian negation—are worked out, without reference to African tribes.

25. Pindar, eighth *Pythian Ode*, 1.95. Anyone with a classical education from this period will have known these lines by rote, and, indeed, Heidegger did.

26. "*Volk*—nie geschichtslos—sowenig wie sprachlos . . . S. S. 34." See Martin Heidegger, *Zum Ereignis Denken*, vol. 73.1 of *Gesamtausgabe*, ed. Peter Trawny (Frankfurt: Klostermann, 2013), 370.

27. Alexandre Kojève, *Introduction à la lecture de Hegel*, ed. Raymond Queneau (Paris: Gallimard, 1947), 372ff.

28. "Der Sinn der Zeitlichkeit ist die Zukunft. Der Sinn der These, die ich vertrete, ist aber diametral dem entgegengesetzt, was Hegel hier sagt." See Martin Heidegger, *Logik: Die Frage nach der Wahrheit*, vol. 21 of *Gesamtausgabe*, ed. Walter Biemel (1976; repr., Frankfurt: Klostermann, 1995), 264–65. The reference is to the lecture published as Martin Heidegger, "Der Begriff der Zeit (Vortrag 1924)," in *Der Begriff der Zeit*, vol. 64 of *Gesamtausgabe*, ed. Friedrich-Wilhelm von Herrmann (Frankfurt: Klostermann, 2004), 118. Heidegger says "*das Grundphänomen der Zeit ist die Zukunft*" (the basic phenomenon of time itself is the future). Emphasis in original.

29. "*Die Zugangsmöglichkeit zur Geschichte gründet in der Möglichkeit, nach der es eine Gegenwart jeweils versteht, zukünftig zu sein.*" Emphasis in original. See Heidegger, "Der Begriff der Zeit (Vortrag 1924)," 123.

30. This, we should remember, was also true for Marx, for whom the proletariat was itself the ground of a coming people, or future "nation."

31. Aristotle, *Physics* 233a23: Πότερον δὲ μὴ οὔσης ψυχῆς εἴη ἂν ὁ χρόνος ἢ οὔ, ἀπορήσειεν ἄν τις.

32. "So würde die Ewigkeit zur Zukunft, einem Momente der Zeit, gemacht." See G. W. F. Hegel, *Enzyklopädie der philosophischen Wissenschaften im Grundrisse (1830)*, vol. 20 of *Gesammelte Werke*, ed. Wolfgang Bonsiepen und Hans-Christian Lucas (Hamburg: Meiner, 1992), §258, p. 248. See, for this whole discussion, §§254–59, pp. 243–51. Heidegger discusses Hegel's presentation of time and space in *Sein und Zeit* [1927], vol. 2 of *Gesamtausgabe*, ed. Freidrich-Wilhelm von Herrmann (Frankfurt: Klostermann, 1977), 571–75.

33. "Und nicht etwa bestimmt [Hegel] das Sein des Raumes *aus* der Zeit, sondern *als* Zeit." Emphasis in original. See Heidegger, *Logik: Die Frage nach der Wahrheit*, 256.

34. "So sehen wir die Gestalten, die wir in der Weltgeschichte als Folge der Zeit sehen, auch perennierend nebeneinander im Raum stehen. Daß diese Gestalten nebeneinander bestehen und ihre Notwendigkeit im Begriff haben, dies ist wesentlich zu bemerken, und davon muß man sich überzeugen." See G. W. F. Hegel, *Vorlesungen über die Philosophie der Weltgeschichte (Berlin 1822/23): Nachschriften von Karl Gustav Julius von Griesheim, Heinrich Hotho und Friedrich Carl Hermann Victor von Kehler*, vol. 12 of *Ausgewählte Nachschriften und Manuskripte*, ed. Karl Brehmer, Karl-Heinz Ilting, and Hoo Nam Seelmann (Hamburg: Meiner, 1996), 40. Something close to this does appear in Hoffmeister's 1955 version of the first volume of Hegel's lectures on world history. See G. W. F. Hegel, *Vorlesungen über die Philosophie der Weltgeschichte*, vol. 1, *Die Vernunft in der Geschichte*, ed. Johannes Hoffmeister (Hamburg: Meiner, 1955), 154.

35. Sikka, "Was Heidegger Racist?," 159.

36. "[Die] Aufgabe, das 'Leben' selbst als die Grundwirklichkeit der Geschichte in seinen Strukturen zu sehen." See Martin Heidegger, *Prolegomena zur Geschichte des Zeitbegriffs*, vol. 20 of *Gesamtausgabe*, ed. Petra Jaeger (Frankfurt: Klostermann, 1979), 19.

37. "Primitive Völker leben, und wir selbst lebten lange Zeit ohne Geschichte." Martin Heidegger, "Wilhelm Diltheys Forschungsarbeit und der gegenwärtige Kampf um eine historische Weltanschauung (16–21 April 1925)," in *Vorträge*, vol. 80.1 of *Gesamtausgabe*, ed. Günther Neumann (Frankfurt: Klostermann, 2016), 111.

38. "Hegel: die Humanität der europäischen Kulturen [ist] verkörpert im Staat." See Heidegger, "Wilhelm Diltheys Forschungsarbeit," 112.

39. "[Der] Gang Gottes in der Welt." See G. W. F. Hegel, *Grundlinien der Philosophie des Rechts* [with *Zusätze* added by Eduard Gans], vol. 7 of *Werke*, ed. Eva Moldenhauer and Karl Markus Michel (Frankfurt: Suhrkamp, 1986), 403, *Zusatz*.

40. Bernasconi lays the blame at Kant's feet: Jon Mikkelsen, in a careful essay provides context (and not a little nuancing) for Kant, and Bernasconi's thesis, noting "the many discussions of this subject that played out in the intellectual discourse of the 'enlightened' societies of Europe" as the eighteenth century progressed. See

Jon Mikkelsen, "Translator's Introduction," in *Kant and the Concept of Race: Late Eighteenth-Century Writings*, ed. and trans. Jon Mikkelsen (Albany: State University of New York, 2013), 19.

41. Robert Bernasconi, "Who Invented the Question of Race?," 11, 12.

42. Faye, *Heidegger: L'introduction du nazisme dans la philosophie*, 169n72.

43. It is from this period on that Heidegger frequently attacks the notion of "culture" in general, together with the claims of people like Spengler.

44. "Man hat gesagt, 1933 ist Hegel gestorben; im Gegenteil: er hat erst angefangen zu leben." See Martin Heidegger, "Anhang II: Protokolle und Mitschriften: 23.1.1935," in *Seminare: Hegel–Schelling*, vol. 86 of *Gesamtausgabe*, ed. Peter Trawny (Frankfurt: Klostermann, 2011), 606.

45. "Erst als der Reichspräsident am 30. Januar 1933, den Führer der Nationalsozialistischen Bewegung, Adolf Hitler, zum Reichskanzler ernannte [. . .] an diesem Tage ist demnach, so kann man sagen, 'Hegel gestorben.' " See Carl Schmitt, *Staat, Bewegung, Volk: Die Dreigliederung der politischen Einheit* (Hamburg: Hanseatische Verlagsanstalt, 1933), 31ff. Schmitt's volume appears in English as *State, Movement, People: The Triadic Structure of The Political Unity; with The Question of Legality*, ed. and trans. Simona Draghici (Corvallis, OR: Plutarch, 2001).

46. "Demnach sind für Hegel die Philosophie als die Selbstentwicklung des Geistes zum absoluten Wissen und die Geschichteder Philosophie identisch. Kein Philosoph *vor* Hegel hat eine solche Grundstellung der Philosophie gewonnen, die es ermöglicht und fordert, daß das Philosophieren sich zugleich in seiner Geschichte bewegt und daß diese Bewegung die Philosophie selbst ist." Emphasis in original. See Martin Heidegger, "Hegel und die Griechen," in *Wegmarken*, vol. 9 of *Gesmtausgabe*, ed. Freidrich-Wilhelm von Herrmann (1976; repr., Frankfurt: Klostermann, 1996), 428ff.

47. "*Geschichtlichkeit* soll *verstanden* und nicht Geschichte (Weltgeschichte) betrachtet werden. Geschichtlichkeit bedeutet Geschichtlich*sein* dessen, was als Geschichte ist." Emphases in original. See Heidegger "Der Begriff der Zeit (Abhandlung 1924)," 3.

48. "Es hat sich also erst und es wird sich aus der Betrachtung der Weltgeschichte selbst ergeben, daß es vernünftig in ihr zugegangen, daß sie der vernünftige nothwendige Gang des Weltgeistes gewesen;—der Weltgeist ist der Geist überhaupt, der die Substanz der Geschichte, der Eine Geist, dessen Natur Eine und immer dieselbe, und in dem Weltdaseyn diese seine Eine Natur explicirt." See G. W. F. Hegel, *Vorlesungsmanuskripte II (1816–1831)*, vol. 18 of *Gesammelte Werke*, ed. Walter Jaeschke (Hamburg: Meiner, 1995), 142.

49. "Das Wissen von einem absoluten Wesen . . . es ist nichts an das Menschliche Anklingende in diesem Charakter zu finden." See Hegel, *Vorlesungen über die Philosophie der Weltgeschichte: Erster Band, Die Vernunft in der Geschichte*, ed. Georg Lasson (Leipzig: Felix Meiner, 1917), 208ff. Several (identical) editions of

Lasson's text were issued from 1917. The passage can be found in Karl Hegel's and Eduard Gans's 1840 edition, *Vorlesungen über die Philosophie der Geschichte*, vol. 9 of *Berliner Ausgabe*, ed. Ludwig Boumann, et al. (Berlin: Duncker und Humblot, 1832–45), 115; also in *Stuttgarter Aufgabe*, vol. 11, ed. Hermann Glockner (1927–41; repr., Stuttgart: Frommans Verlag, 1958), 137, which is very close in form to the 1937 version. See, for the relevant passages in the *Akademie* edition, vol. 27.4 of *Gesammelte Werke*, 1223, and vol. 27.3 of *Gesammelte Werke*, 998.

50. Heidegger gives a full, clear, and very accessible account of this movement and its confusions in the early part of the essay "Zur Seinsfrage (1955)," in *Wegmarken*, vol. 9 of *Gesamtausgabe*, esp. 397ff.

51. This is an argument that Heidegger makes with increasing intensity in a number of places, from about 1936 onwards. See, for one example, Martin Heidegger, *Besinnung*, vol. 66 of *Gesamtausgabe*, ed. Friedrich-Wilhelm von Herrmann (Frankfurt: Klostermann, 1997), 83, where he writes: "Das Seyn—nichts Göttliches, nichts Menschliches, nichts Weltliches, nicht Erdhaftes."

52. "Eine[] grundsätzlichen Sophistik, von der überhaupt Hegels Dialektik lebt," "Hegel kann alles sagen über jedes. Und es gibt Leute, die in einer solchen Konfusion einen Tiefsinn entdecken." See Martin Heidegger, *Logik: Die Frage nach der Wahrheit*, 252, 221, 259. Heidegger explicates, with patient care, Aristotle's geometrical relations in his lectures on *Plato's Sophist*.

53. Alison Stone, "Europe and Eurocentrism," *Aristotelian Society Supplementary Volume* 91, no. 1 (2017): 83–104; "Hegel and Colonialism," *Hegel Bulletin* 41, no. 2 (2020): 247–70.

Her bibliographies contain a thorough appraisal of the literature. One figure strangely absent from this entire debate is Domenico Losurdo, who, despite his concerns about its history, does not mention race in connection with Hegel at all, either in his *Controstoria del liberalismo* or his *Hegel e la libertà dei moderni*. Domenico Losurdo, *Controstoria del liberalismo* (2005; repr., Rome: Editori Laterza, 2006); in English, *Liberalism: A Counter-History*, trans. Gregory Eliot (London: Verso, 2011); *Hegel e la libertà dei moderni*, 2 vols. (1992: repr., Naples: La scuola di Pitagora, 2011); in English, *Hegel and the freedom of Moderns*, trans. Marella Morris and Jon Morris (Durham, NC: Duke University Press, 2004).

54. "Ist die Sklaverei durchaus unrechtlich, so würden [Europäer] Sklaven unmittelbar ihre Freiheit geben." See G. W. F. Hegel, *Die Philosophie der Geschichte: Vorlesungsmitschrift Heimann (Winter 1830/1831)*, ed. Klaus Vieweg (Munich: Fink, 2005), 70.

55. "Das allgemeine planetarische Leben des Naturgeistes besondert sich in die concreten Unterschiede der Erde und zerfällt in die besondern Naturgeister, die im Ganzen die Natur der geographischen Weltheile ausdrücken, und die Racenverschiedenheit ausmachen." See G. W. F. Hegel, *Enzyklopädie (1830)*, vol. 20 of *Gesammelte Werke*, §§393, 392. This is taken over almost unaltered from the edition

of 1817, and also appears in the edition of 1827. See G. W. F. Hegel: *Enzyklopädie (1817)*, vol. 13 of *Gesammelte Werke*, §§312, 311; *Enzyklopädie (1827)*, vol. 19 of *Gesammelte Werke*, §§393, 392.

56. Available as a published text from 1817.

57. See Michael J. Petry, ed., *Hegel's Philosophy of Subjective Spirit*, vol. 2, *Anthropology* (Dordrecht: Reidel, 1978), 51, citing the Kehler manuscript of the lectures of the summer of 1825. See also G. W. F. Hegel, *Vorlesungen über die Philosophie des Geistes (Berlin 1827/28): Nachgeschrieben von Johann Eduard Erdmann und Ferdinand Walter*, vol. 13 of *Ausgewählte Nachschriften und Manuskripte*, ed. Franz Hespe and Burkhard Tuschling (Hamburg: Meiner, 1994), 41.

58. "Was uns näher angeht, ist, wiefern dieses zusammenhängt mit der Beziehung aufs Geistige." See Hegel, *Vorlesungen über die Philosophie des Geistes (Berlin 1827/28)*, 42.

59. "Die Frage von der Racenverschiedenheit hat Bezug auf die Rechte, die man den Menschen zuteilen sollte; wenn es mehrfache Racen gibt, so ist die eine edler, die andere muß ihr dienen. Das Verhältnis der Menschen bestimmt sich durch ihre Vernunft." Petry's translation, from the *Kehler* manuscript of the Summer of 1825. Michael J. Petry, *Hegel's Philosophy of Subjective Spirit*, vol. 2, *Anthropology*, 46–47.

60. "Hegel und der Deutsche Idealismus überhaupt [kann] die Allheit des Seienden in seinem Sein aus der Ichheit als der Unendlichkeit begreifen . . . das Subjekt, das Ich, primär gefaßt ist als 'Ich denke.'" See Martin Heidegger, *Hegels Phänomenologie des Geistes*, vol. 32 of *Gesamtausgabe*, ed. Ingtraud Görland (Frankfurt: Klostermann, 1980), 111.

61. It is here that the connection with Ernst Jünger's *Der Arbeiter: Herrschaft und Gestalt* (1932; Stuttgart: Klett-Cotta, 2013), would, if we had the space, become apparent. Whereas for Hegel the Nordic, Germanic, Protestant race becomes the foremost bearer of Spirit, Jünger attempts to sidestep the "biological" implications of such a theory (as his own rejection of Nazi racial theory), with the "metaphysical" race of the worker. As should by now be abundantly clear, the worker, or any form of *Übermensch*, far from stepping away from Hegel's metaphysics, is in each case a form of its fulfilment.

62. Hegel has in mind here Aristotle's ἐνέργεια, the "setting into work" of the real.

63. However, it becomes immediately clear when we grasp that what Hegel describes is at the same the mirror image of Nietzsche's "will to power."

64. "Indem jetzt das Nichthafte selbst in das Wesen des Seins mithineingenommen werden mußte." See Heidegger, *Aristoteles, Metaphysik Θ 1–3: von Wesen und Wirklichkeit der Kraft*, vol. 33 of *Gestamtausgabe*, ed. Heinrich Huni (1981; repr., Frankfurt: Klostermann, 2006), 27.

65. Julian Young, *Heidegger, Philosophy, Nazism*, 36.

66. Heidegger does this in many places. Two, however, stand out. The first is in Heidegger, *Die Grundbegriffe der Metaphysik: Welt, Endlichkeit, Einsamkeit*, vol. 29/30 of *Gesamtausgabe*, ed. Freidrich-Wilhelm von Herrmann (1983; repr.,

Frankfurt: Klostermann, 1992), in the discussion of "the biological worldview" (39, 283) of animality, and of the zoologists and thinkers von Uexküll and Driesch (374–88 and beyond). The second pervades Heidegger's readings of Nietzsche, but see, especially, Heidegger, "Nietzsche's Alleged Biologism," in *Nietzsche I*, vol. 6.1 of *Gesamtausgabe*, 465–74; also Heidegger, *Nietzsches Lehre vom Willen zur Macht als Erkenntnis*, 47, 58–93.

67. Martin Heidegger, *Die Geschichte des Seyns*, vol. 69 of *Gesamtausgabe*, ed. Peter Trawny (Frankfurt: Klostermann, 1998); in English, Heidegger, *The History of Beyng*, trans. William McNeill and Jeffery Powell (Bloomington: Indiana University Press, 2015), 223. " 'Rasse' ist ein Machtbegriff—setzt *Subjektivität* voraus, vgl. zu Ernst Jünger (GA90) [. . .] wo das Sein des Seienden wenngleich verhüllt und unbegriffen als Macht west [. . .]. Die Rassenpflege ist eine notwendige Maßnahme, zu der das Ende der Neuzeit drängt, [. . .] eine 'Kulturpolitik,' die selbst nur Mittel der Machtermächtigung bleibt." Heidegger's emphasis. The enclosed reference to Jünger is to *Zu Ernst Jünger*, vol. 90 of *Gesamtausgabe*, ed. Peter Trawny (Frankfurt: Klostermann, 2004).

68. "Der metaphysische Grund des Rassedenkens ist nicht der Biologismus, sondern die metaphysisch zu denkende Subjektivität alles Seins von Seiendem." See Heidegger, *Die Geschichte des Seyns*, 71.

69. "Er hat seinen Grund einzig im Ich, das von sich aus, spontan will. Hier ist sein Zusammenhang mit der 'Freiheit.' " See Martin Heidegger, "Seminarprotokolle: Einübung in das philosophische Denken 1941/42," in *Seminare (Übungen) 1937/38 und 1941/42*, vol. 88 of *Gesamtausgabe*, ed. Alfred Denker (Frankfurt: Klostermann, 2008), 299.

70. Heidegger is citing aphorism §619 of the *Will to Power*. See Friedrich Nietzsche, *Nachlaß 1884–1885*, vol. 11, [36] 31]), in *Nietzsche: Kritische Studienausgabe*, ed. Giorgio Colli and Mazzino Montinari, 15 vols. (Berlin: De Gruyter, 1999 [1967]). Martin Heidegger, "Seminarprotokolle: Einübung in das philosophische Denken 1941/42," in *Seminare (Übungen) 1937/38 und 1941/42*, vol. 88 of *Gesamtausgabe* edited by Alfred Denker (2008), 301.

71. "Rassen-pflege ist eine machtmäßige Maßnahme. Sie kann daher bald eingeschaltet bald zurückgestellt warden." See Heidegger, *Die Geschichte des Seyns*, 70.

72. Heidegger, *Logik als die Frage nach dem Wesen der Sprache*, vol. 38A of *Gesamtausgabe*, 73; compare *Logik als die Frage nach dem Wesen der Sprache*, vol. 38 of *Gesamtausgabe*, 72–75.

73. There are other similar indications in the difference between the two texts.

74. See Heidegger, "Hegels 'Rechtsphilosophie' WS 1934/35," in *Seminare: Hegel–Schelling*, 117. The phrase "Staat als Sein des Volkes" is reported from several lectures and protocols of seminars in the summer and winter semesters of 1934.

75. See note 23 above, the title of a short series of politically oriented addresses in late 1934.

76. Heidegger, "Spiegel-Gespräch mit Martin Heidegger, 23 September 1966," 679.

Part III
Life, Identity, and Finitude

Chapter Ten

Dasein and Intersectional Identity

TINA FERNANDES BOTTS

Introduction

In this chapter, Martin Heidegger's concept of Dasein is placed into dialogue with contemporary philosophical discussions about what it means to speak of human identity as "intersectional." In the process, the concept of Dasein is revealed to have deep overlap with the concept of intersectional identity, and in the places where the two theoretical frameworks merge, some truths are arguably reached about the nature of human personal identity.[1]

Dasein is a term Heidegger created to operate as a synonym for the human condition or the human experience for the purpose of, among other things, highlighting certain features about that experience that he thought were not widely acknowledged.[2] Accordingly, and to clear up the confusion and misunderstanding that Heidegger thought surrounded the general understanding of the nature of the human experience, Heidegger's Dasein is defined as much by what it is *not* as by what it is. What Dasein is *not* is the experience of being a mind with a separate body. What Dasein is *not* is existence as an isolated subject in a world of discrete objects. What Dasein *is* is the only entity for whom its own existence is an issue for it. What Dasein *is* is interpretation all the way down.

The idea that, for Heidegger, Dasein is the only entity for whom its own existence is an issue for it can be translated into the idea that, for

Heidegger, the human experience is the only experience that is self-reflexive. In other words, for Heidegger, meaning and the human experience are inextricably intertwined. Similarly, the idea that, for Heidegger, the human way of being (Dasein) is interpretation all the way down is another way of saying that, for Heidegger, (human) existence and the meaning of (human) existence are one and the same topic of discussion. What Dasein *is*, then, for Heidegger, is an attempt to convey something fairly radical about reality itself, about our ability to access reality, and about the role of the human experience in that reality. Specifically, for Heidegger, reality (or knowledge of reality, which is, for Heidegger, effectively the same thing) is nonobjective and the identity of entities (including human personal identity) is not fixed, essential, or timeless but fluid, contingent, and changeable. Moreover, for Heidegger, a given stance on what is real (and what is not real) and a given personal identity are co-constitutive and reciprocally reinforcing.

Following Heidegger's train of thought on the topic of the co-constitutive and reciprocally reinforcing relationship between what is real (and what is not real) and a given personal identity, what there is as a first order of business is what Heidegger calls a "world." I call this an "interpretive landscape" or a system of intelligibility. The logistics of the generation of a given personal identity, for Heidegger, operate within that interpretive landscape according to the same set of dynamics through which any entity in the world comes to be understood as what it is. Stated differently, what happens first is that, once Dasein is familiar with a given landscape, within that landscape, something is *taken up* as one thing or another, usually through actual interaction with other inhabitants of the "world." An object used to drive a nail into a wall becomes (gets taken up as) a "hammer," for example. Similarly, a person may be *taken up*, for example, as "male" or "female" or "black" or "white" or some combination of these or some combination of one or more other traits thought to be dispositive on personal identity.

How a person differs from a hammer, however, for Heidegger, is that a person's self-reflexivity provides an opportunity to either adopt or reject the trait or set of traits. When the trait (e.g., "male") is applied from without by persons in the "world," the given trait, or traits, is, or are, not perfectly applied, but somewhat loosely applied.[3] Being self-reflexive, Dasein (the human way of being) is then able to move toward or away from this/these trait(s), to take them on (to make them meaningful) or not. New traits (e.g., "bricklayer" or "physician" or "nurse") are applied through interactions with the "world" as well, and Dasein can also move toward or away from these traits. It is in this sense that, from a Heideggerian point of view, traditional personal identity markers (such as "female" or "physician") at once define and do not define the human way of being. Philosopher Thomas Sheehan has described this aspect of Dasein as that, for Heidegger, the human way of being is "ontologically bivalent."[4] On the one hand, Dasein is imperfect, a lack, an absence on which the world can write what it will. On the other hand, Dasein is perfect, a presence, a "self-concerned body,"[5] the interpreter and meaning-giver of who and what it is. This "ontological bivalence" results in a tension between difference and synthesis that is "human being itself."[6]

The concept of intersectionality is at the center of much contemporary research in the social sciences and humanities and is at the center of contemporary feminist scholarship. A consistent area of inquiry is intersectional methodology or what some call "intersectional analyses."[7] "Intersectional analyses" are "approaches to issues that reflect the complex interactions among multiple structures and axes of oppression and privilege that are salient in our social identities, for example, race/ethnicity, gender, class, sexual orientation, and ability differences."[8]

Intersectionality, at its core, then, is *a framework for social justice activism*. It is "a theoretical framework for understanding how multiple social identities such as race, gender, sexual orientation, socioeconomic status, and disability status intersect at the micro level of individual experience to reflect interlocking systems of privilege and oppression (i.e., racism, sexism, heterosexism, classism) at the macro social-structural level."[9] The key claim of intersectionality is that oppression is a complex phenomenon that cannot be understood when analyzed through a single lens. According to intersectionality theory, in order to capture the experience of oppression for a particular person, it is necessary to factor in all of the sociocultural rubrics through which they are processed by others, as well as the ways in which being processed through multiple oppressive rubrics limits the person's life options and access to social goods.

The effect of intersectionality on new ways of thinking about the nature of personal identity has been significant, particularly for thinkers interested in deconstructing the phenomenon of institutionalized oppression. For these scholars, and others, intersectionality disrupts the idea that personal identity can be described in terms of neat, monolinear, timeless categories, replacing this idea with a statement about the vast complexity of the nature of personal identity and the extent to which it is affected by, among other things, a plethora of sometimes conflicting environmental forces.[10] At the same time, implicit in the social critique that is at the heart of intersectionality theory is the claim that each of us is something other than, something more than, the labels, traits or personal identity markers that are thrust upon us through the myriad forces of institutionalized oppression. On this view, we are, at a minimum, the ways in which these traits fuse and regenerate to create ways of being that the social institutions at issue have not contemplated.

The implicit, concomitant claim, however, is that each of us is highly unique in terms of our personal identity. Necessarily concomitant to the claim that each of us is a product of the multiple social forces acting upon on us is a second claim about the reality that each of us is, at the same time, *none of* the labels ascribed to us. Instead, each of us is something altogether different from those labels. This aspect of personal identity entails an agency and a sense of responsibility for the choices we make, for example, to either accept or reject these labels, both through our self-concept and through the ways in which we interact with others.

Ange-Marie Hancock touches on this aspect of intersectionality theory when she explains intersectionality as, in part, a "discourse about analytic relationships among categories of difference."[11] Hancock elaborates by using the term "situational contingency" to describe the ontological status of the oppressed in particular.[12] Hancock is saying, I think correctly, that, although context or "situation" is important to describing the lived daily experience of a given oppressed person, "[u]sing situation as a lens does not reify personal experience, for individuals can experience a situation in question in very different ways."[13] Hancock continues, "Nor does [using situation as a lens] reify the structural aspects that shape such situations, assisting in *holding individuals responsible for their actions in a situation.*"[14] In this way, intersectionality captures the same push/pull relationship between what Heidegger calls "the they self" (the socially constructed self) and the authentic self (the core self-reflexivity that describes the human experience) that he describes in *Being and Time* through his discussions of Dasein.[15]

Heidegger's concept of Dasein and the idea that personal identity is intersectional, then, share many of the same features. Through a comparison of Heidegger's concept of Dasein to the contemporary idea that personal identity is intersectional—including a demonstration of the ways in which these concepts overlap—in the discussion that follows, I will make the case that the question of the meaning and significance of Dasein is, in many respects, the same question that is at the root of the problem of intersectional identity, and that is the question of in what human identity (or the human way of being or personal identity) consists. I will also make the case that both concepts answer the question in similar ways. In concluding remarks, I will then offer some ruminations on what I see as the significance of this overlap.

Dasein

For Heidegger, the traditional subject-object model of the nature of reality is flawed. We cannot arrive at an accurate account of the nature of reality through the type of framework used by those accepting the subject-object model. The traditional model of reality, with its focus on "perception" of "objects" as the private experience of an isolated "subject" entails an individualism and solipsism that inaccurately characterizes what it means for anything to be. For Heidegger, what it means for anything to be is inexorably linked to what it means to be human. To be human is not to "perceive" "objects" in a vacuum or even to "know" "objects" in the void, but to inhabit a symbolically structured reality in which everything encountered is encountered *as* something; and in which everything is seen through the eyes of what Heidegger calls a "world" but what can be alternately described as a schema of socially shared interpretive practices.[16] To exist in a "world" is to find oneself in a referential context of significance, a system of meaningful relations toward which one comports oneself (operates or relates) intelligibly.

Heidegger calls an inquiry into what Dasein is "fundamental ontology," which he further describes as an inquiry into *being qua being* or being itself. According to Heidegger, to understand the human way of being is to understand being itself. Heidegger says that fundamental ontology must begin with Dasein because human beings are the only beings for whom their own existence is an issue. The human way of being is not the *source* of *being qua being*, however. Rather, all being gains its *intelligibility* in terms of the *structure* of the human way of being. Structurally, Dasein is *not* as a conscious subject. Instead, Dasein refers to the way in which humans interact with their surroundings and circumstances. This way of *being-in-the-world*, as Heidegger calls it, involves self-interpretation. Heidegger writes, "[Dasein's] ownmost Being is such that it has an understanding of that Being, and already maintains itself in each case as if its Being has been interpreted in some manner."[17] Heidegger calls this self-interpreting way of being *existence*. The human way of being also involves an *understanding* of what it means (for anything) to be in general.

For Heidegger, all social practices entail an ontology. In other words, a given human being always embodies an understanding of its being, an internalization of the learned customs inherent in a given culture. Within a given culture, there are numerous customs and practices that together constitute what it means to be a person, or an object, or an institution, to name some examples of ways of being. In a given culture, there are practices that evidence the way in which what it means to be a person, an object, or a society fit together. Each of these things is an aspect of a given *understanding* of being. Each of us *embodies* a given understanding; that is, we have an ontology, we inhabit a "world," without realizing it at any given time.

In this way, Dasein's understanding of being is not a belief system in the minds of isolated individual subjects but rather a shared way of *behaving*. This rather subliminal, but certainly nonconscious and shared way of behaving must be studied as an *interpretation*, rather than scientifically or objectively, because it is not composed of facts but *practices*. This shared agreement in our practices regarding what entities can show up as, Heidegger calls a *preontological* or *pretheoretical* understanding of being. This shared agreement evidenced by our practices results in things showing up for us always *as* something, and delineates a set of possibilities available to us. A given entity shows up as a "pen," for example, or a given person shows up as "friendly" or "threatening." Still, our preontological understanding of being is neither direct nor obvious. The more we try to get at it, the more elusive it becomes.

Heidegger calls the preontological understanding of being that occurs in shared social practices a *hermeneutic* ontology. It is an ontology practiced against a horizon of intelligibility inhabited by Dasein. In other words, there is no essential human way of being, on this view. To exist is to take a stand on what is essential about one's own being and to be defined by that stand. Heidegger writes, "[W]e cannot define *Dasein*'s essence by citing a 'what' of the kind that pertains to a subject matter, . . . its essence lies rather in the fact that in each case it has its Being to be, and has it as its own."[18]

This means that Dasein is self-interpreting, and this process always takes place inside a given social structure or context of intelligibility, or inside of what Heidegger calls Dasein's *facticity* or factual circumstances. Dasein has no essential nature. Instead, Dasein always understands itself within a given culture that has already decided on specific possible ways to be human, on what human beings are essentially. In other words, Dasein believes itself to have an essence. It believes itself to be an object. Its everyday preontological understanding of its own being is thus erroneous.

Inside of a given culture, a certain interpretation of what human nature is prevails. Each of us is born into and then socialized into a particular cultural understanding of being. At this point, Dasein has not yet taken a stand on itself. At some point, Dasein focuses on the question of what it means to be. This first takes the form of actively accepting or identifying with a given prevailing cultural interpretation or role, like doctor or teacher or mother. But if Dasein ever gets to the point of realizing that it can never find meaning by identifying with a socially created role, however, it achieves what Heidegger calls *authentic* being, which means understanding the *groundlessness* of one's own existence. Authenticity means *choosing* oneself and one's own individuality and proactively rejecting or choosing the culturally created and socially reinforced roles in which one found oneself and then allowed oneself to adopt earlier on.

Within this framework, cultures are "worlds." They are the schemas of intelligibility in which we find ourselves. Humans grow up within cultures, and cultures are things that are interpreted and understood rather than perceived. Cultures as "worlds" provide intelligibility to lived experience. For Heidegger, on a day-to-day level, human beings are a set of meaningful social practices and these social practices give rise to intelligibility. Human beings are essentially self-interpreting and therefore interpretation is the proper method for studying them. Human being is interpretation. But Dasein hides from this truth about its being and this means that we cannot directly determine the human way of being from human practices. Instead, Dasein must begin where it finds itself, in the midst of misunderstanding its way of being. It must examine itself in its "average everydayness."[19] From there, Dasein can make headway, indirectly, into discovering its more primordial way of being.

Heidegger describes what he means by *being-in*, or the relation between Dasein and the world. When Heidegger speaks of Dasein's *being-in-the-world*, he does not mean spatially in the traditional sense of the word. Instead, to be in the world is to be acquainted with the context or system of intelligibility in which one resides, to understand it, to interact with the entities that show up in that "world." There are three compartments (ways in which Dasein interacts with the world) that play fundamental roles in the relation of Dasein to its "world": state-of-mind [*Befindlichkeit*], understanding [*Verstehen*], and discourse/talk [*Rede*]. Together these constitute what Heidegger calls the structural features of *being-in* that are common to what Heidegger calls both the *authentic* and the *inauthentic* modes of being.[20]

To understand something on a particular occasion, for Heidegger is to engage in *projection*. To use something in a particular way is to assign to it one of its possibilities. The item is made intelligible through being chosen for a use. It becomes understood. The same is true of self-understanding. As stated at the top of this chapter, to be Dasein is to have one's own being as an issue for one. Who one is *is not* a matter of who one says one is or even of who one thinks one is, but of *how one lives, how one interacts with the world*. To understand oneself, to make oneself intelligible to oneself, is to exist in a certain way, to "press forward into possibilities."[21] Additionally, the purposes or reasons why one lives the way one does amount to what Heidegger calls one's *for-the-sakes-of-which*, or our identities. In other words, what motivates us is *who we are*. When Dasein realizes that its essence is interpretation, it realizes that it is whatever it takes itself to be.

Heidegger engages the question of what it means to be anything, as well as the related question of what Dasein is, with a bit more specificity in his discussion of the neutrality of Dasein in *The Metaphysical Foundations of Logic*.[22] Here, Heidegger relates the neutrality of the concept of Dasein to Dasein's emancipatory potential. Heidegger explains that he did not use the word "man" for "that being which is the theme of the analysis" but used the word *Dasein* instead in order to make clear that the human mode of being "is not indifferent."[23] Heidegger elaborates:

> The peculiar *neutrality* of the term "Dasein" is essential, because the interpretation of this being must be carried out prior to every factual concretion. This neutrality also indicates that Dasein is neither of the two sexes. But here sexlessness is not the indifference of an empty void, the weak negativity of an indifferent ontic nothing. In its neutrality Dasein is not the indifferent nobody and everybody, but the primordial positivity and potency of the essence. [. . .] Neutrality is not the voidness of an abstraction, but precisely the potency of the *origin*, which bears itself in the intrinsic possibility of every concrete factual humanity.[24]

Heidegger goes on to explain that Dasein exists only concretely, only "in its factual concretion,"[25] and "prior to all prophesying and heralding worldviews."[26] "This neutral Dasein," Heidegger elaborates, is not the egocentric individual. Reinforcing the anti-Cartesianism of *Being and Time*, Heidegger goes on to say that, although thoughtful, Dasein ("the one philosophizing") is not the center of the world. Instead, Dasein represents a description "of the multiplication [. . .] which is present in every factically individuated Dasein as such."[27] Importantly, for Heidegger, Dasein entails an "intrinsic possibility of multiplication which [. . .] is present in every Dasein and for which embodiment is an organizing factor."[28]

Moreover, for Heidegger, Dasein is primordially *thrown*. "This thrown dissemination into a multiplicity is to be understood metaphysically," Heidegger tells us.[29] Each Dasein, while still remaining neutral, is at the same time pushed into a particular factical direction, "where other possibilities are faded out or remain closed."[30] Dasein is, Heidegger tells us, involved. Heidegger writes that the metaphysical neutrality of Dasein "is only possible on the basis of the extreme existentiell *involvement* [Einsatz] of the one who [. . .] projects."[31] What Heidegger calls Dasein's "essential finitude" is something, according to Heidegger, that "can only be understood existentially in the inessentiality of the self that only becomes concrete [. . .] through and in the service of each possible totality."[32]

En route to tying all of the above together, Heidegger offers, "The basic intent of the analysis is to show the intrinsic possibility of the understanding-of-being, which means at the same time the possibility of transcendence."[33] What Heidegger means by "transcendence" here is somewhat unclear. Dermot Moran provides some clarity. For him, while on the one hand Heidegger is "specifically critical of Husserl's Cartesian construal of the traditional concepts of 'transcendence' and 'immanence,'" at the same time Heidegger uses the concept of transcendence throughout *Being and Time* and throughout the work in such a way that indicates that, for Heidegger, transcendence simply *is* being.[34] But Heidegger's transcendence, for Moran, is new and distinctive from the way the term has been used in the history of philosophy to that point, and in fact, "evolves" over time. According to Moran, while transcendence, for Heidegger, constitutes selfhood, it is something that belongs uniquely to Dasein as what fundamentally constitutes its being.[35] Moreover, according to Moran, transcendence, for Heidegger, in fact names something essential about the human condition, while at the same time revealing the historicity of that existence.

For Moran, what that something essential is is transcendence understood as entailing a radical rethinking of the nature of intentionality. According to Moran, Heidegger "recognize[s] that intentionality is possible only against a backdrop of a world which always is presumed but which is never presented as an object of experience."[36] But if Dasein is essentially transcendent, then, Dasein is, at a minimum, beyond the body. Withy speaks of this aspect of Dasein in chapter 12 of this volume. There, Withy highlights that Dasein represents or connotes the entities that make sense of entities. Making sense of things is something that Dasein does. We do not do this as embodied beings, according to Withy. In fact, "the human body is so displaced in the existential analytic that not only is it not a central site of our finitude, but it is not even required by Dasein's way of being." At the same time, on Heidegger's own terms, it logically follows from Heidegger's description of Dasein that in order to use the tools that are ready-to-hand, Dasein must have a body. More to the point, in order to interact with entities in general that are ready-to-hand, Dasein must have a body. Perhaps it is safest to say, then, that at a minimum there is a tension in Heidegger's concept of Dasein between Dasein as meaning-maker and Dasein as situated entity whose being is being-in-the world.

Farin articulates a kind of resolution of this tension in chapter 1 of this volume. There Farin argues that Dasein does indeed refer to the individual human being that each one of us is, which means that we are Dasein qua sense-making *and* being situated in the world, namely, by means of our bodies. Farin writes, "In *Being and Time*, Dasein is the ontological and transcendental sine qua non." Quoting Heidegger, Farin writes that Dasein is the "ontic-ontological condition for the possibility of all ontologies." Dasein is, for Farin, "nothing other than the 'understanding' of beings and Being as such." At the same time, the analytic of Dasein is directed toward laying the groundwork for exploring the discussion of "what man is" philosophically, and, for Farin, this means that Heidegger is still engaged with the question, "What is man?" Part of that, for Farin, is Dasein's finitude and the fact that Dasein "is certainly not to be confused with a Cartesian cogito, for it is thrown into the world not of its own making, and it is exposed to other beings and Being at large, always within the horizon of its own limited time."

Intersectional Identity (Personal Identity as Intersectional)

One of the key recurring questions in feminist philosophy is the question of whether there is any one trait that all women share, that is, whether it is the case that a single distinguishing characteristic (or a set of distinguishing characteristics) can be found that signifies with absolute certainty that what we have before us in a given situation is a "woman." On the one hand, to argue that such a characteristic (or set of characteristics) can be located at all subjects one's argument to the charge of biological determinism, that is, to the charge that one is asserting that women's biology is the source of their "womanness." Such an argument is also subject to the criticism that it universalizes something that is not universalizable, that is, the argument unjustifiably takes what is true of some women and universalizes it out to all women. On the other hand, to argue that such a distinguishing characteristic (or set of characteristics) cannot be found is to allow for the possibility that the word "woman" has a multiplicity of meanings. In the realm of intersectionality theory, the possibility that the word "woman" has not a single meaning but a multiplicity of meanings is the more viable option, given the fact that women's experiences vary so widely across social identity markers such as race, ethnicity, class, socioeconomic status, and disability status. From the point of view of intersectionality theory, then, it is social experiences, and not biology, that most primarily affect questions of personal identity.

One form of social experience, and incidentally the form with which intersectionality theory is primarily concerned, is the experience of being oppressed (or privileged, as the case may be). According to Ann Garry, "Intersectional analyses make a fundamental point that we all have many important facets to our identities and are differently impacted by multiple interacting systems of oppression and privilege depending on our various facets."[37] Although, for Garry, intersectionality alone "provides neither any structural analyses of oppressions and privileges nor any particular analysis of anyone's complex identity or experiences," at the same time intersectionality does "point out what kinds of analyses might be useful, namely ones that consider mutually constructed or intermeshed axes of oppression or facets of identities."[38] Garry's deployment of the metaphor of facets (on, for example, a mirror ball) captures well the key intersectional insight that we are none of us monodimensional but in fact splendidly multidimensional or multifaceted vis-à-vis those aspects of what we refer to when we try to capture something on the order of a unified self. According to standard intersectional identity theory, none of us is adequately captured or characterized by any one so-called identity marker (like race, gender, or class), but instead we are all composites of complex, interlocking, and overlapping pressures placed on us from without, each one of us uniquely forged through these interactions.

At the same time, and as Garry importantly highlights, intersectional identity theory does not provide an explicit analysis of anyone's personal identity outside of the ways in which personal identity is forged in the crucible of structural oppression. At the surface level, the work of the concept of intersectionality is to deconstruct the ways in which oppression and privilege operate to forge (often problematically) that aspect of personal identity that exists and operates within oppressive social systems. But more substantively, intersectional identity theory implicitly entails a recognition that what each of us *is* (male, female, or otherwise) is something beyond externally imposed descriptors, something beyond the oppressive forces that act upon us, something that is free and has agency and autonomy, particularly in the realm of personal identity. To the extent that intersectional identity theory describes personal identity as forged both by the interaction of different axes of oppression upon us and through each of our individual autonomous choices, then intersectionality theory, like Heidegger's Dasein, entails a rejection of the mind-body problem, a critique of traditional ontology, and a statement about the effect (and noneffect) of environment on personal identity.

To speak of intersectionality theory as taking a stance on the nature of reality may seem unusual to some. The traditional, historical, or at least most fundamental understanding of what intersectionality *is* is that it is a description of the fact that societies contain several different systems of oppression, subordination, or domination that interact (or "intersect") with one another in such a way as to alter the effect of the experience of oppression of the person upon whom the various systems of domination act. For example, Angela Harris, Kimberlé Crenshaw, and Patricia Hill Collins, among others, have all argued since the late twentieth century that for black women gender subordination is also at the same time racial subordination.[39] Angela Harris and Zeus Leonardo elaborate upon this theme through arguing that the experiences (and therefore existences) of racialized women are different from the experiences (and therefore existences) of nonracialized women.[40] The question is what any of this has to do with the mind-body problem.

Contemporary scholarship in philosophy has opened up the vista of interpretations or uses for the concept of intersectionality in such a way as to unearth and lay bare its theoretical assumptions and foundations. I have tried to do this in some of my philosophical work.[41] The work of philosophers Linda Martín Alcoff, Anna Carasthasis, Kristie Dotson, and Ann Garry, among others, arguably also operates in the service of this objective.[42] Although it would not be fair to claim that any of us have achieved a definitive answer to the question of just in what intersectionality or intersectional identity consists (e.g., none of us have been able to identify its essential elements or key features), it is fairly well settled that one reason for this state of affairs is that it is the nature of intersectionality and intersectional identity to be unsusceptible to traditional analytic scrutiny, with all of its distinctions and assumptions and definitions.[43]

Instead, intersectionality theory and intersectional identity stand for the proposition that each human experience is unique, and further that it is the nature of the human experience that each of is unique, distinctive. We are each distinctive, at a minimum, in terms of the way that each of our experiences of being human is far more complex and multifaceted than any of the categories of oppression, standing alone or even in concert, can capture. When advocates for the existence of intersectional identity claim that singular and externally imposed identity markers are not a good fit for members of oppressed groups, that such markers do not describe the experiences of such persons, they are at the same time claiming that the personal experiences of oppressed persons, and first-person testimony about such experiences, should carry more weight than is presently the case in the assessment of who or what (oppressed) people are. A necessary correlate of this idea is that we are none of us simply one thing or another thing (or still another thing, and on and on). Instead, we are both-and. We are all. Paradoxically, at the same time we are none of the things or characteristics ascribed to us from without.

The mind-body problem in philosophy takes many forms, but the form at issue in the present discussion is the form according to which the basic building blocks of reality are substances and substances must be purely one thing. Traditionally, there were two main substances in the history of philosophy: mind and body, also known as ideas and the physical world.[44] As regards the nature of the self, or the problem of personal identity, the mind-body problem traditionally asks questions such as whether the self is primarily a mind or a body, how mind and body interact, and what relationship the self has to mind or body. Underlying all of these questions is an assumption that entities must be one thing or another, never both.[45] This idea is known as "substance dualism." The intersectional proposition, however, is that each human being is at once not one but multiple things, and in addition that we are whatever emerges as these traits merge and interact in our lives. The messy hodgepodge of experiences (and the interactions between these experiences) that intersectionality claims makes up each of our personal identities (at least on the social level) is implicitly a rejection of both substance monism and substance dualism.

The deeper intersectional claim is not just that each of us is a hodgepodge of experiences (usually of oppression or privilege) and the product of the interactions between these experiences, but also that each of us is actually, at the same time, *none* of these experiences. The idea that each of us could both be a conglomeration of things as a result of our varied personal experiences (with oppression and privilege, among other things) *and* none of the things ascribed to us by society violates the law of noncontradiction, and is, in this way, arguably a critique of traditional ontology. Traditional ontological questions concern what exists and what it means for something to exist. These questions presume that there is something there (that is, over there, outside of self and outside of interpretation) that is objective and susceptible to analysis at arm's length. The law of noncontradiction in logic, of course, stands for the proposition that contradictory statements cannot both be true. Aristotle extended the principle into the realm of metaphysics through his ontological version: "It is impossible for the same thing to belong and not belong to the same thing at the same time and in the same respect."[46] In this way, intersectionality theory is a critique of traditional ontology.

The intersectional critique of traditional ontology is different from Heidegger's but is similar in important respects. Heidegger's critique of traditional ontology (defined, in part, as holding, at a minimum, that what things are is an objective matter) is that what things are (being) and how they are interpreted (i.e., what things mean) are intimately connected. That is, his explanation of Dasein entails a claim about the difficulty of getting at reality immediately.[47] The difficulty he describes is ubiquitous and applies to every situation in which our goal is to have knowledge of something, including knowledge of personal identity.

Intersectionality theory, then, both claims that we (our personal identities) are the products of social forces external to the self (primarily forces of oppression and privilege) and that we are each something completely different from those social forces. The oppression lies in the failure on the part of powerful social forces to acknowledge this second aspect of who we are. Instead, the oppressed are seen in terms that fit the mold of a given oppressive lens, or multiple oppressive lenses, understood as always and already clouded and cracked. The lens through which we see ourselves, however, is clear and strong. We understand that the labels applied to us are not applied appropriately or fairly, that somehow a different prescription is required to see us properly. This understanding is the source of our being able to identify when the process of oppression is happening to us.

Conclusion

Heidegger's interlocutors seem to be at odds, at times, over the question of whether Dasein is, as Withy describes, primarily an entity that makes sense of other entities, or, as Farin describes, the embodied individual human being that each one of us is. However, a close reading of Heidegger himself on the topic finds support for each of these interpretations of Dasein. Within the pages of *Being and Time* and subsequent works, Dasein is arguably revealed as some sort of combination of both of these interpretations, entailing the features of each at different times and in different contexts (in keeping with what Sheehan has called Dasein's "ontological bivalence"). K. M. Stroh develops the idea of a complex and multifaceted Dasein a bit further.[48] For Stroh, Dasein contains an inherent form of intersubjectivity to which we must "return" in order to achieve authenticity. Stroh takes very seriously, in other words, Heidegger's claim to be moving past the isolated Cartesian subject, and sees Dasein as also moving toward a view of authentic human existence that is cognizant of the way our identities are always and already formed within a preexisting community. Stroh thus sees a coherence between what appear to be two divergent concepts of Dasein through a reinterpretation of Dasein as community. The idea of a human way of being that reaches toward authenticity within a factic context that is both preexistent and "communal" (or collectively generated) is compatible with theories of human identity based in intersectionality.

Heidegger's Dasein and intersectional identity share at least three features in common: a negative assessment of the legitimacy of the mind-body problem, a critique of traditional ontology, and a statement about the relationship between environment and personal identity. More specifically, they both reject the mind-body problem as nonsensical, reject the idea that to exist is to be static, timeless, and changeless, and understand personal identity as a product of a reciprocal and ongoing relationship between external or cultural forces and individual agency. Who we are *socially* is the product of social forces. The races, genders, ability statuses, socioeconomic statuses, and other personal identity markers or labels assigned to us through social interaction deeply affect both the degree to which and the manner in which we are oppressed in society (or not). On the one hand, both Heidegger's identification of the human way of being, or Dasein, with social constraints that arise out of social practices and intersectionality theory's acknowledgment of the degree to which forces of oppression operate in complex ways on the options made available to us and our access to social goods, capture the constraints on personal identity. On the other hand, who we are more fundamentally is something else indeed. For both Heidegger and intersectional identity theory, we are, in addition, self-reflexive agents, interpreters of our own experiences and identities, quite beyond anything imposed from outside of ourselves. This is reflected both in Heidegger's concept of authenticity and in the implicit intersectional claim that we are each something beyond the systems of oppression that act upon us.

Some possible lessons to be gleaned from this overlap between Heidegger's conception of the human way of being and the nature of personal identity coming in from intersectionality theory are as follows. First, the fact that these two seemingly theoretically divergent, or at least, foreign prisms of analyzing the world (and the human way of being) arrive at similar conclusions about the nature of existence, and especially about the nature of what it means to be a human being, should at least give the responsible reader pause to consider the likelihood that these conclusions are legitimate. Second, if these conclusions are legitimate, then it seems it is incumbent upon us to inquire into the implications of these conclusions for the pressing social problems that face us.[49]

In these times of social unrest, it seems particularly important that scholars engaged in the project of trying to use their work to make positive social change should be mindful of the effect their work may have on either untangling or exacerbating the pernicious social problems underlying this unrest.[50] The lesson that the human way of being is complex, polydimensional, and takes on certain shapes in response to social forces (such as the forces of institutionalized racism and other oppressive forces)—and particularly the lesson that said shape can change and take unique forms in response to the particularized contextual pressures placed upon each of us—can possibly operate as an eye-opener for those resistant to being receptive to the idea that the actions of others can, and often are, induced and generated by oppression rather than autonomous choice. If one accepts, in other words, that the actions of a protestor, or even a looter, may be more a product of a life of alienation from the halls of privilege and status than of personal choice, if every fairly nonoppressed person can see themselves in someone alienated from society, then the problem of human beings' inhumanity against other human beings may lose some its energy and power.

Third, the same is true, perhaps, for a global recognition that each of us is more than, or at least other than, a conglomeration of externally imposed labels, or even a set of intersecting, externally imposed labels, in terms of the power we have over who we choose to be and how we choose to live our lives. Fourth, and I think compellingly, perhaps the lesson is that the human experience, that is what it means to be a human being, on both the macro ("the human way of being") and micro (personal identity) levels, is made up of both of these apparently divergent characterizations and that's okay. That is, maybe it is *both* the case that the human way of being is constrained by what Heidegger called our "they" self, by the "worlds" into which we have been thrown (including systems of oppression, intersectional and otherwise), *and* it is also the case that we have the power to accept or reject the resulting labels and constraints, should we choose to do so. Attempting to remove the labels (engaging in self-reflexive interpretation regarding personal identity), the suits of constraint and privilege, may be difficult or uncomfortable, but until we at least try to do so, arguably, we will continue to find ourselves unable to see the commonalities that can bring us together in the service of peace and common interests.

Notes

1. My method here is borrowed from Karl Mannheim in his *Ideology and Utopia*, trans. Lewis Wirth (London: Routledge, 1991). There, Mannheim argues that it is the task of the intellectual to unmask or place into dialogue the surface meanings (or what Mannheim called the "ideologies") of seemingly divergent interpretive frameworks to reveal a kind of knowledge that has a legitimacy grounded in the places where the seemingly divergent frameworks merge.

2. The translation of Dasein, as "the human way of being," comes from Hubert L. Dreyfus, *Being-in-the-World: A Commentary on Heidegger's Being and Time, Division I* (Cambridge, MA: MIT Press, 1991).

3. This is because the claim that "Socrates is a philosopher" presumes that Socrates has the traits thought to be essential to the class of entities known as philosophers, but the claim also presumes that Socrates has other traits as well, since if this were not the case, "Socrates is a philosopher" would not be a meaningful statement, but a tautology.

4. Thomas Sheehan, "Dasein," in *A Companion to Heidegger*, ed. Hubert L. Dreyfus and Mark A. Wrathall (Oxford: Blackwell, 2007), 193–213, 206.

5. Sheehan, "Dasein," 206.

6. Sheehan, "Dasein," 206.

7. See, for example, Ann Garry, Serene J. Khader, and Alison Stone, introduction to *The Routledge Companion to Feminist Philosophy*, ed. Ann Garry, Serene J. Khader, and Alison Stone (New York: Routledge, 2017), 1–10.

8. Garry, Khader, and Stone, introduction to *Routledge Companion to Feminist Philosophy*, 6.

9. Lisa Bowleg, "The Problem with the Phrase 'Women and Minorities': Intersectionality—an Important Theoretical Framework for Public Health," *American Journal of Public Health* 102, no. 7 (2012): 1267–73, esp. 1267.

10. See Laurie Shrage, ed., *You've Changed: Sex Reassignment and Personal Identity* (New York: Oxford University Press, 2009); Ann Garry, "Intersectionality,

Metaphors, and the Multiplicity of Gender," *Hypatia* 26, no. 4 (2011): 826–50; Cynthia Levine-Rasky, *Whiteness Fractured* (Burlington, VT: Ashgate, 2013); Tina Fernandes Botts, ed., *Philosophy and the Mixed Race Experience* (Lanham, MD: Lexington Books, 2016).

 11. Ange-Marie Hancock, *Intersectionality: An Intellectual History* (New York: Oxford University Press, 2016), 32.

 12. Hancock, *Intersectionality*, 110.

 13. Hancock, *Intersectionality*, 110.

 14. Hancock, *Intersectionality*, 111. Emphasis added.

 15. Martin Heidegger, *Being and Time*, trans. John Macquarrie and Edward Robinson (New York: Harper and Row, 2008).

 16. "World" in what Heidegger calls an "everyday" sense, by contrast, means simply the extended objects we find around us.

 17. Heidegger, *Being and Time*, H15.

 18. Heidegger, *Being and Time*, H12.

 19. Heidegger, *Being and Time*, H16.

 20. *Authentic* being (*Eigentlichkeit*) is being in which Dasein takes responsibility for its being, in which Dasein becomes an individual, in which Dasein owns up to its ability to decide its own being for itself. *Inauthentic* being is being in conformity with a "world"; it is *not* taking responsibility for one's own being, *not* owning up to one's responsibility for deciding one's own being.

 21. Heidegger, *Being and Time*, H145.

 22. Martin Heidegger, *The Metaphysical Foundations of Logic*. trans. Michael Heim (Bloomington: Indiana University Press, 1992).

 23. Heidegger, *The Metaphysical Foundations of Logic*, 136.

 24. Heidegger, *The Metaphysical Foundations of Logic*, 136–37.

 25. Heidegger, *The Metaphysical Foundations of Logic*, 137.

 26. Heidegger, *The Metaphysical Foundations of Logic*, 137.

 27. Heidegger, *The Metaphysical Foundations of Logic*, 137.

 28. Heidegger, *The Metaphysical Foundations of Logic*, 138.

 29. Heidegger, *The Metaphysical Foundations of Logic*, 138.

 30. Heidegger, *The Metaphysical Foundations of Logic*, 139.

 31. Heidegger, *The Metaphysical Foundations of Logic*, 140.

 32. Heidegger, *The Metaphysical Foundations of Logic*, 140.

 33. Heidegger, *The Metaphysical Foundations of Logic*, 141.

 34. Dermot Moran, "What Does Heidegger Mean by the Transcendence of Dasein?," *International Journal of Philosophical Studies* 22, no. 4 (2014): 491–514, esp. 496.

 35. Moran, "What Does Heidegger Mean by the Transcendence of Dasein?," 497.

 36. Moran, "What Does Heidegger Mean by the Transcendence of Dasein?," 510.

37. Garry, "Intersectionality, Metaphors, and the Multiplicity of Gender," 826–50, esp. 827.

38. Garry, "Intersectionality, Metaphors, and the Multiplicity of Gender," 830.

39. See, for example, Angela Harris, "Race and Essentialism in Feminist Legal Theory," *Stanford Law Review* 42, no. 3 (1990): 581–616; Kimberlé Crenshaw, "Demarginalizing the Intersection of Race and Sex: A Black Feminist Critique of Antidiscrimination Doctrine, Feminist Theory and Antiracist Politics," *University of Chicago Legal Forum*, no. 1 (1989): 139–67; Patricia Hill Collins, *Black Feminist Thought: Knowledge, Consciousness, and the Politics of Empowerment* (New York: Routledge, 2000).

40. Angela Harris and Zeus Leonardo, "Intersectionality, Race-Gender Subordination, and Education," *Review of Research in Education* 42, no. 1 (2018): 1–27.

41. See, for example, Tina Fernandes Botts, *Philosophy and the Mixed Race Experience*; "The Genealogy and Viability of the Concept of Intersectionality," in Garry, Khader, and Stone, *Routledge Companion to Feminist Philosophy*, 343–57.

42. See, for example, Linda Alcoff, *Visible Identities: Race, Gender, and the Self* (Oxford: Oxford University Press, 2006); Anna Carastathis, *Intersectionality: Origins, Contestations, Horizons* (Lincoln: University of Nebraska Press, 2014); Kristie Dotson, "Making Sense: The Multistability of Oppression and the Importance of Intersectionality," in *Why Race and Gender Still Matter*, ed. Namita Goswami, Maeve O'Donovan, and Lisa Yount (London: Pickering and Chatto, 2016), 13–25; Garry, "Intersectionality, Metaphors, and the Multiplicity of Gender," 826–50.

43. See, generally, Namita Goswami, Maeve O'Donovan, and Lisa Yount, eds., *Why Race and Gender Still Matter* (London: Pickering and Chatto, 2016).

44. Of course, for many modern philosophers, "God" was also a substance, but for our purposes, we need not engage that aspect of the history of philosophy.

45. We need not ask how mind and body interact, for example, if they are not separate "substances."

46. Aristotle, *Metaphysics* 4.3.1005b19–20. As it happens, Aristotle articulated three versions of the principle: the "ontological" version, listed here, the "doxastic" version, and the "semantic" version. The "doxastic" version is, "It is impossible to hold (suppose) the same thing to be and not to be." (*Metaphysics* 4.3.1005b24, cf. 1005b29–30). The "semantic" version is, "Opposite assertions cannot be true at the same time" (*Metaphysics* 4.6.10011b13–20).

47. Heidegger, *Being and Time*.

48. See K. M. Stroh, "Intersubjectivity of Dasein in Heidegger's Being and Time: How Authenticity is a Return to Community," *Human Studies* 38 (2015): 243–59.

49. I want to take a brief moment to acknowledge that Martin Heidegger was affiliated, for a time, with National Socialism (Nazism). I raise this point because I feel a responsibility to make readers aware that the creator of the concept of Dasein is known to have said things and written things that are racist. For some, this may

raise a specter of suspicion around anything Heidegger or his philosophy may have to say about the human way of being. I am sympathetic to this viewpoint to the extent that I believe attempts to lop off philosophical ideas from the political or personal views of their creators should be handled with care and attention. However, I also find Heidegger's concept of Dasein to have a high degree of explanatory power. In any event, for me, at this point in my relationship with Heidegger's thought, I am comfortable working with Heidegger's thought on its own terms. This may not be true for others and, if not, I understand why. The reader should note that scholars disagree about the exact nature of Heidegger's affiliation with National Socialism, as well as about the extent to which Heidegger's political convictions or personal views may have affected his philosophy of being. For some, Heidegger's notion of historicity, for example, problematically operated as the driving force behind the racial purity fueling National Socialism. See, for example, Thomas Sheehan, "Reading a Life: Heidegger and Hard Times," in *Cambridge Companion to Heidegger*, ed. Charles Guigon (Cambridge: Cambridge University Press, 1993), 70–96. Others focus on the fact that Heidegger invited his contemporaries to rethink the phenomenon of race so as to reject biological reductionism, in keeping with Heidegger's general project of overcoming Western metaphysics. See, for example, Robert Bernasconi, "Race and Earth in Heidegger's Thinking During the Late 1930s," *Southern Journal of Philosophy* 48, no. 1 (2010): 49–66. Additional information on Heidegger's relationship with National Socialism can be found in Victor Farias, *Heidegger et le nazisme*, trans. Myriam Benarroch and Jean-Baptiste Grasset (Lagrasse, France: Éditions Verdier, 1989); Bernhard Radloff, *Heidegger and the Question of National Socialism: Disclosure and Gestalt* (Toronto: University of Toronto Press, 2007); Rüdiger Safranski, *Martin Heidegger: Between Good and Evil*, trans. Ewald Osers (Cambridge, MA: Harvard University Press, 1998); Julian Young, *Heidegger, Philosophy, Nazism* (Cambridge: Cambridge University Press, 1998); and Johannes Fritsche, "Heidegger's 'Being and Time' and National Socialism," *Philosophy Today* 56, no. 3 (2012): 255–84.

    50. At the time of this writing, in various cities across the United States (and, indeed, the entire world), protests against racial injustice on the part of the (American) police force, including police brutality, murder, and other injustices against African Americans, have cropped up with an amazing frequency and energy in response to the apparent murder (I say "apparent" murder because there has as yet been no trial) of George Floyd by police officers in Minneapolis. A vast, international public outcry in the streets, in the news media, and in social media has erupted with a marked intensity, persistence, and frequency. Public statements offered in support of Black Lives Matter are being issued on the part of countless businesses and other social institutions. Calls for the changing of the names of institutions named after historical figures known to have been involved in racial injustice are taking place as well as demands for the removal of statues and plaques dedicated to similar historical figures.

Chapter Eleven

Natality vs. Mortality
Turning Heidegger Inside Out

ANNE GRANBERG

Heidegger defines the objective in his magnum opus, *Sein und Zeit*, as clarifying "the meaning of Being" as such, but this ontological question can only be answered by investigating the being that we ourselves are—the human being. Instead of approaching the question as a question about *what* the human being is, Heidegger focuses on *how* the human being is; the human being is "being-there" (*Dasein*), "an issue for itself" and the being that understands Being.[1] Furthermore, Dasein is essentially Being-in-the-world, and Heidegger defines the structural totality of being-there as care (*Sorge*). Once the concept of Dasein is established, however, Heidegger tends to avoid talking about "the human" except to criticize traditional concepts such as *animal rationale* and philosophical dichotomies. While he is careful to point out that the analytic of Dasein is intended as a preparation for working out the question of the meaning of Being and not as a philosophical anthropology, he also holds the door ajar for regarding it—although incomplete—as comparable to "an existentially a priori anthropology."[2] Heidegger's reservations notwithstanding, it is safe to say that the main impact of *Sein und Zeit* has been precisely as a kind of philosophical anthropology, albeit one that challenges traditional dichotomies—of man and world, subject and object, inside and outside, reason and emotion, body and soul. This is not particularly surprising, given that *Sein und Zeit* tells us rather more about the human being than about Being.

In contrast to Heidegger's reticence, "the human" is explicitly placed at the front and center of Arendt's thought—as intimated in the title of *The Human Condition*. Although often seen as a political theorist (a label she also preferred),[3] Arendt was self-admittedly also "a sort of phenomenologist,"[4] and it is my suggestion that her portrayal of how and who we are as human beings is useful for shedding light on a blind spot in Heidegger's analytic of Dasein, considered as a philosophical anthropology. This blind spot is the "in-between" human beings, which is the *topos* of all of Arendt's thinking. In contrast to the tradition's tendency to focus either on the individual or on some kind of collective totality, when approaching the question of the human from an Arendtian point of view, both the individual and the totality are abstractions—the concrete is the *in-between*.

While the ontological aspirations of *Sein und Zeit* might seem a far throw from Arendt's more explicit anthropological take on human existence, it is worth keeping in mind that Heidegger insists that the *Seinsfrage* (the question after the meaning of Being) is not abstract but rather the most basic and concrete.[5] We always already maintain ourselves within a tacit understanding of Being (of the world, ourselves, and entities within the world) inherent in our activities and interactions. There are different interpretations of precisely what Heidegger means by "Being" (and different interpretative angles give slightly different definitions), but if we think of the Being of beings as "meaningful presence to Dasein" (Sheehan),[6] or as "intelligibility" (Dreyfus),[7] or as the sense that things make to us (both as "what" and "how") in our concrete experience,[8] and think of the meaning of Being (*Sinn von Sein*) as what makes this sense-making itself possible, the definition of the human being as the being that understands Being is not that alien to Arendt's perspective after all. She would agree that human beings disclose Being (are engaged in making sense of the world and ourselves), but links this "sense-making" to fundamental activities and capacities that respond to and enact basic conditions.[9]

In Arendt's thought, the kinship to Heidegger is both substantial and methodological. They both reject the notion of an ahistorical human nature on the one hand, and the recourse to a detached worldless *cogito* on the other hand—and both see the human being as a self-interpretive, situated, and radically historical *Being-in-the-world*, always already inhabiting a pretheoretical forestructure of practical and social relations. Methodologically, her penchant for etymological analyses in order to get to originary experiences,[10] her use of the ancient Greek *polis* as a reference point, and, perhaps most importantly, her use of concepts that are drawn from experience and denote a "how" rather than a "what," all owes much to the influence of Heidegger's lecture courses on Aristotle in the 1920s.[11] As Ingo Farin points out in this volume, the main topic of the early Heidegger is the self-understanding of "factical life," rather than the established academic problems of epistemology or ontology. What Heidegger in this period calls "factical life experience" (*Faktische Lebenserfahrung*) corresponds roughly to the preontological level in *Sein und Zeit*, and the early Heidegger stresses that the task of phenomenology is to analyze the "how" of relating-to (*Verhalten*) as such; how the world is always revealed in a certain light and under certain aspects. For Heidegger in this period, the task of philosophy is the "self-interpretation" of factical life, and his commitment to avoid theoretical constructions and stay close to the phenomena is echoed in Arendt's statement that "thought itself arises out of incidents of living experience and must remain bound to them as the only guideposts by which to take its bearings."[12] These similarities aside, I agree with Taminiaux and Villa who claim that although deeply inspired by Heidegger, Arendt is also engaged in a continuous—although not always explicit—debate with him.[13] While Taminiaux's and Villa's focus is mainly on Arendt and Heidegger's different retrieval of the Aristotelian distinction between *praxis* and *poiesis*, what I will attempt to do here is to unpack her debate with Heidegger through a very un-Aristotelian and un-Greek[14] concept, namely, *natality*, and show how they differ "on common ground," as it were, in their appeal to fundamental experiences (mortality and natality) as the basis for conceptualizing human existence.

Arendt never gave any detailed critique of Heidegger's Dasein-analytic, but in her 1946 article "What Is Existential Philosophy?"[15] she presents the core of her criticism in a rather polemical and condensed fashion. What Arendt reacts to most vehemently is the way the Heideggerian "Self" in her view is cut off from plurality: "The essential character of the Self is its absolute Self-ness, its radical separation from all its fellows." While the Kantian concept of man or humanity is transindividual, the Heideggerian Self carries no such reference to others with it: "being-a-Self has taken the place of being human" and hence is the "total opposite of man," she claims. The question of the meaning of the Self is, however, "truly unanswerable, because a Self, taken in absolute isolation, is meaningless."[16] "Existence itself is, by its very nature, never isolated. It exists only in communication and in an awareness of the other's existence. [. . .] Existence can develop only in the shared life of human beings inhabiting a given world common to them all."[17] According to Arendt, it is the focus on death as the *principium individuationis* in *Sein und Zeit* that leads Heidegger to this impasse, and I suggest that we can read her concept of natality as an attempt to turn the "inverted" Heideggerian self "the right side out" as it were.

"Fact of Life" or Metaphor?

In *The Human Condition*, natality and mortality are introduced as the "most general conditions of human existence." She also states that, "since action is the political activity par excellence, natality, and not mortality, may be the central category of political, as distinguished from metaphysical, thought."[18] However, Arendt also frequently refers to natality as a "fact"; in *The Human Condition* we are told that "action as a beginning corresponds to the fact of birth,"[19] and in *Between Past and Future* natality is said to be "the fact that human beings are *born* into the world."[20] This fact is then a condition for freedom, given that action "is the actualization of the human condition of natality"[21] and "being free and to act are the same."[22] The description of natality as a "fact" gives us pause: Given that the faculty of action is said to be *ontologically rooted* in the fact of natality,[23] in what way can we say that being born—a biological fact if there ever was any—is the ontological root of action and freedom? To state that in order to act, one must first be born is trivially true, but not very informative, and given the general anti-biological tenor of Arendt's thought, her reference to the "fact of birth" as both the most central political concept and the ontological root of action is puzzling, to say the least. A quite common interpretation is therefore to read natality purely *metaphorically* as a stand-in for our capability for spontaneous action.[24] After all, to act, to insert oneself into the world through speech and action, is, according to Arendt, "like a second birth."[25] But in *what sense* is action *like* a second birth? Why is a raven like a writing desk? (As the Mad Hatter said to Alice.) Taken as a metaphor it appears flawed: giving birth is labor, and being born is no activity at all, and furthermore something we have in common with all mammals and thus obviously ill fitted as a metaphor for a specific *human* capacity.[26] Furthermore, as Totsching points out, if "natality" were merely a metaphor for the capacity to act or begin, the claim that the "faculty of action is ontologically rooted in the fact of natality" would be plainly circular and nonsensical.[27] A purely metaphorical reading also severs the ties to actual births that Arendt repeatedly refers to. The connection between entering the world through birth and possessing the capacity to act or begin is not self-explanatory, we need to clarify precisely *how* the capacity to begin, spontaneity, new beginnings (the metaphorical meanings of "natality"), relates to natality as concrete factual births as a *condition* for action in a nontrivial sense.

Natality as Thrownness?

Another quite common interpretation is to see natality as an existentiale along the lines of Heidegger's *thrownness* or *Geworfenheit* in §72 of *Sein und Zeit*.[28] My first objection to this rather influential Heideggerian reading is that, while it solves the problem of circularity mentioned above, it obscures the link between natality and plurality, and thus risks turning natality into what Arendt would consider a "metaphysical" rather than a "political" concept, and thus miss its critical role vis-à-vis Heidegger. Secondly, the explicit association that Arendt makes between natality and *beginnings* underscores an important difference between natality and thrownness. *Geworfenheit* refers to facticity, that we are always-already thrown into a world not of our own making, with its specific language, tradition, heritage, and way of life (i.e., a finite range of possibilities), and thus denotes our dependency on the *past*, while natality is consistently described by Arendt as a *rupture* with the past and the unpredictable and "miraculous" appearance of the new.[29]

Furthermore, Heidegger's existentialia are always structures of *my own* existence, but when natality is introduced in *The Human Condition* it is not as *my* having-been-born, but as something one foresees and reckons with in labor and work, namely, "the constant influx of newcomers."[30] From this perspective, natality refers to a phenomenon in common human experience—that of receiving new humans. I find this noteworthy, especially in light of the marked tendency among otherwise perspicuous commentators to identify natality with thrownness. There is no methodological solipsism in Arendt, nor any presupposed "mineness" or *Jemeinigkeit* framing the investigation from the outset. In fact, we could say that natality is a phenomenon that precisely *resists* the move that Heidegger makes in insisting on the "mineness" of death; it would sound preposterous—if not outright silly—to claim that "birth is always essentially my own" or "birth is constituted by mineness."[31] Natality is, first of all, experienced as the birth of others, the arrival of plural newcomers. What I will suggest here is that plurality is built into the concept of natality from the start, in that it refers to a phenomenon that demands to be seen from a *plurality of perspectives*—from the general perspective of the world (third person plural), of those who receive the newcomers (first person plural), as well as from the first-person singular perspective. To associate natality with my "having-been-born," as most commentators do, is therefore too narrow. It is not totally off the mark, however, since this aspect plays a role in what we (in want of a better word) might call the Arendtian version of authenticity. Natality connects several interrelated, nonhierarchical conditions of human existence—appearance, worldliness, and plurality—that together condition and make possible the human way of being as "natals"—newcomers who have the capacity to begin.

Birth as Appearance

From a certain point of view, birth belongs to the same biological processes that we share with other living beings, what Arendt describes as a cyclical reproduction of the same—that is, the human species. It is tempting to read this as implying a radical split between a "first," merely physical birth belonging to biological life, and natality proper as the "second birth" into language, but this would render the importance Arendt ascribes to concrete, factual births incomprehensible. I will suggest that Arendt's point is not so much to differentiate between a "first" (physical) birth and a "second" (linguistic) birth, but to shift our perspective from nature to world. It is in relation to the world that birth can become a beginning of *somebody*, a biography, and it is from the perspective of the world that the newborn enters, that his or her birth is the beginning of something new and unique.[32] To live is to "be among men," and birth is appearing and death disappearing from a common space.[33]

Although Arendt is appreciative of Heidegger's notion of "world" as a step toward conceptualizing plurality,[34] her emphasis on the world as a common "space of appearance" marks a difference from Heidegger who bases his ontological concept of "worldhood" on an analysis of the handling of equipment in what can be described as a workshop-environment structured upon relations between tools and tasks rather than relations between people.[35] In Heidegger's descriptions, the analysis of the ready-to-hand and present-at-hand methodically precedes the analysis of *Mitdasein* and the *Mitwelt*, and others are first and foremost encountered "at work," as it were, as producers and users of things.[36] Arendt, on her part, stresses that the human-made world, with its "reifications" and its instrumental relations, is *also*—and at the same time—an *in-between*: "To live together in the world means essentially that a world of things is between those who have it in common, as a table is located between those who sit around it; the world like every in-between, relates and separates at the same time."[37] To this world of reifications (be it buildings, tools, or institutions) Arendt adds a second layer, a second in-between—"the web of human relationships"—consisting of intersubjective connections created and maintained by speech and action. This web is intangible but no less real than the structure of material things and it "exist wherever men live together."[38] What makes the world of reifications a human home is that it is a stage for action and speech—as she expresses it in *Men in Dark Times*: "The common world remains 'inhuman' in a very literal sense unless it is constantly talked about by human beings. For the world is not humane just because it is made by human beings, and it does not become humane just because the human voice sounds in it, but only when it has become the object of discourse."[39]

The birth of human beings are thus not natural occurrences but *worldly* phenomena in the sense that being born is to *appear* on this scene as a "stranger and a newcomer."[40] We can here see the contrast to Heidegger's analysis of death, where death—properly understood—is a structure of Dasein's own being, and thus not a worldly event at all. That is, he does not merely prioritize a first-person perspective on death, but appears to want to do away with *all* generality and universality whatsoever in relation to death, since the specific "mineness" of death is not captured by the insight that "I too, must die" or "we are all mortals"—rather, death *is* just as my own: "In so far as it is, death is always essentially my own."[41] In contrast, Arendt insists that there is a *genuine objectivity* to birth and death as appearances in—and disappearances from—a common world, in line with her view expressed in *Life of the Mind* that being and appearance coincide.[42] What we experience as *real* is what can be seen and heard from a multiplicity of vantage points and for a plurality of people, since it is the presence of others "who see what we see and hear what we hear [that] assures us of the reality of the world and ourselves."[43]

The Mutual Dependence of World and Natality

Being-in-the-world implies, for Arendt, to appear to others in the world, which implies that we are not just *in* the world, but *of* it—embodied and visible, perceiving and being perceived at the same time.[44] In order for birth to be an appearance of something new in the world, the newcomer must be received, named, and guided into the "web of human relationships" and into language. As appearance in an intersubjective web, the "naked fact of birth" is always-already relational and linguistic. Although not particularly stressed by Arendt herself, to be *of* the world also betokens vulnerability; to be born means to be dependent on the care and goodwill of others:[45] "Every man is born a member of a particular community and survives only if he is welcomed and made at home in it."[46] To welcome the newcomer creates new interpersonal relationships, new threads in the web and connections between people; first between the infant and the caretakers in the closest environment, and later between the child and further parts of the web. As Totsching points out, the "naked fact" of birth itself creates, alters, and shakes up relationships even *before* the newcomer is able to act on her own account: "[T]he birth of every child stirs up the web of relationships and so prevents it from petrifying."[47] There is therefore a relation of mutual dependence between natality as a "fact" (births, arrival of newcomers) and the world—the world as a stable frame is a condition for the appearance of the newcomer as a unique "somebody," and the influx of newcomers is a condition for the durability of the world; as Arendt expresses it, "[N]atality daily *renews* this world itself, which otherwise would end along with the death of individuals."[48]

Given that the durability of the world not only depends on the persistence through time of its "reifications," but also on stories, practices, and cultural traditions being handed down and preserved, the influx of newcomers is a fundamental condition for our care for the world: if it were not for the constant appearance of new human beings, the world would cease to be an object of common concern for us. Natality in its concrete mundane sense as the arrival of newcomers is constitutive for our sense of meaning and hope. This point is poignantly illustrated by Schott, who draws on the P. D. James science fiction novel *Children of Men*: if there were to be no more births, there would be no more interest in maintaining the world for new generations and no interest in the past, since all knowledge gained about the past would be without a future.[49] It is the influx of newcomers that makes preserving the memory of the past and taking care of the present meaningful activities. That is, caring for the world links us to present and future generations: "[T]he common world is what we enter when we are born, and what we leave behind when we die. It transcends our lifespan into past and future; it was there before we came and will outlast our brief sojourn with it. It is what we have in common not only with those who live with us, but also with those who were here before and with those who will come after us."[50]

The First-Person Perspective: Existing as a Beginner

From the viewpoint of the world, natality represents the new; ruptures and beginnings, but from a first-person singular perspective, my own birth is an irretrievable past. The facticity of my birth signifies not just that I am always-already "thrown" into a preexisting world of preestablished meaning, but simultaneously that my arrival—though completely opaque for me—was an *appearance of something new from the perspective of others*. There is a structural parallel between Arendt's "action" and Heidegger's authenticity in that both are conceived as a *confirmation* or an *attestation* of a ground not stemming from ourselves: Dasein cannot get "behind" its own thrownness,[51] its historical contingent and limited horizon, and my own beginning in birth is likewise inaccessible to me. I find it conspicuous that Heidegger, in his discussion of "guilt" and "conscience," uses terms like "voice," "call," and "answer," which indicates a relation to others without ever allowing this relationship to enter into the analysis itself. The call of conscience has a vertical character, it comes "from me and yet from beyond me,"[52] but in the last instance it remains a form of auto-affection. Both Heidegger and Arendt introduce a "call-and-response" structure, where facticity demands a response, but for Arendt this response is instigated by—and directed at—others:

> With word and deed we insert ourselves into the human world and this insertion is like a second birth, in which we *confirm and take upon* ourselves the naked fact of our original physical appearance. This insertion is not forced upon us by necessity[. . . .] [I]ts impulse springs from the beginning which came into the world when we were born and *to which we respond* by beginning something new on our own initiative.[53]

To insert oneself into the human world "with word and deed" is a confirmation of our original appearance for others, and what we attest to is the *promise of the new* that we—as newcomers—embodied in the eyes of others.

Arendt repeatedly claims that every human being is capable of new beginnings,[54] but this capacity is not at the disposal of the individual (like creativity, for instance), because the capacity to begin is not really a "property" of the subject at all.[55] This is due to certain features of action itself, first and foremost that it is never possible in isolation. Action is always action in concert, and while a single individual may be the instigator, action differs essentially from production in that the agent—unlike the producer—never attains full control over the outcome. This is due to the fact that action always takes place within a network of relations between other acting and speaking persons: "Since action acts upon beings who are capable of their own actions, reaction, apart from being a response, is always a new action that strikes out on its own and affects others."[56] What *makes* the beginner's deed an instance of beginning, is that others *take* it as an occasion to begin themselves, and acting is thus (in contrast to producing) essentially and necessarily intersubjective. Action—if it is to be a real beginning—requires not only the presence of others but their action as well, which is why Arendt can claim that action, "no matter what its specific content, always establishes relationships."[57] Since it always takes place within a web of relationships among plural individuals where new players and new ways of playing the game continuously enter the scene, the outcome of action is unpredictable in principle—even for the agent herself, and what an action finally amounts to, is therefore not under the agent's sovereign control. Thus, as agents we never quite know what we are doing when we act "into the web of inter-relationships and mutual dependencies that constitute the field of action."[58] To do and to suffer are therefore opposite sides of the same coin, since not only the outcome, but also the meaning of our actions depends on others: the deed vanishes, but in being witnessed, judged, and talked about, the witnesses and storytellers testify to its meaning. The full meaning of actions is therefore only revealed retrospectively.[59] In other words, the meaning of our actions depends on how they are received and interpreted by contemporary others *and* future newcomers. As acting beings, we are anything but sovereign: "Sovereignty, the ideal of uncompromising self-sufficiency and mastership, is contradictory to the very condition of plurality."[60]

The Daimon on the Shoulder

Although Arendt—like Heidegger—poses the question of the self as a "who" rather than a "what," the difference between them is striking. In *Sein und Zeit*, becoming an authentic self consists in facing up to mortality and heeding the call of conscience, which stems from Dasein itself, and the call is answered by "reticent resoluteness which exacts anxiety of itself" in which Dasein is authentically itself.[61] Heidegger repeatedly describes the confrontation with death as *nonrelational*, and he does not differentiate between sociality in general and "publicness" as a specific degenerate form. When Dasein confronts its "ownmost" possibility—that is, death—"all its relations to any other Dasein has been undone."[62] Resoluteness is according to Heidegger an openness or "disclosedness" and as such constituted by discourse (*Rede*), attunement (*Befindlichkeit*), and understanding (*Verstehen*), but each of these constitutive moments now appear in a *completely nonrelational mode*: the attunement of *Angst* severs our relations to others, understanding projects itself upon its ownmost-Being-Guilty and the discourse is silent. The nonrelational character of the call of conscience is further underlined in that the call is said to be all the more authentically understood the more it is heard in a nonrelational way.[63] The call of conscience—as well as the response to it—is silent as opposed to the loud chatter of *das Man*, and the whole process remains a completely internal and private affair.

Regarding the self or the "who," Arendt goes in the complete opposite direction and takes the "superficial"—that which appears—seriously. According to her, what does not appear in a common world might be exclusively our own, but remains dreamlike and without reality.[64] Arendt conceives of the "who" that is disclosed in action as a response to a question—Who are you?—posed to the newcomer by the world.[65] As to the nature of this "who," she draws on the image of "the Greek *daimon* who accompanies each man throughout life, who is his distinct identity," "always looking over his shoulder from behind and thus only visible to those he encounters."[66] In other words, this identity that we cannot help but reveal in speech and action, is not under our control; we disclose ourselves without being able to calculate beforehand who we reveal.[67] In acting we can surprise ourselves, and we do not always know who we are before we act. It is therefore risky and demands courage and trust.[68] The self is in other words relational through and through for Arendt, and what is unique about us (our *daimon*) is something that manifests itself in an intersubjective "in-between" space. To that point, she makes a provocative comparison in *The Life of the Mind* between our psychic life and our inner organs, and suggests that if action and speech were direct manifestations of our inner life, we would all act and speak alike, since our desires, needs, pains, and pleasures are no more unique than our inner organs.[69] Our inner lives must be articulated and deindividualized to a shape fit for public appearance in order to communicate the individual "who,"[70] and action and speech is therefore a revealing that creates identity and uniqueness rather than presuppose it.

Heidegger's Contempt for the Public

That Heidegger's existential analytic displays conspicuous blind spots in the description of intersubjectivity and the self-other relation is a fairly common criticism.⁷¹ While Heidegger is clear that the world is always a "with-world" (*Mitwelt*) and that *Mitdasein* (others) is "existentially constitutive for Being-in-the-world,"⁷² the actual descriptions of intersubjectivity in *Sein und Zeit* appear somewhat impoverished, and fall mainly into two types: that of a work-community (what Sartre would call a crew)⁷³ or the publicness dominated by *das Man*.⁷⁴ Heidegger's characterizations of *die Öffentlichkeit* is consistently pejorative, it is dominated by distantiality, averageness and levelling down, idle talk (*Gerede*), curiosity (*Neugier*), and ambiguity (*Zweideutigkeit*).⁷⁵ Although Heidegger acknowledges that our being-with others can take place in different modes, he does not provide any phenomenological account of how others can appear to us in various degrees of visibility *within* the everyday, since his descriptions are dominated by productive contexts rather than face-to-face relations. While *Mitsein* is a necessary condition for the significance of entities within the world (since both dealing with equipment and using language is unthinkable without a certain "averageness" inherent in social practices), Being-with-others is never seen as a condition for achieving authenticity, it is first *after* Dasein has become *eigentliches Selbstsein* that a more authentic relation to others is possible, far removed from "talkative fraternizing."⁷⁶

Arendt's claim is here exactly the reverse: "The revelatory [i.e., revealing the 'who' of somebody] quality of speech and action comes to the fore where people are *with* others, and neither for nor against them—that is in sheer human togetherness."⁷⁷ In so far as we can talk about authenticity in Arendt, it is as a specific mode of being with one another or *Miteinandersein*. The different basic activities of labor, work, and action let the world, ourselves, and others appear in different ways, and, while the being-together in labor and work erases individual uniqueness, speaking, acting, and judging (especially—but not only—in public) is the form of togetherness in which we appear to each other *qua men*, as Arendt phrases it.⁷⁸

Conditions and Actualizations

What Arendt calls "the original interdependence of action"⁷⁹ encapsulates the mutual dependence of the conditions of plurality and natality. They are—to speak Heideggerian—equiprimordial (*gleichursprünglich*) and we cannot establish a hierarchical foundational relation between them.⁸⁰ Arendt introduces the human condition of plurality as "the fact that men, not Man, live on the earth and inhabit the world."⁸¹ This is of course trivially true. However, as several commentators have pointed out, there is more to the concept of plurality than a mere multiplicity of human beings or qualitative differentiations (diversity) within a multiplicity. Plurality is not something that is just "present at hand," but something more akin to an achievement.[82] Loidolt has recently argued—quite convincingly in my opinion—that Arendt's conditions are not just empirical conditions but must be read as basic ways in which existence actualizes itself, or ways of "happening" of "factical life," to use the vocabulary of the early Heidegger. Life is actualized or enacted through labor,[83] worldliness through work, and plurality and natality through speech and action, and these basic activities open up what Loidolt calls different "meaning-spaces."[84] As concrete multiplicity and diversity, plurality is a "fact," but then there is how plurality is concretely experienced through specific forms of being with one another. Arendt links plurality to *uniqueness*, revealed by speech and action where human beings "can communicate themselves and not merely something."[85] Loidolt argues that uniqueness should be understood as each person's "being a perspective" as an embodied "openness to the world,"[86] which we all *are* as conscious subjects. However, this unique viewpoint is in need of articulation and expression and, not least, recognition by others in order to *appear as such*. Uniqueness can therefore only fully appear as a worldly reality in what Loidolt calls *actualized plurality*—a mode of being-with-one-another (*Miteinandersein*) where we speak, act, and judge with others as equals, that is, as a certain form of "we." If we return to the statement that action is the "actualization of natality," it points to an experience of existing as beginners: in acting we *appeal* to others through words and deeds and are *responded to* by them in turn in a common "space of appearances" created by actualized plurality in which we appear as *fully human* to each other. It is here that Arendt's valorization of the public and the political comes in: speaking and acting in a public space, as distinct and equal (in a political sense),[87] represent the fullest actualization of plurality and natality. There is of course a matter of more or less here: we cannot refrain totally from speaking and acting and still live a human life,[88] but not all instances of communication or action are genuine beginnings or reveals a "who." Speaking and acting in a deficient or inauthentic mode—what Arendt dubs *behavior* (acting in conformist, repetitive, and predictable ways)—does not reveal anything or introduce anything new. Action can be an actualization of natality when we affirm the beginning that we were (for others) in acting as nonsovereign beginners in a public sphere that *allows for plural uniqueness to appear*. By now we might provide an answer to how action is "like a second birth":

action—like birth—is a matter of *appearing to others who respond to this appearance*. Action can therefore be "like" a second birth because both the "first" and "second" birth is a relation of interdependence.

For Arendt, the "who"—although "plainly visible"—nevertheless retains a "curious intangibility." When we try to describe who somebody is, we tend to end up with describing traits and qualities—a "what," a type or a character.[89] The unique "who" (being-a-perspective) that shows itself in words and deeds escapes objectification, as it were. To the extent that we can talk about personal identity as a "tangible totality" at all, it is only in retrospect, as a story of the person's life.[90] The meaning of this totality remains unpredictable and inaccessible for the agent; I cannot know beforehand the outcome of my life story, and while stories (the results of action and speech) reveal an agent, this agent is not an author or producer.[91] I can thus never "own" or "be" myself as a totality. In contrast, Heidegger's rather complex descriptions of authenticity (*Eigentlichkeit*) as involving resoluteness, Self-constancy (*Selbständigkeit*), *potentiality-for-being-a-whole* (*Ganzseinkönnen*), and appropriation of what is most one's own, are—as mentioned above—a wholly internal affair and as such completely illusory for Arendt, since without acknowledgment by others we would not even be able to put faith in the way we appear to ourselves.[92] From her perspective it simply does not make sense to talk, like Heidegger does, about a "constancy of the Self" as "steadiness and steadfastness"[93] except as a relation to others, since it is the presence of actual concrete others "who confirm the identity between the one who promises and the one who fulfills."[94]

In short: The Arendtian response to Heidegger's *Eigentlichkeit*—the "who" of Dasein—is the Heideggerian Self turned inside out: not tacit or internal, but appearing, and intersubjective rather than intrasubjective. Our "who" is not under our control, and to the extent we can talk about it as a "totality" at all, this totality is always deferred. Arendt's conception of selfhood and identity is thus—unlike the Heideggerian version—profoundly worldly and in opposition to any notion of ownership.

Future: Closed and Open

Arendt suggests that Heidegger's thinking about death is based on a flawed assumption: "the idea that once I no longer exist my interest in what is must also come to an end. It is altogether characteristic of modern philosophy that so many thinkers have accepted this assumption innocently, as it were, and without closer inspection."[95] We could of course counter that Heidegger is quite clear that authentic existence is not something floating above everydayness; on the contrary, resoluteness pushes the resolute self into taking care of things and solicitous Being with others.[96] The problem is, however, that authenticity is a way of relating to one's *own* finitude. The authentic future as anticipation of death (*Vorlaufen-zum-Tode*) is *closed*,[97] Heidegger claims, in contrast to the everyday conception of time as endless on both sides. Ordinary, public time is infinite, because das Man *cannot* die, and "public time" belongs to everyone—and hence to nobody.[98] Originary time, Heidegger states, is finite: "Die ursprüngliche Zeit ist Endlich."[99] Existing as a whole in a specific way in which Dasein "stretches itself along" temporally, and since the "how" of authentic temporalizing is anticipation of death—the ownmost nonrelational possibility—authentic futurality becomes closed in on itself, excluding anything alien or external. This closure stands in tension, however, with the notion of Dasein and Mitsein as equiprimordial. While Being-in-the-world always implies Mitsein, the futural character of Dasein is only associated with a finite time that is exclusively one's own. As equiprimordial with Dasein, we would expect Mitsein to have an authentic temporal dimension as well—a "Mitzeit," if you like.[100] If others are an essential part of my Being-there—not merely as its "content" but as part of its formal structure—should not Dasein be able to be *toward* a time after its own death, a Being-toward-a-time-*after*-the end, a time when I am not?

Arendt's notion of "natality" points us precisely in this direction. As said above, it is the influx of newcomers that opens the future and makes our activities—action, work, labor, and preservation—meaningful here and now. *If* our temporal horizon were wholly finite, Arendt argues, the world would simply lose all reality,[101] since what makes the world real and a common concern for us is precisely that it transcends our "brief sojourn with it." This opening toward the future also carries with it an ethical demand—we are *responsible* for the world that we hand over to the next generation. The very unboundedness of action points to a time "after my end," since the consequences of my actions do not come to an end with my death, and the *meaning* of our lives are only "tangible" retrospectively. The future is therefore not closed in on itself, but that does not mean that it is infinite—merely that there is no absolute border between my future and the future of others. Arendt's comment in "What Is Existential Philosophy?" that death functions as "the guarantor that all that matters ultimately is myself"[102] might at first glance seem superficial and offhanded, but I think she puts her finger on an essential problem in Heidegger's account, namely, the equalizing of "being an issue" with "Umwillen seiner selbst." By linking futurity (ahead-of-itself) to Being-towards-death, care (*Sorge*) can be expressed as Dasein existing *for the sake of itself*.[103] Moreover, the "ownness" of existence gets an emphatic character through the pathos of nonrelationality and loneliness.[104] There is an essential, albeit subtle, difference between one's own existence "being an issue" (i.e., that Dasein always stands in some kind of understanding relationship to itself) and existing primarily *for the sake of* one's own individual existence.[105]

Finding Meaning

Heidegger's description of the world as a hermeneutical referential structure of equipmental relations is mirrored in Arendt's description of the "meaning-space" inhabited by *homo faber* (she even uses Heidegger's concepts of "in order-to" and "for-the-sake-of"),[106] but there is a hierarchy between work and action in *The Human Condition*, which has to do with the activities' capacity to create meaning. According to Arendt, the way work discloses the world is dominated by an instrumental, means-ends orientation, and she claims that this utilitarian attitude has become dominant in modernity. The inherent problem for the instrumental outlook is that it is unable to find a final end to the chain of means and ends, with the result that the "in order to" becomes the content of the "for the sake of," as she phrases it. In other words, meaningfulness is conflated with utility. However, utility established as meaning only generates meaninglessness. According to Arendt, the only solution to the limitless instrumentalization[107] within this outlook is the Kantian one, that is, to declare man as an end in himself. Heidegger does something similar in establishing Dasein (the being for which, in its Being, that very Being is essentially an issue) as an ultimate end, a "for-the-sake-of" that itself does not partake in the referential totality of means and ends.[108] Arendt's critique of the Heideggerian Self in *Sein und Zeit* is therefore double: on the one hand, Dasein as the ultimate "Umwillen seiner" is not a real analogue to the Kantian "end in itself," since the "for the sake of" when individualized in anticipation of death refers to one's *own* Dasein and not to humanity generally, and on the other hand, this move does not transcend the attitude of *homo faber*, and is therefore not able to solve the problem of meaninglessness. Not unlike the later Heidegger, Arendt points out that to establish man as an end in himself does not counteract the "limitless devaluation" and "instrumentalization of the whole world,"[109] because it is precisely this move that permits *homo faber* to "degrade nature and the world into mere means, robbing both of their independent dignity."[110] Productive comportment cannot discover meaning, only utility, and we can only be rescued from the meaninglessness inherent in *homo faber*'s means-ends orientation by the faculties of action and speech "which produce meaningful stories"[111] as a part of the web of human relationships. An important difference between Arendt and Heidegger is that for Arendt, *the very Being together in speech and action* (what we called "actualized plurality" above) is *the* "for-the-sake-of-itself" where meaningfulness can be found within a common space of appearances where we judge and talk about the world and what happens in it: "Men in the plural, that is men in so far as they live and move and act in this world, can experience meaningfulness only because they can talk with and make sense to each other and to themselves."[112] Labor and work are activities that can be performed in solitude and these activities do not really need language in order to be performed,[113] while speech is indispensable for acting in a public space. Action and speech disclose and illuminate the world according to other standards than utility or functionality—of beauty, greatness, virtuosity, and virtue, as well as the principles inherent in deeds worth remembering. It is when we "humanize the world by talking about it" that we can find meaning in it. The common "space of appearances" is a space where words can resonate, deeds "shine," and events be talked about and turned into stories.[114] What is for the sake of itself is meaningful, and political speech and action—the actualization of natality and plurality—is an inherently meaningful activity independent of any concrete "results."

On Being Human

In the "Letter on 'Humanism,'" Heidegger suggests that the humanity of the human being is not something *in* man, but must be sought elsewhere, and I think Arendt would agree—although not with Heidegger's answer as to *where* to find the "essence" of the human. According to Arendt, what we conceive of as essentially human, be it meaning, language, freedom, action, individuality, or selfhood are all *relational* phenomena that can only be fully developed in a *Miteinandersein* of actualized plurality. The reason she stresses that "natality, and not mortality, may be the central category of political, as distinguished from metaphysical, thought"[115] is that the "metaphorical" sense of natality (freedom as the capacity for action or spontaneity) is a phenomenon born from the *in-between* and not a property of the subject, Dasein, or Man in the singular. As she phrases it in *The Promise of Politics*:

> "[Freedom's] place of origin is never inside man, whatever that inside may be, nor is it in his will, or his thinking, or his feelings; it is rather in the space between human beings, which can arise only when distinct individuals come together, and continue to exist only as long as they remain together."[116]

Arendt (who self-admittedly had "joined the ranks of those who for some time now have been attempting to dismantle metaphysics, and philosophy with all its categories")[117] can thus be said to present us with a humanism that is nonmetaphysical in the sense that the locus of the human is not human nature or the subject, that is, our humanness is not something "present-at-hand" that resides "inside" the human being like intellect or compassion—but something that comes into existence in-between human beings. Referring to Jaspers, she suggests that there is a new, although not fully developed, approach to the concept of humanity in the concept of communication,[118] and it is a recurring theme for her that we *make* each other human[119] through the act of communicating that teaches us to see each other as unique viewpoints on a shared world: "We humanize what is going on in the world and in ourselves only by speaking of it, and in the course of speaking of it we learn to be human."[120] To see each other as human is in this sense an achievement, we are most humane when we have an attitude of trust, respect, openness and a willingness to share the world with others, but we cannot achieve this kind of *humanitas* in solitude.[121]

When Arendt takes pains to elaborate the obvious—that men, not Man inhabits the earth, that new human beings are constantly being born, and that actions cannot be undertaken alone, this is in line with the fundamental tenet of phenomenology as an "everyday anamnesis" (in Critchley's elegant phrase).[122] That is, the kind of thinking that points out what is normally passed over, that which is right under our noses, and therefore not normally noticed. When asking after the meaning of Being in *Sein und Zeit*, Heidegger's point of departure in concrete, "hands-on" dealings with tools and implements resulted in a groundbreaking new vocabulary for conceptualizing the tacit understanding inherent in our everyday practices. If we look at Heidegger's definitions of the human being in *Sein und Zeit* (as Dasein, as the being that understands Being, as Being-in-the-world, and as care) we could—from an Arendtian standpoint—argue that these general ontological determinations of the human way of being as "sense-makers" in fact *presuppose* natality and plurality. The overlooked and unnoticed that Arendt wants to illuminate is the fundamental relational and intersubjective character of all human reality and meaningfulness, and her claim is that this relationality must also be addressed when we ask what makes sense-making possible. This in-between is what is passed over by Heidegger, both in *Sein und Zeit* and in his later Being-historical thinking. Although many facets of Heidegger's thinking change after the so-called "turn" or *Kehre*, the relation between the essence of Dasein and Being is a constant, but in the "Letter on 'Humanism,'" we are told that all questions about "the humanity of the human" must be subordinated to the question about Being: "[W]hat is essential is not the human being but being."[123] Dasein is still thought as "thrown project," but the emphasis has now shifted squarely to the "thrownness" aspect. His deep suspicion of the public is, however, unchanged. Heidegger famously states, in the "Letter on 'Humanism,'" that "Language is the house of Being"; that "[i]n its home human beings dwell,"[124] and that "in thinking being comes to language." But he is—if anything—even more dismissive of the communicative aspect of language than in *Sein und Zeit*.[125] Neither before nor after the *Kehre* is there a source for new meaning in horizontal relations, action in concert or communicative *praxis*: "the clearing" is never public.

Notes

1. Martin Heidegger, *Sein und Zeit* (1927; repr., Tübingen: Niemeyer, 1986), 12; or *Being and Time*, trans. John Macquarrie and Edward Robinson (New York: Harper and Row, 1962), 32.

2. See Heidegger, *Sein und Zeit*, 17, 131, 183, 200; *Being and Time*, 38, 170, 227, 244.

3. Hannah Arendt, *Essays in Understanding, 1930–1954: Formation Exile and Totalitarianism*, ed. Jerome Kohn (New York: Schocken, 1994), 1.

4. Quoted in Elisabeth Young-Bruehl, *Hannah Arendt: For Love of the World* (New Haven, CT: Yale University Press, 2004), 405.

5. See Heidegger *Sein und Zeit*, 9; *Being and Time*, 29.

6. Thomas Sheehan, *Making Sense of Heidegger: A Paradigm Shift* (London: Rowman and Littlefield, 2015), xiv–xviii.

7. Hubert L. Dreyfus, *Being-in-the-World: A Commentary on Heidegger's Being and Time, Division I* (Cambridge, MA: MIT Press), 1991.

8. As I see it, the "being of beings" cannot be given a simple definition but must be seen as a complex relational structure encompassing intelligibility, mode

of givenness, and the fact that something is given in experience at all; that is, the being of an entity encompasses its "what," its "how," and its "that." In the case of a hammer, its "what-being" is "something-in-order-to-hammer-in-nails-with," but its "how-being" depends on how it shows up in a particular context as more or less handy or unhandy, depending on how I relate to it in light of my project.

9. Hannah Arendt, *The Human Condition* (1958; repr., Chicago: University of Chicago Press, 1989), 9. To the most general conditions "under which life is given to man on earth," Arendt adds man-made conditions created through our own activities, which possess the same conditional power as natural things.

10. The point of Arendt's etymologies is not to suggest that the original meaning of a word is somehow more "authoritative" in itself, but to reawaken an experience that has been lost: "The word [. . .] is something like a frozen thought that thinking must unfreeze." See Hannah Arendt, *Thinking*, vol. 1 of *The Life of the Mind* (New York: Harcourt Brace Jovanovich 1978), 171. She here echoes Heidegger's approach to the history of philosophy as a dismantling of rigidified concepts in order to get to original experiences, that is, what the early Heidegger meant by "destruction."

11. These texts are from Martin Heidegger, *Phänomenologische Interpretationen zu Aristoteles: Einführung in die phänomenologische Forschung* [winter semester 1921–22], vol. 61 of *Gestamtausgabe*, ed. Walter Bröcker and Käte Bröcker-Oltmanns (Frankfurt: Klostermann, 1985); "Phänomenologische Interpretationen zu Aristoteles: Anzeige der hermeneutischen Situation" [1922], in *Dilthey-Jahrbuch für Philosophie und Geschichte der Geisteswissenschaften* 6 (1989): 235–74; *Ontologie: Hermeneutik der Faktizität* [summer semester 1923], vol. 63 of *Gesamtausgabe*, ed. Käte Bröcker-Oltmanns (Frankfurt: Klostermann, 1988); *Grundbegriffe der aristotelischen Philosophie* [summer semester 1924], vol. 18 of *Gesamtausgabe*, ed. Mark Michalski (Frankfurt: Klostermann, 2002); *Platon: Sophistes* [winter semester 1924–25], vol. 19 of *Gesamtausgabe*, ed. Ingeborg Schüssler (Frankfurt: Klostermann, 1992).

12. Hannah Arendt, *Between Past and Future* (London: Penguin, 2006), 14.

13. See Jacques Taminiaux, *The Thrachian Maid and the Professional Thinker: Arendt and Heidegger* (New York: State University of New York Press, 1997), ix; and Dana Villa, *Arendt and Heidegger: The Fate of the Political* (Princeton, NJ: Princeton University Press, 1996), 115–17.

14. Arendt, *The Human Condition*, 247.
15. Arendt, *Essays in Understanding*, 163–88.
16. Arendt, *Essays in Understanding*, 181–82.
17. Arendt, *Essays in Understanding*, 186.
18. Arendt, *The Human Condition*, 9.
19. Arendt, *The Human Condition*, 8–9, 178.
20. Arendt, *Between Past and Future*, 171.
21. Arendt, *The Human Condition*, 178.
22. Arendt, *Between Past and Future*, 151.
23. Arendt, *The Human Condition*, 247.

24. See, for example, Richard J. Bernstein, "Provocation and Appropriation: Hannah Arendt's Response to Martin Heidegger," *Constellations* 4, no. 2 (1997): 162; Patricia Bowen-Moore, *Hannah Arendt's Philosophy of Natality* (London: Palgrave Macmillan, 1989), 23; Mary G. Dietz, "Hannah Arendt and Feminist Politics," in *Hannah Arendt: Critical Essays*, ed. Lewis P. Hinchman and Sandra K. Hinchman (New York: State University of New York Press 1994), 235.

25. Arendt, *The Human Condition*, 176.

26. Hannah F. Pitkin, *The Attack of the Blob: Hannah Arendt's Concept of the Social* (Chicago: University of Chicago Press, 1998), 308ff.

27. See Wolfhart Totsching, "Arendt's Notion of Natality: An Attempt at Clarification," *Ideas y Valores* 66, no. 165 (2017): 340–41.

28. Benhabib, Villa, and Birmingham all associate natality with *Geworfenheit*. See Seyla Benhabib, *The Reluctant Modernism of Hannah Arendt* (Oxford: Rowman and Littlefield, 2000), 109; Villa, *Arendt and Heidegger*, 141; Peg Birmingham, *Hannah Arendt and Human Rights: The Predicament of Common Responsibility* (Bloomington: Indiana University Press, 2006), 29.

29. Arendt, *Between Past and Future*, 169.

30. Arendt, *The Human Condition*, 8.

31. Compare: Heidegger, *Sein und Zeit*, 240, 265; *Being and Time*, 284, 309.

32. Arendt, *Between Past and Future*, 182; *The Human Condition*, 96–97.

33. Arendt, *The Human Condition*, 7, 20, 97.

34. Arendt suggests that Heidegger's concept of "world" gives "philosophical significance to structures of everyday life that are completely incomprehensible if man is not primarily understood as being together with others." See Arendt, "Concern with Politics in Recent European Philosophy," in *Essays in Understanding*, 443.

35. See, for example, *Sein und Zeit*, 74–75, 117; *Being and Time*, 105, 153.

36. See, for example, *Sein und Zeit*, 74–75, 117, 120; *Being and Time*, 105, 153, 156. However, we can find descriptions of the everyday that are far more similar to Arendt's approach in some of Heidegger's texts predating *Sein und Zeit*, for example, in *Ontologie: Hermeneutik der Faktizität*, 90–91.

37. Arendt, *The Human Condition*, 52.

38. Arendt, *The Human Condition*, 182–84.

39. Hannah Arendt, "On Humanity in Dark Times: Thoughts about Lessing," in *Men in Dark Times* (New York: Harcourt, 1968), ebook ed. (Boston: HMH, 1970), locations 417–19. See also *The Human Condition*, 204, 236.

40. Arendt, *The Human Condition*, 96–97.

41. Heidegger, *Sein und Zeit*, 240; *Being and Time*, 284.

42. Arendt, *Thinking*, in *The Life of the Mind*, 1:20.

43. Arendt, *The Human Condition*, 50, but also 51, 57. For a discussion of Arendt's debt to Husserl's transcendental intersubjectivity for her notion of reality as appearance to several subjects, see Sophie Loidolt, *Phenomenology of Plurality: Hannah Arendt on Political Intersubjectivity* (New York: Taylor and Francis, 2018), 162–67.

44. Arendt, *Thinking*, in *The Life of the Mind*, 1:20, 22.

45. This point is elaborated in Birmingham, *Hannah Arendt and Human Rights*, 23–29; Benhabib, *The Reluctant Modernism of Hannah Arendt*, 109, 137.

46. Hannah Arendt, *Crises of the Republic* (San Diego: Harcourt Brace, 1972), 87–88.

47. Totsching, "Arendt's Notion of Natality," 342. See also Benhabib, *The Reluctant Modernism of Hannah Arendt*, 112–13.

48. Arendt, *The Human Condition*, 246–47.

49. Robin May Schott, introduction to *Birth, Death, and Femininity: Philosophies of Embodiment*, ed. Robin May Schott (Bloomington: Indiana University Press, 2010), 8.

50. Arendt, *The Human Condition*, 55.

51. "Grundsein besagt damnach, des eigenstens Seins von Grund auf nicht mächtig sein." See Heidegger, *Sein und Zeit*, 284; *Being and Time*, 330.

52. Heidegger, *Sein und Zeit*, 275; *Being and Time*, 320.

53. Arendt, *The Human Condition*, 176–77. MY emphasis.

54. Arendt, *The Human Condition*, 204.

55. Arendt, *Willing*, in *The Life of the Mind*, 2:217; also Hannah Arendt, *On Violence* (New York: Harcourt, 1970), 44.

56. Arendt, *The Human Condition*, 190.

57. Arendt, *The Human Condition*, 190.

58. Hannah Arendt, *The Promise of Politics*, ed. Jerome Kohn (New York: Schocken Books, 2005), 56.

59. Arendt, *The Human Condition*, 192.

60. Arendt, *The Human Condition*, 234; also *Between Past and Future*, 163.

61. Heidegger, *Sein und Zeit*, 322; *Being and Time*, 369.

62. Heidegger, *Sein und Zeit*, 250; *Being and Time*, 294.

63. Heidegger, *Sein und Zeit*, 280, 296–97; *Being and Time*, 325, 343.

64. Arendt, *The Human Condition*, 199.

65. Arendt, *The Human Condition*, 178.

66. Arendt, *The Human Condition*, 179–80, 193.

67. Arendt, *The Human Condition*, 192.

68. Arendt, *Essays in Understanding*, 23.

69. Arendt, *Thinking*, in The *Life of the Mind*, 1:29, 34

70. Arendt, *The Human Condition*, 50.

71. See, for example, Michael Theunissen, *The Other: Studies in the Social Ontology of Husserl, Heiddeger, Sartre, and Buber*, trans. Christopher Macann (Cambridge, MA: MIT Press, 1984); Jürgen Habermas, "Work and Weltanschauung: The Heidegger Controversy from a German Perspective," *Critical Inquiry* 15, no. 2 (1989): 431–56; Taminiaux, *The Thrachian Maid and the Professional Thinker*; Jacques Taminiaux, *Heidegger and the Project of Fundamental Ontology*, trans. Michael Gendre (Albany: State University of New York Press, 1991); Emmanuel Levinas, *Totality and Infinity* (Pittsburg: Duquesne University Press, 1991).

72. Compare: Heidegger, *Sein und Zeit*, 118, 121, 125; *Being and Time*, 155, 157, 163.

73. Jean-Paul Sartre, *Being and Nothingness*, trans. Hazel E. Barnes (New York: Simon and Schuster, 1966), 332.

74. Heidegger's ambivalent portrayal of *das Man* and its possible political ramifications is one of the oldest debates among Heidegger commentators. I will not go into the details here, suffice it to say that one can be justified in claiming, with Bernstein, that Heidegger remained unable to properly conceptualize anything resembling plurality. See Bernstein, "Provocation and Appropriation."

75. Heidegger, *Sein und Zeit*, §27, §§35–38.

76. Heidegger, *Sein und Zeit*, 298; *Being and Time*, 344–45 [274]. Interestingly, we find a much closer resemblance to Arendt's position in an earlier text, *Grundbegriffe der aristotelischen Philosophie* (1924), where Heidegger, in §9, links the Aristotelian *logon echon* and *Miteinandersein* (*koinoia*). Heidgger here emphasizes that Being-with-One-Another (*koinoia*) is a fundamental mode of Being-there in the sense of Being-as-speaking-with-One-Another. For a comparison to Arendt, see Loidolt, *Phenomenology of Plurality*, 171–72.

77. Arendt, *The Human Condition*, 180.

78. See Arendt, *The Human Condition*, 176, 212.

79. Arendt, *The Human Condition*, 189.

80. "Das Phänomen der *Gleichursprünglichkeit* der konstitutiven Momente ist in der Ontologie oft mißachtet worden zufolge einer methodisch ungezügelten Tendenz zur Herkunftsnachweisung von allem und jedem aus einem einfachen Urgrund." See Heidegger, *Sein und Zeit*, 131. Arendt is more faithful to this warning than Heidegger himself, who in my opinion moves awfully close to a notion of *einfachen Urgrund* with originary temporality as an ultimate transcendental ground. See Anne Granberg, "'Die Seinsfrage' som et hypertranscendentalt spørsmål," in *Cassirer og Heidegger i Davos*, ed. Hein Berdinesen and Lars Petter Storm Torjussen (Oslo: Dreyer Forlag, 2013), s. 307–19.

81. Arendt, *The Human Condition*, 7.

82. Loidolt, *Phenomenology of Plurality*, 221–33; see also Bernstein, "Provocation and Appropriation," 160–66.

83. Loidolt points out that the term for actualized or enacted, used in the German version *Vita Activa*, is *Vollzug*, undoubtedly a notion of Heideggerian origin.

84. Loidolt, *Phenomenology of Plurality*, 129. In a similar vein, Hinchman and Hinchman have suggested that labor, work, and action should be read as existentials and not categories. Lewis P. Hinchman and Sandra K. Hinchman, "In Heidegger's Shadow: Hannah Arendt's Phenomenological Humanism," *Review of Politics* 46, no. 2 (1984): 197.

85. Arendt, *The Human Condition*, 176.

86. Loidolt here talks about a "specific form of non-objectifying experience of others" as the basic structure of political intersubjectivity. This "we" of plurality

is fragile, however, and "actualized plurality" is neither necessary nor automatic. See Loidolt, *Phenomenology of Plurality*, 178–79, 200.

87. Equality is thus not our natural state but an achievement, since we are not born equal but have the ability to make each other equal through artificial institutions. See Hannah Arendt, *On Revolution* (New York: Penguin, 1963), 21.

88. Arendt, *The Human Condition*, 176.

89. Arendt, *The Human Condition*, 181.

90. This is also why outcomes *do* matter. Arendt is sometimes read as if the outcome of an action is completely irrelevant, but outcomes are nevertheless an essential part of the structure of any story. See Roy T. Tsao, "Arendt against Athens: Rereading the Human Condition," *Political Theory* 30, no. 1 (2002): 97–123. However, what counts *more* than outcomes or results are the "principles" inherent in the action. It is the principles that "shine" and inspire through time, and a failed action might inspire future generations.

91. Arendt, *The Human Condition*, 184.

92. Arendt, *Essays in Understanding*, 174.

93. Heidegger, *Sein und Zeit*, 322; *Being and Time*, 369.

94. Arendt, *The Human Condition*, 237.

95. Arendt, *Essays in Understanding*, 174.

96. See Heidegger, *Sein und Zeit*, 123, 398; *Being and Time*, 160, 344.

97. Heidegger, *Sein und Zeit*, 330; *Being and Time*, 378–79.

98. "Das Man stirbt nie, weil es nicht sterben *kann*, sofern der Tod je meiner ist und eigentlich nur in der vorlaufenden Entschlossenheit existenziell verstanden wird." See Heidegger, *Sein und Zeit*, 424; *Being and Time*, 477.

99. Heidegger, *Sein und Zeit*, 331; *Being and Time*, 380.

100. One could argue that the notion of cohistorizing and *Geschick*, in the infamous §74, serves this function in *Sein und Zeit*, and historicity as a kind of collective "Mitzeit" becomes more pronounced in Heidegger's lectures in the 1930s. However, this "with-time" is linked to a notion of the German *Volk* as a "self," marked by the same preoccupation with the "own" and the "un own" and lack of plurality that characterizes Heidegger's discussion of *Eigentlichkeit* in *Sein und Zeit*. For a striking example, see Martin Heidegger, *Logik als die Frage nach dem Wesen der Sprache* [summer semester 1934], vol. 38 of *Gesamtausgabe*, ed. Günter Seubold (Frankfurt: Klostermann, 1998), 128.

101. Arendt, *The Human Condition*, 55, 120.

102. Arendt, *Essays in Understanding*, 180–81.

103. Compare: Heidegger, *Sein und Zeit*, 181, 192–93, 330; *Being and Time*, 225, 236–37, 378.

104. See Heidegger, *Sein und Zeit*, 250, 263; *Being and Time*, 294, 308.

105. It is my hunch that the problematic and quasi-solipsistic traits of the authentic Self in *Sein und Zeit* results from Heidegger's attempt to give the meaning of Being a unitary ground in originary temporality, where the analysis of death,

authenticity and selfhood is subservient to this search for an ultimate transcendental ground. Heidegger tries, so to speak, to do too much at once in combining fundamental ontology with an account of personal identity. When finite temporality is also thought as what makes up the "subjectivity of the subject," as he phrases it a year later—in *Metaphysische Anfangsgründe der Logik im Ausgang von Leibniz* [summer semester 1928], vol. 26 of Gesamtausgabe, ed. Klasu Held (Frankfurt: Klostermann, 1978), 205–6; and in *Phänomenologische Interpretation von Kants Kritik der reinen Vernunft*, vol. 25 of *Gesamtausgabe*, ed. Ingtraud Görland (Frankfurt: Klostermann, 1977), 394—it makes sense that he should later comment that the path taken in *Sein und Zeit* was in danger of "unwillingly becoming merely another entrenchment of subjectivity." See, for instance, Martin Heidegger, *Nietzsche*, vol. 4, *Nihilism*, trans. David Farrell Krell (New York: HarperCollins, 1982), 141; Martin Heidegger, *Überlegungen II–VI (Schwarze Hefte 1931–1938)*, vol. 94 of *Gesamtausgabe*, ed. Peter Trawny (Frankfurt: Klostermann, 2014), 41–43, 74–76, 81–82. Another example of this overzealous search for unity can be seen in Heidegger's claim, in §70 of *Sein und Zeit*, that space is founded on time rather than being equiprimordial with it. Heidegger's turning from temporality to thinking in terms of "place" is discussed by Jeff Malpas in this volume.

106. Arendt, *The Human Condition*, 154.
107. Arendt, *The Human Condition*, 157.
108. See Heidegger, *Sein und Zeit*, 84, 192; *Being and Time*, 116–17, 236.
109. Arendt, *The Human Condition*, 157.
110. Arendt, *The Human Condition*, 156.
111. Arendt, *The Human Condition*, 236.
112. Arendt, *The Human Condition*, 4.
113. Arendt, *The Human Condition*, 179.
114. Arendt, *Between Past and Future*, 154–55.
115. Arendt, *The Human Condition*, 9.
116. Arendt, *The Promise of Politics*, 170.
117. Arendt, *Thinking*, in *The Life of the Mind*, 1:212.
118. Arendt, *Essays in Understanding*, 186.
119. Arendt, *The Human Condition*, 176, 204, 212, 236. See also "On Humanity in Dark Times: Thoughts about Lessing," and "Karl Jaspers: A Laudatio," in *Men in Dark Times*.
120. Arendt, *Men in Dark Times*, ebook locations 421–22.
121. See Arendt, *Men in Dark Times*, ebook locations 1361–63, 271–72.
122. Simon Critchley and Reiner Schürmann, *On Heidegger's Being and Time* (London: Routledge, 2008), 47.
123. Martin Heidegger, "Letter on 'Humanism,'" trans. Frank A. Capuzzi, in *Pathmarks*, ed. William McNeill (Cambridge: Cambridge University Press, 1998), 254.
124. Heidegger, "Letter on 'Humanism,'" 239.
125. Heidegger, "Letter on 'Humanism,'" 242.

Chapter Twelve

Having Some Regard for Human Frailty

On Finitude and Humanity

KATHERINE WITHY

> You'll never be a first-class human being [. . .] until you've learned to have some regard for human frailty.
>
> —C. K. Dexter Haven, character in *The Philadelphia Story*

As Heidegger presents it in the existential analytic in *Being and Time*, the primary challenge of being the sort of entity that we are is having the right sort of regard for our frailty. We usually think of human frailties as arising from the vulnerabilities of the body—to injury, sickness, debility, and death. But for Heidegger our frailty is not tied to our embodiment, since we are not essentially bodies but instead cases of Dasein, the entity that understands being. The understander of being will be vulnerable in a distinctively existential-ontological way. I argue that our existential-ontological finitude rests not on our human bodies but on our being-amidst-entities and being-with-others, and I suggest—by appeal to the 1940 film *The Philadelphia Story*—that having proper regard for this finitude is what allows us to manifest the very best of our humanity.

Being a Case of Dasein

The existential analytic analyzes the being of Dasein, the entity that we each are.[1] Who are we? "We" are, first of all, readers of Heidegger's text. With him, we raise the question of the meaning of being. We can do so because we already have a sense of what it is to be: what it is for an entity to be what it is (rather than something else), what it is for an entity to be there (rather than not), and what it is for the entity as such to be at all. We are the entities that understand entities in their being.[2] Even those of us who do not practice ontology or read Heidegger understand entities in their being, if we go about making sense of them in terms of that and what they are. In this broader sense, "we" are sense-making entities.

From the fact that Dasein is the entity that "we" each are, and the fact that "we" are each also human beings, I do not conclude, with (for example) Farin, that "'Dasein' refers to individual human beings."[3] To conclude this, we would need to establish that the "we" of humanity is coextensive with the "we" who are sense-makers, and this remains to be established. Indeed, there is good reason to think that these two modes of "we" are not coextensive. There are human beings who do not or cannot make sense of entities: very young infants, people with severe cognitive disabilities, people in certain types of comas. These human beings are not cases of Dasein. Further, it is likely that there are times in our own lives when we are human beings but not cases of Dasein—as when, for example, we enter non-REM sleep.[4] Non-REM sleep involves no sense-making activity, so when we are in this stage of sleeping our being Dasein has been suspended in some way. Finally, we can at least imagine cases of Dasein who are not human beings—as does every science fiction story in which intelligent (i.e., sense-making) alien life figures. These are initial reasons to believe that "Dasein" and "human being" are not necessarily coextensive.

That the identity of "Dasein" and "human being" cannot be assumed is obscured by Heidegger's frequent use of shorthands such as "human Dasein."[5] Heidegger casually equates the human and Dasein throughout *Being and Time*[6] (although he later denies this).[7] After *Being and Time* (as before it), he drops "Dasein" and speaks directly of the human being (*Mensch*). But this complicates rather than simplifies matters. For it is not always clear what "human being" refers to. Sometimes, for example, it refers not to us but instead to our essence (and sometimes to the essence of a specifically Western "us").[8] The same problem afflicts "Dasein," which also sometimes names not us but our essence.[9] I suspect that, like many of

Heidegger's terms, both "Dasein" and "human being" do not mean what we ordinarily take them to mean but are formally indicative. Both, I suggest, indicate "us"—whomever "we" turns out to encompass—with regard to our being as sense-makers. Thus, "when we designate this entity with the term 'Dasein,' we are expressing not its 'what' (as if it were a table, house, or tree) but its being."[10] The point is to direct us to the fact that we are not *homo sapiens*, persons, or consciousnesses but entities that make sense of entities, understanding them in their being. It may turn out to be the case that this entity's "way of being is proper only to the human being," but that is an empirical claim, true only "as far as our experience shows."[11] The sense-making entity might be most familiar to us as the human being, but—like Kant's practically rational agent—it is not the same as it.

My aim is not to establish that "Dasein" and "human being" are not coextensive. That would take a lot more argument and evidence. I want only to loosen up the assumed connection between the two in order to suggest that thinking of us as human beings is different from thinking of us as cases of Dasein. Thinking of us as sense-making entities *displaces* or *replaces* some of the features that we are accustomed to taking as essential to our humanity—and, in particular, to our finitude. The helplessness and rapid development of infancy, for example, are important dimensions of human life—but they are not central to the existential analytic, since the infant is not yet a case of Dasein. Sleeping without dreaming is something that we do as human beings, but it is not something that a case of Dasein does.

The reason is that dreamlessly sleeping belongs to our human embodiment rather than to our sense-making. As the sense-maker, a case of Dasein makes sense of that and what things are (i.e., discovers entities, or interprets) on the basis of who it takes itself to be.[12] Taking oneself to be someone (i.e., projecting onto an ability-to-be) involves committing to some identity and throwing oneself forward into the project of going about *as* that sort of figure—as a seamstress, a sailor, or a student. Going about as a seamstress, a sailor, or a student consists in making sense of things as such figures do: as buttonholes (to be sewn), berths (to be docked in), or books (to be read). One does this by reading books, docking in berths, and sewing buttonholes. Dreamlessly sleeping, however, is not a way of going about as a seamstress, sailor, or student. It is not something that we do as a case of Dasein, even if it is something that we do as an embodied human being.

In fact, the human body is so displaced in the existential analytic that not only is it not a central site of our finitude, but it is not even required by Dasein's way of being. This is perhaps a surprising claim. It seems to many that the human body is everywhere present, unacknowledged, in Heidegger's account of Dasein's engaging with the ready-to-hand. What is ready-to-hand is a tool, and Heidegger's primary examples are hand tools: the hammer, needle, door latch.[13] One would think that such hand tools require a hand. But strictly, reference to the hand is not what makes something ready-to-hand.[14] Heidegger argues that what is ready-to-hand is what it is by virtue of mutually referring to other entities—such as nails, thread, and doors—within an entire context of practical intelligibility. This context is itself organized and made intelligible by reference to the identity that a case of Dasein has taken up[15]—say, that of a sailor. The project of being a sailor brings with it a context of paraphernalia, each item of which refers to others, and through which the sailor lives out their life as a sailor. Thus, needles and thread repair sails and clothing, hammers secure planks and hammocks with nails, and so on, all in the service of being a sailor. What makes the needle or hammer ready-to-hand is its role in the sailor's world, not that it is wielded by a hand.

Of course, *wielding* the needle or hammer requires a hand. One might extrapolate: all comporting toward ready-to-hand entities is embodied, skillful coping of the sort that we find in craft production and manual trades. But the extrapolation fails, because not everything that is ready-to-hand is a hand tool. Thus, I disagree with Hubert Dreyfus and others who take comporting toward entities to be embodied, skillful coping.[16] As Sacha Golob has argued, Dreyfus's interpretation of Heidegger reads too much Merleau-Ponty into his text.[17] Heidegger's account of the ready-to-hand is not an account of unreflective, embodied coping but instead an account of meaning. What is ready-to-hand is so not because it is wielded by a hand but because of its role in the life of the sailor, student, or seamstress. Following Aristotle,[18] Heidegger distinguishes two broad ways in which ready-to-hand entities can be coordinated with the project of a case of Dasein: they can be usable or detrimental—a help or hindrance—to it.[19] Thus the ready-to-hand includes not only hand tools but whatever can help or hinder: traffic jams, lighting conditions, bank deposits, deadlines, emotional resilience, conceptual distinctions, and so on. It requires neither hand nor body to comport toward deadlines or conceptual distinctions. While a body might be an ontic condition of there *being* traffic jams, lighting conditions, and emotional resilience, comporting toward these helps and hindrances is not a matter of embodied, skillful coping with one's hands, or any other body part.

Even Dasein's essential spatiality is analyzed in a way that displaces the importance of the human body. To be spatial is (1) to bring things near, by *desevering* or *circumspective bringing-close*, and (2) to be directionally oriented.[20] Heidegger discusses human Dasein's directionality in terms of its orientation towards left and right,[21] but he makes clear that directionality as such concerns how things are intelligibly oriented or placed within a meaningful world.[22] This is the orientation that we track, for example, when we draw mind maps. We see the same focus on meaning and displacement of embodied spatiality in the account of bringing entities close. One might assume that such proximity must necessarily be bodily, but—again—Heidegger understands it in terms of the space of meaning opened up by projecting on some identity. He gives the example of a friend approaching, who is existentially closer to us than the very street under our feet. He explains:

> If Dasein, in its concern, brings something close by, this does not signify that it fixes something at a spatial position with a minimal distance from some point of the body. When something is close by, this means that it is within the range of what is proximally ready-to-hand for circumspection.[23]

If to be ready-to-hand is to be a help or hindrance to a case of Dasein living out its identity, then to be *proximally* ready-to-hand is to be an *immediately relevant* help or hindrance. The approaching friend is closer to us than the street because she is more immediately relevant to who we are trying to be. (Of course, the friend is not an entity ready-to-hand but another case of Dasein. Heidegger does not seem to notice this difference—perhaps because the proximity of the proximate ready-to-hand entity does not differ from the proximity of the proximate case of Dasein.) To be proximate is to be immediately relevant, but being immediately relevant does not depend on proximity in space—as pay cheques, deadlines, and marriage proposals well attest. So too, bringing something close—that is, making it relevant to my immediate concern—does not require that I inhabit physical space. Heidegger allows it to be carried out "purely cognitively,"[24] for instance; no body required. All that Dasein's spatiality requires is commitment to an identity, and the "space" of mattering that that commitment opens up.

So, neither comporting toward the ready-to-hand nor being spatial requires that a case of Dasein have a body. Of course, "Dasein harbors the intrinsic possibility for being factically dispersed into bodiliness."[25] But nothing in the existential analytic *requires* a body, even if Heidegger's examples do.[26] It follows that there may be cases of Dasein, such as artificial intelligences, that are not embodied at all. (Whether there actually are is, of course, an empirical question—as is whether artificial intelligence is even possible.) Such cases of Dasein would be very different from us, and we likely need the help of science fiction storytelling even to begin to imagine them—whether they are distributed networks of intelligence, cosmic consciousnesses, or entities living outside of space-time. They will not wield hammers or approach friends on the street, but they will have their own (scarcely conceivable) modes of comporting toward what helps and hinders their projects. Committing to such projects and making sense of things in terms of them (and, thereby, living out Dasein's distinctive temporal structure) is what makes for a case of Dasein.

It is such disclosing and discovering being-in-the-world that makes a case of Dasein "alive"[27] in an existential-ontological, rather than a biological, sense. And that means, too, that it is our being-in-the-world, as cases of Dasein, that makes *us* alive, in addition to our "abysmal bodily kinship with the beast."[28] Heidegger associates life with being-in-the-world rather than with "dependen[ce] on a fragile material body," as (for instance) Martin Hägglund does.[29] Hägglund argues that for a "form of life [to be] intelligible as *living*," it must make an effort to maintain itself, and he holds that an effort at maintenance presupposes a fragile body. But Hägglund's reasoning is flawed: while an effort to maintain something requires that that thing be fragile, it does not require that that thing be material or embodied. To be alive is quite plausibly to be required to make the effort to maintain oneself, yet for Heidegger that effort goes into a living that is not biological but meaningful. "Life is a being-in-a-world."[30] And life is a being-in-a-world such that "*in its being as such, this very being is a question.*"[31] The struggle of being-in-the-world as a form of living is the struggle of committing to being who one is. It is not the struggle against bodily mortality but the struggle of commitment. What, then, necessitates this struggle, if not a fragile body? What finitude or fragility attends the effort that we make to maintain our lives as committed cases of Dasein?

Being Finite

We saw that an entity is ready-to-hand by virtue of helping or hindering a life project. This is true whether or not that entity is brought close so as to be immediately relevant to that project. If it is brought close, however, a further possibility is opened up: it might come so close that it touches or moves us. To be touched or moved by something is for it to be the object of a mood or emotion and, so, for that entity to matter.[32] What matters (most) to a sailor, for instance, is the weather. Foul weather moves her to fear, while she is moved to hope by fair weather and fair winds. Fair winds hasten progress to the destination, and fair weather permits repairs and relaxation. Relaxation, repairs, and getting to one's destination quickly all help her to be a sailor successfully. What enables them is thus an object of hope. Foul weather, in contrast, is an object of fear because it threatens life, limb, ship, and cargo, and losing one's cargo, ship, limb, or life might be the end of a sailor's ability to be a sailor.

In fearing, something that is ready-to-hand *qua* detrimental—in this case, foul weather—"reaches what is threatened [. . .] with definite regard to a special factical ability-to-be."[33] Moods such as fear take what has been brought close in existential spatiality and *bring us back to*[34] our life project as something that is put at stake by that thing.[35] Thus it is when the sailor's ability to be a sailor is put at risk by a storm that she fears the storm. A storm that is not an existential risk is not an object of fear—even though it may be immediately relevant and a hindrance of some sort. Even though it is proximately ready-to-hand as detrimental, a mild storm does not *matter*. A storm matters only when it puts at stake for the sailor the very fact *that* she is a sailor and that she *has* a sailor's life to go on living.[36] It matters, that is, when it puts at stake Dasein's thrown ability-to-be.

A bad storm puts the sailor at risk of existential death. This is not to say that the sailor might perish on the high seas. "Perishing" is the type of dying that befalls biological things, including *Homo sapiens*, but not cases of Dasein.[37] Cases of Dasein do demise, which I take to be a sort of social death.[38] Macquarrie and Robinson point out that Heidegger's term, *Ableben*, has legalistic connotations, which suggests that demise is the set of events in which a community releases one of its members—informing the coroner, holding a funeral, passing assets to one's heirs, and so on.[39] In this sense, our sailor might demise to her friends and family if she is counted lost at sea, even if she does not perish but lives on in an isolated port. But as long as she continues to live out her life as a sailor, she has not yet died in the way that Dasein dies. What it means to say that Dasein dies is disputed in the scholarship.[40] What stand one takes on the question depends in part on what one thinks Dasein *is*. I have argued that Dasein's living is not a matter of its biological embodiment but of its being-in-the-world—committing to a project and making sense of entities on the basis of the space of meaning thereby opened up. If that is what living is, then dying is some version of no longer being able to do *that*. If this is right, then for our sailor to die is for her no longer to be able to be a sailor and make sense of things in a sailory sort of way. Perhaps she has not perished or demised but has recklessly lost her cargo in a storm, or done something dishonorable and against the sailor's code. If either of these eventualities make it such that our sailor can no longer go on as a sailor, then she has died an existential-ontological death.

Existential death is the constant, imminent, certain possibility of Dasein's own impossibility.[41] It is the constant possibility that entities ready-to-hand will make it impossible to go on as a sailor, or seamstress, or student. This constant possibility is less of an event that might come to pass—although, it is that, too—and more of a permanent vulnerability that belongs to the structure of Dasein's being. Such existential risk arises not from biological embodiment but from the fact that Dasein, in carrying out its projects, depends on other entities. When Heidegger explains what it is to be amidst (*bei*) entities, he finds that such facticity "implies that an entity 'within-the-world' has being-in-the-world in such a way that it can understand itself as bound up in its 'destiny' with the being of those entities which it encounters within its own world."[42] We live our lives in concert with other entities, on which the success, failure, development, and character of our life projects depend.[43] It is because we depend on entities in this way that existential death belongs to us as Dasein.

But being-amidst-entities is not the only ground of existential death. We are also subject to existential death because we are amidst entities *with others*. I mentioned earlier that our sailor might have done something dishonorable and against the sailor's code. Because of this, the crew might reject her—in fact, all crews might reject her. In the best case, she is a sailor without a crew, and in the worst case, she is no longer a sailor at all. She has died an existential death. Alternatively, our sailor might breach no sailor's norm but the sailing profession and lifestyle might become obsolete—perhaps because of increasing automation. In that case, it becomes impossible for anyone, including our sailor, to be a sailor. All sailors then die an existential death.

Being-with-others subjects Dasein to existential death because, first, being recognized by others is part of what it takes to be living out a particular life project. One cannot *be* a sailor unless the crew—or any crew, and people in general—recognize one as such. To be recognized *as* a sailor is for one's day-to-day goings-about to be given uptake *as* the sort of goings-about that characterize a sailor. One must be seen to do what a sailor does. One might do this poorly and, so, be a *bad* sailor—perhaps by swearing ineptly, or tying knots badly, or following orders too slowly. But to refuse any order, to not know any knots, or to blush when words turn blue—well, in that case, no one would think you a sailor at all. Nor would you be one.

We need others to recognize us as meeting the standards for who we are trying to be, and we also need others for those very standards to be. Whether the sailor's code is a written rule book or a set of unspoken social norms (or both), it is constituted, instituted, and revised socially. Thus, while it might be up to me whether I am a sailor rather than a seamstress or a student, it is not up to me what it takes to *be* a sailor, a seamstress, or a student. It is in this sense that Dasein most fundamentally "belongs to" and "stands in subjection to" others[44]—not only in that it falls prey to fashions and trends, but in that it depends on others for the normative standards governing its life projects. This dependence is nowhere more apparent than when the standards change. If swearing ceases to be part of being a sailor, then no individual's defiant cursing will change that. Or, if automation renders the identity obsolete, the fact that there are no intelligible standards for being a sailor is a fact that belongs to the community. No mariner can stand as a counter-example to it.

The community broadly and the crew specifically are grounds of our sailor's existential death, alongside the weather. In general, the weather symbolizes the ways in which ready-to-hand entities can make it impossible to go on as who we are. Entities can withdraw their support for our projects or actively undermine our ability to carry them out. Notice that this existential death based on being-amidst-entities resembles perishing, in which the biological body withdraws life support. So too, existential death based on being-with-others, in which others cease to recognize us as who we are, resembles demise, in which the community constitutes us as deceased. And, just as perishing and demise frequently travel together, so too an existential death might be attributable to both ready-to-hand entities and other cases of Dasein. Indeed, the one might cause the other. For example, Jonathan Lear argues that the Crow people might have experienced a Heideggerian existential-ontological death at the hands of European colonizers.[45] This death was brought about by particular detrimental ready-to-hand entities—namely, laws passed by the United States government, the violence that enforced those laws, and the social geography of reservations—which, in turn, rendered obsolete traditional social identities and, so, made it impossible to recognize one another in terms of who they were trying to be. When others cannot recognize you as who you are, and entities do not help you to live out your life as who you are, then you cannot be who you are. This impossibility of being who you are is your death.[46]

Dasein dies, then, not because it inhabits a fragile body but because it is amidst entities, with others. These together are its essential dependence and vulnerability, and, so, Dasein's proper finitude. Now we can finally ask: What does it take to have the right regard for this finitude? And how will having this right regard help us to manifest the best of our humanity?

Being in Love

In addition to fearing and hoping, our sailor loves. She loves her crew, she loves the sea, and she loves the sailor's life. Loving the sailor's life, in fact, consists in loving one's crew and loving the sea. By "loving the sea," I mean not only loving the ocean—its boundless, traversable expanse, its tides and swells, its changing colors—but loving the entire region of ready-to-hand entities that come with a life on the ocean. Some of these will help the sailor to be a sailor, some will hinder her, and some of those will even threaten existential death. Our sailor loves them all. Loving one's crew also requires accepting both the "good" and the "bad": criticism as well as esteem, normative constancy and clarity as well as change and obscurity—and even change and criticism that amount to existential death. In thus embracing others and entities, including as sources of existential death, our sailor faces up to the fact that her life as a sailor is made both possible and vulnerable by its being-amidst-entities and its being-with-others. Embracing that—loving the sailor's life—is having proper regard for Dasein's finitude.[47]

Such loving regard is not any sort of affect, positive or otherwise. It is instead "the essential will for what is of the essence."[48] It wills for the object of love—the beloved—that it or they come into and persist in their essence, as what or who they are. To love others is to allow them to *be* others, and that means: to recognize their normative authority with regard to the standards for counting as a sailor (or a seamstress, or a student)—both what the standards are, and whether one meets them. So too, to love entities is to allow them to *be* what they are, whether they are helps or hindrances, and even whether they are existential threats. It might seem perverse to allow an existential threat to be as it is. But allowing a storm, for example, to be what it is does not mean wishing for it, pursuing it, or not preparing for it. Allowing a storm to be a storm in fact consists in (among other things) taking the appropriate precautionary measures and trying to avoid it as much as possible. Appropriate respect for and fear of the weather and water are part of the love of the sea, which the sailor loves for both better and worse.

A love that frees entities for their being, allowing them to show themselves as they are, is a specifically phenomenological love. On the one hand, this loving is the special task of the philosopher or phenomenologist.[49] On the other hand, freeing entities for their being is precisely the sense-making that is the distinctive mark of any case of Dasein. So, there is a sense in which every case of Dasein loves others (i.e., is characterized by solicitude[50]) and loves a region of entities ready-to-hand (i.e., is characterized by concern[51]). Every sailor loves the sea. And yet, some sailors do not fear the storm, in the sense that they do not acknowledge the ways in which entities ready-to-hand are detrimental to their project of being a sailor and put them at risk of existential death. Like Aristotle's rash and hopeful soldiers, they overestimate their own abilities, "think[ing] they are stronger and nothing could happen to them."[52] Taking oneself—that is, one's life-defining project—to be invulnerable to ready-to-hand entities is failing to acknowledge one's essential dependence on entities ready-to-hand and failing to face up to the possibility of existential death. Similarly, one fails to face up to the possibility of existential death at the hands of others if one insists that being who one is is entirely up to one's decision: *I am a sailor, even if all crews reject me*; or, *I am a sailor, even if there are no more sailors*. Not every sailor is willing to accept the potential obsolescence of the sailor's life or the possibility of being rejected by the seafaring world. But living with these possibilities and, so, the possibility of existential death amounts to recognizing one's being as amidst entities and with others. In thus recognizing itself and becoming transparent to itself,[53] a case of Dasein frees itself, as an entity, for its own finite being. It loves itself, in both its ability and its vulnerability.

Committing to a life-defining project, such as being a sailor, in full recognition of its vulnerability—and, so, the possible necessity of having to give it up—is what Heidegger calls "anticipatory resoluteness." A case of Dasein resolves upon a way of life while anticipating (but not awaiting) existential death. Having this proper regard for its finitude makes a case of Dasein authentic. And, perhaps surprisingly, being an authentic case of Dasein in turn allows us, as human cases of Dasein, to be first-class human beings. I thus conclude by returning to our humanity.

Becoming a First-Class Human Being

In the "Letter on 'Humanism,'" Heidegger complains that we do not think "the *humanitas* of the human being high enough" if we do not think ourselves as cases of Dasein, in our existential-ontological openness.[54] I have defended a version of this point in this chapter, by showing how the existential analytic displaces the body and identifies a more profound finitude in Dasein's existential structure. Now, however, I want to suggest that Heidegger does not think our humanity quite *far* enough. By pushing his analysis a little further, we can recapture the core idea that is traditionally associated with our humanity. To show this, I turn to *The Philadelphia Story* (which I quoted at the outset) and its portrayal of coming to "have some regard for human frailty."[55] Human frailty is represented in the film by drunkenness, both the loss of self-control in inebriation and the loss of the self in addiction. Other sorts of vulnerabilities are mentioned throughout, but overall the film leaves it open precisely what our true vulnerabilities are. What it does insist on is that coming to accept one's own and others' frailties is what it takes to love, and further, that such love opens the possibility of claiming our full humanity.

Tracy Lord comes to "feel like a human being" after a night of drunkenness, emotional vulnerability, and possible premarital infidelity. She realizes that she is not the "tower of strength" and invulnerability that she (perhaps despite herself) took herself to be. She is instead needy, vulnerable, and dependent. In particular, Tracy finds that alcohol can negatively affect her and that she depends on the esteem and recognition of others in order to be who she is. Interpreted existentially-ontologically, this amounts to recognizing her finitude as amidst entities and with others. This is Tracy's authentic self-disclosing or self-loving.

As she comes to love herself in this way, Tracy is also able to love others. This love of others differs from the love that I discussed in the previous section, which involved recognizing others as normative authorities. That sort of love uncovers someone as a representative of *das Man* (an "other" in Heidegger's technical sense[56]). It is different from uncovering someone as a case of Dasein. Doing that requires uncovering someone in their existential structure, and especially in their vulnerable being-amidst-entities and being-with-others. Thus Tracy, first, allows her father the need for admiration from others that led him to infidelity and, so, uncovers him in his being-with-others. This repairs their relationship and restores her filial love. Second, Tracy rekindles her love for her ex-husband, C. K. Dexter Haven, who had previously repulsed her with his dependence on alcohol. Dexter no longer drinks but he needs Tracy to have some "understanding of [his] deep and gorgeous thirst"—that is, of his risky being-amidst-entities. In acknowledging Dexter's vulnerability to entities and her father's dependence on others, Tracy can be interpreted as recognizing them as amidst entities and with others, and, so, as cases of Dasein. This loving uncovering is plausibly what Heidegger calls "authentic solicitude," which "pertains essentially to authentic care—that is, to the existence of the other, not to a '*what*' with which he is concerned; it helps the other to become transparent to himself *in* his care and to become *free for* it."[57]

But the film takes Tracy one step beyond authentic solicitude when she remarries Dexter. Why must she marry him rather than simply love him? The film ends immediately prior to the couple's vows, which would have presumably included a commitment to remain together "in good times and bad" or to love one another "for better or worse." I invoked the latter phrase when I spoke of loving the sea as accepting that region of entities as including both helps and hindrances, and I hinted at the former when I described accepting others as accepting the good (esteem, praise) with the bad (criticism, rejection, obsolescence). Authentic solicitude goes beyond these by uncovering another case of Dasein as themselves "bound up in [their] destiny with the being of" ready-to-hand entities and others,[58] and, so, as themselves subject to both good times and bad. I want to suggest that the commitment of a marriage vow takes this one step further: in it, one commits to taking on the helps and hindrances of another. It says not merely, *I will be there for you through fair weather and foul*, but instead: *Let what counts as fair and foul weather for you count so for me, too*. And it is in this, I will suggest, that we find our humanity. We also move beyond the account of what it takes to be us that Heidegger gives. As I have told it here, that account holds that a case of Dasein is open only to those types of ready-to-hand entities that are coordinated with the identity that it takes up. It shares this world of meaningful entities with those with whom it shares an identity, and with those with socially-coordinated identities (port workers, weather forecasters, rope makers). This is a shared world, yet it is rather solipsistic. I fear the storm because it is a threat to me, and you fear the storm because it is a threat to you. The storm is a threat to each of us, and there is a sense in which we fear it together. But—and Heidegger is explicit about this—I can never fear the storm as a threat to *you*.[59] I can fear it only as a threat to myself, whether to my ability to be me or to my ability to continue my relationship with you.[60]

Yet every day we distinguish this sort of selfish fear from a genuinely com-passionate or sym-pathetic fear, and we think that the latter is worth aspiring to. What do we take ourselves to be doing in this? I do not think that we are strictly aspiring to sympathy or compassion in the sense of a shared affective experience. Rather, we aspire to a radical expansion of our openness to mattering, such that we are open not only to what helps or hinders us in our own projects but also to what helps and hinders others. We aspire to genuinely fear *for* others—to be moved by what is detrimental to them, even if it is not detrimental to us. We aspire to, in a profound sense, share a world together—without sharing an identity. I am not entirely sure how we do this, but I do think that it is what a marriage vow commits us to doing.[61]

What we aspire to in enlarging our openness is neither passion nor matrimony but humanity. When we speak of humanity aspirationally, we often gloss it in terms of compassion, sympathy, or kindness, while having the sense that these words are too weak. Thinking of us as cases of Dasein, and so in terms of our finite being-in-the-world, amidst entities and with others, allows us to better articulate what humanity demands of us: not merely feeling with or for others (sympathy, compassion), not merely accepting the normative authority of others (solicitude), not merely acknowledging the existential-ontological structure of others (authentic solicitude), but beyond that, enlarging our openness to meaning beyond ourselves, so that we can be open—genuinely open—to what matters to others.[62]

After Tracy and Dexter marry, we anticipate that they will spend their second honeymoon as they did their first: sailing their boat, now the *True Love II*. Having come to have the right regard for Dasein's finitude, and having expanded their openness to encompass one another's fields of mattering, they can now truly sail a single ship and encounter fair and foul weather together.

Notes

1. Martin Heidegger, *Being and Time*, trans. John Macquarrie and Edward Robinson (New York: Harper and Row, 1962), H41. Note that I decapitalize terms, such as "Being," that are capitalized in the translation.

2. Heidegger, *Being and Time*, H4.

3. Ingo Farin, "Heidegger's Engagement with and Critique of Philosophical Anthropology," ch. 1 of this volume.

4. Contra Taylor Carman, *Heidegger's Analytic: Interpretation, Discourse, and Authenticity in "Being and Time"* (Cambridge: Cambridge University Press, 2003), 232.

5. Heidegger, *Being and Time*, H51, H198, H382, H401.

6. For example, Heidegger, *Being and Time*, H11, H14, H197, H212.

7. "The term 'man' was not used for that being which is the theme of the analysis. Instead, the neutral term *Dasein* was chosen." See Martin Heidegger, *The Metaphysical Foundations of Logic*, trans. Michael Heim (Bloomington: Indiana University Press, 1984), 136.

8. For example: "When we speak of "human being" [*Mensch*] here and throughout these remarks, we always mean the essence of the historical human being [*Mensch*] of that history to which we ourselves belong: the essence of Western humankind." See Martin Heidegger, *Hölderlin's Hymn "The Ister,"* trans. William McNeill and Julia Davis (Bloomington: Indiana University Press, 1996), 51. Translation modified.

9. To take just one clear example of many: "We name the being of man being-there, Da-sein." See Martin Heidegger, *The Fundamental Concepts of Metaphysics: World, Finitude, Solitude*, trans. William McNeill and Nicholas Walker (Bloomington: Indiana University Press, 1995), 63.

10. Heidegger, *Being and Time*, H42. I take it that this is what Farin is picking up on when he situates Dasein at the base of the human being. See Farin, "Heidegger's Engagement with and Critique of Philosophical Anthropology," n40.

11. Martin Heidegger, "Letter on 'Humanism,'" trans. Frank A. Capuzzi, in *Pathmarks*, ed. William McNeill (Cambridge: Cambridge University Press, 1998), 247.

12. Heidegger, *Being and Time*, H145.

13. Heidegger, *Being and Time*, H67–70.

14. Contra Jacques Derrida, "Geschlecht II: Heidegger's Hand," in *Deconstruction and Philosophy: The Texts of Jacques Derrida*, ed. John Sallis (Chicago: University of Chicago Press, 1989), 176.

15. Heidegger, *Being and Time*, H84, H86, H144.

16. See, for example, Hubert L. Dreyfus, *Skillful Coping: Essays on the Phenomenology of Everyday Perception and Action*, ed. Mark A. Wrathall (Oxford: Oxford University Press, 2014).

17. Sacha Golob, *Heidegger on Concepts, Freedom, and Normativity* (Cambridge: Cambridge University Press, 2014).

18. See Aristotle, *Politics* 1253a15.

19. Heidegger, *Being and Time*, H83. See also Martin Heidegger, *Basic Concepts of Aristotelian Philosophy*, trans. Robert D. Metcalf and Mark B. Tanzer (Bloomington: Indiana University Press, 2009), 41.

20. Heidegger, *Being and Time*, H105.

21. Heidegger, *Being and Time*, H108–9.

22. Heidegger, *Being and Time*, H11.

23. Heidegger, *Being and Time*, H107.

24. Heidegger, *Being and Time*, H105.

25. Heidegger, *The Metaphysical Foundations of Logic*, 137. In fairness, Heidegger goes on to make the point again in a way that apparently does not support

my claim: "As factical, Dasein is, among other things, in each case dispersed in a body" (137). I read this as saying that cases of Dasein (as far as we know) do, in fact, have bodies, even though in principle they might not.

26. For an interpretation of finding (*Befindlichkeit*) that makes no essential reference to the body, while allowing for contingent embodiment, see my "Finding Oneself, Called," in *Heidegger on Affect*, ed. Christos Hadjioannou (Cham, Switzerland: Palgrave Macmillan, 2019). For an interpretation of thrownness that makes no essential reference to the body, see my "Situation and Limitation: Making Sense of Heidegger on Thrownness," *European Journal of Philosophy* 22, no. 1 (2014): 61–81; and "Thrownness," in *The Cambridge Heidegger Lexicon*, ed. Mark Wrathall (Cambridge: Cambridge University Press, 2021).

27. Heidegger, *Being and Time*, H50, H194, H246ff.
28. Heidegger, "Letter on 'Humanism,' " 248.
29. Martin Hägglund, *This Life: Secular Faith and Spiritual Freedom* (New York: Pantheon, 2019), 32.
30. Heidegger, *Basic Concepts of Aristotelian Philosophy*, 16, cf. 14.
31. Heidegger, *Basic Concepts of Aristotelian Philosophy*, 31.
32. Heidegger, *Being and Time*, H137.
33. Heidegger, *Being and Time*, H186. Translation modified. In *Being and Time*, Heidegger classifies weather phenomena and, more broadly, natural phenomena, sometimes as present-at-hand (H118, H250) and sometimes as ready-to-hand (H70ff., H95). Here, I follow him in holding that "the wind is wind 'in the sails' " (H70) and, so, ready-to-hand.
34. Heidegger, *Being and Time*, H340.
35. For more on this, see Withy, "Finding Oneself, Called," 166.
36. See Heidegger, *Being and Time*, H134.
37. Heidegger, *Being and Time*, H247.
38. Heidegger, *Being and Time*, H247.
39. Macquarrie and Robinson, H247 trans. n1, in Heidegger, *Being and Time*.
40. For a helpful overview of interpretive possibilities, see Hubert L. Dreyfus, foreword to *Time and Death: Heidegger's Analysis of Finitude*, by Carol White, ed. Mark Railowski (London: Routledge, 2005), ix–xxxvi.
41. Heidegger, *Being and Time*, H250, H258.
42. Heidegger, *Being and Time*, H56.
43. Recall that an entity is anything that *is* (meaningful); therefore, an entity need not be material or physical. Depending on other entities thus does not entail depending on bodies and, so, does not require that Dasein be embodied.
44. Heidegger, *Being and Time*, H126, H163.
45. Jonathan Lear, *Radical Hope: Ethics in the Face of Cultural Devastation* (Cambridge, MA: Harvard University Press, 2006).
46. There is also a deeper form of death in which I cannot go on, not only as who I am, but *as a case of Dasein*. This has precisely the same structure as the

phenomenon that I discuss here, in that it depends on my being-amidst-entities and being-with-others. This death occurs when others do not recognize me as a case of Dasein or entities cease to be meaningful in terms of my projects. A full account of Heidegger on death would work out this phenomenon. I do not discuss it here because my goal is to locate Dasein's finitude in its being-amidst-entities and being-with-others, which is most easily done with the more readily recognizable phenomenon of death.

47. My argument in this section is deeply indebted to two people. The first is John Haugeland, who also associated love and death in his interpretation of Heidegger. See John Haugeland, *Dasein Disclosed: John Haugeland's Heidegger*, ed. Joseph Rouse (Cambridge, MA: Harvard University Press, 2013), 274; Joseph Rouse, "Love and Death," in *Giving a Damn: Essays in Dialogue with John Haugeland*, ed. Zed Adams and Jacob Browning (Cambridge, MA: MIT Press, 2017), 131–57. While my account of love as (authentic) discovering is much the same as Haugeland's account of love as an instance of and model for the phenomenon of (authentic) intentionality, and while we both hold that properly loving requires facing up to death, we differ on how to understand death. Inspired by Kuhn, Haugeland takes existential death to be a breakdown in an understanding of being precipitated by an anomalous entity that does not make sense within that understanding of being. In contrast, I take it to be precipitated by entities that *do* make sense within an understanding of being, as in some way detrimental. I am inclined to take Haugeland's anomalous entities as a special class of the detrimental, but I think that he would insist—and correctly so—that the breakdown that they precipitate is of a distinctive sort.

The second person to whom I am indebted is Martin Hägglund, who, inspired in part by Heidegger—see Hägglund, *This Life*, 394n19—has argued that there is a deep connection between our finitude and our ability to love. I disagree with many aspects of his argument—including his reliance on bodily mortality as a basis and model for what I have called existential death, and his vision of love as a sort of desperate clinging to something at risk of slipping away—and I do not find it particularly Heideggerian. But thinking through this disagreement has been invaluable to me in working out my own argument.

48. Martin Heidegger, *Hölderlin's Hymn "The Ister,"* 131. See also Martin Heidegger, *Nietzsche*, vol. 2, *The Eternal Recurrence of the Same*, trans. David Farrell Krell (New York: Harper Collins, 1991), 207.

49. Heidegger, *Being and Time*, H34.

50. Heidegger, *Being and Time*, H121.

51. Heidegger, *Being and Time*, H57.

52. The quote, describing the hopeful soldier, is from Aristotle, *Nichomachean Ethics*, trans. Terence Irwin, 2nd ed. (Indianapolis: Hackett, 1999), 1117a14. The rash soldier is discussed at 1115b29.

53. Heidegger, *Being and Time*, H146

54. Heidegger, "Letter on 'Humanism,'" 234. Translation modified to read "human being" instead of "man."

55. *The Philadelphia Story*, dir. George Cukor (Beverley Hills, CA: Metro-Goldwyn-Mayer Studios, 1940). Stanley Cavell has an interpretation of *The Philadelphia Story* that is quite different from mine but which, nonetheless, originally inspired me to engage philosophically with this film. See Stanley Cavell, "The Importance of Importance," in *Pursuits of Happiness: The Hollywood Comedy of Remarriage* (Cambridge, MA: Harvard University Press, 1981).

56. Heidegger, *Being and Time*, H118.

57. Heidegger, *Being and Time*, H122.

58. Heidegger, *Being and Time*, H56.

59. Heidegger, *Being and Time*, H141–42.

60. Heidegger, *Being and Time*, H142.

61. Of course, no actual marriage vow is required. Nor is it required that the cases of Dasein in question be romantic partners. I am less certain whether this expanded openness is possible only in the context of two cases of Dasein. I see no reason why it should be, and yet any examples I generate of deep, nonromantic commitments among members of groups—such as those found in seafaring crews, the military, or orchestras—are cases where members share identities and projects in common.

62. Heidegger did not achieve this humanity personally, and perhaps that is why he did not think us far enough, philosophically.

Chapter Thirteen

Dwelling after 1945

Heidegger among the Architects[1]

TOBIAS KEILING

Reconstruction? Technologically, financially not possible; what am I saying?—spiritually impossible!

—Otto Bartning, 1946

Heidegger's "Letter on 'Humanism'" is his first major philosophical statement after World War II. The "Letter," first published in 1947, is not only a response to the question Jean Beaufret posed to Heidegger—"Comment redonner un sens au mot 'humanisme'?" (How to give back meaning to the word "humanism"?)—but Beaufret's questions also give Heidegger occasion to contribute to a central intellectual debate of the time: the attempt to renew a normative meaning of our shared humanity after the atrocities of the war. Among the most prominent philosophical contributions to this debate were two German émigrés' books: Ernst Cassirer's *Essay on Man* (1944) and Hannah Arendt's *The Human Condition* (1958). But the debate was not restricted to philosophy.

The renewal of European culture was also the explicit aim of *Merkur*, established as *Journal for European Thought* (*Zeitschrift für europäisches Denken*) in 1947 and a leading German-language intellectual medium of the time. Here not only philosophers and anthropologists such as Maurice Merleau-Ponty, Arnold Gehlen, and Arnold Bergsträsser, but also writers and literary scholars, Hans Egon Holthusen, Ernst Nossack, and Gabriel Marcel among them, contributed texts that reference our common humanity already in the title. These discussions are quite justly referred to in scholarship today as "postwar humanism" (*Nachkriegshumanismus*), for most of its protagonists argued that some form of humanism could serve as a focal point for rethinking Europe after two world wars.[2] Max Bense, a regular contributor to the early issues of the *Merkur* who was to become a stern critic of Heidegger's thought on technology and a prominent philosopher of technology in his own right, nevertheless wrote a respectful review of the "Letter" for the journal. Its opening lines summarize well the intellectual concerns of the day:

> It is one of the consequences of the war that the question as to our ethical convictions is posed in a more radical and fresher way than before. The experience of the in-humane [*Unmenschlichkeit*] forces on us a new passion for humanity [*Menschlichkeit*]. But in our experimental century, progressing so slowly from one theory to the next, from one ideology to another ideology, in the hope that they provide us with personal, social, and spiritual norms—in this century, there emerges a consciousness of the aporias, of the difficulties of humanism, and it is those difficulties we need to address both in theory and in practice. It is the task of philosophers to dissolve these aporias—or at least that they tell us how we are to live with them.[3]

To understand the "Letter" in its immediate historical context is to understand it as a philosophical comment on how to renew European or Western culture, and after 1945 this also quite literally meant how to *rebuild* it, and thus the question of the human was also a question for the architects. The aim of this chapter is to lay out how Heidegger's critique of humanism relates to his philosophy of architecture and its contemporary reception. In the first two sections, I concentrate on the "Letter" and the form of thinking about the human that is the target of Heidegger's critique. I will contrast this account with what I take to be the decisive concept in his positive proposal for how to understand the human being, namely, as "dwelling" (*Wohnen*). For Heidegger, humans are essentially dwellers.

Others have written on Heidegger's central essay in the philosophy of architecture, "Building Dwelling Thinking," where his account of the human as dweller is developed.[4] Instead of discussing the many themes Heidegger associates with dwelling in that text, the third section will be devoted to the immediate context of its presentation. I wish to show here that both in the "Letter" and in the lecture to the architects, Heidegger does not break completely with a specific form of rethinking the human, namely, with a sequential model in which an intellectual or spiritual transformation is to *precede* a different ethos and a transformed form of action. I argue in the first two sections that the general thrust of Heidegger's discussion of human nature is to move from an inside out model to an outside in model, where what is genuinely human can no longer be separated from its surrounding. This outside in model can be used productively in the philosophy of architecture, yet no genuine dialogue between architects and the philosophers took place when Heidegger first presented "Building Dwelling Thinking." In the third section, I show that both Heidegger and his most outspoken critic fall back on the sequential model for cultural renewal. The architects present, however, assumed a reflective or dialogical model, as I aim to show in the concluding fourth section.

As is the case for the "Letter," historical context makes clear that "Building Dwelling Thinking" presents another element in Heidegger's contribution to the question of the human. The lecture was delivered in 1951 at the second of the so-called Darmstädter Gespräche, a series of conferences and exhibitions in the industrial city of Darmstadt, which had been largely destroyed by air bombings in the last years of the war.[5] While the topic of the first of these conferences had been "The Image of Man in Our Time" (Das Menschenbild in unserer Zeit), the second conference was devoted to "Man and Space" (Mensch und Raum). Lectures were accompanied by an exhibition of architectural projects, which were at the center of discussion during the conference.[6] Heidegger was invited by the architect Otto Bartning, organizer of the conference and the exhibition, and delivered his lecture in the presence of the most important architects from German speaking countries. Other delegates to the conference include the political scientist and journalist Dolf Sternberger, the sociologist Alfred Weber, and the philosophers Hans-Georg Gadamer and José Ortega y Gasset. Ortega also gave a lecture, speaking in the afternoon on the same day as Heidegger.[7] The conference thus presents one of the occasions where Heidegger intervened directly and publicly in the question how to respond to the cultural crisis induced by the war, and, to my knowledge, it is the only event where the immediate response to his ideas is documented in detail.[8] I draw from the transcript of this discussion to develop Sternberger's criticism of Heidegger and the discussion of dwelling following Heidegger's presentation of "Building Dwelling Thinking."

Inside Out: Heidegger's Critique of Humanism

A pivotal moment in Heidegger's response to Beaufret's question is the provocative rejection of "humanism," a term Heidegger views as merely a product of the "market of public opinion."[9] This rejection is best understood as part of Heidegger's larger attempt to present an argument for a revision of our way of thinking, and this revision is less dismissive of the category of the human than Heidegger's comment on "humanism" may suggest. This revision indeed begins with the very first line of the "Letter," when Heidegger responds to Beaufret's question how philosophy can be applied practically with the injunction that "we are still far from pondering the essence of action decisively enough."[10] Instead of developing some genuinely philosophical thought to be put into action subsequently, Heidegger rejects a conception of philosophy where it would merely serve as a theoretical means to practical ends. The alternative Heidegger offers is for philosophy to make explicit the meaning of actions we are already engaged in, including and beginning with the idea of agency itself. Rather than as sequential, where theory simply precedes practice, Heidegger here understands the relation of thought and action as circular or reflexive: the task of thinking is not to guide action by telling us what to do, but to make transparent what we are already doing, which may or may not lead to acting differently. Because of its reflexive character, thinking is neither theoretical nor practical but, as Heidegger puts it, "comes to pass [*ereignet sich*] before this distinction."[11]

Most consequential for the question of humanism among the themes Heidegger engages with in the "Letter" is his attempt to articulate a normative contrast between different ways of thinking, which in turn represent different ways to understand what it means to be human. For despite his criticism of the idea that the human is the *zoon logon echon* or *animal rationale*, Heidegger continues to conceive of the human in view of some idea of *logos* in the sense of language. The human capacity to use language and to think rationally is nothing simply given with the constitution of the human as the kind of animal "having" *logos*. That very description is rather based on presuppositions associated with a set of philosophical assumptions

Heidegger calls "metaphysical," and much of the first half of the "Letter" is devoted to showing that not only the history of philosophy from Plato to Marx but also Sartrean existentialism is entangled in this way of thinking.[12] Throughout most of the history of thought, "the essence of humanism is metaphysical."[13] It is for this reason that the word "humanism" has ceased to have any action-guiding meaning, and that is what prompted, according to Heidegger at least, Beaufret's desire to "give back" to it its genuine meaning.

A claim as wide-ranging as this is not only disputable but may be impossible to make good on in the interpretation of the history of ideas. Yet whether or not Heidegger's understanding of the "metaphysical" trajectory of the history of philosophy is correct, what drives this interpretation is the search for another way of thinking and a corresponding alternative to understanding ourselves as human beings. Rather than motivating its rejection, Heidegger wants to make the weaker point that the "essence of humanism" is "questionable;" what is needed is to rethink "more primordially" the "essence of the human being."[14] Yet if we are called to *think*, and to think *better*, the problem with humanism is not with its substantial claim, with the idea that language, reason, *ratio*, or *logos* is characteristic of our humanity. The proper response to the loss of meaning diagnosed by Beaufret is reflexive in the way sketched above: it is to engage in thinking in order to understand how it is that our thinking shapes us as human beings, thus reclaiming *in actu* the fact that we are involved in the development of these ideas as thinkers. Humanism is problematic only to the extent that the notion of a rational capacity defining our shared nature has come in opposition to an essential element in exercising that capacity, namely, that we do so in committing freely to our true beliefs, including our understanding of ourselves as "thinking beings." Because they relate as the theory and practice of thinking, *understanding* what it is to be human cannot be separated from *becoming* human. In Hegelian terms, understanding the human being is of the structure of self-consciousness rather than consciousness.

Realizing that the humanist doctrine can be questioned is thus a first step toward recovering a free relation to our human nature. The next step is to reconceive the two defining notions of humanism, " 'freedom' and 'nature' of the human being," in such a way that they align with the reflexive model instead of merely contradicting each other.[15] But if a more "primordial" thinking of these categories were to succeed, nothing stands in the way of again endorsing humanism as "concern that the human being become free for his humanity and find his worth in it." Eventually, Heidegger's discussion of language will provide a better understanding of what defines the human, and, although it is little discussed in the "Letter," "dwelling" is Heidegger's name for what it means to actualize this nature deliberately and reflectively. Setting the quarrels with the history of philosophy aside, then, and perhaps somewhat simplifying matters, the alternative to a "metaphysical" view of the human is not simply another doctrine *about* the human being but a different and preferable ("primordial") mode of *being* human, that is, of thinking. The challenge of Heidegger's "Letter" to philosophy is not in its forceful attack on much of the history of philosophy but in its attempt to retrieve some form of free choice between these different ways of actualizing our being in thinking.[16]

What this freedom amounts to, emerges most clearly by contrasting different ways in which the genuinely human can be understood as being located in the world. One such understanding is generated by a strategy of addition or extension. This argumentative pattern aims to identify a trait of the being of the human that is to be taken as defining our humanity, typically an internal, mental, or intellectual capacity, and then to add further elements and larger contexts to the phenomenology of human life thus begun. The classic version of this idea is a dualistic view of subjectivity, the separating of mind and body, where the mind defines the genuinely human, the locus of cognition, deliberation, and decision, while the body is conceived as a mere addition to the mind, as that part of us we have in common with animals and that therefore cannot define our being human. Heidegger quite explicitly addresses this point:

> Are we really on the right track toward the essence of the human being as long as we set him off as one living creature among others in contrast to plants, beasts, and God? [. . .] We must be clear on this point that if we do this we abandon the human being to the essential realm of *animalitas* [animal being] even if we do not equate him with beasts but attribute a specific difference to him. In principle, we are still thinking of *homo animalis*—even when the *anima* [soul] is posited as *animus sive mens* [spirit or mind], and this in turn is later posited as subject, person, or spirit. Such positing is the manner of metaphysics.[17]

What is problematic about the attempt to determine a specific difference between humans and animals, then, is that it forces the thinker to isolate the defining human element in contrast to a mere animal part of our being, which in turn raises the question where this genuinely human part is to be located. No matter how this essence is identified in a particular philosophical system, the problem with this model of the human is that it conceives of the being of the human as distributed among essential and nonessential elements that can be considered independently from one another. The attempt to begin with the essential is further taken as equivalent to beginning with some notion of interiority in order to then move to the outside. The first, and problematic, option in our choice how to understand ourselves as thinking beings is defined by versions of this inside out model.

To see the pertinence of this model, consider a contemporary example. Although its aim is precisely to overcome a dualism of mind and body, contemporary cognitive psychology continues to use the extension strategy in the paradigm of so-called "4E cognition."[18] As the name indicates, this body of theory is defined by the idea that the mind must be seen as essentially intertwined with its surroundings: *embodied* in a lived body, *embedded* in a situational context, *enacted* in relation to its environment, and *extended* into the world of objects with which it interacts. An adequate description of the mind requires considering these different contexts. But despite the effort to overcome the tendency of closing in the human being in its interior mind, the development of this body of theory over the last decades suggests that it nonetheless follows a strategy of adding to or extending what most genuinely defines our inner cognitive capacity. The series of enlargements of the mind still begins at what is considered both central and interior to it.

Since there is no explicit anthropological or metaphysical claim associated with this body of scientific theory, Heidegger's worry may appear relevant only for the philosopher hoping for a complete account of human being but not for a cognitive psychologist, who is happy to embrace the incompleteness of her account. Heidegger's problem, however, is not with the scope of such a theory but with its explanatory structure. As long as the account is premised on the idea that there are different moments in the human being that can become an object of theory independently from one another, such an account cannot be integrated into a coherent theory of human nature. Even a still more encompassing, more extended theory cannot lay claim to completeness in the relevant sense. That could only be achieved by explaining the human all at once, and this is what Heidegger's alternative aims to offer, beginning, as it were, outside rather than inside.

Outside In: Heidegger's Alternative

Consider a passage from "Building Dwelling Thinking," which most directly reveals Heidegger's alternative to the inside out model of extending or adding to the essentially human. Heidegger here reiterates two basic phenomenological ideas when he criticizes a representationalist account of conscious thought and a dualism of mind and body, but the way he presents these ideas shows his attempt to avoid and invert the strategy just discussed. On the picture Heidegger is advocating, merely adding additional contexts around the locus of thinking as central, defining element of the human can never be sufficient:

> If all of us now think, from where we are right here, of the old bridge in Heidelberg, this thinking toward that locale is not a mere experience inside the persons present here; rather, it belongs to the essence of our thinking *of* that bridge that *in itself* thinking persists through [*durchsteht*] the distance to that locale. [. . .] And only because mortals pervade, persist through, spaces by their very essence are they able to go through spaces. [. . .] When I go toward the door of the lecture hall, I am already there, and I could not go to it at all if I were not such that I am there. I am never here only, as this encapsulated body.[19]

Striking about this passage is that Heidegger sees an embodied mind as still "encapsulated," as not extended enough into the world. So it would seem that he demands an even further extension of the mind. But even to conceive of the possibility of bodily movement as an affordance of my surroundings will not do, for not only is the range of perception more extended than that of my movement, as when I see the door before I move toward it; our acquaintance with the world is such that even remembering or imagining a far removed entity requires that that entity allows or affords to be remembered or imagined.[20] There must *be* an old bridge in Heidelberg independent of my relation to it for me to intend it. What is more, on Heidegger's example, nothing in the entity itself motivated remembering or imagining it, as that conscious act was prompted merely by the address expressed in the words of the lecture. What allowed a competent speaker to have at least some understanding of what is here asked of her, is the referential linguistic expression Heidegger uses in his thought experiment: "[i]f all of us now think [. . .] of the old bridge in Heidelberg." The condition of possibility for my intentional action is not merely that the bridge and the thinking humans *are*, but that despite all difference in their constitution, both are beings *in language*. As a consequence, any instance of "thinking" is in some sense conceptual or linguistic.[21]

Although Heidegger uses the broad sense of the term found in Descartes's *Meditations*, where "thinking" means any conscious act, reflecting on what we do when we are "thinking" of the bridge reveals a very un-Cartesian understanding of that activity. Rather than internal or intimate, bound first to myself as thinking substance, thinking is revealed as the most extended mind-world relation. It not merely extends into but begins in the world, in a capacity actualized free from any ontic constraints: the old bridge affords to think of it, but it does not force me to. Beginning outside, the world is disclosed not as a realm of determinacy opposing my freedom, but as the genuine locus of freedom. As free orientation into the world, thinking is at least rational in the minimal sense that it is actualized in the space of discourse; it discloses both the world in its meaning and ourselves as beings thus "dwelling" in the world. In this way language has a constitutive function for our being in the world.[22]

Many of these ideas may be common to any phenomenological or hermeneutical understanding of consciousness and intentionality. What is defining Heidegger's account in "Building Dwelling Thinking" is the further step of describing conscious and linguistic intentional activity as "persisting through spaces" (*Räume durchstehen*), emphasizing that space is not a metaphor for describing rational thought and action but the actual medium in and by which meaning is encountered. Heidegger's positive view for understanding the idea that human beings are essentially thinkers is conditioned on a redefinition of thinking that reveals its essentially *spatial* nature, and it is this idea that Heidegger associates with "dwelling" as the name for the being of the human: "To say that mortals *are* is to say that *in dwelling* they persist through spaces by virtue of their stay among things and locales."[23] One should be clear that this constitutes a paradigm shift: the idea that there is an elementary form of "spatial thinking"[24] has had forerunners in discussions in Husserl, the early Heidegger, and Merleau-Ponty, and a parallel can be found in Davidson's discussion of understanding as triangulation.[25] Yet the idea that our being-in-the-world is not merely linguistic through and through but, being so, is essentially spatial, is the characteristic and most consequential idea in Heidegger's later philosophy.[26]

Although Heidegger also reverses the inside out model in the "Letter," the spatial character of our thinking or hermeneutic being is much less explicit here than in the lecture to the architects. Heidegger merely says that language is neither "the utterance of an organism; nor is it the expression of a living thing"[27] but notoriously "language is the house of being."[28] The problem with this, however, is that it produces merely an image for the spatial nature of language rather than a plausible description; as in many discussions of "logical space" or the "space of reason," the "house" in Heidegger's dictum is merely a metaphor.[29] It is by fleshing out the idea of dwelling that the lecture to the architects makes good on what was only developed metaphorically in the "Letter."

To see this, compare the uses of "dwelling" in the two texts. When Heidegger, in the lecture to the architects, claims that the being of humans is in "*dwelling*," where "dwelling" means to "persist through spaces by virtue of their stay among things and locales," it is clearly us, the humans, who dwell. A more fine-grained account can easily be given: we dwell by living in houses, interacting with objects, traveling on roads, and so forth. Yet whether humans are dwellers in this sense is much less clear in the "Letter." There, Heidegger emphasizes that the house of being "is propriated by being and pervaded by being," and, although the human being is said to dwell in this house, what this means is that the human being "belongs to the truth of being, guarding it."[30] Being itself and the human being are both in the house of language, but it appears being can more properly be said to be "dwelling." This is brought out most clearly in a passage where Heidegger makes use of a contrast between two German terms easily obscured in translation: language is the "house" (*Haus*) of being, yet to the "essence of the human being" it merely provides a "provisional abode" (*Behausung*).[31]

In 1947, when the letter was first published in Switzerland, or in 1949, when it was published in Germany, this contrast between a genuine home, reserved, as it were, to being, and a merely provisional abode will not have been lost on the reader. The function of this contrast seems equally clear: to indicate that "dwelling" is not merely a name for what humans in fact do, but a normative notion, where how we dwell is inadequate with respect to how being is in language. That "language is the house of being" will always sound "anthropomorphistic," as if being were a person who could serve as exemplar for how humans are to act and to live, or "mystical," as if human actions are ultimately nothing but events in the world.[32] What defines Heidegger's account of dwelling in the "Letter" is that it embraces the ambiguity of its axiomatic phrases; with respect to the genitive in the phrase "house *of being*" (*Haus des Seins*), Heidegger even admits to intentionally shaping this ambiguity.

Only at the very end of the "Letter" does Heidegger hint at his motivation to make such deliberate use of ambiguity and to leave indeterminate the nature of the form of thinking he advocates. Responding to the question, as Beaufret puts it, how thinking can "preserve the element of adventure that all research contains without simply turning philosophy into an adventuress,"[33] Heidegger refers to the idea of purely ontological understanding. Being is said to provide "the first law of thinking,"[34] and although Heidegger only briefly alludes to it in response to Beaufret's last question, it falls to poetry to serve as example for how thinking can thus be claimed by being. The alternative to the inside out account of thinking and its genuine measure is with the last turning of the "Letter" explained in a jointure of ontology and poetry, what Heidegger calls "simple saying."[35] This immediate normative force of being is articulated in the attempts at "simple saying" that are the most memorable expressions from the "Letter": in thinking, the human ought to act as "shepherd of being"[36] and "neighbor of being."[37]

These remarks are not merely obscure and deliberately ambiguous and, I take it, in this sense poetic. They also harbor a difficulty resulting from Heidegger's idea of a purely ontological normativity, and, although Heidegger offers various accounts of an experience of being over the course of his works, in the "Letter" poetic language stands in for such an experience.[38] The problem with this idea, however, is that, in some way or other, it falls back on a sequential model for the transformation of thinking, where we modify our basic, purely ontological understanding of being, perhaps in an encounter with poetry or some other "simple saying," *before* we can appropriately engage in any other, merely ontic endeavor. With regard to dwelling, this becomes explicit when Heidegger promises that "one day we will, out of thinking the essence of being in a way appropriate to its matter, more readily be able to think what 'house' and 'dwelling' are."[39] This suggests that a genuine understanding of being, most directly encountered in poetic and genuinely philosophical language, must precede any genuine dwelling. Despite Heidegger's initial disavowal of the sequential model in the opening passages of the "Letter," by end of the text, the normativity of being is again taken as *preceding* any specific human action such as thinking and dwelling. Given that to dwell and to understand ourselves as dwellers is Heidegger's proposal for how to understand our humanity, this may lead to the idea that we are to suspend, as it were, our being merely human in order to first undergo a modification of ontological understanding.

The worry with this can be expressed as a worry with the form Heidegger's reversal of the inside out model takes in the "Letter." Heidegger endeavors to rethink several basic concepts (language, thinking, dwelling) in such a way that they are to offer alternative descriptions for our being in the most extended contexts, farthest out, so to speak. In describing the genuinely human, we are to reverse direction and to move from the outside in, beginning with the most encompassing, absolute context grasped in ontological understanding. But the simple saying of poetry or philosophy, effective as it may be in capturing our relation to the world as a whole through phrases such as that of "language as the house of being," fails to make sense of the possibility and the need to return to and create some form of interiority. Heidegger has good reasons to reject and to avoid the inside out model for understanding the human being. But to the extent that the "Letter" offers an alternative description at all, it is in danger, as it were, to get stuck on the outside. The orientation toward the outmost context of ontological understanding fails to make plausible a desire to create and to shape a space rightly considered as mine or ours, as that place where I or we live, a home—in the literal sense.[40] It is in the discussion following the lecture to the architects and in contrasting Heidegger's approach to that of the practitioners, that this worry emerges most clearly.

Heidegger among the Architects

Few of the contributions in the discussion during the "Man and Space" conference directly address the lectures given, as most of the conversation is among the architects who attack each other's ideas about the nature, function, and task of building, often referencing examples of good building or engaging in criticism of the work of others. The tone of discussion is civilized, although the debate is controversial at times and includes outspoken, if friendly, polemic. Of the philosophers on the panel, Ortega y Gasset speaks once, while Heidegger remains silent even when, in the discussion following Ortega's lecture, he is criticized quite explicitly by Sternberger. I will focus on this critique here because it is the only direct response to Heidegger's ideas. This, in fact, is most striking about the discussion: the contrast between the lively discussion among the architects, and the absence of any dialogue between them and the philosophers.

Although having only recently been appointed a lecturer in political science at the University of Heidelberg, Sternberger had had some renown working as a journalist at the *Frankfurter Zeitung* in the years before and after the war. Having completed a doctorate on the understanding of death in *Being and Time* under the supervision of the Protestant philosopher of religion Paul Tillich, Sternberger was well acquainted with Heidegger's philosophy, and it is most likely that he would also have taken notice of the "Letter," Heidegger's most important postwar publication.[41] Closely associated with Karl Jaspers, Sternberger in his own academic publications drew from the work of Hannah Arendt and her reading of Aristotle to develop a version of republicanism suited for Germany's postwar politics. Sternberger later called this view "constitutional patriotism" (*Verfassungspatriotismus*), a term still prominent in accounts of the normative foundations of the German state today.[42] In comparison to Heidegger, born in 1889, and many other delegates to the conference, Sternberger, born 1907, represents a younger generation.

After much of the time allotted to discussion has passed, Sternberger is the first not only to address the lectures by the philosophers, but also to speak directly of the immediate social and historical context of the discussion, the very fact of the destruction of much of continental Europe and the immediate need for housing for millions of people. The time is, in Sternberger's words, "an epoch of forced relocations, of resettlements, of barrack camps, of refugees, of *Heimatvertriebene* [persons expelled from their homes in former German territories], and of *displaced persons* [English in the original]."[43] Sternberger goes on to accuse some thinkers—and here he is referring to Heidegger—of catering to the "yearning for rest and safety"[44] of those who have been without home, exploiting what he calls their *horror mobilitatis*, their fear of being forced again from their abodes or newly found homes. The target of Sternberger's critique is not a specific political, aesthetic, or ideological program, and it is not directed against the idea of describing humans as dwellers as such. Sternberger rather accuses Heidegger of advancing a problematic notion of *Heimat*: "home as the place of the final sedentariness of man in himself, the walling-off of one's home, sedentariness as rootedness on one's own piece of land."[45]

This comment may be taken to suggest that Sternberger's worry is with the danger of enclosure, with an individual or a group separating some territory from all outside land. To understand one's home in such a way would be to follow the inside out model, though somewhere drawing a line where one would cross from what is home to what is foreign. Husserl conceives of home in this way when he suggests that there is a distinction between a "home world" (*Heimwelt*) into which one is born and a "foreign world" (*Fremdwelt*) an individual encounters in the course of her life. But if Husserl understood this as a successive discovery of more extended contexts and as a formative experience for the individual, what Heidegger would advocate is to stop exploring and remain at home. This picture does not do justice to Sternberger's critique, though, for when he rephrases his point, it becomes clear that his worry is not simply with an embrace of a provincial localism. Sternberger endorses the inside out model no more than Heidegger, and their disagreement emerges only because of the shared assumption that one's understanding of home is of metaphysical or ontological import.

Sternberger's point is merely to retrieve as a matter of choice and debate our understanding of ourselves as dwellers. Referring to Heidegger's and Ortega's lectures, Sternberger goes on to contrast two alternative views. There are two fundamentally distinct kinds of thinkers,

> the one [. . .] thinking of the possibility that man might dwell in paradise, in an ontological paradise of meaningful order, in an ontological paradise with all its coziness [*Gemütlichkeit*], with the arch-coziness [*Ur-Gemütlichkeit*] of Paradise. The others think of and do not forget that the earth is not this Garden of Eden or at least that we actual humans have, on that memorable day, been chased from the Garden of Eden.[46]

Although Sternberger's polemic is clearly intended as an affront to Heidegger, this should not occlude that he shares the assumption that there is a fundamental background understanding of all there is, and that the historical situation demands a reflection and possibly a revision of this understanding. Sternberger only rejects as a self-deception what he takes to be Heidegger's account of what the whole of being is, an "ontological paradise of meaningful order," and contrasting Heidegger's to Ortega's lecture, Sternberger finds in the latter the better alternative. Rather than *finding* ourselves already at home in the world, we have to think of it as a place we must *make* our home: "[B]y its own nature [*von Haus aus*], the earth is [. . .] I don't want to say absolutely unlivable, wholly unsuited for dwelling [*absolut unwohnlich*] but at least not livable [*wohnlich*] enough."[47]

Already rendering Ortega's position in such a way, however, emphasizes that dwelling can be used to describe the fundamental form of being-in-the-world, since Ortega himself had not said anything about dwelling. His presentation rather begins with a direct endorsement of the inside out model:

> The human, life—that is evident—is an interior event [*inneres Geschehen*] and nothing more. Therefore one can only speak of the human and of life if one speaks from the inside [*von drinnen aus*]. If one wants to speak of the human in earnest, one can only do so *from* one's *own* interior [*vom eigenen Drinnen her*], one can only speak *of one self*. Everything else, what we can say of the other human being, of other life, or of the human in

general, one must regard as secondary, derived and abstract rather than as evident [. . .] propositions.[48]

Ortega consequently contrasts the "inner image" of the human with the "outer image," and, although he holds that only the "inner image" the individual has of herself is the "fundamentally true" one, he turns to a description of the (bodily) movement and behavior of humans.[49] Because we can observe humans to be often engaged in "*technical* movements" (*technische Bewegungen*) as in the production of artifacts, Ortega advances the central "thesis" of his presentation: "The human being is a technician" (*Der Mensch ist Techniker*), constantly at work in "creating a new world for himself" by reshaping the natural world.[50] Although not a creation out of nothing but a creation out of something, *creatio ex aliquo* rather than *creatio ex nihilo*, technology is a "creation" (*Schöpfung*) nonetheless.[51] While animals are simply immersed in the natural world, the capacity to create their own world is what sets humans apart from animals. From the perspective of the "transcendental behaviorist" (*transzendentaler Verhaltensforscher*), as Ortega calls himself, the human is "the being that does *not* belong to this and within this spontaneous and actual world."[52] Sternberger is correct, then, when he summarizes Ortega's view as the idea that the human being is not originally at home in the world. Assimilating Heidegger's account of dwelling to the animal life, as analogy would require, is hardly a fair assessment.

Sternberger's endorsement of Ortega's position also seems more interested in polemic than in developing his proposal for how to dwell and how to build, although, with regard to these questions, Ortega's presentation is even less consequential than Heidegger's, as there is no explicit comment about either dwelling or the task of architecture. Only in the closing words does Ortega address the architects as eminent creators of the genuinely human world: "This new world of technology is like a huge orthopedic apparatus, that is what you want to create, and all of technology has this wonderful but—as with all human affairs—also dramatic movement and quality: to be a fabulous, great orthopedics."[53] This image of orthopedics may or may not give a plausible account of the general function of technology for the human being, but it certainly helps little with regard to the questions discussed among the architects; it implies nothing about how to build. Ortega's dualism of a natural and technological world even leads him to deny that the current crisis is a genuinely cultural crisis at all. After providing a brief account of evolutionary history and emphasizing the role technology has played for the survival of the human species, Ortega concludes by asking what the morale of this "narration" has been, answering that "this myth provides us with a new victory over technology: it wants to create a new world for us because the actual world is not fit for us, we have become sick because of this world [*weil wir an dieser Welt krank geworden sind*]."[54]

While the idea that dwelling requires some way of making oneself at home in the natural world, the idea to which Sternberger referred, is certainly worthy of discussion, Ortega's further claim that the crisis of the time is merely a sickness of our natural constitution is more difficult to appreciate, and it directly opposes the conviction of Sternberger and many other delegates. Ortega denies rather than addresses the worry that two world wars have revealed the ambivalence of human reason, of human agency, or of the role of technology in the history of mankind. The implication of the closing words is rather that what is genuinely human lives in a kind of innermost sanctum that could not be affected by any destruction in the outside world. But if this is so, then, despite Sternberger's rendering of Ortega's position, his ultimate proposal is not that making the natural world more habitable can serve as a norm for dwelling. Rather, what is genuinely human, for Ortega, does not dwell at all, if this means to live in an essential relation to an outside. If the substance of Sternberger's criticism lies in identifying the genuine measure for dwelling, this question is not even broached by Ortega.

With a view to the reception of Heidegger's philosophy, however, Sternberger anticipates a criticism often put forward later, namely, that it identifies the measure of dwelling too easily with a provincial rootedness at the expense of a more cosmopolitan idea of being-in-the-world, devaluating other forms of dwelling and implicitly portraying life outside the city as preferable because it unburdens the dweller from any relation to others.[55] The rejoinder to this critique, also formulated in the literature, is that Heidegger does in fact recognize a normative contrast in ways of dwelling, and what he is after is an understanding of dwelling that avoids the modern equalization and uniformization of dwelling;[56] in such a way, Heidegger's philosophy can even serve as template for a positive ethical understanding of architecture.[57] Looking back at the initial moment of this discussion, however, it may seem more plausible to regard this disagreement as a calculated result of Heidegger's own writing. Similar to Heidegger's writing in the "Letter," the ambivalence in his account of dwelling may not be incidental but carefully designed.

Consider the last comments of the lecture, when Heidegger acknowledges the problem of a "housing shortage" (*Wohnungsnot*) but quickly adds that the current lack of housing is not the "genuine plight of dwelling" (*eigentliche Not des Wohnens*).⁵⁸ True plight, Heidegger continues, summing up ideas from his reading of the history of thought, is "older than the world wars with their destruction;" it consists of no actual shortage of housing but "in this that mortals ever search anew for the essence of dwelling, that they *must ever learn to dwell.*"⁵⁹ Heidegger here acknowledges the extraordinary circumstances of the time, but at the same time denies their relevance for the lasting question how we are to dwell. The real issue is not the merely technical or practical problem of how to provide proper housing but a deeper, intellectual one: the question how we ought to dwell is not recognized as the fundamental problem it is, "*as the* plight."⁶⁰ In a move that effectively displaces all practical concerns into questions of ontology, Heidegger goes on to suggest that recognizing the proper difficulty of dwelling is already overcoming it.⁶¹ This is what Sternberger a few hours later called out as a false promise and ridiculed as the ontological Garden of Eden: "[A]s soon as man *gives thought* to his homelessness, it is a misery no longer."⁶² Rather than a threat to one's very life, homelessness "rightly considered and kept well in mind . . . is the sole summons that calls mortals into their dwelling."⁶³

The ambivalence of this proposal is striking, and it is unsurprising that it has received such varied responses: although Heidegger has just argued that the question as to the genuine measure of dwelling is enduring and fundamental, he gives little direction as to how to address it, offering instead a form of spiritual recovery from the "misery" (*Elend*) of the present. As Sternberger pointed out, to the person in need of housing or the architect asking herself how to provide for that person's needs, this offers too much in consolation. But it also offers too little in guidance for the task at hand, and this is a worry Sternberger does not voice.⁶⁴ What is obscured when Sternberger singles out and attacks Heidegger is that both the promise of overcoming homelessness and the alternative of Ortega's view, to which Sternberger refers, represent a return to the sequential model, where a transformation of thought must occur *before* consequences in action can follow. Not because Heidegger and Sternberger agreed on a specific ontological understanding adequate to the times, but because that is what they disagreed about, they further the transformation of the question of dwelling from a practical or aesthetic problem to a spiritual or intellectual one. This move is not peculiar to either Heidegger or Sternberger, however, but an idea fundamental to the conference and the exhibition. Consider the preamble of the conference, shown at the entrance to the exhibit: it not only describes building as "a basic activity of the human" but also states that "homelessness is the plight of our time."⁶⁵ Thus ideas today's reader may quickly associate with and take as peculiar of Heidegger's philosophy of architecture are in fact drawn from the immediate circumstances of its presentation, if not common ideas of the time.

The spiritual cast of the conference can indeed be traced back to Bartning, the conference organizer and influential president of the Bund deutscher Architekten (Association of German Architects) at the time. Bartning, born in 1883, belonging to the same generation as Heidegger, was known in particular for his association with the Protestant church, having designed the so-called *Notkirchen*, provisional church buildings that were industrially manufactured and erected especially in Northern Germany, in the Protestant regions most affected by the war. At the conference, Bartning emphasizes this spiritual implication of what only seem to be practical questions when he frames the discussion following Heidegger's and Ortega's lectures as an attempt to determine "the part that architecture can play in overcoming homelessness, both the bodily and the spiritual homelessness."[66] In Bartning's own academic writing, the notion of an ideal spiritual "community" (*Gemeinschaft*) is prominent. It not only informed Bartning's design of the churches built after the war but also his understanding of the task of architecture generally, laid down as early as 1919 in a draft curriculum for architects that strongly influenced the Bauhaus manifesto authored by Walter Gropius.[67] The promise of both an actual and spiritual home that Sternberger is attacking with a view to Heidegger thus dates back to the end of the First World War, although it returned with new urgency after 1945. Reconstructing European cities and building for a new community appeared, as Bartning wrote in an article quoted as the motto to this chapter, not merely "technologically" and "financially" but first "spiritually impossible."[68]

With the privilege of hindsight, what returns here is a problem discussed with regard to the "Letter" above, namely, the worry with a sequential model for cultural renewal, where an intellectual or spiritual transformation has to *precede* a different way of practical engagement. Despite the rejection of that model in the opening paragraphs of the "Letter," to which I referred in the first section, Heidegger quite explicitly endorses this model not only in the closing passages of that text but also in the lecture to the architects when he discusses the relation between dwelling and building. Proper dwelling, as "the basic character of Being"[69] must *precede* proper building: "*Only if we are capable of dwelling, only then can we build.*"[70] The idea is reiterated in "... Poetically Man Dwells ... ," a talk given a few months after "Building Dwelling Thinking." Heidegger here formulates more explicitly the idea that the notion of dwelling functions as a basic term for all human life, but also falls back on the sequential model, for an encounter with poetry is to occur *before* we can engage in any merely ontic activity relating to dwelling: "Man does not dwell in that he merely establishes his stay on the earth beneath the sky, by raising growing things and simultaneously raising buildings. Man is capable of such buildings only if he already builds in the sense of the poetic taking of measure."[71] It is fair to say, then, that Heidegger is torn between the reflective and the sequential model of cultural renewal, and that when it comes to building and architectural design, these activities are clearly second to a poetical or philosophical transformation of ontological understanding. Despite Sternberger's fervent critique, the two of them as well as Bartning share some version of the sequential model for the renewal of European architecture and culture more generally. This is what separates all three of them from the architects in the auditorium.

A Missed Opportunity?

The irony of this situation is that Heidegger's own critique of the sequential model in the opening paragraphs of the "Letter" can help to explain why no dialogue between theory and practice took place on the days of the conference. Ortega's and Heidegger's lectures implied little, if anything for how to build, and neither did Sternberger's comments. To the extent that they addressed the idea that dwelling is part of human nature at all, the philosophers did so without engaging with the practice that is already the genuine reflection of dwelling and the task of architecture: building. The only hint as to how one *should* build can be glimpsed from Heidegger's reference to the "Black Forest farm" as an example of dwelling, a choice that triggered Sternberger's polemic response and has been met with scorn since. Although Heidegger clarifies at the closing of the lecture that this reference is intended as an example for a *past* form of dwelling ("a dwelling that *has been*, how it was able to build"[72]), the fact that no other example is discussed may still be taken as a longing for a past rather than as a demand to think of a *future* form of dwelling. But if Heidegger's mood was of such melancholy, those present at his lecture did not share in this feeling.

Although there is little general comment by the architects on the relation of their profession to history, the following remark by Sep Ruf sums up well much of what was said: "You see, we are indeed interested in the old things and want to take over and continue tradition, but only to the extent that it shows us our own intellectual path, just as earlier times have attempted to realize and design their own spiritual world view."⁷³ Quite explicitly, albeit not formulated in an abstract way, Ruf here endorses the reflective or dialogical model for a relation of architecture to its past. But such dialogue takes place in the medium of genuinely architectural meaning, by endorsing or rejecting certain elements of how homes have been built in the past. What is more, if the general thrust of both the "Letter" and Heidegger's lecture can be described as an inversion of the inside out model, as I have argued in the first two sections, there is good reason why Heidegger's later philosophy has been of such interest to theorists of architecture. Heidegger is approaching what, from a phenomenological perspective at least, is indeed the central problem of architecture: the separation of an inside from an outside and the formation of a livable and agreeable inside space.⁷⁴ Even if they make no explicit reference to the idea of the philosophers, the architects also broach this topic, and it is with regard to this question that an exchange between philosophers and architects might have begun.

The relation between inside and outside is indeed quite directly addressed in the opening statement by Hans Schwippert, member of the Werkbund and architect of the provisional German parliament, the Bundeshaus in Bonn. The statement sets the tone for much of the following discussion and is repeatedly, though also critically, referred to. Schwippert begins by looking at the historical situation not as a disengaged thinker, but as a practitioner would, commenting on how others solved the architectural problem: "[A] round the world, the good architects are building tents, light open things." Schwippert is well aware of the hardships of the time, however, for he goes on to comment that "this in a strange way contradicts what common sense demands of us."⁷⁵ A reflection of dwelling always already happens in how human build their homes, and under the circumstance of the time and in response to the need to renew, European building culture renews itself by building homes responsive to this situation:

> Something remarkable has happened to us, that our spaces want to have openness, lightness, not the rigorous and hard boundaries of dark caves. [. . .] The spatial constitution [*das Räumliche*] that corresponds to our dwelling is something light [*ein Helles*], something mobile, a light and open sequence of rooms, and this idea persistently asserts itself in these times, even if, on the face of it, they intend something different.⁷⁶

What sets a comment like this apart from both Heidegger's at least alleged preference for rural life and Sternberger's sympathies for Ortega's somewhat austere idea of dwelling as process of appropriating hostile nature is that Schwippert is clear that building requires aesthetic and practical choices not equivalent to ontological ones. Whether or not one agrees with Schwippert's preferences in this regard, how we should *build* is the question that must be answered, and this cannot be a merely spiritual or intellectual question. Because Heidegger took it as such and returns to a model for cultural renewal he elsewhere rejects, the Darmstadt conference is a missed opportunity for a dialogue between philosophy and architecture. But, just as such, it shows where a more fruitful dialogue might begin: by asking how inside and outside can and should be related in building, dwelling, and thinking. This is a question about which both architects and philosophers will have something to say.

Notes

1. The title of this chapter is inspired by Andrew J. Mitchell, *Heidegger Among the Sculptors: Body, Space, and the Art of Dwelling* (Stanford, CA: Stanford University Press, 2010), which in turn harks back to William J. Richardson, 'Heidegger among the Doctors,' *Reading Heidegger: Commemorations,* ed. John Sallis (Bloomington: Indiana University Press, 1993), 49–63. For very helpful comments, thanks are due to Ian Alexander Moore and the editors of this volume.

2. For recent research on this discourse in Germany and France, see Matthias Löwe and Gregor Streim, eds., *"Humanismus" in der Krise: Debatten und Diskurse zwischen Weimarer Republik und geteiltem Deutschland* (Berlin: De Gruyter, 2017); Thomas Ebke and Caterina Zanfi, eds., *Das Leben im Menschen oder der Mensch im Leben? Deutsch-Französische Genealogien zwischen Anthropologie und Anti-Humanismus* (Potsdam: Universitätsverlag Potsdam, 2017). For the discussion in the USA, see Mark Greif, *The Age of the Crisis of Man: Thought and Fiction in America, 1933–1973* (Princeton, NJ: Princeton University Press, 2015).

3. Max Bense, "Heidegger's Brief über den Humanismus," *Merkur* 3, no. 20 (1949): 1021–26, esp. 1021. Where German texts are referenced, translations are my own.

4. A very good introduction is David Sharr, *Heidegger for Architects* (Abingdon, UK: Routledge, 2007). Also see Pavlos Lefas, *Dwelling and Architecture: From Heidegger to Koolhaas* (Berlin: Jovis, 2009). For the place of dwelling in the broader context of Heidegger's later philosophical system, see Julian Young, *Heidegger's Later Philosophy* (Cambridge: Cambridge University Press, 2002). For an overview of literature on Heidegger's philosophy of architecture, see the appropriate section in Tobias Keiling, "Martin Heidegger: Later Works," in *Oxford Bibliographies,* ed. Duncan Pritchard (Oxford: Oxford University Press, 2021), https://doi.org/10.1093/OBO/9780195396577-0426.

5. Published as Otto Bartning, ed., *Mensch und Raum: Darmstädter Gespräch*, Darmstädter Gespräche 2 (Darmstadt: Neue Darmstädter Verlangsanstalt, 1952); reprint, *Mensch und Raum: Das Darmstädter Gespräch 1951*, Bauwelt Fundamente 94 (Braunschweig: Vieweg, 1991). The presentation has been recorded and is available on a compact disc, published as part of Eduard Führ, *Bauen und Wohnen: Martin Heideggers Grundlegung einer Phänomenologie der Architektur* (Münster: Waxmann, 2000).

6. See Regine Heß, "Display, Discuss, and Build: German Architectural Congresses and Exhibitions between Continuity and Cold War," in *Rethinking Postwar Europe: Artistic Production and Discourses on Art in the later 1940s and 1950s*, ed. Barbara Lange, Dirk Hildebrandt, and Agata Pietrasik (Berlin: Böhlau, 2020), 235–60.

7. Sharr, *Heidegger for Architects*, 36. Ortega comments on his presentation in Darmstadt and the following discussion in José Ortega y Gasset, "Anejo: En Torno Al 'Coloquio de Darmstadt, 1951,'" in *Obras Completas*, vol. 9, 2nd ed. (Madrid: Revista de Occidente, 1965), 625–44. Heidegger describes his meetings with Ortega in "Begegnungen mit Ortega y Gasset," in *Aus der Erfahrung des Denkens, 1910–1976*, vol. 13 of *Gesamtausgabe*, ed. Hermann Heidegger, 2nd ed. (Frankfurt: Klostermann, 2002), 127–29.

8. But see the protocol of a discussion following a presentation of ". . . Poetically Man Dwells . . . ," in 1952. Martin Heidegger, *Leitgedanken zur Entstehung der Metaphysik, der neuzeitlichen Wissenschaft und der modernen Technik*, vol. 76 of *Gesamtausgabe*, ed. Claudius Strube (Frankfurt: Klostermann, 2009), 383–94. Also, there exists an opinionated anonymous report on Heidegger's lecture—"Einblick in das was ist" [Insight into That Which Is], *Der Spiegel*, April 6, 1950, 35–36—which relates some but not all of the discussion following the presentation in Bühlerhöhe.

9. Martin Heidegger, "Letter on 'Humanism,'" trans. Frank A. Capuzzi, in *Pathmarks*, ed. William McNeill (Cambridge: Cambridge University Press, 1998), 239–76, esp. 239.

10. Heidegger, "Letter on 'Humanism,'" 239.

11. Heidegger, "Letter on 'Humanism,'" 272.

12. Heidegger, "Letter on 'Humanism,'" 244–54.

13. Heidegger, "Letter on 'Humanism,'" 262.

14. Heidegger, "Letter on 'Humanism,'" 262.

15. Heidegger, "Letter on 'Humanism,'" 245.

16. A similar contrast between different ways of thinking defines Heidegger's account of *Gelassenheit* as norm for human agency. See Tobias Keiling, "Letting Things Be for Themselves: *Gelassenheit* as Enabling Thinking," in *Heidegger on Technology*, ed. Aaron Wendland, Christos Hadjioannou, and Christopher Merwin (London: Routledge, 2018), 96–114, https://doi.org/10.4324/9781315561226.

17. Heidegger, "Letter on 'Humanism,'" 246.

18. See the introduction and the chapters in Albert Newen, Leon de Bruin, and Shaun Gallagher, eds., *The Oxford Handbook of 4E Cognition* (Oxford: Oxford University Press, 2018), https://doi.org/10.1093/oxfordhb/9780198735410.001.0001; Richard Menary, "Introduction to the Special Issue on 4E Cognition," *Phenomenology and the Cognitive Sciences* 9, no. 4 (2010): 459–63, http://dx.doi.org/10.1007/s11097-010-9187-6. For a systematic exposition, see Shaun Gallagher, *Enactivist Interventions: Rethinking the Mind* (Oxford: Oxford University Press, 2017).

19. Martin Heidegger, "Building Dwelling Thinking," in *Basic Writings*, ed. David Farrell Krell (London: Routledge, 1977), 343–64, esp. 358–59.

20. Peters develops a similar argument with regard to the encounter with other people: Heidegger does not emphasize the embodied nature of intersubjectivity because, on his view, embodied face-to-face encounters are not explanatorily more basic than other forms of intersubjectivity. Rather, the very distinction and hierarchy between so-called "primary intersubjectivity" (face-to-face interaction between embodied subjects) and "secondary intersubjectivity" (mediated by other persons, symbols, or objects) already follows from a privileging of the individual (embodied) mind, from what I have called the inside out model. See Meindert E. Peters, "Heidegger's Embodied Others: On Critiques of the Body and 'Intersubjectivity' in *Being and Time*," *Phenomenology and the Cognitive Sciences* 18 (2019): 441–58. The distinction between these two forms of intersubjectivity comes from Shaun Gallagher and Rebecca Seté Jacobson, "Heidegger and Social Cognition," in *Heidegger and Cognitive Science*, ed. Julian Kiverstein and Michael Wheeler (New York: Palgrave Macmillan, 2012), 213–45.

21. Sacha Golob has argued that, although Heidegger rejects the idea that all intentional states have a propositional structure, he defends the idea that all instances of intentionality are conceptual. See Sacha Golob, *Heidegger on Concepts, Freedom, and Normativity* (Cambridge: Cambridge University Press, 2014).

22. See Charles Taylor, "Heidegger on Language," in *A Companion to Heidegger*, ed. Hubert L. Dreyfus and Mark A. Wrathall (Oxford: Blackwell, 2005), 433–55. For the implications of this idea for a thinking of the human being, see Charles Taylor, *The Language Animal* (Cambridge, MA: Harvard University Press, 2016).

23. Heidegger, "Building Dwelling Thinking," 359.

24. Günter Figal, "Spatial Thinking," *Research in Phenomenology* 39, no. 3 (2009): 333–43.

25. Jeff Malpas, *Place and Experience: A Philosophical Topography* (Cambridge: Cambridge University Press, 1999). For a reading of Heidegger as thinker of space, see Jeff Malpas, *Heidegger's Topology: Being, Place, World* (Cambridge, MA: MIT Press, 2006); Jeff Malpas, *Heidegger and the Thinking of Place: Explorations in the Topology of Being* (Cambridge, MA: MIT Press, 2012).

26. To be sure, division 1 of *Being and Time* includes a detailed discussion of the "spatiality of Dasein" (§§22–24). In division 2, §70, however, Heidegger

presents his further claim that this spatiality can be reduced to Dasein's temporal constitution. Although the theme of spatiality is thus already present in the early Heidegger, Dasein is not spatial in an ontologically relevant way. Importantly, this is one of the few claims Heidegger explicitly retracts later, in the lecture "Time and Being." For discussion, see Malpas, *Heidegger's Topology*, 39–146.

27. Heidegger, "Letter on 'Humanism,'" 248.

28. Heidegger, "Letter on 'Humanism,'" 243. For a discussion of this infamous "slogan," see Mark A. Wrathall, *Heidegger and Unconcealment: Truth, Language, and History* (Cambridge: Cambridge University Press, 2011), 156–76, https://doi.org/10.1017/CBO9780511777974.

29. On spatial metaphors in the description of rationality ("logical space," "space of reasons"), see Tobias Keiling, "Logische und andere Räume: Wittgenstein und Blumenberg über Unbestimmtheit," *Deutsche Zeitschrift für Philosophie* 64, no. 5 (2016): 720–37, https://doi.org/10.1515/dzph-2016-0053.

30. Heidegger, "Letter on 'Humanism,'" 254.

31. Heidegger, "Letter on 'Humanism,'" 274. In the translation in *Basic Writings*, Capuzzi translates *Behausung* as "home," missing the implication of the provisional and insufficient character of this abode.

32. The appearance of such a paradox in Heidegger's writing is, itself, likely an influence of an idea prominent in the writings of Meister Eckhart, namely, that the human being *is* indeed God such that the norm for becoming human is to realize one's prior ontological union with God. See Ben Morgan, *On Becoming God: Late Medieval Mysticism and the Modern Western Self*, Perspectives in Continental Philosophy (New York: Fordham University Press, 2013); Ian Alexander Moore, *Eckhart, Heidegger, and the Imperative of Releasement* (Albany: State University of New York Press, 2019).

33. Heidegger, "Letter on 'Humanism,'" 275.

34. Heidegger, "Letter on 'Humanism,'" 275–76.

35. Heidegger, "Letter on 'Humanism,'" 276.

36. Heidegger, "Letter on 'Humanism,'" 260.

37. Heidegger, "Letter on 'Humanism,'" 261.

38. This attempt to identify a purely ontological experience follows from Heidegger's merger of phenomenology and ontology, which motivates the idea that claims about being must be cashed out in a phenomenology of the experience of being. Throughout his works, Heidegger locates this experience in various phenomena. In the context of his philosophy of history, similar to the anticipation of a future change in the meaning of "dwelling," it is pushed into the expectation of an indeterminate future. For a sketch of the development of Heidegger's philosophy, along these lines, and the problems emerging from it, see Tobias Keiling, "Heidegger's *Black Notebooks* and the Logic of a History of Being," *Research in Phenomenology* 47, no. 3 (2017): 406–28; Tobias Keiling, "Phenomenology and Ontology in the Later Heidegger," in *The Oxford Handbook of the History of Phenomenology*, ed. Dan

Zahavi (Oxford: Oxford University Press, 2018), 251–67, https://doi.org/10.1093/oxfordhb/9780198755340.013.17.

39. Heidegger, "Letter on 'Humanism,'" 272. Translation modified.

40. Steven Crowell, "Interiors: The Space of Meaning and the Great Indoors," in *Raum erfahren*, ed. David Espinet, Tobias Keiling, and Nikola Mirkovic (Tübingen: Mohr Siebeck, 2017), 129–47, https://doi.org/10.1628/978-3-16-154963-2.

41. Adolf Sternberger, *Der verstandene Tod: Eine Untersuchung zu Heideggers Existenzialontologie*, Studien und Schriften zur Gegenwartsphilosophie 6 (Leipzig: Hirzel, 1934); reprinted in Dolf Sternberger, *Über den Tod*, Schriften 1 (Frankfurt: Insel, 1977; Frankfurt: Suhrkamp 1981), 69–264.

42. Jan Werner Müller, *Constitutional Patriotism* (Princeton, NJ: Princeton University Press, 2007).

43. Bartning, *Mensch und Raum*, 124.
44. Bartning, *Mensch und Raum*, 124.
45. Bartning, *Mensch und Raum*, 124.
46. Bartning, *Mensch und Raum*, 124.
47. Bartning, *Mensch und Raum*, 124.
48. Bartning, *Mensch und Raum*, 111.
49. Bartning, *Mensch und Raum*, 111.
50. Bartning, *Mensch und Raum*, 112.
51. Bartning, *Mensch und Raum*, 112.
52. Bartning, *Mensch und Raum*, 113.
53. Bartning, *Mensch und Raum*, 117.
54. Bartning, *Mensch und Raum*, 117.

55. Albert Borgmann, "Cosmopolitanism and Provincialism: On Heidegger's Errors and Insights," *Philosophy Today* 36, no. 2 (1992): 131–45; Neil Leach, "Forget Heidegger," *Scroope* 12 (2000): 28–32; Christian Illies and Nicholas Ray, *Philosophy of Architecture* (Cambridge: Cambridge University Press, 2014), 37–46; Richard Sennett, *Building and Dwelling: Ethics for the City* (London: Allen Lane, 2018), 121–43.

56. Kenneth Frampton, "Towards a Critical Regionalism: Six Points for an Architecture of Resistance," in *The Anti-Aesthetic*, ed. Hal Forster (Seattle: Bay Press, 1983); Kenneth Frampton, "On Reading Heidegger," in *Theorizing a New Agenda for Architecture: An Anthology of Architectural Theory, 1965–1995*, ed. Kate Nesbitt (New York: Princeton Architectural Press, 2000), 440–46; Christian Norberg-Schulz, *Existence, Space & Architecture* (London: Studio Vista, 1971); Christian Norberg-Schulz, *Genius Loci: Towards a Phenomenology of Architecture* (London: Academy Editions, 1980).

57. Karsten Harries, *The Ethical Function of Architecture* (Cambridge, MA: MIT Press, 1996), ch. 10. In discussing the American reception of "Building Dwelling Thinking," Martin Woessner shows that Harries's selective appreciation of its supposed ethical outlook is typical for philosophers and architects, including such

prominent figures as Daniel Libeskind. See Martin Woessner, *Heidegger in America* (Cambridge: Cambridge University Press, 2011), 230–62.

58. Heidegger, "Building Dwelling Thinking," 363. Translation modified.

59. Heidegger, "Building Dwelling Thinking," 363.

60. Heidegger, "Building Dwelling Thinking," 363.

61. This argument is foreshadowed in the lecture "Poverty," Heidegger's first appearance in a smaller public setting after the end of the war, on June 27, 1945. In reference to a line from Hölderlin, Heidegger recognizes the actual plight as one of *Geist* rather than basic needs. This is further connected with a specific vision of European renewal: "Viewed from the entirety of, and the actual destiny of the West, the danger of famine for example and of the years of scarcity consists, not only in the fact that perhaps many human beings perish, but in the manner in which those who survive live only in order to eat so that they may live. [. . .] Only when the European nations are attuned to the overtone of poverty do they become the richest peoples of the West—the West that does not and cannot go under because it has not yet risen at all. Rather, the beginning of the West's rising lies in the fact that the people of the West alternately awaken themselves to their ownmost, learn to have a knowing awareness of the ownmost of poverty so that they can be poor." See Martin Heidegger, "Poverty," in *Heidegger, Translation, and the Task of Thinking: Essays in Honor of Parvis Emad*, ed. Frank Schalow, Contributions to Phenomenology 65 (Heidelberg: Springer, 2011), 3–10, esp. 8.

62. Heidegger, "Building Dwelling Thinking," 363.

63. Heidegger, "Building Dwelling Thinking," 363.

64. Karsten Harries has commented directly on Sternberger's critique, arguing that it was unfounded, because Sternberger misinterpreted the closing passage of Heidegger's lecture. For the reasons developed in the last paragraph, I disagree with this. See Karsten Harries, "In Search of Home," *Cloud-Cuckoo-Land: International Journal of Architectural Theory* 3 (1998), https://www.cloud-cuckoo.net/.

65. Bartning, *Mensch und Raum*, 33.

66. Bartning, *Mensch und Raum*, 85.

67. Both Bartning and Gropius were active in the Workers' Council for Art (Arbeitsrat für Kunst), and Gropius knew and commented on Bartning's draft curriculum. See Joseph Imorde, "Otto Bartning: Spiritualität und Modernes Bauen," in *Raum für Bildung: Ästhetik und Architektur von Lern- und Lebensorten*, ed. Hildegard Schröteler-von Brandt, Thomas Coelen, Andreas Zeising, and Angela Ziesche (Bielefeld: transcript Verlag, 2012), 305–18; Paul Betts, *The Authority of Everyday Objects: A Cultural History of West German Industrial Design*, Weimar and Now (Berkeley: University of California, 2004), ch. 2.

68. Otto Bartning, "Ketzerische Gedanken am Rande des Träummerhaufen," *Frankfurter Hefte: Zeitschrift für Kultur und Politik* 1, no. 1 (1946): 63–72. Excerpt available in *Architekturheorie 20: Jahrhundert, Positionen, Programme, Manifeste*, ed. Vittorio Lampugnani, Ruth Hanisch, Ulrich Maximilian Schumann, and Wolfang

Sonne (Ostfildern-Ruit: Hatje Cantz, 2004), 174–77. The epigraph to this chapter is taken from this text.

69. Heidegger, "Building Dwelling Thinking," 362.
70. Heidegger, "Building Dwelling Thinking," 361.
71. Martin Heidegger, ". . . Poetically Man Dwells . . . ," in *Poetry, Language, Thought* (New York: Harper and Row 1971), 213–29, esp. 227. On this passage, see Günter Figal, "On Dwelling: Considerations on Human Life, Buildings, and Space," in *Freiräume: Phänomenologie und Hermeneutik* (Tübingen: Mohr Siebeck, 2017), 154–65.
72. Heidegger, "Building Dwelling Thinking," 362.
73. Bartning, *Mensch und Raum*, 107.
74. This point is argued by Günter Figal in his discussion of Frank Lloyd Wright's Falling Water. See Günter Figal, *Aesthetics as Phenomenology* (Bloomington: Indiana University Press, 2015), ch. 4.
75. Bartning, *Mensch und Raum*, 86.
76. Bartning, *Mensch und Raum*, 87.

List of Contributors

Babette Babich is Professor of Philosophy at Fordham University, New York. She is the author, among many other works, of *Günther Anders' Philosophy of Technology* (2022) and editor of *Reading David Hume's 'Of the Standard of Taste'* (2020).

Tina Fernandes Botts is Professor of Law at the San Joaquin College of Law. She has a law degree from Rutgers University and a Ph.D. in philosophy from the University of Memphis. She is the author, among other works, of *For Equals Only: Race, Equality, and the Equal Protection Clause* (2018).

Ingo Farin is an independent scholar working in Hobart, Tasmania. He is the co-editor of *Reading Heidegger's Black Notebooks* (2018) and *Hermeneutical Heidegger* (2016).

Anne Granberg is Associate Professor of Philosophy at the University of Bergen. She has published on topics in existentialism and phenomenology, especially the phenomenology of embodiment.

Sara Heinämaa is Professor of Philosophy at the University of Jyväskylä. She is the author of *Birth, Death, and Femininity* (2010) and *Toward a Phenomenology of Sexual Difference* (2003), and editor of *Contemporary Phenomenologies of Normativity* (2022) and *Phenomenology as Critique* (2022).

Laurence Hemming is Honorary Professor at Lancaster University. He is the author, among other works, of *Heidegger and Marx* (2013) and the editor and co-translator of Ernst Jünger, *The Worker* (2017).

Bruce Janz is Professor of Philosophy at the University of Central Florida. He is the editor, among other works, of *Place, Space and Hermeneutics* (2017) and the author of *African Philosophy and Enactivist Cognition* (2022).

Niall Keane is Senior Lecturer in Philosophy at the University of the West of England, Bristol. He has published widely in the areas of phenomenology and hermeneutics and is the co-author of *The Gadamer Dictionary* (2012) and co-editor of *The Blackwell Companion to Hermeneutics* (2016).

Tobias Keiling is Associate Professor of Philosophy at the University of Warwick. He is the co-editor, among other works, of *The Routledge Handbook of the Phenomenology of Agency* (2020) and *Paths in Heidegger's Later Thought* (2020).

Jeff Malpas is Emeritus Distinguished Professor at the University of Tasmania, and Honorary Professor at Latrobe University and at the University of Queensland. He is the author, among many other works, of *Rethinking Dwelling: Heidegger, Place, Architecture* (2021), and *In the Brightness of Place* (2022).

Hans Ruin is Professor of Philosophy at Södertörn University. He is the co-editor of the Swedish edition of the *Collected Works* of Friedrich Nietzsche, and author, among many other works, of *Being with the Dead: Burial, Ancestral Politics, and the Roots of Historical Consciousness* (2019).

Thomas Schwarz Wentzer is Professor of Philosophy at Aarhus University. He has published extensively on topics in phenomenology, hermeneutics, and philosophical anthropology, and is the co-editor, among other works, of *Philosophy on Fieldwork: Case Studies in Anthropological Analysis* (2022).

Katherine Withy is Associate Professor of Philosophy at Georgetown University. She is the author of *Heidegger on Being Uncanny* (2015) and *Heidegger on Being Self-Concealing* (2022).

Index

4E cognition, 331

abode, 110n, 334, 337, 348n; *see also* dwelling, house
Abraham, 228
absolute, 11, 14, 161, 162, 220, 234, 236–241, 243–246
Adam, 228
Adorno, Theodore, 48, 56, 60, 67
action, 130, 187, 195, 216, 219, 284, 285, 287, 289–299, 328, 332, 333, 335, 341
aeon, 191–193
Africa/Africans, 232, 233, 234, 241, 242, 245
Agamben, Giorgio, 47, 206, 207, 208, 212, 217, 219, 220
agency, 67, 159, 264, 272, 275, 328, 340
agent, 116, 130, 159, 163, 275, 289, 290, 294, 309
Alcoff, Linda Martín, 272
aletheia, 144, 218
analytic of Dasein/existential analytic, 13–14, 15, 16, 53, 92, 96, 111, 210, 237, 270, 281, 282, 283, 307, 308, 309, 311, 318
Anders, Günther, 47–51, 53, 57, 59, 60, 63, 66, 67, 68, 69, 70, 71
Angelus Silesius, 192

animal/animality, 3, 17, 18, 48, 51, 54, 60, 66, 67, 94, 97, 99, 100, 103, 197, 206, 207, 208, 214–222, 234, 241, 245, 247, 328, 330, 339; animal-Da-Sein, 66
animale rationale (rational animal), 15, 51, 103, 211, 241, 245, 281, 328
animalization, 207, 220, 223n
animal studies, 207, 220, 221
animate beings/entities, 97, 98, 126, 214
Anthropocene, 1, 146, 147
anthropocentric/anthropocentrism, 22, 23, 50, 93, 94, 206, 208, 221
anthropological machine, 7, 207, 219, 220
anthropologism, 7, 8, 18, 19, 22, 24, 25, 27, 30, 31, 32, 33–34, 35, 53, 54, 55, 113, 153n, 168, 176, 206, 233
anthropology/anthropological thought, 9, 12, 15–16, 51, 53, 54, 59, 112, 211, 234, 245; *see also* philosophical anthropology
anti-humanism/anti-humanist, 7, 32, 146, 147, 151, 205; *see also* humanism/humanist
anti-metaphysical/nonmetaphysical, 205, 298
anti-Semitism/anti-Semitic, 3, 67, 228, 231

anxiety, 9, 176, 213
appearance, 150, 161, 162, 163, 164, 166, 172, 190, 286, 287, 288, 289, 291, 294, 296, 297
a priori/apriority/apriorism, 11, 156, 171–173
Aquinas, Thomas, 56
architects, 325, 326, 327, 333, 334, 336, 341–345
architecture, 3, 326, 327, 339, 340, 342, 343, 344, 345
Arendt, Hannah, 47, 67, 84, 206, 282–299, 325, 337
Aristotle, 51, 55, 56, 59, 66, 69, 95, 159, 165, 212, 228, 236, 242, 244, 274, 283, 310, 317, 337
artificial intelligence, 1, 311, 312
atheism, 50, 206; *see also* theism
attitude; *see* natural attitude, naturalistic/natural-scientific attitude, personalistic attitude, phenomenological attitude
Augustine of Hippo, 47, 51, 52, 56
Auschwitz/Auschwitz-Birkenau, 1, 49, 70, 71
authentic/authenticity, 47, 48, 57, 66, 100, 232, 264, 267, 275, 276, 286, 289, 290, 291, 292, 294, 295, 317, 318, 319, 320; *see also* inauthenticity
Axelos, Kostas, 185, 192, 193, 194, 195, 198, 200, 201

Barash, Jeffrey, 228
Bartning, Otto, 325, 327, 342, 343
Basic Problem of Phenomenology, 163
Baudrillard Jean, 48
Bauhaus, 342
Beaufret, Jean, 68, 101, 137–138, 325, 328, 329, 334, 335
beginning/beginner, 284, 285, 286, 289, 290, 293
being/Being (*Sein*), 3, 8, 9, 12, 13–15, 19–21, 23, 25–26, 28, 31, 33, 34, 35, 40n, 44n, 50, 53, 68, 85, 90, 93, 101, 103, 111, 139, 142, 143, 145, 146, 150, 156, 157, 159, 171, 186, 187, 189, 192, 193, 199, 200, 205, 206, 210, 227, 265–267, 282, 298, 299n, 307, 308, 334, 335; *see also* beings/entities, beyng/*Seyn*, Dasein, Da-sein, metaphysics, ontology, question of being/Being, truth of being/Being, understanding of being/Being
being-amidst-entities, 307, 314–320
being-in-the-world, 30, 33, 55, 156, 159, 162, 163, 168, 171, 176, 186, 213, 214, 222, 265, 267, 270, 281, 282, 287, 292, 295, 298, 312, 313, 314, 320, 333, 338, 339, 340
being-with (*Mitsein*)/being-with-one-another (*Miteinandersein*)/being-with-others, 218, 292, 293, 295, 303n, 307, 314–320
beings/entities (*Seiendes*), 13, 14, 17, 18, 19, 20, 21, 22, 25, 26, 29, 31, 34, 66, 93, 98, 114, 118, 120, 143, 163, 164, 165, 176, 210, 214, 218, 219, 262, 266, 267, 270, 273, 275, 282, 292, 308–319; *see also* living entities
Being and Time/Sein und Zeit, 8, 9, 12–16, 19, 20, 27, 33–35, 51, 56, 57, 59, 60, 64, 84–86, 88, 90, 92, 93, 96, 98, 101, 111, 114, 138, 139, 141, 143, 144, 148, 164, 170, 174, 175, 176, 177, 210, 211, 213, 214, 217, 218, 229, 232, 234, 235, 237, 264, 268, 269, 270, 275, 281–283, 285, 290, 292, 296, 297, 298, 299, 307, 308, 336
Bense, Max, 326
Bergson, Henri, 209, 210
Bergsträsser, Arnold, 326
Bernasconi, Robert, 228, 230, 232, 238, 239, 242
beyng/*Seyn*, 140, 141, 188, 247

biology, 26, 51, 208, 211, 212, 214, 219, 245, 271
biological determinism, 270
biologization, 208, 222
bio-philosophical, 94
biopolitical, 207, 221, 223n
birth, 11, 66, 217, 284–289, 294
Black Lives Matter, 280n
Black Notebooks, 3, 4n, 56, 58, 138, 140, 146
Blumenberg, Hans, 40n
body/bodies, 40n, 49, 63, 67, 68, 95, 97, 98, 100, 115, 116, 118, 124, 125, 269, 270, 273, 307, 309, 310, 311, 312, 315, 316, 318, 321n; *see also* embodiment
boredom, 213, 221
Boumann, Ludwig, 242
boundary realization, 96–100, 103
Boss, Medard, 34
Browning, Robert, 62, 71
Buber, Martin, 141
Buddha, 49
Building Dwelling Thinking, 327, 328, 331, 333, 342
Bultmann, Rudolf, 57
Byron, George Gordon, 62

Camper, Pieter, 242
Capobianco, Richard, 34, 44n
Carasthasis, Anna, 272
care, 9, 59, 64, 86, 95, 98, 144, 159, 162, 163, 176, 179, 281, 296, 298, 319
Cartesian/Cartesianism, 17, 30, 87, 95, 112, 162, 166, 205, 220, 221, 268, 269, 270, 275, 333
Cassirer, Ernst, 16, 85, 88–91, 92, 94, 100, 325
Cavell, Stanley, 324n
Char, René, 3
child/children, 68, 191–194, 197, 198, 200, 288

Christian/Christianity, 37n, 112, 211, 228
class, 263, 271
clearing, 31, 86, 102, 142, 144, 188
cogito, 10, 14, 15, 18, 29, 30, 282; *see also* Descartes
cognitive psychology, 331
Collins, Patricia Hill, 272
colonialism/post-colonial, 227–228, 315
commitment/committing, 309, 311, 312, 313, 317, 319, 329
communication/communicative, 119, 134, 283, 293, 298, 299
community, 235, 236, 275, 292, 313, 315, 342
compassion, 298, 319, 320
Conrad-Martius, Hedwig, 159
consciousness, 10, 26, 27, 30, 31, 32, 43n, 51, 115, 117, 121, 156, 157, 158, 160, 163, 166, 169, 170, 174, 211, 212, 237, 309, 329, 333
constitution/constitutive (transcendental), 31, 113, 120, 121, 123, 124, 130, 131, 141, 155, 156, 162, 164, 166, 167, 168, 174, 176, 177, 179, 207, 262, 269, 288, 291, 328, 333
Contributions to Philosophy/Beiträge zur Philosophie, 56–58, 187, 139, 141, 187
creator/creators, 64, 339
Crenshaw, Kimberlé, 272
Critchley, Simon, 298
Crowell, Steven Galt, ix, 32, 44n, 112
culture, ix, 48, 214, 233, 239, 266, 267, 325, 326
Cumming, Robert Denoon, 138

Dahlstrom, Daniel O., 55
daimon, 290, 291
Davidson, David, 333

Dasein, 8, 13–16, 19–21, 23–24, 25, 26, 28, 31–32, 33, 34–35, 37n, 40n, 66, 90, 92, 93, 94, 95, 97, 100, 159–166, 169, 170, 173–177, 210–214, 234, 241, 261, 262, 264, 265–269, 272, 274, 275, 287, 289, 290, 291, 294, 295, 296, 299, 307–320; see also analytic of Dasein, being/Being, there being/being there, Da-sein, metaphysics of Dasein
Da-sein, 47, 51, 53, 54, 55, 57, 60, 66, 68, 71, 71n, 112, 141, 177
death, 11, 48, 66, 190, 217, 218, 220, 284, 285, 286, 287, 290, 294, 295, 296, 307; see also existential death
deiform; see *imago dei*
demise, 313, 314, 315
Descartes, René, 18, 28, 31, 48, 59, 246, 332; see also Cartesianism
destiny, 207, 234, 235, 247, 248, 314
Derrida, Jacques, 185, 206, 217, 220
Dilthey, Wilhelm, 9, 85, 95, 96, 161, 162, 165, 175, 209, 210, 211, 237
dogmatic/dogmatism, 2, 3, 4n, 117, 120
Dotson, Kristie, 272
Dreyfus, Hubert, 282, 310
Driesch, Hans, 86, 97, 216
dualism (of mind and body), 330–332
dwelling (*wohnen*), 103, 138, 143, 144, 149, 326, 327, 328, 329, 333, 334, 335, 338–345; see also abode, house

ego/egoic, 26, 31, 32, 112, 117, 121, 124, 159, 166
Einleitung in die Philosophie, 7, 186, 188, 190, 195
Elden, Stuart, 192, 194
emancipatory, 9, 207, 268
embodiment, 60, 95, 96, 116, 125, 158, 185, 195, 216, 238, 265, 266, 270, 275, 287, 289, 307, 309, 310–314, 331, 332, 347n
Emerson, Ralph Waldo, 62
emotion/emotive, 130, 163, 281, 313
emplacement, 92, 95
Engelland, Chad, 173
Enlightenment/enlightened, 9, 12, 35n, 221, 219
epoché, 26, 131–132n
Ereignis, 34, 235
Erörterung, 138
essence, 3, 7, 13, 15, 20, 23, 28, 31, 32, 33, 66, 71, 92, 93, 94, 102, 103, 142, 149, 157, 160, 164, 166, 171, 176, 199, 207, 208, 218, 219, 221, 231, 238, 266, 268, 297, 299, 308, 316, 330
eternal, 11, 193, 240
eternity, 236
ethical/ethics, 95, 143, 145, 205, 208, 219, 220, 222, 295, 340
ethnicity, 263, 271
ethnography, 53–54, 76n
Europe/European, 2, 228, 236, 238, 239, 242, 245, 315, 325, 326, 337, 342, 343, 344; see also non-European(s)
excentric/excentricity, 91, 92, 93, 94, 100, 104
excentric positionality, 91, 92, 99, 100
existence; see human existence
existential death, 313, 314, 315, 316, 317, 323n
existentiale/existentialia, 9, 96, 97, 285
experience, 26, 96, 119, 121–127, 132n, 155–159, 160–175, 177, 187, 188, 191, 199, 209, 218, 235, 236, 261–267, 271, 272, 273, 276, 282, 283, 285, 287, 293, 300n, 320, 335, 337, 348n
expression, 113, 117, 122, 125, 209

Index | 359

expressive/meaningful whole, 113, 120, 122, 123, 125, 126, 127; see also person

factical life/factical existence/facticity, 8–9, 10, 11, 27, 33, 39n, 96, 132n, 212, 234, 245, 266, 283, 285, 289, 293, 314
factuality, 162
Farin, Ingo, 54, 105n, 128n, 153n, 179n, 224n, 270, 275, 283, 308, 321n
Faye, Emmanuel, 229, 230, 238
Fell, Joseph, 140
feminist philosophy, 270
Feuerbach, Ludwig, 9–10, 11, 12, 43n
finitude, 4, 14, 27, 91, 92, 94, 150, 159, 177, 212, 218, 220, 244, 270, 295, 307, 309, 312, 315, 316, 317, 318, 320, 323
Fink, Eugen, 38n, 185, 192, 193–196, 198, 200, 201
Firenze, Antonio, 206, 207, 208
First Nations/First Peoples, 234, 236, 242
Fischer, Joachim, 88, 89
foreign, 337
Foucault, Michel, 206
frailty/frailties, 307, 318
Frankfurt School, 48, 59, 88
freedom, 16, 21–23, 34, 190, 214, 238, 239, 244, 247, 284, 297, 330, 333
Frege, Gottlob, 53
Fundamental Concepts of Metaphysics: World, Finitude, Solitude, 85, 94, 206, 213
fundamental ontology, 13, 54, 84, 85, 90, 145, 176, 265; see also philosophical anthropology
future, 11, 59, 98, 102, 200, 234, 235, 244, 288, 290, 294, 295

Gadamer, Hans-Georg, 185, 198, 209, 327
game, 186, 187, 189, 193, 194, 195, 290; see also language game
Gans, Eduard, 238, 239
Gates Bill, 60
Garry, Ann, 271, 272
Gehlen, Arnold, 326
Gelassenheit, 145, 217
geistig/Geist, 11, 236, 240, 243, 350n
gender, 263, 271, 272, 275
German Idealism, 234, 238, 241, 243, 244
Ge-stell, 48
God, 17, 48, 52, 197, 211, 228, 238, 241, 244, 246
Goethe, Johann Wolfgang, 62, 63, 64, 69, 70
Golob, Sacha, 310, 347n
Grassi, Ernesto, 146, 154n
Gropius, Walter, 342
ground, 14, 15, 20–23, 26–27, 31, 33, 37n, 95, 96, 123, 157, 190, 236, 239, 241, 289

Haar, Michel, 176, 186
Hägglund, Martin, 312, 323n
Hancock, Ange-Marie, 264
Harris, Angela, 272
Haugeland, John, 323n
Hebel, Johann Peter, 62
Hegel, Georg Friedrich Wilhelm, 49, 70, 232–247
Hegel, Karl, 239, 240
Heimat, 337
Heraclitus, 191, 192, 194
Herder, Johann Gottfried von, 9, 12, 35n, 64, 238
here/now, 10, 11, 120, 121, 124, 125, 126, 295; see also there (*Da*)
heritage, 285

hermeneutics/hermeneutical, 10, 13, 20, 33, 53, 55, 59, 85, 90, 91, 95, 96, 101, 104, 109n, 111, 209, 225n, 266, 296, 333
hermeneutical anthropology, 8, 12
Hiroshima, 1, 60, 70, 71
historical, 1, 9, 11, 12, 22, 101–104, 111, 123, 155, 160–168, 174, 176, 177, 217, 229, 232, 234, 237, 239, 243, 245, 247, 272, 282, 289
historicality/historicity (*Geschichtlichkeit*), 11, 15, 22, 102, 160, 161, 179n, 217, 220, 240, 269, 280, 304
historicism, 8, 161, 237
history, 2, 11, 26, 34, 66, 173, 217, 230–240, 245, 247, 248, 329, 330, 339
history-less (*geschichtslos*), 232, 233, 237, 251n
history of Beyng/being, 234, 247–248
Hitler, Adolf, 239, 240
Hölderlin, 62, 63, 64, 65, 69, 138, 247, 248
Hodge, Joanna, ix
Holthusen Hans Egon, 326
home, 21, 287, 299, 334, 336, 337, 338, 399, 340, 342, 344; *see also* abode, dwelling
homelessness, 341
Homer, 193
homo sapiens, 51, 65, 309, 313; *see also* human/human being, humankind/human race
house, 148, 334; *see also* abode
house of being (*Haus des Seins*), 103, 110n, 148, 299, 333, 334
Huizinga, Johan, 185
human/human being, 1, 2, 9–10, 13, 14–16, 17–18, 19, 21, 23–24, 28, 31–32, 33, 34–35, 37n, 48–50; 51, 55, 59, 60, 61, 63, 64, 65, 66–68, 69, 70, 84, 91–93, 94, 98, 99, 100, 101, 118, 141, 145, 147, 164, 165, 171, 172, 174–176, 190, 191, 194, 196, 197, 227, 229, 230, 239, 241, 263, 265, 266, 273, 308, 326, 328, 330, 333; question of, 1–3, 14, 50–51, 62, 90, 92, 142, 143, 167, 177, 187, 232, 247, 281, 297; *see also* Dasein, Da-sein, human condition, human existence, humankind/human race, humanness, humanity, man, newcomers, posthuman, overhuman, transhuman
human engineering, 60
human existence, 34, 35, 99, 100, 101, 103, 111, 160, 161, 162, 165, 168, 176, 177, 197, 208, 210, 211, 212, 217, 218, 219, 222, 262, 275, 282, 283, 286
human condition, 15, 47, 99, 101, 261, 269, 292; *see also* posthumanism, transhumanism
humanism, 2–3, 29, 32, 42n, 48, 49–50, 56, 59, 62, 68, 69, 71, 94, 101, 103, 137, 141, 143, 145–147, 149, 150, 151, 186, 196–198, 199, 200, 205–207, 220–221, 237, 298, 325, 326, 328, 329; *see also* anti-humanism, post-humanism, postwar humanism, Renaissance humanism, Roman humanism, über-humanism
humanitas, 100, 101, 102, 103, 205, 206, 298
humanity, 55, 59, 66, 163, 199, 207, 232, 234, 235, 238, 240, 241, 248, 283, 296, 297, 298, 307, 308, 309, 316–320, 325, 326, 329, 330, 335
humanization, 223n
humankind/human race, 63, 94, 102, 238
humanness, 185, 298
Humboldt, Wilhelm von, 238

Husserl, Edmund, 7–8, 24–27, 30–32, 40–41n, 43n, 44n, 52, 53, 54, 59, 85, 96, 111–126, 155–170, 173, 174, 175, 176, 177, 209, 210, 333, 337
Hyginus, Gaius Julius, 64

ideal/ideality, 155, 156, 159, 160, 162, 173, 177, 244
idealism, 87, 96, 166, 167, 170, 182n, 234; *see also* German Idealism
identity, 3, 4, 32, 166, 173, 174, 228, 245, 261–277, 291, 294, 309, 310, 311, 315, 319, 320; *see also* personal identity
identity marker, 263, 264, 271, 273, 275
imago dei, 48, 66, 211
immanence, 159, 170, 171, 194, 269
in-between, 97, 282, 286, 287, 291, 298, 299
inauthentic/inauthenticity, 51, 57, 232, 267, 293
indeterminacy, 17, 18, 22, 114, 116, 151
indigenous/indigeneity, 227, 234
individuation, 113, 117, 120, 121, 122, 126, 130n
Ingarden, Roman, 159
inhuman, 3, 151
injustice; *see* racial justice/injustice
inside out (model), 97, 212, 281, 294, 327, 328, 331, 333, 335, 336, 337, 338, 344, 345; *see also* outside in model
intelligibility, 262, 265–268, 310
intentionality, 30, 156–165, 167, 169, 170, 174, 269, 333
interiority, 98, 159, 231, 331, 336
interpersonal, 123, 288
inter-play, 187, 191, 198; *see also* play
interpretation, 8, 261, 262, 265–268, 274, 277

interpretive landscape, 262
intersectional/intersectionality, 261, 263, 264, 270–276
intersubjectivity, 168, 173, 179, 275, 291, 292
Introduction to Metaphysics, 57, 61, 103
intuition, 30, 96, 171, 172, 174, 240
irrationalism, 95
Islam, 228

James, P. D., 288
Janicaud, Dominique, 56
Jaspers, Karl, 56, 138, 209, 298, 336
Jünger, Ernst, 246, 256n
justice; *see* racial justice/injustice

Kaffern, 232, 251n
Kant, Immanuel, 3, 4, 9, 12, 13, 20, 31, 35n, 51, 53, 54, 59, 62, 89, 91, 96, 186, 237, 238, 242, 246, 309
Kant Society, 24, 87
Kant and the Problem of Metaphysics, 1, 17, 24, 92, 93, 141
Keane, Naill, 105n, 128n
Kehre (turn/turning), 100, 139, 299
Klages, Ludwig, 214
Koffka, Kurt, 97
Köhler, Wolfgang, 97
Kojève, Alexandre, 235
Kusch, Martin, 54
Kurzweil, Ray, 60
Krell, David Farrell, 192, 194

language, 103, 123, 144, 145, 148, 149, 211, 218, 232, 236, 241, 286, 292, 297, 299, 329, 332, 333, 334, 335
language games, 186
Lear, Jonathan, 315
Leonardo, Zeus, 272
Letter on Humanism, 68, 85, 101, 103, 104, 137–139, 143, 146–151, 197,

Letter on Humanism (continued) 198, 205, 297, 299, 317, 325–330, 333 336, 342–344
Levinas, Emmanuel, 67, 68, 89
liberalism/liberal, 86, 147, 207, 221, 240, 248
life (*Leben*), 8–12, 58, 60, 85, 93–96, 98, 99, 100, 102, 103, 104, 111, 112, 114, 115, 117, 120, 122, 123, 124, 125, 156, 158, 159, 161, 165, 169, 171, 175, 192, 193, 194, 205, 206, 207, 208–214, 217, 218, 219, 220, 221, 222, 241, 263, 286, 291, 293, 294, 308, 312, 313, 315, 316, 340, 344; *see also* Dasein, natural life/organic life
life-philosophy, 9, 10, 12, 207, 208, 211, 214
life project, 312–315
Lindstrom, Randall, ix
living beings/entities, 95, 97, 103, 122, 216, 286
localism, 337
logos, 103, 189, 218, 219, 328, 329
Loidolt, Sophie, 293
Lotze, Hermann, 56
love/loving, 316, 317, 318, 319, 323n
Lucian of Samosata, 64
Luther, Martin, 56

Malpas, Jeff, 133n, 305n, 347n
man, 9–10, 14–18, 22, 25, 26, 29, 32, 39n, 53, 91, 92, 112, 197, 206, 207, 214, 215, 217, 220, 270, 281, 283, 291, 296, 297; *see also* human/human being
das Man (the they/the one), 55, 291, 292, 295, 318
Mann, Thomas, 88, 100
materialism, 120
Matarana, Humberto, 199
mattering, 311, 320
Marcel, Gabriel, 326

Marquard, Odo, 22
Marx, Karl, 10, 43n, 241, 329
mathematics, 53, 131, 132, 159
meaning, 123, 125, 156, 158, 162–165, 167, 169, 170–175, 197, 209, 262, 264, 288, 296, 297–299, 311, 313, 329, 333
meaning of being/Being; *see* being/Being, question of being/Being, understanding of being/Being
Meinong, Alexius, 159
Meister Eckhart, 56, 348n
Merleau-Ponty, Maurice, 95, 310, 326, 333
metaphor/metaphorical, 148, 149, 154n, 284, 333
Metaphysical Foundations of Logic, 163, 268
metaphysical, 2, 3, 92, 94, 102, 147, 159, 198, 199, 200, 207, 208, 220, 236, 239, 241, 242, 243, 245, 256n, 269, 285, 328, 329, 330, 331, 338, *see also* anti-metaphysical, nonmetaphysical
metaphysics, 2, 10, 19, 20, 28, 91, 92, 103, 143, 149, 241, 243–246, 248
metaphysics of Dasein, 21, 22, 25, 84, 90, 92, 177
Middle Ages, 233
Milton, John, 62
mind-body problem/separation, 272, 273, 275, 330
mineness, 51, 52, 95, 285, 287
Misch, Georg, 87
Mitchell, Andrew J., 345n
modernity, 8, 28, 29, 30, 150, 173, 246, 296
mood, 186, 213, 313
Moran, Dermot, 269
Moore, Ian Alexander, 345n
mortality, 66, 217, 218, 281, 283, 284, 290, 312, 323
Most, Glenn, 192

Nagasaki, 1, 60, 70, 71
natality, 66, 281, 283–289, 292, 293, 295, 296, 297, 299
National Socialism/Nazism, 1, 58, 146, 147, 154n, 205, 228, 229, 231, 235, 236, 237, 239, 240, 243, 246, 247, 248, 279n, 280n
natural attitude, 32, 115, 125
natural life/organic life, 85, 93–104, 208
naturalism/naturalistic, 10, 33, 35, 96, 113, 117, 118, 119, 155; *see also* natural attitude, naturalistic/natural-scientific attitude
naturalistic/natural-scientific attitude, 117, 118, 119, 125
naturalization, 94, 95, 130–131n, 206
necessity, 190, 239, 240, 247, 248
Nenon, Thomas, ix
neo-Kantian/neo-Kantians, 10, 85, 101, 163, 165, 209
newcomers/newborns/new human beings, 285–291, 295, 298
Nietzsche, Friedrich, 48, 49, 50, 51, 52, 54–57, 63, 64, 66, 69, 70, 185, 209, 231, 246
non-Europeans, 199; *see also* Europe/Europeans
normative standards/authority, 315, 316, 318, 320
normativity, 104, 335
Nossack, Ernst, 326

objectivity, 23, 159, 162, 173, 245, 287
objectivism, 35, 146, 168
ontology, 10, 15, 17, 18, 20, 37n, 59, 89, 95, 115, 150, 167, 186, 187, 192, 208, 211, 220, 222, 265, 266, 272, 274, 275, 283, 335, 341
onto-anthropology, 103
onto-historical/Being-historical, 8, 30, 299

openness, 4, 21, 23, 35, 90, 150, 157, 159, 161–177, 218, 221, 222, 291, 293, 298, 318, 320
oppression, 263, 264, 271–277
organic modals, 96, 98
organisms, 48, 94, 95, 98, 99, 103, 114, 120, 216, 217
orientation, 97, 98, 143, 311, 333
Ort; see *topos*
Ortega y Gasset, José, 327, 336, 338, 339, 340, 343, 344
outside in model, 97, 327, 331, 335, 344; *see also* inside out model
overhuman, 64
ownness, 121, 123, 124, 125, 296

pandemic, 2, 47, 58
Parmenides, 56, 244
past, 11, 193, 233, 234, 235, 285, 288, 289, 343, 344
Pathmarks (Wegmarken), 139
people, 235, 236, 247; see also *Volk*
perish/perishing, 220, 313, 315
person, 113–119, 122, 123, 125, 126, 168, 193, 262, 263, 264, 266, 272, 273, 276, 286, 290, 293, 294, 309, 341; *see also* interpersonal
personal identity, 261–264, 270 277, 294, 310, 319, 320
personalism/personalistic, 111, 113, 115, 162; *see also* attitude, personalistic
personalistic attitude, 117, 118, 119, 120, 122, 125
personal traits, 262, 264, 294
phenomenology, 24–25, 31, 53, 54, 56, 59, 94, 111–126, 130–131n, 157–162, 166, 172, 173, 187, 200, 201, 209, 211, 283, 298, 330
phenomenological attitude, 118
phenomenological (transcendental) reduction, 8, 115 125, *see also* phenomenological attitude

philosophical anthropology, 4, 7–45, 84, 85, 86–104, 111–115, 121, 126, 141, 167, 211, 281, 282
philosophy, 2, 8–12, 17–19, 20–21, 25, 26, 27, 29–30, 39n, 53, 66, 67, 84, 85, 88, 89, 104, 112, 177, 206, 209, 228, 234, 239, 283, 294, 298, 328, 329, 345
philosophy of culture, 89, 90, 94
philosophy of life, 95, 96, 111, 112
Pindar, 234
place, 4, 86, 97, 98, 137–151, 213, 336, 338; of being/thinking, 140–142; *see also* emplacement, topology/topological, *topos*
plants, 17, 18, 51, 54, 86, 99, 224n
Plato, 14, 51, 143, 144, 244, 329
play/playing, 185–201; *see also* interplay
playfulness, 185
Plessner, Helmuth, 83–104
plurality, 117, 283, 285, 286, 287, 292, 293, 297, 299
poetry, 138, 335, 336, 343
poiesis, 193, 283
Pope, Alexander, 61, 62, 63, 64
Porphyry, 56
positionality, 95, 98, 103; *see also* excentric positionality
possibility, 21, 99, 103, 120, 125, 160, 172, 175, 210, 212, 218, 271, 290, 295, 314, 317
posthuman/posthumanism, 47, 205, 221, 223n
postwar humanism, 326
power, 119, 120, 122, 150, 234, 239, 246, 247, 276; *see also* will to power
practice, 53, 119, 147, 164, 186, 228, 265–267, 275, 288, 292, 298, 328, 329, 343
presence, 98, 244, 245, 263, 287, 290, 294
present, 3, 11, 20, 27, 211, 235, 236, 240, 243, 245, 288
present-at-hand, 19, 20, 27, 31, 34, 97, 286, 293, 298
psychology, 16, 26, 53, 95, 130, 156, 211
psychologism, 8, 53, 54, 155–158
psychophysical, 118, 126, 169
Promethean shame/Promethean inadequacy, 48, 59
public, 291, 292, 293, 295, 297, 299

question of being/Being, 8, 12, 13, 20, 50, 53, 68, 111, 140, 142, 145, 146, 150, 186, 192, 199, 200, 308; *see also* being/Being, understanding of being/Being

race/racism, 3, 227–248, 263, 271, 279n–280n
racialization/racialized, 247, 248, 272
racial justice/racial injustice, 227, 280n
rational/rationality, 156, 159, 162, 185, 214, 220, 221, 240, 329, 333
rational/rationalistic, 87, 111, 127n, 128
rational animal; *see* animal
ready-to-hand, 270, 286, 310–319
realism, 68, 159, 167, 182n
reason, 22, 127n, 189, 190, 192, 211, 212, 219, 234, 281, 329, 340
reality/real, 11, 13, 29, 171, 172, 175, 210, 213, 219, 262, 265, 272, 273, 287, 291, 295, 299
realism/realists, 68, 159, 167, 178n, 182n
Rée, Paul, 70
reflective (dialogical) model, 327, 343, 344; *see also* sequential model
reflexive/reflexivity, 99, 328, 329
Reinach, Adolf, 159

relationality/nonrelationality, 164, 169, 174, 213, 288, 290, 291, 295–297, 299, 299n
releasement, see *Gelassenheit*
religion, 48–50, 240, 242, 245
Renaissance humanism, 42n, 154n, 198, 199, 200
renewal, 101, 325, 327, 342, 343, 345, 350n
resolute/resoluteness, 290, 294, 295
responsible/responsibility, 200, 220, 221, 264, 278n, 295
Richardson William John, 54, 345n
Rickert, Heinrich, 210
Rilke, Erich Maria, 66
Roman humanism, 197
romantic/Romantics, 194, 197, 246, 324n
rootedness, 90, 340
Rosenberg, Alfred, 146, 243
Rousseau, Jacques, 51
Roux, Wilhelm, 100
Ruf, Sep, 343, 344

Sartre, Jean-Paul, 56, 138, 292
scepticism, 18
Scheler, Max, 24, 41n, 51, 84–92, 100, 102, 114, 165–169, 172, 173, 209, 210, 214
Schiller, Friedrich, 185
Schmitt, Carl, 71, 239
Schneider, Ilona, ix
Schott, Robin May, 239
Schürmann, Reiner, 54–60, 65, 66, 69
Schwippert, Hans, 344, 345
science, 2, 13, 15, 19, 50, 52, 53, 54, 55, 60, 61, 75n, 96, 127n, 161, 209, 210, 212, 243, 245, 263
self, 4, 31, 55, 117, 121, 124, 125, 126, 177, 246, 264, 271, 273, 274, 283, 284, 290, 291, 294, 295, 296, 318; *see also* self-reflexive/self-reflexivity
self-reflexive/self-reflexivity, 209, 262, 264, 275, 277
self-understanding, 10, 13, 146, 268
sense-bestowal, 164, 165, 166
sense-making, 270, 282, 297, 299, 308, 309, 314, 317
sense-transference, 124, 126
sequential model, 327, 328, 335, 341, 342; *see also* reflective model
Sheehan, Thomas, ix, 54, 66, 152n, 263, 275, 282
Sikka, Sonia, 228, 229, 230, 237
Simmel, Georg, 209
situatedness, 140, 155, 213
slavery, 242
solicitude, 319, 320
Sophocles, 61–62, 63
space-time, 120, 121, 213, 312
space/spatiality, 19, 30, 97–99, 124, 125, 126, 149, 150, 162, 177, 188, 189, 191, 193, 196, 215, 236, 237, 242, 286, 291, 293, 297, 310, 311, 313, 333, 336, 347n
specific difference, 103, 330
speech, 103, 126, 234, 284, 287, 291, 292, 293, 294, 297
Spengler, Oswald, 214
Spiegel interview, 41n, 231, 248
Sportpalast, 40–41n
Stalinism, 235
Stanley, Wendell, 60, 67
state (theory/philosophy of), 238–240, 245, 246, 247
Stein, Edith, 114
Sternberger, Dolf, 327, 328–341, 343, 344
Stone, Alison, 242
Stroh, K. M., 275
Strong, Tracy Burr, 47, 81n

subjectivity, 28, 29, 30, 32, 57, 114, 115, 121, 159, 160, 161, 162, 164, 165, 166, 168 170, 171, 172, 173, 176, 215, 221, 236, 238, 240, 241, 245, 246, 330
subjectivism, 8, 18, 27–28, 30, 35, 42n, 54, 88, 112, 146, 147, 149
surroundings, 97, 119, 124, 216, 265, 327, 331, 332

Taminiaux, Jacques, 283
Taubes, Jacob, 71
technology, 2, 29, 48, 52, 54, 60, 66, 150, 197, 326, 339, 340
technoscience, 50, 63
teleonomy/teleonomical, 212, 216, 218, 224n
theism, 50; *see also* atheism
theology/theological, 26, 48, 50, 56, 112, 211, 228
there (*Da*), 3, 19–20, 55, 66, 124, 126, 141, 142, 150, 245, 274; *see also* here, now
there being/being there, 21, 54, 68, 112, 125, 126, 133n, 213, 218, 281, 295, 303n; *see also* Dasein, Da-sein
thinking, 32, 139–143, 145–151, 157, 174, 220, 230, 244, 246, 328, 329, 330–335
thrown/thrownness, 14, 23, 65, 176, 230, 269, 270, 277, 285, 289, 299, 313
Tillich, Paul, 24, 336
time/temporality, 21, 52, 93, 94, 98, 99, 124, 158, 159, 160, 173, 175, 177, 192–194, 220, 233, 235, 236, 237, 240, 295, 312; *see also* space-time, time together with others, time-space
time-space/time-play-space (Zeit-Raum/ Zeit-Spiel-Raum), 189

time together with others (*Mitzeit*), 295, 304n
topographic, 94, 149
topology/topological, 34, 92, 138, 141–150
topos, 140, 176; *see also* place
Totsching, Wolfhardt, 284, 288
tradition, 233, 285, 288
transcendence, 43n, 55, 91, 93, 94, 159, 162–164, 168, 175, 176, 179, 186, 221, 269
transcendental, 12, 13, 15, 26–27, 31–32, 33, 112, 113, 115, 116, 125, 126, 155, 157–172, 175, 176, 177, 186, 187, 189, 197, 209
transcendental consciousness, 26, 27, 31, 32, 158, 160
transcendental constitution; *see* constitution
transcendental ego, 26, 31, 32, 166
transcendental idealism, 166
transcendental subject (subjectivity), 160, 164, 166, 168
transcendental reduction, 32, 115
transformation (intellectual, spiritual), 327, 335, 341, 342
transhuman/transhumanism, 47, 50, 58, 59, 60, 63, 69
truth, 14, 143, 144, 156, 162, 211, 221, 267
truth of being/Being, 34, 140, 176, 188, 197, 198, 266
turn/turning; see *Kehre*

über-humanism, 63
understanding of being/Being, 13–15, 19–21, 25, 26, 28, 34, 40n, 90, 91, 93, 247, 265–267, 282, 291, 292, 293, 298, 307, 323, 335
Uexküll, Jakob Johann, 100, 214, 215, 216

uncanny (*unheimlich*)/uncanniness (*Unheimlichkeit*), 22, 28, 61, 62
unique/uniqueness, 111, 160, 165, 207, 214, 222, 264, 269, 271, 273, 276, 286, 288, 291–294, 298

vaccines, 47, 49, 59, 60, 63, 67
Vallega-Neu, Daniela, 187
validity, 25, 26, 155, 156, 161, 162
Varela, Francisco, 199
Villa, Dana, 283
vitalism/vitalist, 97, 207, 214, 216, 221, 224n
Virilio, Paul, 49, 67
von Herrmann, Friedrich-Wilhelm, 211
Volk 229, 236, 249n
vulnerable/vulnerability, 66, 288, 307, 314, 316, 317, 318

Weber, Alfred, 327
Weber, Max, 94
West/Western, 48, 50, 59, 88, 100, 227, 229, 230, 234, 236, 237, 238, 239, 308, 326
What is Called Thinking, 61, 147
will to power, 15, 246, 256n
Withy, Katherine, 269, 270, 274

Wittgenstein, Ludwig, 186
world, 2, 3, 9–12, 14, 15, 19, 23, 25–27, 29–30, 31, 32, 35, 49, 55, 59, 63, 117, 118, 147, 155–177, 185–201, 208, 213–222, 246, 261–263, 265, 268, 270, 281–299, 311, 319, 320, 330, 333, 337, 339, 340
worldly/worldliness, 27, 117, 155, 156, 158, 165, 166, 167, 172, 173, 174, 176, 177, 179, 195, 286, 287, 293, 294
world-disclosing, 32, 159, 164
world-openness, 91, 168, 169
world-history, 237, 238, 239, 240, 242
World War I/First World War, 1, 342
World War II/Second World War, 1, 85, 205, 325
Wynter, Sylvia, 186, 198–200

Yorck von Wartenburg, Paul, 209
Young, Julian, 229, 230, 245

Zammito, John, 12
Zollikoner Seminare, 34
Zulus, 232

www.ingramcontent.com/pod-product-compliance
Lightning Source LLC
Chambersburg PA
CBHW031703230426
43668CB00006B/92